D1736290

THE POLITICS OF ARMS CONTROL TREATY RATIFICATION

Also by Michael Krepon

Commercial Observation Satellites and International Security* (*co-editor*)
Arms Control and the Reagan Administration (*author*)
Verification and Compliance: A Problem-solving Approach (*co-editor*)
Strategic Stalemate: Nuclear Weapons and Arms Control In American Politics* (*author*)

Also by Dan Caldwell

American-Soviet Relations: From 1947 to the Nixon-Kissinger Grand Design (*author*)
Henry Kissinger: His Personality and Policies (*editor*)
Soviet International Behavior and U.S. Policy Options (*editor*)
The Dynamics of Domestic Politics and Arms Control: The Salt II Treaty
    Ratification Debate (*author*)

*also published by St. Martin's Press

THE POLITICS OF ARMS CONTROL TREATY RATIFICATION

edited by

Michael Krepon
President
Henry L. Stimson Center

and

Dan Caldwell
Professor of Political Scienc
Pepperdine University

St. Martin's Press
New York

in association with the
Henry L. Stimson Center

© Henry L. Stimson Center 1991

First Published in the United States of America in 1991

Printed in the United States of America

ISBN 0-312-06604-X

Library of Congress Cataloging-in-Publication Data

The Politics of arms control treaty ratification / edited by Michael Krepon
    and Dan Caldwell.
        p.   cm.
    Includes index.
    ISBN 0-312-06604-X
    1. Arms control—United States—History. 2. Treaties—
    Ratification—History. 3. United States—Foreign relations—
    Treaties. 4. United States—Politics and government—20th century.
I. Krepon, Michael, 1946-   . II. Caldwell, Dan.
JX1974.P6238   1991
341.3'7'0941—dc20   91-34787
                                                            CIP

Contents

Acknowledgments

This book has been made possible through the grant support of the Ford Foundation. We are deeply grateful to Enid C.B. Schoettle for supporting the Stimson Center's treaty ratification project and for helping us to disseminate our findings. Stanley Heginbotham was instrumental in shaping our inquiry into executive-congressional relations. He also provided wise counsel during the formative stages of the project.

Many individuals played important roles in the creation of this book. Any study of this kind is only as good as its case studies, and we have been fortunate to enlist the services of Thomas H. Buckley, Benjamin S. Loeb, Rodney J. McElroy, Janne E. Nolan, Alan Platt, and William C. Widenor who helped refine the list of questions addressed in each case and who adapted to the focused comparison method of inquiry admirably well.

We also wish to thank the case study reviewers for their efforts to sharpen the analysis of individual cases: George Bunn, Linda Brady, Lynn Davis, I. M. Destler, Elisa Harris, Pat Holt, Robert Hoover, David Kennedy, Herbert F. Margulies, and John Stewart. We are grateful to James M. Montgomery for steering us in the right direction at the outset of our inquiry.

Most of the essays in this book were presented to a conference on executive-congressional relations and the treaty ratification process convened at the Woodrow Wilson International Center for Scholars. We wish to thank Charles Blitzer, Robert Litwak, and Samuel Wells of the Wilson Center and Enid C.B. Schoettle of the Ford Foundation for providing this opportunity to broadcast our findings to a Washington audience and to receive useful comments from a knowledgeable audience.

Special thanks go to McGeorge Bundy, Terry Deibel, Alexander George, Lynn Meininger, John Rielly, Stanley Riveles, Gaddis Smith, and Larry K. Smith. We are grateful to Richard Baker, Jo Anne McCormick Quatannens, and Donald A. Ritchie of the Historical Office of the United States Senate. Dan Caldwell would like to thank the Seaver College Reassigned Time Committee of Pepperdine University for granting him support while working on this project. Most important, we wish to thank Page Fortna, Steven Irwin, Nancy McCoy, John Parachini, Amy Smithson, Lisa Tepper, and Fred von Lohmann, whose research and administrative support made this project possible.

M.K., D.C.

Introduction
Dan Caldwell

This book presents a critical examination of executive-congressional relations and the domestic politics of arms control treaty ratification within the United States during the twentieth century. The starting point of this study is the hypothesis that the politics of treaty ratification can be as important as the negotiations leading up to agreements. Benefits to international peace and security sought in years of painstaking diplomatic effort can be lost without Senate consent, as was the case with the Treaty of Versailles and the second treaty arising from the Strategic Arms Limitation Talks (SALT II). Despite the substantial importance of this subject, the politics of treaty ratification is a relatively unexplored area, particularly compared with the volumes of studies and memoirs concerning past arms control negotiations.

With the simultaneous pursuit of a number of arms control agreements and a weakened political leadership in the Soviet Union, it is appropriate to assess the ways in which the executive and congressional branches have handled past arms control treaties. How have treaties been dealt with in the past? What domestic political factors within the United States have been the most important in determining whether a treaty has won the Senate's approval or not? How can an administration improve the chances for ratification by paying attention to these factors?

The existing literature on executive-congressional relations and the politics of treaty ratification does not deal extensively with these questions. The topic of the ratification process has been overlooked by historians, political scientists, and practitioners of public policy. Only the Versailles Treaty has been carefully analyzed, but much of the scholarship surrounding this ratification battle was written decades ago.[1]

No prior effort has been made to analyze and draw conclusions from case studies of the treaty ratification process. This is unfortunate, for lessons can be distilled from previous debates that provide important suggestions on avoiding pitfalls and ameliorating divisiveness during the ratification process. For example, it obviously helps for the president to have strong national security credentials, for the agreement in question to offer tangible security benefits to the United States, and for the treaty partner(s) to behave in an acceptable way before and during the Senate's deliberations. But these are obvious and somewhat superficial observations concerning the politics of treaty ratification, and it is the assumption of this study that richer, more differentiated lessons can be learned by delving deeper into the historical record.

There are few theoretically informed analyses of treaty ratification. One of the best, by Professor Robert D. Putnam, presents a stimulating analysis of the relationship of domestic politics and international relations, including the politics of treaty ratification.[2] Putnam distinguishes between the bargaining among negotiators that may lead to an agreement and the subsequent discussions within the domestic constituency of each of the negotiating parties. In the present volume the focus is on the latter set of negotiations. Putnam notes, "A more adequate account of the domestic determinants of foreign policy and international relations must stress *politics*: parties, social classes, interest groups (both economic and noneconomic), legislators, and even public opinion and elections, not simply executive officials and institutional arrangements."[3] The study has sought to focus on these domestic political factors, with the exception of social classes, in each of the case studies.

This project seeks to identify the elements of an effective ratification strategy by analyzing the ratification experience with the following arms control treaties: the Versailles Treaty of 1919, the Washington Naval treaties of 1922, the Geneva Protocol of 1925, the Limited Test Ban Treaty of 1963, the

Anti-Ballistic Missile (ABM) Treaty of 1972, the SALT II Treaty of 1979, and the Intermediate-range Nuclear Forces (INF) Treaty of 1987.

Research Objectives and Rationale of the Study

During the first 200 years of the United States' existence, the Senate approved more than 1,500 treaties, approximately 90 percent of all that were submitted to the Senate. Of these, 177 failed to be implemented after being signed by the president and sent to the Senate for its advice and consent. Most of these unratified treaties never came to a vote; either they were withdrawn from the Senate's consideration by the president or the Senate's leadership chose not to bring them to a vote because it appeared unlikely that they would be approved. The Senate approved about 25 percent of the unimplemented treaties, which were left unratified by the president because of amendments or other changes included in the Senate's resolution of ratification. Only 17 treaties were actually rejected by the Senate.[4]

The failure of the United States to ratify particular treaties has occasionally had serious consequences. For example, the failure of the United States to participate in the international security system established by the Treaty of Versailles undermined the League of Nations' peacekeeping arrangements, and the United States' failure to ratify the SALT II Treaty had a corrosive effect on American prestige, particularly since both the U.S. and USSR observed the treaty's terms informally for almost a decade after its signing.

In the 1973–86 period, arms control treaty ratification was extraordinarily difficult: the three agreements signed before the INF Treaty all languished in the Senate. The INF Treaty broke this pattern because it was championed by the most conservative and anticommunist president since Richard M. Nixon, and because a dynamic, new Soviet leadership confounded all expectations by accepting President Ronald Reagan's proposals virtually intact. The Kremlin could do so because it understood that U.S. proposals happened to coincide with long-standing Soviet strategic objectives of denuclearizing the European continent and undermining the strategy of flexible response espoused by NATO (the North Atlantic Treaty Organization). In order to realize these objectives, the new Soviet leadership under Mikhail Gorbachev was willing to scrap a numerical superiority built on new weapons systems, a tactic that surprised the Reagan administration officials who had crafted the U.S. negotiating positions.

These unique circumstances are not likely to be duplicated in the foreseeable future. With the fall of communism in Eastern Europe and its weakening in the Soviet Union, anticommunism has lost much of its meaning and salience in U.S. domestic politics. Thus, President George Bush and his successors cannot simply rely on their anticommunist credentials (as presidents Nixon and Reagan did) in order to gain support for particular arms control agreements.

Just as it appeared that the "end of history" was nigh, Saddam Hussein invaded Kuwait and complicated the future of international politics. Before the Persian Gulf War, there was discussion of deep cuts in the military forces of the United States, the Soviet Union, and other major powers. Following the outbreak of the war, history appeared to be very much "alive," and the need for significant military forces and for efforts to reduce military burdens and risks by treaty instruments continues.

The contributors to this book assume that history matters and that the politics of arms control treaty ratification will matter a great deal in the years ahead. For a long-term process of increased national and international security to occur, prudent defense postures will have to be supplemented with newly ratified arms control agreements.

Policy-Relevant Theory and the Structured, Focused Comparison Methodology

This study proposes to fill the existing void in the literature in a way that is accessible to both policymakers and scholars. The late, eminent British historian Arnold Toynbee once commented, "History not used is nothing, for all intellectual life is action, like practical life, and if you don't use the stuff—well, it might as well be dead." In keeping with Professor Toynbee's admonition, the research objectives and the variables analyzed in the study have been selected in part for their relevance to the concerns and needs of policymakers.

In recent years a number of historians and political scientists have sought to analyze particular aspects of foreign policy and international relations in ways that contribute to the diagnosis of actual policy problems. Based on the systematic assessment of various historical cases, analysts have attempted to reach contingent generalizations, which, according to Alexander L. George and Richard Smoke, are "generalizations which may or may not be true, according to the contingency, and which specify the contingencies that 'activate' or 'validate' them."[5] Such generalizations must not only be relevant to actual policy problems; they must also be applicable to the diagnosis of particular situations and to the selection of better strategies by policymakers for the achievement of their desired objectives.

This volume builds on scholars' interest in the development of policy-relevant theory, which has increased in recent years. Interest has also increased in the comparative case study approach. Seeking to avoid the disappointing experiences of both single case studies and quantitative studies of hundreds or even thousands of cases and variables, researchers have adopted the comparative case study approach as a way of analyzing particular phenomena in foreign policy and international relations and as a means of focusing on policy-relevant variables.

The authors have borrowed heavily from Alexander L. George and his collaborators, who have developed a comparative case study methodology that they call the "structured, focused comparison" approach.[6] According to this method, the analyst prepares a set of standardized, general questions that reflect the theory-related objectives of the study at hand. These questions are then asked of each of the cases under investigation. This methodology borrows from both the quantitative and single case study approaches: the analyst treats each case as if it were a unique case—the approach historians normally adopt—in order to examine in what ways it is similar and dissimilar from the other cases under examination. At the same time, posing the same set of questions for each case resembles the statistical or survey research approaches that many social scientists employ. Based on the results of posing the standardized set of questions for each case, the analyst modifies the original questions and hypotheses to account for previously neglected factors. Thus, the process is an iterative one.

Once an acceptable set of questions is developed, the analyst explains the outcome in each case in terms of the general independent variables in the study. A comparison of the results of the findings of each case can be made, owing to the common framework used for analysis. This comparison enables the analyst to develop context-dependent generalizations about the particular phenomenon under investigation. It should be noted that this methodology is not a "cookbook" or "off-the-shelf" research approach; rather, the analyst must carefully formulate questions and select cases with reference to the theoretically relevant research objectives of the study. To date, studies employing the focused comparison methodology have been published on deterrence, coercive diplomacy, escalation, détente, crisis prevention, and U.S.-Soviet security cooperation.[7] Although comparative assessments of arms control negotiating experiences have been published, analyses of arms control treaty ratification efforts have yet to be published.[8] This study seeks to fill this gap in the existing literature.

The selection of cases is vital when employing the structured, focused comparison approach. This study focuses solely on arms control treaties. Of all the treaties placed on the Senate calendar for that chamber's advice and consent, arms control compacts have traditionally been viewed by the executive and congressional branches as having a special character. The stakes involved, usually inflated by friend and foe alike, are deemed worthy of the most solemn and independent judgment. The fate of treaties governing trade or the foreign relations of the United States may also have far-reaching consequences, but not in the same way as compacts involving central components of military power. Here, errors of judgment can directly affect the nation's physical security. Senators are therefore granted an unusual degree of independence in judging the merit of the treaty, and much of the usual bargaining that accompanies legislation of lesser importance is minimized. Treaties concerned with strategic weapons—capital ships in the 1920s and 1930s or nuclear weapons in the 1970s, 1980s, and 1990s—are thus assured a unique place in U.S. political discourse and in the ceaseless tug-of-war between the White House and Capitol Hill. For this reason, the study has focused solely on arms control ratification debates, broadly enough defined to include the Versailles Treaty, which demilitarized Germany after World War I.

Given the research objectives of this study, the coeditors wanted to select treaties that limited weapons in some way and that were negotiated in the twentieth century. Even limiting the selection to treaties that met these criteria nevertheless provided a number of potential "candidate cases," including the Antarctic Treaty, the Outer Space Treaty, the Latin American Nuclear Free Zone Treaty, the Nuclear Nonproliferation Treaty, the Seabed Arms Control Treaty, the Biological Weapons Convention, the Threshold Test Ban Treaty, the Peaceful Nuclear Explosions Treaty and the Environmental Modification Convention.[9]

To winnow the list of candidate cases, two selection criteria were added: cases were to be considered important by both the academic and policymaking communities and to reflect a mix of treaties that either succeeded or failed to secure the Senate's consent. Based on these criteria, the following cases were selected for analysis: the Versailles Treaty, the Washington Naval treaties, the Geneva Protocol, the Limited Test Ban Treaty, the ABM Treaty, the SALT II Treaty, and the INF Treaty. In order that these cases might be analyzed systematically, the coeditors of this book drafted a set of questions related to the research objectives of the study. These questions were presented to the participants in the study for their input and were used as the basis for the initial case study drafts. The questions were then reformulated and the revised questions were used as the organizational foundation of the final chapter drafts. The coeditors asked authors not only to answer common questions but to structure the organization of their particular case according to a standard outline. As a result, the case studies contained in this volume have been written on the basis of a common analytical and organizational framework, and comparison across cases has thereby been facilitated.

The authors of the case studies were requested to present first a brief, historical introduction to the case indicating why the case was important, the background concerning the origins of the treaty, and the treaty's major provisions. The purpose of the introduction to the case was not to provide a complete picture of the negotiating record but to set the stage for a more in-depth discussion of the events that followed after the treaty was signed. After the introduction, authors were asked to address five substantive areas: (1) the international political context of the treaty, (2) the domestic political context, (3) the role of the president, (4) executive-congressional relations, and (5) public opinion and the role of interest groups. The questions and issues concerning each of these areas are briefly summarized below.

International Political Context

What was the international context of the treaty ratification debate, and how did this shape ratification efforts? How did the ratification effort relate to the administration's other national security objectives? Did prior ratification debates or major historical events shape this particular ratification effort? Did contemporaneous events abroad affect the ratification debate? If so, were these events directly related to the subject of negotiations, or were they unrelated? Did the structure of the international system and alliance relationships affect the ratification process? Was "world opinion" a factor in the ratification debate? Did the executive or legislative branch or both link the treaty to other international issues, either directly or indirectly? If so, what impact did such linkage have in the ratification process?

Domestic Political Context

What was the domestic political context of the treaty ratification debate? How did the ratification effort relate to the administration's other domestic objectives? Which prominent political figures and constituencies were heavily involved? How did electoral politics shape the executive branch's approach to the negotiations and the arguments it used during the ratification campaign? Were there substantial divisions within the executive branch over negotiating the treaty? If so, how did these divisions affect the negotiations and the ratification debate? How did domestic perceptions of the U.S. negotiating partner(s) shape the ratification process? Did the executive or legislative branch or both link the treaty to domestic issues, either directly or indirectly? If so, what impact did such linkage have in the ratification process?

Role of the President

How popular was the president during the negotiation and ratification process? How did the president's popularity or lack of same affect the executive branch's strategy? How vigorous and skillful was the president in resolving differences and enlisting cooperation within the executive branch during the negotiating process? How vigorous and skillful was the president in enlisting the support of key members of Congress during the negotiations and the ratification debate? How did the president employ his subordinates to secure the Senate's consent? What roles were military leaders, cabinet officers, the national security adviser, and other key individuals asked to play? What techniques did the president pursue to influence members of Congress and mobilize public opinion? How successful were these techniques?

Executive-Congressional Relations

What was the state of executive-congressional relations during the negotiations, congressional hearings, and the Senate floor debate, and how did these relations affect the ratification effort? Did the constitutional requirement for a two-thirds majority affect the administration's strategy in dealing with the Senate? What techniques did the executive branch employ to smooth the ratification process and to gain the Senate's consent? Were there trade-offs made on related or unrelated issues? What was the relationship between the administration, the Senate leadership, and key members of Congress during the negotiations and the ratification process? Did these relationships affect the outcome of the Senate's deliberations? What was the basis for senatorial support of and opposition to the treaty? Was opposition based on principled disagreements over treaty provisions, irreconcilable opposition to a negotiating partner, party politics, personal antipathy, or other reasons? Did the administration's strategy and tactics affect the nature of the opposition? How did the process of Senate amendments and reservations affect the outcome? How well did the administration manage this process?

Public Opinion and the Role of Interest Groups

What was public opinion toward the treaty during the negotiations, congressional hearings, and the Senate floor debate? What motivated the public to express its opinion? How important was public opinion in affecting the votes of key "fence-sitting" senators? How well informed were the president and his key advisers about public opinion toward the treaty? What strategy and tactics did the administration pursue to influence public opinion? Did these efforts matter? Are there apparent reasons for success or failure? Which interest groups were prominent in their support of or opposition to the treaty? What strategy and tactics did these groups employ? Do any of these strategies and tactics appear to have swayed votes in the Senate? Do any of these strategies and tactics appear to have swayed public opinion during the negotiations and during the ratification process?

Organization of the Book

The case studies are presented chronologically. The first case study, therefore, is William C. Widenor's chapter on the Versailles Treaty. Dr. Widenor is currently professor of history and chairman of the department at the University of Illinois at Urbana-Champaign and the author of *Henry Cabot*

Lodge and the Search for an American Foreign Policy.[10] Thomas H. Buckley, professor of history at the University of Tulsa and author of *The United States and the Washington Conference, 1921-1922*, wrote the chapter on the Washington Naval treaties.[11] Rodney J. McElroy, a doctoral candidate at the University of Sussex, is the author of the chapter on the Geneva Protocol. Benjamin S. Loeb, a retired civil servant with thirty years of experience with the Nuclear Regulatory Commission, the Atomic Energy Commission, and the International Atomic Energy Commission, analyzes the politics of the ratification of the Limited Nuclear Test Ban Treaty. He is especially well qualified for this task, having assisted Glenn T. Seaborg in writing his accounts of arms control activities during the Kennedy and Johnson administrations.[12] Alan Platt, former legislative assistant to Senator Edmund Muskie (D-Maine) and U.S. Arms Control and Disarmament Agency (ACDA) official, focuses on the ABM Treaty.[13] Dan Caldwell, professor of political science at Pepperdine University, is the author of the chapter on SALT II and a coeditor of this volume. He recently completed a book on the domestic politics of the SALT II Treaty ratification debate.[14] Janne E. Nolan, a visiting fellow at The Brookings Institution and the author of *Guardians of the Arsenal: The Politics of Nuclear Strategy*, is the author of the chapter on the INF Treaty. Dr. Nolan has also served as an official in ACDA and as senior defense and foreign policy adviser to Senator Gary Hart (D-Colo.).

Michael Krepon, coeditor of this study and director of this project, is currently president of The Henry L. Stimson Center in Washington, D.C. He previously served as an official in ACDA and is the author of *Strategic Stalemate: Nuclear Weapons and Arms Control in American Politics*.[15] The Stimson Center was founded in 1989 as a nonprofit organization to pursue research and public education on vital issues of arms control and international security.

As one can see from this brief description, the participants in this project have a mix of educational and professional backgrounds. Five of the eight participants (Krepon, Loeb, Nolan, Platt, and Widenor) have served in either the executive or legislative branch of government; three (Krepon, Nolan, and Platt) have served in both branches; three were trained in political science (Caldwell, Nolan, and Platt); and five were trained in history (Buckley, Krepon, Loeb, McElroy, and Widenor). This mix of historians and political scientists, former policymakers, and academics is unusual for an undertaking of this sort and has contributed to the intellectual vitality of the project. This is not to say that it has been easy to develop a common research approach and to extract common themes and lessons learned from the seven cases studied, for different academic disciplines—even those as closely related as history and political science—have their own vocabularies and particular methodological concerns. In addition, both policymakers and academics are often quick to dismiss one another as irrelevant to the analysis of their particular concerns, needs, and interests.

Attempts to extrapolate the findings of this study to other types of treaties require the utmost caution; as historians are wont to note, history never repeats itself, and each historical case possesses unique aspects. This caveat aside, the analyses and conclusions contained in this study should be most relevant to other arms control treaties. Some of the conclusions may be relevant to agreements covering trade or foreign relations, but these issue areas require separate study. Those who wish to draw such conclusions are invited to adapt and use the focused comparison methodology employed in this study.

Notes

1. See Kenneth Colegrove, *The American Senate and World Peace* (New York: Vanguard Press, 1944); Alan Cranston, *The Killing of the Peace* (New York: Viking Press, 1960); Royden Dangerfield, *In Defense of the Senate: A Study in Treaty Making* (Norman: University of Oklahoma, 1933); and

Denna Frank Fleming, *The Treaty Veto of the American Senate* (New York: G. P. Putnam, 1930). For more recent studies, see Lloyd Ambrosius, *Woodrow Wilson and the American Diplomatic Tradition: The Treaty Fight in Perspective* (Cambridge: Cambridge University Press, 1987), and William C. Widenor, *Henry Cabot Lodge and the Search for an American Foreign Policy* (Berkeley: University of California Press, 1980).

2. Robert D. Putnam, "Diplomacy and Domestic Politics: The Logic of Two-Level Games," *International Organization* 42, no. 3 (Summer 1988): 427–60.

3. Ibid., 432 (emphasis in the original).

4. Mary H. Cooper, "Treaty Ratification," *Editorial Research Reports* (January 29, 1988): 42.

5. Alexander L. George and Richard Smoke, "Appendix: Theory for Policy in International Relations," in *Deterrence in American Foreign Policy: Theory and Practice* (New York: Columbia University Press, 1974), 636.

6. George and Smoke, *Deterrence in American Foreign Policy*, 95–97; Alexander L. George, "Case Studies and Theory Development: The Method of Structured Focused Comparison," in *Diplomatic History: New Approaches*, ed. Paul Gordon Lauren, (New York: Free Press, 1979), 107–20; and Alexander L. George and Timothy J. McKeown, "Case Studies and Theories of Organizational Decision Making," in *Advances in Information Processing in Organizations: A Research Annual*, ed. Robert F. Coulam and Richard A. Smith, vol. 2 (Greenwich, Conn.: JAI Press, 1985), 21–58.

7. George and Smoke, *Deterrence in American Foreign Policy*; Alexander L. George, David K. Hall, and Williams R. Simons, *The Limits of Coercive Diplomacy: Laos, Cuba, Vietnam* (Boston, Mass.: Little, Brown & Co., 1971); Richard Smoke, *War: Controlling Escalation* (Cambridge: Harvard University Press, 1977); Dan Caldwell, *American-Soviet Relations: From 1947 to the Nixon-Kissinger Grand Design* (Westport, Conn.: Greenwood Press, 1981); Alexander L. George, *Managing U.S.-Soviet Rivalry: Problems of Crisis Prevention* (Boulder, Colo.: Westview Press, 1983); and Alexander L. George, Philip J. Farley, and Alexander Dallin, eds., *U.S.-Soviet Security Cooperation: Achievements, Failures, Lessons* (New York: Oxford University Press, 1988).

8. Hedley Bull, "Strategic Arms Limitation: The Precedent of the Washington and London Naval Treaties," in *SALT: Problems and Prospects*, ed. Morton A. Kaplan, (Morristown, N.J.: General Learning Press, 1973), and Roger Dingman, "Statesmen, Admirals and SALT: The United States and the Washington Conference, 1921–1922" (Santa Monica: California Arms Control and Foreign Policy Seminar, December 1972).

9. For the texts and brief descriptions of these agreements and others, see U.S. Arms Control and Disarmament Agency, *Arms Control and Disarmament Agreements: Texts and Histories of Negotiations* (Washington, D.C.: GPO, 1982).

10. See note 1.

11. Thomas H. Buckley, *The United States and the Washington Conference, 1921-1922* (Knoxville: University of Tennessee Press, 1970).

12. Glenn T. Seaborg with the assistance of Benjamin S. Loeb, *Kennedy, Khrushchev and the Test Ban* (Berkeley: University of California Press, 1981), and Glen T. Seaborg with Benjamin S. Loeb, *Stemming the Tide: Arms Control in the Johnson Years* (Lexington, Mass.: Lexington Books, 1987).

13. Dr. Platt is also the author of *The U.S. Senate and Strategic Arms Policy, 1969-1977* (Boulder, Colo.: Westview Press, 1978), and the coeditor (with Lawrence Weiler) of *Congress and Arms Control* (Boulder, Colo.: Westview Press, 1978).

14. Dan Caldwell, *The Dynamics of Domestic Politics and Arms Control: The SALT II Treaty Ratification Debate* (Columbia: University of South Carolina Press, 1991).

15. Michael Krepon, *Strategic Stalemate: Nuclear Weapons and Arms Control in American Politics* (New York: St. Martin's Press, 1984).

1   The League of Nations Component of the Versailles Treaty

William C. Widenor

Though both the inception of the League of Nations and its constitutional shape may clearly be attributed to the influence of Woodrow Wilson, the concept of "a league to keep the peace" was not original with him. The idea of a league had long been a staple of American internationalist thought, and even former President Theodore Roosevelt had touted the league idea in the course of his Nobel Peace Prize acceptance speech in Norway in 1910.[1] In internationalist circles, however, there had never been any consensus about how such a league should be constituted; some Americans favored a great power league (Roosevelt's idea), others opted for the idea of a universal collective security organization, while still others were committed to a juridically based internationalism. Even so, until World War I kindled renewed interest in the idea, it is probably fair to say that the idea of a league remained anathema to most Americans, that it was considered too drastic a departure from the prevailing isolationist tradition. Americans still tended to think in terms of American exceptionalism and of the necessity for protection from the evil wiles of European diplomacy. The strength and pervasiveness of this kind of thinking can perhaps best be gauged by viewing even Wilson's league idea as an insistence that the world order be fundamentally overhauled as a precondition to sustained American participation therein.

Consequently, it should not be surprising that when President Wilson embraced the league idea in 1916 as part of his campaign to bring about a negotiated settlement in Europe, a so-called "peace without victory," he did so gingerly and without crossing many bridges. Speaking before the First Annual National Assemblage of the League to Enforce Peace (a pro-league pressure group headed by A. Lawrence Lowell, president of Harvard, and former President William Howard Taft), Wilson went no further than to claim that future peace would depend upon "a new and more wholesome diplomacy," upon "some sort of agreement among the great nations," "some feasible method of acting in concert," and to call upon the nations of the world to "in some way band themselves together to see . . . that right prevails. . . ."[2]

Despite his audience, Wilson did not even endorse the use of force to maintain the world's peace. According to the testimony of his secretary of state, Robert Lansing, Wilson, "after preparing his address . . . went over it and erased all reference to the use of physical force in preventing wars."[3] The result was that when the president came to his punch line ("I feel that the world is even now upon the eve of a great consummation, when some common force will be brought into existence which shall safeguard right"), it was certainly not clear to his listeners whether he was talking about an international military force or about the force of worldwide public opinion strengthened by a great international conversion to the principles of democracy and peace.

Even the fact of the United States' entry into World War I lent little clarity to Wilson's intentions. In his War Message to Congress on April 2, 1917, Wilson declared that one of the things the United States would be fighting for would be "a universal dominion of right by such a concert of free peoples as shall bring peace and safety to all nations and make the world itself free."[4] Though his enunciation of U.S. war aims was specific in some respects, his famous fourteenth point went only so far as to declare that "a general association of nations must be formed under specific covenants for the purpose of affording mutual guarantees of political independence and territorial integrity to great and small states alike."[5] There was no suggestion about how that might be done. Not once did Wilson discuss the constitutional problems inherent in international organization or even hint about what the covenants would specify or how the guarantees would be enforced. Regarding what was perhaps the most basic issue of all, Wilson never made it clear whether he contemplated an international army of enforcement or merely a self-denying ordinance. Some tough decisions were involved, and though it may have been politic in the immediate sense to avoid them, to do so was to miss an opportunity to garner public and congressional support for something more tangible than the idea of "a league" and to invite the reappearance at a later and less opportune time of the problems involved in constructing a viable international organization to keep the peace.

Though in retrospect it seems perfectly clear that Wilson had long since determined to make the league the cornerstone of the peace treaty and that this intention had much to do with his decision to head personally the U.S. delegation to Paris, it is also true that in November of 1918, as the war ended and a peace settlement loomed on the horizon, it would have been very hazardous to predict the precise nature of such a settlement. The armistice arrangement itself left considerable doubt about whether the peace would be imposed or negotiated. The role of a league in future international relations remained highly problematic.

First, there was the matter of its scope and membership. Wilson's original conception had been formulated when the United States was still determined to stand aside from World War I and when the United States was still attempting to arrange "a peace without victory." Once the United States entered the war, however, the stock image of a league began inexorably to change from that of a universal league to a league of victors. For some Americans this presented few problems. U.S. entry into the war led former President Taft to proclaim that a world League to Enforce Peace had been formed.[6] The watchword of the League to Enforce Peace readily became: "We are engaged with our Allies in precisely the kind of war the League's program holds to be both justifiable and necessary."[7] President Wilson, however, disdained such a path and clung to the fiction of a universal league because he was distrustful of the war aims of the Allies (he could never bring himself to call them more than "Associates") and probably also because he was mindful of the views of William Jennings Bryan, who still commanded a large following in the Democratic party and who argued that the prevalent war psychology had made a universal league that much more difficult to achieve.[8]

A second question pertained to the league's potential powers. On the one hand, many Americans still in the thrall of the isolationist tradition were frightened by the prospect of any league, especially one with substantial power. On the other hand, French leaders, while still thinking in terms of traditional international power politics, were beginning to see that a league if strong enough and if possessing its own army, might serve their primary purpose of keeping Germany in check. In short, from the outset the question was not whether there was going to be *a* league but rather how much power that league would have and how it would function. As Senator Henry Cabot Lodge (R-Mass.) told the Senate on December 21, 1918, he had been ruminating for several years (actually since the establishment of the League to Enforce Peace in 1915) on the subject of the relationship between force and peace and had come to the following conclusion:

> If . . . there is to be a league of nations in order to enforce peace, one thing is clear. It must be either a mere assemblage of words, an exposition of vague ideals and comforting hopes, or it must be a practical system. If such a league is to be practical and effective, it can not possibly be either unless it has authority to issue decrees and force to sustain them. It is at this point that the questions of great moment arise.[9]

Early on, it was clear that Wilson's task as a peacemaker would be a formidable one. From the outset he faced the dilemma inherent in the taunt made by Senator William E.

Borah (R-Idaho), "What will your league amount to if it does not contain powers that no one dreams of giving it?"[10] Senator Lodge, who would assume the role of Senate majority leader and of chairman of the Senate Foreign Relations Committee in the new Congress, was initially skeptical about constructing any league at all, believing that the nations could never agree on the practical details of the league's constitution. As he told his friend Theodore Roosevelt, "I think the practical difficulties are so great that it will be a long day before they really do anything about it."[11]

Nevertheless, harking back to his earlier definition, "a mere assemblage of words," Lodge began to worry that Wilson was not sufficiently concerned with enforcing the peace against Germany and that he and those who had not been thoroughly pro-Ally from the beginning of the conflict would seek to substitute some weak league for the exaction of physical guarantees against the resurrection of German military power. Just as Wilson was arriving in Paris and holding his first preliminary diplomatic discussions, Lodge sought both to clarify the issue and to pressure the president. Both privately in a memorandum prepared to be shown to British, French, and Italian leaders (Arthur Balfour, Georges Clemenceau, and Francisco Nitti, respectively) and publicly in the Senate Lodge warned that the consequences of Wilson's persistence with his league idea would be dire.

> Under no circumstances must provisions for such a league be made a part of the peace treaty which concludes the war with Germany. Any attempt to do this would not only long delay the signature of the treaty of peace, which should not be unduly postponed, but it would make the adoption of the treaty, unamended, by the Senate of the United States and other ratifying bodies, extremely doubtful.[12]

Long before the negotiations in Paris were even under way and long before anyone turned a hand to the drafting of a league constitution, political battle lines were being drawn in such a way as to presage a momentous conflict.

International Political Context

As historian Arthur Walworth has so aptly put it, late 1918 was definitely "America's moment."[13] U.S. arms had turned the tide of battle against the Central Powers, the Allies were all heavily in debt to the United States, and most of Europe was a supplicant for U.S. supplies and foodstuffs. In fact, the war had destroyed most of the traditional European order and had resulted in what historian Raymond J. Sontag once called "a broken world."[14] There was great political and social turmoil, especially in the defeated countries. The Bolsheviks had already seized power in Russia, and there was a widespread fear, inflamed by temporary Bolshevik successes in both Bavaria and Hungary, that the Red menace was spreading westward, and, of course, there would be many at the peace conference who would seek to turn that fear to their own national advantage. As Ray Stannard Baker once claimed, Paris cannot be understood without Moscow.[15] Europe was in a dangerous state of flux; in the words of Czech leader Thomas Masaryk it was now just "a laboratory resting upon a vast cemetery."[16] The United States had gone to war according to President Wilson to make the world "safe for democracy," and what so many Europeans now wondered was whether that would be the end result of the war, whether the United States could indeed bring peace to their troubled continent.

If it was "America's moment," it was also democracy's moment. The four great empires of central and eastern Europe were in a state of collapse. As a result, for the first time in European history, democratic governments were to bear full responsibility for constructing a lasting peace. It was inevitable that democracy would make some embarrassing demands on diplomacy and complicate the efforts of the world's statesmen. What only time would tell was whether democracy would facilitate or hinder a statesmanlike peace.

Perhaps the "moment" belonged above all to President

Wilson. At the outset of the peace conference Wilson was enormously popular. He was so well received in France initially that he caused serious consternation in the highest circles of the French government.[17] In truth he had risen to an extraordinary position of moral leadership and now was at the very height of his worldwide popularity. His eloquent statements of idealistic war aims had made him a hero to liberals everywhere and had led war-weary and oppressed populations throughout the world to hail him as their deliverer, as the one person capable of making a just peace. Moreover, in addition to this transcendent moral influence, all the traditional instruments of national power lay in Wilson's hands. As one of Wilson's severest critics, John Maynard Keynes, once put it:

> The American armies were at the height of their numbers, discipline, and equipment. Europe was in complete dependence on the food supplies of the United States; and financially she was even more at their mercy. Europe not only already owed the United States more than she could pay; but only a large measure of further assistance could save her from starvation and bankruptcy. Never had a philosopher held such weapons wherewith to bind the princes of this world.[18]

That, however, was no guarantee that such weapons would suffice. There were also many obstacles to a Wilsonian peace. Though Wilson's moral power was great, it tended to dissipate quickly when weighed on the cruel scales of national interest and Weltpolitik. In addition, Wilson's economic power over the Allies took the form principally of control over credits and foodstuffs. Had he used that power aggressively, he would also have punished American farmers at home, still a very powerful constituency in 1918–19.

Some obstacles were inherent in the very organization and approach of the U.S. delegation. Wilson had plenty of good advice; his often heralded commission of experts, frequently called the Inquiry, studied most of the international problems likely to arise in the course of the conference and overall supplied Wilson with some two thousand reports. Yet those reports never coalesced into a philosophy of international relations or a coherent approach to the construction of a lasting peace and the advent of general disarmament. In several important ways the United States was as unprepared for bringing about peace as it had originally been unprepared for war. Americans had little experience in making other than bilateral peace treaties, and they were more accustomed to looking at issues as a matter of justice than they were to looking at them as a part of a pattern dictated by the requisites of a lasting peace. To compound matters, Wilson never succeeded in imposing any organization on the huge U.S. delegation. There was almost no liaison between the other U.S. delegates and Wilson, and the president tended to be isolated both because he preferred to operate alone and because "nobody dared to tell him the truth."[19]

Moreover, despite Wilson's initial ascendant popularity, there was never any agreement—either among the delegates or the respective public opinions that they represented—as to what was requisite for an enduring peace. Public opinion, never unitary, soon divided into thirty-two separate opinions, the number of nations in actual attendance. There were from the outset two major strands of thinking about how to construct a durable peace. One, especially appealing to English-speaking diplomats, sought to avoid harsh peace terms that might incite revanchism among the vanquished and to provide for a continuing process of adjustment and negotiation. The other, strongly advocated by the French, would create alliances with a preponderance of military power so that Germany would never dare "break out" on the world again.

Though Wilson was to have serious problems with all the other major Allies (the British, the Italians, and the Japanese), his principal antagonist at the peace conference was destined to be Georges Clemenceau of France, whose philosophy of international relations was almost the reverse image of his own. From the French premier's conservative, skeptical point of view, conflicts between states were inevitable. France had prevailed in the latest conflict only by assembling a powerful coalition against Germany, an alliance that it would surely need again because the recent long war had only worsened the French deficiency in military personnel and had only made it crystal clear that France fighting alone could never even hope to withstand another onslaught of German might. From the French perspective, a Wilsonian peace might very well shorten the interval of Germany's recovery and hasten the day when the Germans would feel strong enough to attempt to avenge their present defeat. The only real security for France lay in the reduction of German power, in all its manifestations, and the exaction of guarantees against its ever rising again. As Keynes once explained:

> So far as possible, therefore, it was the policy of France to set the clock back and to undo what, since 1870, the progress of Germany had accomplished. By loss of territory and other measures her population was to be curtailed; but chiefly the economic system, upon which she depended for her new strength, the vast fabric built upon iron, coal, and transport, must be destroyed. If France could seize, even in part, what Germany was compelled to drop, the inequality of strength between the two rivals for European hegemony might be remedied for many generations.[20]

Such a program represented a distinct challenge to Wilson's conception of what was required for a lasting peace at every fundamental point: a league of victors determined to prevent Germany from ever "breaking out" again versus a universal collective security organization, disarmament of Germany versus general disarmament, physical exactions versus paper-guarantees, indemnities designed to cripple Germany versus simple reparations, and some dismemberment of Germany in violation of Wilson's commitment to the principle of self-determination. In short, just beneath the surface of practically every problem confronting the peace conference lay the question of how France could best be protected against Germany.

Another obstacle to a Wilsonian peace was the group of secret treaties and agreements that the Allies had contracted between themselves before the United States entered the war, treaties of which Wilson was aware but about which he continued to feign ignorance. France had been promised by all the Allies the return of Alsace-Lorraine. The Russians had even promised France possession of the Saar Valley and the construction of an independent buffer state out of German territory on the west side of the Rhine. Italy had been promised considerable accessions of Austrian territory, both about the head of the Adriatic Sea and in the southern Tirol. Moreover, Japan had been promised not only all the German islands in the North Pacific but also the takeover of all German rights in the Shantung province of China. These claims were the real headaches; all tended to compromise both the spirit and the letter of Wilson's Fourteen Points promise of self-determination and to demonstrate that self-determination was not necessarily the panacea it was touted to be.

Another obstacle, and one that Wilson could never surmount, was the vindictive spirit prevalent among the peoples of all the Allied countries, including the United States, a spirit that, precisely because these were mostly democratic countries, had to be taken into account. The domestic politics of Britain and France were such that few politicians could resist the temptation to seek domestic political advantage by upping the ante regarding what should be demanded from the Germans by way of compensation. The people wanted revenge and retribution, and their strong backing strengthened the hand of those who, like Clemenceau, had little interest in a Wilsonian peace of reconciliation. Thus the very democracy that Wilson thought a safeguard against war proved to be a formidable barrier to a statesmanlike peace.

Perhaps the principal reason why Wilson was unable to translate U.S. power into a settlement that would have conformed to the Fourteen Points was that he was not as disinterested as he pretended to be. All Wilson's actions in Paris point to the conclusion that the League of Nations was what he really cared about; all other considerations were secondary. To get the League Covenant adopted was an achievement so precious that he was willing to pay for it with concessions on other issues that in many cases contravened the principles of the Fourteen Points. Clemenceau, first and foremost, but the other Allied leaders as well, let it be known, just as did the Soviets toward the end of the World War II, that they would swallow the U.S. plan for international organization, but at a price. Therein may lie the key to understanding how to find one's way through the labyrinthine negotiations that led to such a complex and inconsistent peace treaty. As Colonel House, who had to go about the dirty business of purchasing support for Wilson's league, once explained the ensuing pattern of negotiations, "The fact is that the League of Nations in which he has been more deeply interested than anything else from the beginning . . . has been played to the limit by the French and Japanese in extracting concessions from him; to a certain extent by the British too, and the Treaty as it stands is the result."[21]

Before his vision of what could be achieved by a league of nations, Wilson sacrificed his Fourteen Points one by one. Suffice it to say that at the outset Wilson conceded the South Tirol to Italy for supposedly strategic reasons, thereby incorporating 225,000 Austrians into Italy and violating the principle of self-determination. From there on it was all downhill. To persuade France to give up its plans for an independent buffer state on the Rhine, Wilson was forced to sign a special treaty pledging the United States to protect France against invasion, a treaty derogatory of the league idea, since it implied that the league might not be effective and that separate and special guarantees were required. Wilson never liked the French Guarantee Treaty and made no effort to secure its ratification. The Japanese threatened not to join his league, and as a result, Wilson gave in on Shantung, despite the long tradition of U.S. concern for the preservation of the territorial integrity of China. Not only were the Germans deprived of all their colonies and of considerable territory in Europe that contained large German populations, but they also were saddled with an exceptionally high bill for reparations and were forced, in a war guilt clause that was anathema to the German people and ran contrary to the common sense of most Americans, to accept exclusive blame for starting the conflict.

Wilson thought he could bend Europe to his will, and initially he was probably too successful for his own good. He not only got his much vaunted league but pulled off his greatest diplomatic coup and made his most costly political mistake at one and the same time, when the Paris Peace Conference decided to make the League of Nations an integral part of the Treaty of Versailles, something that Wilson's American opponents had long warned should not be done. This was a fateful step. In transcending the immediate business of concluding hostilities and looking to reform the whole international system, Wilson loaded his treaty with an inordinate amount of political and ideological difficulty. His opponents, having little faith in the efficacy of a league, wanted to postpone the matter to some indefinite future. He thwarted and frustrated them, but by tying his league to the peace treaty, he made it carry a large and growing burden, for it was initially the peace treaty itself that came under the sharpest attack. Both with respect to their provisions and to the prospects for their ratification the Versailles Treaty and the League Covenant would have had smoother sailing if they had not been linked.

Wilson did not succeed in producing a treaty consonant with his own principles. He may even on occasion, as Keynes once complained, have simply been "bamboozled" by Clemenceau and David Lloyd George. It is understandable that Wilson would be reluctant to admit to that but less understandable that he refused to admit that the treaty was seriously flawed. Keynes's explanation is that Wilson assumed a self-righteous attitude that invited a hypocritical treaty. Wilson's attitude, as depicted by Keynes, was supposedly "I see your difficulties and I should like to be able to agree to what you propose; but I can do nothing that is not just and right, and you must first of all show me that what you want does really fall within the words of the pronouncements which are binding on me." Keynes's point is that European draftsmen were certainly up to the challenge.[22]

In this regard another British critic, Harold Nicolson, may have been even more perceptive. He saw Wilson as a man "obsessed," even "possessed." To him "the League Covenant was his own Revelation and the solution of all human difficulties." So what mattered some injustices here and there if the world in the league actually had machinery to prevent war and to correct wrongs by peaceful process? The covenant "became for him the boxroom in which he stored all inconvenient articles of furniture" in the hope that they would somehow simply go away.[23] In thus attempting to diffuse criticism of the treaty's many inequities, however, Wilson was only creating further difficulties for himself and his treaty. He was causing attention to be focused on the actual constitution of the league—on the questions of how and if it could accomplish even part of what was claimed for it. The vagueness of his original conception and the vagueness of Article 10 of the League Covenant, which suggested the use of force to maintain the status quo, were coming to haunt him. League members pledged "to respect and preserve as against external aggression the territorial integrity and existing political independence of all members," but such important questions as how those pledges would be carried out and to what extent member states were bound to accede to the wishes of the League Council were left dangerously unanswered.

Domestic Political Context

Wilson remained optimistic about the chances for ratification of the Versailles Treaty, believing that public opinion would demand ratification of his League Covenant for world peace and that the Senate could be bludgeoned into favorable action, but both his own political future and the ratification of his treaty were in more jeopardy than he realized.[24]

Even before going to Paris to negotiate the peace, Wilson had received a severe political setback in the congressional elections of late 1918. Some of his more prominent Republican opponents, such as Lodge and his friend Theodore Roosevelt, fought that campaign as a "khaki election," attempting to turn it into a referendum for "unconditional [German] surrender and complete victory just as Grant stood."[25] Wilson, in response, fearing that his plans for a "just" peace were being undermined, launched an appeal for the election of a Democratic Congress so that he might serve as the American people's "unembarrassed spokesman in affairs at home and abroad." A Republican victory, he declared, would "certainly be interpreted on the other side of the water as a repudiation" of his leadership.[26] Lodge and Roosevelt wanted desperately to believe that the election turned on foreign policy issues and that their appeal for a complete Allied victory and a peace resting on permanent Allied military predominance had turned the tide. Though some scholars have attributed the Democratic loss to Wilson's mistake in issuing such a partisan election appeal, historian Seward W. Livermore assembled persuasive evidence that the election actually turned in the Midwest on domestic, bread-and-butter issues and overall on a significantly lower than usual voter turnout.[27]

Whatever the reasons for the outcome, the Republican victory not only weakened Wilson but forced him for the first time in his presidency to face a Congress controlled by the opposition party. Even before a single line of the Versailles Treaty was written, both Wilson and his ideas concerning what would constitute a proper and just peace settlement were in trouble. Lodge, looking ahead to a Republican victory in 1920, was determined to reassert the authority of Congress in foreign affairs and to impose his version of a proper peace settlement. Like Clemenceau, Lodge thought that keeping the Germans permanently in check should be the peace conference's primary concern.[28] Though the president still enjoyed great stature, the senator, by virtue of his chairmanship of the Senate Foreign Relations Committee and his chairmanship of the Republican Conference in the next Senate, would hold positions of considerable strength and advantage and was going to have to be reckoned with.

Wilson, however, was undaunted. As he then told his daughter: "I think the Republicans will find the responsibility which they must now assume more onerous than joyful, and my expectation is that they will exercise it with some circumspection. I shall see to it that they are put in a position to realize their full responsibility and the reckoning in 1920 may hold disappointing results for them." Wilson envisaged a scenario in which the Senate Republicans could be charged with breaking the peace of the world, thereby giving him an issue on which he might be reelected—a somewhat fantastic vision, given the strength of the two-term tradition at the time.[29] Wilson once again saw himself as a progressive crusader fighting the country's reactionaries against the odds. That was the kind of fight—one between a progressive peace and a reactionary peace, and between a progressive president and the conservative Senate majority leader—that Wilson relished. It was also precisely the kind of battle that he waged throughout 1919 and 1920, a battle that, had it corresponded to political realities, he might have won.

Unfortunately for Wilson, the political realities were other than what he thought. As historian Robert M. Crunden has reminded, just because Wilson was a progressive and Lodge a conservative, there is no reason to define the fight over the treaty as at heart a battle over a progressive issue. Progressives were deeply divided over the treaty and the league. The opposition, the irreconcilables or the "Battalion of Death," was led by some of the most progressive men in Washington—Senators Borah, Hiram Johnson (R-Calif.), and Robert M. La Follette (R-Wis.). "In fact, the fight over the

Treaty of Versailles was also the last great battle within progressivism."[30]

No sooner were the terms of the peace treaties published than the editors of the *New Republic* forsook Wilson and reembraced isolationism. In an editorial on May 17, 1919 written by Walter Lippmann, the *New Republic* declared, "We do not see how this treaty is anything but the prelude to quarrels in a deeply divided and hideously embittered Europe." The following week the editors recommended that the United States withdraw from all commitments to Europe and took sharp aim at Article 10 of the League Covenant, which to their mind would only serve to perpetuate all the inequities of the overall treaty.[31] Wilson's decision to join with the Allies in interventions against the Bolsheviks stirred the liberals against him even further. Continued turmoil in Europe combined with the repression of labor and the onset of the Red Scare in the United States also caused many on the Left to take issue with Wilson's preoccupation with foreign policy and his beloved league and to demand that the administration think about America first and reestablish a progressive agenda at home.

Moreover, almost every major immigrant group within the United States found some fault with the treaties. Wilson was to learn that the "hyphenates" were also a force to be reckoned with. German-Americans resented the discrimination they had endured during the war and blamed Wilson for U.S. intervention, for the notorious war guilt clause, and for the terrible financial burden imposed on the German people by the treaty. Italian-Americans were bitter about Wilson's opposition to further Italian territorial aggrandizement. They ignored the fact that he had waived the principle of self-determination in order to give Italy the South Tirol district and concentrated their fire on his opposition to Italian claims to the city of Fiume. Millions of Irish-Americans, so important to Democratic prospects in the cities of the North, were also indignant because the president had not affronted the United Kingdom by pressing the cause of Irish independence at Paris. They particularly disliked Article 10 of the League Covenant, which suggested the use of force to maintain the status quo, because they feared that it might hinder the realization of independence for Ireland. In short, the political landscape was complex and fraught with pitfalls for a president who sought to impose a traditional liberal-conservative dichotomy on viewpoints with respect to what he saw as the crowning achievement of progressive reform, namely his League Covenant.

Despite these growing and impending desertions, most historians still believe that in the spring of 1919 most Americans were ready to approve the Treaty of Versailles and accept U.S. membership in the League of Nations. Of course, one cannot be sure, as there was in this period no objective public opinion polling, and even had there been, it is problematic whether any information of value could have been obtained from a poll that might have asked Americans whether they favored a league to guarantee the world's peace. The point, as historian Herbert F. Margulies so aptly puts it, is that support for the league was "broad but shallow."[32] Yes, most Americans probably wanted a league to keep the peace, but behind that initial support was a host of qualifications. They wanted a league, yes, but not one that could do certain things. They wanted a league, yes, but they still found many provisions of the treaty unacceptable. It was this situation that shaped the political strategies of both Wilson and Lodge.

Wilson's strategy was geared toward creating an irresistible public demand for immediate ratification by the Senate. Consequently, he had little interest in detailed discussion of the workings of the league or the multifarious other provisions of the treaty. He was not even interested in trying to persuade the American people to accept new international responsibilities knowingly or in trying to convince them that their vital interests were involved in the maintenance of peace in Europe. Rather, Wilson saw that his only chance was in engendering in the American people a sense of moral urgency that would overwhelm all specific criticism of either the League Covenant or the treaty. First in Boston, and then two weeks later in his New York opera speech, Wilson avoided discussing the specifics of league organization and made no attempt to answer his opponents' arguments. Rather, he spoke of the league in highly exalted tones as the only way to keep the peace and to restore prosperity. Never once did he mention the possibility of the league's having to employ physical force; his emphasis was always on the great moral force of world public opinion and on the cleansing and clarifying influences of publicity. Progressive reform had at last been brought to the whole world![33]

This strategy had an important ancillary aspect, which was developed in a cablegram from Joseph Tumulty, Wilson's press secretary, to the president and dated January 6, 1919. Tumulty, arguing that Wilson's personal contact with the peoples of Europe had done much to advance his program, thought that the president should use the occasion of his return "to strike in favor of [the] League of Nations." Specifically, he suggested: "Could you not consider stopping upon your return at port of Boston instead of New York? The announcement of your stopping at Boston would make ovation inevitable throughout New England and would centre attack on Lodge."[34] Wilson followed Tumulty's advice and was very well received in Boston. The league idea was initially very popular in New England, and Wilson's visit produced considerable pressure on Lodge to soft-pedal his opposition to the league idea. Wilson, by seizing the initiative, set the framework within which Lodge had to respond.[35]

Lodge scarcely needed his friend Albert J. Beveridge (former Republican senator from Indiana) to remind him that "the future of the [Republican] party is in your hands more than in those of any other man," that Republican prospects would suffer greatly if the Democrats could claim that Wilson had brought about "the greatest constructive world reform in history."[36] It appeared that Wilson was seeking to make the league a vehicle for a Democratic victory and even perhaps for his own election to a third term, something that Lodge wanted at all costs to prevent.

Many of those who ended up in the irreconcilable camp (opposed to the league under all circumstances) thought that the league could be a winning political issue for the Republicans, but Lodge was not so sure and worried that that advantage might initially accrue to Wilson and the Democrats.

advantage might initially accrue to Wilson and the Democrats. He warned Beveridge that the situation required careful handling and that he did "not think it would be wise for us at this stage to make it a party issue, nor to confront it with a blank negative."[37] He allegedly also told Senator Borah that he did not believe the League could be defeated outright, that "the best we can do is to get changes that will emasculate it as much as possible."[38] Politics clearly dictated a strategy of amendment and reservation.

The political situation also dictated a strategy of delay. Lodge, the intellectual heir of the Federalists, did not trust the American people's first thought on an issue involving perhaps "the most momentous decision that this country has ever been called upon to make."[39] Like the Federalists, he viewed the Constitution, and especially the powers of the Senate, as a means of ensuring that "the operation of the popular will depend for its final expression upon the calm second thought of the community and not be governed by the passions of the moment."[40] Believing that to give a decision on the League Covenant "hastily and without complete knowledge of what we are to agree to would be almost criminal," Lodge determined to await the community's "calm second thought," optimistic that once the people understood "what the practical difficulties and dangers are," they would desert the president's cause in great numbers.[41]

Accordingly, there would have to be a great educational campaign among the people on the league issue and such a campaign would obviously take time. Wilson's problem was that Lodge, in his dual capacity of chairman of the Senate Foreign Relations Committee and Senate majority leader, was in a position to dictate the pace of treaty consideration and thereby ensure that the time for such a campaign would be found. Moreover, as Lodge had suspected, as the American people learned more of the details of the league constitution and more about how it would operate, as the vague Wilsonian ideal became a concrete reality demanding specific American pledges and sacrifices, they began to lose their enthusiasm for Wilson's great cause.

Role of the President

President Wilson played such a prominent role both in the negotiation of the treaty and in the attempt to secure its ratification that many Americans perceived the Versailles Treaty as "Wilson's treaty" rather than as a treaty negotiated by the government of the United States. This perception clearly served to damage the treaty's prospects for ratification.

Wilson had been a very successful president in getting progressive legislation passed; for years he had commanded and Congress had enacted, perhaps consciously simulating the relationship between a British prime minister and the members of the House of Commons of his own party. Wilson's successes, however, had not brought great popularity. Wilson had originally been elected president in 1912 because of the insurgent-standpatter split in Republican ranks. He had been reelected in 1916 only by an extremely narrow margin. The Republican party remained the majority party in the country, a fact underlined by the Republicans' recapture of control of both houses of Congress in the congressional elections of 1918, despite Wilson's appeal that Democrats be elected so as to strengthen his position in the forthcoming peace negotiations. The situation called for a policy of accommodation with the political opposition; many Republican votes would be necessary to secure ratification of the peace treaty by the Senate. Wilson, however, as David Lloyd George once put it, had "rather an ecclesiastical than a political type of mind"; he "was a bigoted sectarian who placed in the category of the damned all those who belonged to a different political creed and excluded them forever from charitable thought or destiny."[42]

In addition, Wilson tended to be a loner. He trusted in himself alone or in someone like Colonel House, whom he deemed to be loyal (at least until their break in the spring of 1919) to his designs. These two things, his partisanship and his distrust of others, had much to do both with his decision to go to Paris and do the primary negotiating himself and with the makeup of the rest of the U.S. delegation. Logical choices would have been prominent Republican senators or at least the leaders of the League to Enforce Peace, former President Taft and President Lowell of Harvard, both of whom were Republicans. The League to Enforce Peace was the major pressure group advocating a league and ought to have been encouraged rather than neglected. Yet Wilson throughout the war had kept his distance from those who advocated specific proposals, with the result that "Taft and his colleagues were never to know precisely where they stood with Wilson or to what degree he really believed in their League to Enforce Peace."[43] It is hard to resist the conclusion that by shunning such natural allies, Wilson was endeavoring to make sure that he would be in total control and that it would be "his" league that emerged from the conference both in design and in responsibility and credit. It was for that reason that he was convinced that he himself had to go to Paris and that he surrounded himself in the peace delegation, despite Taft's advice to the contrary, with men of such limited stature that there was no possibility of any challenge to his leadership.[44]

Henry White, a fairly obscure but nevertheless talented diplomat, but also one with little political standing, was the only Republican named to the delegation. Colonel House and a number of other advisers had suggested that Wilson appoint former President Taft or Elihu Root, who was a former secretary of state and who had recently served in the Senate. Taft still had a substantial political following, and Root enjoyed great prestige among senators. Wilson, however, thought that their views diverged too far from his own and that they could not be trusted. House was convinced that in passing them by Wilson "made again one of his common mistakes."[45] Even with those who were appointed to the delegation, such as Secretary of State Robert Lansing, he had very little contact. Wilson and Lansing conferred only once during their transatlantic crossing, and Lansing could only conclude that the Department of State, like the Senate, was to have little do to with the actual negotiations in Paris.[46] With respect to the all-important constitution for the League of Nations, Wilson took absolutely no one into his confidence except the trusted Colonel House.[47]

Wilson's pattern of isolation and of feeling that he had to do everything himself was buttressed by a feeling of moral arrogance, which he had displayed on previous occasions but which now manifested itself in a particularly acute form.[48] The actual negotiations have been described above, but here it is important to understand the attitude with which Wilson approached his European counterparts, for it bears a striking resemblance to that which he later displayed toward his senatorial opposition. Wilson encouraged his advisers to view the Paris Peace Conference as a great moral battle between the new world and the old.[49] Discarding the traditional tenets of diplomacy, he arrogated to himself a higher authority than that of the leaders with whom he had to negotiate. The United States, he told members of the Inquiry (the staff of academic experts he and House had assembled), would be the only disinterested nation at the conference, and consequently he was under a moral compulsion to make sure that justice was served in all matters, even with respect to boundary disputes in which the United States had no interest.

Moreover, Wilson (who had a dubious political mandate from his own people) dared to assert that the statesmen of the Allies did not truly represent the temper of their own peoples.[50] Implicit in that assumption was the idea that if necessary, he could go over their heads and appeal directly to the peoples of Europe. This kind of thinking was no doubt encouraged by the tremendous receptions Wilson received on his initial visits to the various European countries. Yet when in the case of Fiume he appealed to the Italian people directly, he found that the Italian people wanted exactly what their leaders wanted, namely, additional territorial acquisitions around the head of the Adriatic Sea. Moreover, Wilson found that such appeals not only did not work but served to strengthen the hand of those who opposed him.[51] Again one can see a certain parallel between the manner in which Wilson dealt with the leaders of the Allied powers and the manner in which he subsequently dealt with the leaders of the Senate. He would brook no opposition. The Allies had other priorities, and there would have been no League of Nations and certainly no Article 10 but for Wilson's insistence. His role in Paris was paramount; he got what he wanted, though, as recounted above, the cost was considerable. In addition, throughout the ratification fight he continued to be the principal player. He set the agenda and strongly influenced the outcome. In the end the treaty was not ratified, because he came to no agreement with those senators who wanted ratification—but with certain reservations—and because he controlled enough Democratic votes to prevent ratification with reservations attached. The story of his relations with the Senate follows below, but it is important to consider first the questions of why Wilson could accept no compromise with the large group of moderate Republicans who really wanted ratification and why he resorted instead to an appeal to the people over the heads of their senators, an appeal that angered the very lawmakers he should have been courting. Why, against the advice of his doctors, did he embark on a Western speaking tour to rally support for the league, seemingly seeking martyrdom and telling Joseph Tumulty that "even though in my condition, it might mean the giving up of my life, I will gladly make the sacrifice to save the Treaty"?[52]

Wilson was taken severely ill in Paris in April 1919, long before his debilitating stroke in October of that year. Because of his having to do everything himself, he no doubt simply wore out his body. His doctor, Cary Grayson, and the historian of the great flu epidemic both believe that the flu was chief among Wilson's problems. The most informed scholar of Wilson's medical history has suggested the possibility of a cerebral vascular occlusion, possibly complicated by a viral inflammation of the brain.[53] Newly uncovered medical records now "indicate that Wilson suffered from a disease of the carotid arteries in the neck, which hindered blood flow to the brain, and hypertension, which worsened his condition."[54] From this time on he was a changed man. On that point most historians can agree. "Convinced of his own rectitude, convinced too that the treaty was the best one negotiable under difficult circumstances, he seemed to calcify."[55]

Does this new evidence of disability before Wilson's 1919 stroke mean, as historian Arthur Link contends, that one should now "lay to rest the theories that Wilson's problems were psychological"? Link claims that Wilson's unwillingness to comprise was "uncharacteristic" and that "in his normal healthy state, Wilson would have found compromise with the large group of moderate Republicans."[56] Despite this new evidence, the matter remains unresolved. The Wilson who had to do it all himself so as to ensure that right would triumph, the Wilson who had so little regard for the views of other statesmen and who tended to believe that public opinion was always with him and could be called upon to throttle his opposition, was not a man likely to compromise with mere senators. There is a continuity in Wilson's manner of dealing with his opponents that stretches back beyond April 1919 and suggests that not all of his problems were medical.

Executive-Congressional Relations

Wilson never served in the Senate and had little regard for its prerogatives. As Senator Robert La Follette pointed out in one of the preliminary debates, Wilson, in his book *Constitutional Government*, had written that "to guide diplomacy is to determine what treaties must be made if the faith and prestige of the Government are to be maintained; he [the president] need disclose no step of negotiation until it is complete, and when in any critical matter it is completed the Government is virtually committed; whatever its disinclination, the Senate may feel itself committed also."[57] Worse still from the standpoint of executive-congressional relations, Wilson did not respect the members of Senate nor its leaders. He had so little confidence in Democratic leader

Gilbert Hitchcock (D-Nebr.) that he had once tried to have him removed from the position of chairman of the Senate Foreign Relations Committee and had characterized him and the other Democratic   as "a rum lot."[58] As for the Republican leader, Henry Cabot Lodge, soon to become majority leader in the new Congress, Wilson hated him deeply,[59] and that condition blinded him both to Lodge's abilities and the influence he could exert on the outcome of the treaty ratification battle.

Wilson, seeing little prospect of dealing effectively with the Senate beforehand, felt justified in negotiating a treaty without paying attention to the Senate's advice and in seeking consent to it as a fait accompli. "He could not conceive," historian Arthur Walworth has written, "that the senators would dare to defeat a treaty of peace after victory in the First World War."[60] Despite the outcome of the 1918 elections, Wilson was so confident of his mandate that he remarked to the French ambassador that "the Senate must take its medicine."[61]

The man who assumed the position of majority leader in the Senate when the new Congress convened on March 4, 1919, Henry Cabot Lodge, was not only a long-standing enemy of Wilson and of his foreign policy but a skillful parliamentary strategist and tactician as well. As historian W. Stull Holt once wrote of Lodge: "No one can read extensively in the *Congressional Record* during his career without being impressed by his mastery of parliamentary technique. . . . No one in 1919 knew better than he the various devices and methods by which a treaty could be killed, nor had anyone had more practice in the use of them."[62]

Lodge was also a student of the Senate's prerogatives and had written extensively on that subject. He had long lamented the growth of executive power and had celebrated the Senate's treaty-making power as a means of halting executive aggrandizement, at least in the realm of foreign relations. Historically, the chairmen of the Senate Foreign Relations Committee have been particularly sensitive to the subject of the prerogatives of the Senate, and Lodge was certainly no exception. "War can be declared without the assent of the Executive, and peace can be made without the assent of the House," he once pointed out, "but neither war nor peace can be made without the assent of the Senate."[63] Lodge thought that President James Polk's message to the Senate of June 10, 1846, seeking advice in advance upon important measures of foreign policy was the requisite approach. In his writings he emphasized that a treaty is "still inchoate, a mere project for a treaty until the consent of the Senate has been given to it" and that the Senate might act "at any stage of negotiation."[64] Lodge set the stage for a renewal of the long-standing battle between the executive and the Senate for control over the nation's foreign relations when, even before World War I was over, he warned "that the responsibility of a Senator in dealing with any question of peace is as great in his sphere as that of the President in his."[65]

Lodge's priorities were very different from those of the president. He worried much about the introduction of the league idea, worried that an ineffective league might be substituted for exaction of physical guarantees against a recurrence of German aggression. He doubted that an effective league could be formed but knew that even if it was possible to form one, what would be required for the construction of an effective collective security organization was never politically feasible at home. Any way he looked at it, the league idea was an unnecessary and complicating factor.[66]

Wilson took no cognizance of the advice of such adversaries as Lodge, and immediately upon reaching Paris, he announced that the formation of a League of Nations would be the first and foremost task of the conference. Wilson left Washington without establishing any agreement with the Senate Foreign Relations Committee, indeed without any consultation on the best way to proceed in the negotiations. Lodge could only draw the conclusion that Wilson was ambitious to dictate the terms of peace and he lost no time in informing his British friends that the Republican party would not give Wilson a free hand.[67] Theodore Roosevelt was also in touch with British leaders and urged them to look to Congress and not to the president as the genuine policymaker in the United States.[68] Even those few senators of Wilson's own party whom he saw before departing for Europe were unhappy, believing that Wilson was not interested in their views, that he had no considered plan and was giving way to undigested idealism, and that they would be asked to approve a treaty about which they had had nothing to say.[69] There was even an effort in the Senate Foreign Relations Committee to force Wilson to include eight senators in the peace delegation, but the temporary Democratic majority in the committee succeeded in killing such a suggestion. The overall tenor of early discussions both in the committee and on the Senate floor, however, did not augur well for a sympathetic reception of the eventual treaty.

Wilson did not seem to grasp that in the next Congress the Republicans would control the institutions of the Senate and that he was going to need a substantial number of Republican votes if his treaty was going to be ratified. If ever the country needed a bipartisan foreign policy, it was at this moment, but if Wilson understood that intellectually, he could not bring himself to act on that fact.

Lodge, believing that Wilson could be forced "as we forced him before, to do what ought to be done but which he is not planning to do," made one last effort just before the life of the Sixty-fifth Congress expired. On the eve of his assuming control of the command posts of the new Republican Congress (chairman of the Senate Foreign Relations Committee, where Wilson's treaty would first be considered, and chairman of the Republican Conference, with control over all committee assignments), Lodge sent a strong message to Wilson and at the same time took a long step toward forging a position on which the diverse elements composing the Republican membership of the Senate could comfortably stand. Just before midnight on March 3, 1919, Lodge rose in the Senate to introduce a motion, quickly dubbed the "round-robin," stating that "the constitution of the league of nations in the form now proposed to the peace conference should not be accepted by the United States" and that it was the sense of the Senate that the peace treaty with Germany be concluded expeditiously and the league proposal be taken up only after the negotiation of a satisfactory peace.[70]

The rules specified that such a resolution could be considered only by unanimous consent, and when a Democrat objected, as Lodge had anticipated, he simply read into the record a statement signed by thirty-seven Republican senators and senators-elect indicating that they would have voted for the resolution had they had the opportunity. Two names were subsequently added to the list. By this device Lodge accomplished two purposes at once. He sent Wilson a forceful message to the effect that on matters of foreign policy and especially those involving treaties, the president's policy could be blocked. Even more significant, Lodge demonstrated that he was now in charge of the disposition of the treaty and that the vast majority of Republican senators (certainly more than one third of the total membership of the Senate) were now committed to a policy of united and partisan action on the treaty.

Lodge's next coup came at the outset of the new Congress and involved the composition of the Senate Foreign Relations Committee. The Republicans' narrow overall majority of only two seats in the Senate seemed to call for only a 9–8 (Republican to Democrat) ratio on that crucial committee. That would mean that the vote of one of the continuing members, Porter McCumber (R-N.Dak.), might well be decisive, and Lodge knew that McCumber harbored pro-league sympathies and that he was far from subscribing to Lodge's hardheaded, pro-Ally approach to the peace settlement. Lodge was able to persuade the Senate to authorize a 10–7 (Republican to Democrat) ratio on the Foreign Relations Committee. He appears to have sounded out prospective new appointees and to have extracted from them pledges to support him in handling the League Covenant and in pursuing a strategy of amendment and reservation.[71] In this manner he succeeded in neutralizing McCumber and in greatly strengthening his own position.

The four new Republican appointees were George Moses (R-N.H.) and Hiram Johnson (R-Calif.) (both of whom became irreconcilables on the league issue) and Warren G. Harding (R-Ohio) and Harry New (R-Ind.), both strict party regulars. As there were already four irreconcilable holdovers on the committee, Lodge's appointments gave the committee a rather irreconcilable cast. What really mattered, however, was that Lodge and his two party loyalists (Harding and New) now occupied the decisive middle ground on the committee and were in a position to tilt its decisions as they saw fit.

Lodge's control of the Senate Foreign Relations Committee also meant that he could control the pace of its deliberations. The first two weeks of hearings were devoted to Lodge's reading the entire treaty aloud. Holding the reins of committee power also permitted Lodge to summon to testify exactly those persons whose testimony was likely to embarrass the president, especially Secretary of State Lansing, who testified that the president need not have yielded on Shantung to secure Japanese adherence to the league, and William C. Bullitt, who resigned from the peace delegation to return to Washington and trumpet the fact that Lansing had told him that he considered the league "entirely useless."[72] Also called to testify were many representatives of hyphenate groups who had some quarrel with certain provisions of the treaty. Irish-Americans were particularly virulent in their denunciation of the league, and they were heard frequently and at length.

As time went on the importance of controlling the Senate Foreign Relations Committee became increasingly evident. The committee was able to create a ground swell of opposition to Wilson and his league by means of the kind of testimony mentioned above and by continually asking the president for detailed information on the actual negotiations, information that would likely embarrass both Wilson and the

Allied leaders if supplied. If it was not supplied (which was usually the case), the committee could then decry the president's lack of cooperation. As long as the committee felt that opposition to the league was being created, it was prepared to see the hearings stretched out. Democratic leader Gilbert Hitchcock made repeated efforts to have the treaty reported to the full Senate, but he never had the votes to compel the committee to report. It finally did so of its own accord but only after sentiment in favor of the League Covenant had long since passed its zenith.

This is not to say that the outcome was foreordained. Despite Lodge's many successes, opinion within his own party remained deeply divided, and he found it necessary to engage in many a balancing act. As he once told Elihu Root, the situation was "not an easy one for anybody who is forced as I am to be the leader and in a sense manager. Forty-nine men, ranging from Borah to Colt [a mild reservationist from Rhode Island] presents [sic] a variety of subjects to deal with and one not always easy to grasp."[73] There were about a dozen Republican senators who vowed they would not vote for any league, while there were also a substantial number who really wanted to see the league experiment tried and who wanted only a few so-called "mild" reservations to the League Covenant. In the middle were Lodge and a large group of party regulars who could be reconciled to U.S. entry into the league only under the cover of "strong and effective reservations," reservations that would make the league less of a collective security organization and more of a mere world forum.[74]

Eschewing the irreconcilable position that he deemed politically dangerous, Lodge devoted his every effort to uniting the Republicans on truly effective reservations.[75] "Beyond that," he calculated, "a majority in the Senate is not to be found able to control."[76] The key word is "control." Lodge seized it early and never relinquished it. Working with Elihu Root and National Republican Chairman Will Hays, Lodge made sure that his party was officially on record as favoring "*a* league of nations."[77] Though he continued to support a few amendments (which would have necessitated a renegotiation of the whole treaty), he used that tack primarily as a means of appeasing the irreconcilables and forcing the mild reservationists back toward middle ground.

The key to Lodge's maintaining control in the Senate was his ability to work with the mild reservationists. Historian Thomas A. Bailey once speculated on what might have been the result if Wilson and his followers had opened their arms to the Republican mild reservationists.[78] When they finally made a move in that direction, they found they were much too late. By the late summer of 1919, Lodge had them committed to him and to the reservations that bore his name. Interestingly, the so-called Lodge reservations were a cooperative effort, more the work of Elihu Root and such mild reservationists as Senator Irvine Lenroot (R-Wisc.), than they were of Lodge himself.[79] That is why the mild reservationists stood so strongly behind the Lodge reservations throughout the protracted treaty fight and why even Senator Frank B. Kellogg (R-Minn.) (whom Lodge had kept off the Senate Foreign Relations Committee) had no qualms about claiming on the Senate floor that the reservations had "not been drawn by the enemies of the treaty" but rather "by its friends, who want to save it. . . ."[80] So it was that by early September Lodge could report the following to Root: "Our people were united on his four central points, including the all important reservation to Article X declaring that no American troops could be despatched without Congressional authorization."[81] Even the vast majority of the mild reservationists felt that Article 10 entailed dangerous and unrealistic commitments and were not prepared to accept it without substantial qualifications. Lodge recognized that and built his strategy around it. Wilson, perhaps because Article 10 was his own inspiration, did not recognize that fact or consider it consequential.

It is not that the president did not confer with the Senate. He had many conferences with individual senators, and he invited the Senate Foreign Relations Committee to the White House upon the occasion of his first return from Europe in February. There was a second White House conference on August 19, 1919, at the request of the committee. The timing of this second conference was particularly unfortunate, for it came only four days after Wilson had reiterated to Senator Hitchcock his objection to the attaching of any reservations to the treaty on the basis that they would indicate a halfhearted American acceptance of the league, which would destroy its possibilities of preserving the peace. Wilson said that if the Senate amended the treaty text, he would not ratify the treaty but would instead send Senators Lodge and Philander C. Knox (R-Pa.) to Berlin to negotiate a new treaty with Germany.[82]

In these meetings the president managed to create a cordial atmosphere, but he also tended to lecture rather than listen. Moreover, there was no bargaining. The president opened the second conference with a prepared statement urging early approval of the treaty so that economic prosperity might return and the world be stabilized. He reminded the committee that he had been flexible and had met many of their concerns, that he had succeeded in getting the League Covenant amended to meet their objections regarding the Monroe Doctrine, domestic questions, and the right of withdrawal. This was of course true, but only in a limited sense. Wilson had secured changes on those subjects, but the changes had not met all of the senators' objections. Then Wilson switched his attention to Article 10, which, he believed, was entirely clear in its meaning. The advice of the League Council, which had to be unanimous, was only advisory, he explained. Each government was free to reject it. Nevertheless, Article 10 was the very backbone of the covenant, and without it the league would be hardly more than a debating society. Further, the obligation was moral, not legal; it was binding in conscience only, not in law. The Congress was left free to put its own interpretation upon the obligation in all cases that called for action, Wilson said, but he went on to claim that a moral obligation was superior to a legal obligation and had greater binding force and that the guarantee was so strong that in practically every case the United States would probably act under the advice of the League Council. Most of the senators were left unsatisfied because Wilson's interpretation seemed to beg the question of whether the council's advice was binding and that point, of course, was crucial to understanding what kind of international organization the league would be. They were left feeling that Article 10 was indeed of doubtful meaning. Even more disconcerting was Wilson's concluding pronouncement. "If the United States were to qualify the document in any way, I am confident from what I know of the many conferences and debates which accompanied the formulation of the treaty that our example would be followed in many quarters, in some instances with very serious reservations, and that the meaning and operative force of the treaty would presently be clouded from one end of its clauses to the other."[83]

The president and the Senate had reached an impasse. As the *New York Times* reported: "A careful canvass of the Committee on the return of the Senators to their offices showed an absolutely unchanged alignment. The President did not convince any Senators who are opposed to the League or Treaty, or any of those who want reservations. But on the other hand, he inspired with more enthusiasm, apparently, those who favor ratification without change."[84] From this point on the question really became one of whether Wilson would accept the treaty with the major Lodge reservations (including the one to Article 10 stating that the United States accepted no responsibility under that article unless Congress should so determine in a particular case) or whether the United States would be a part of the treaty at all. Wilson, unable to accept that he had been politically outmaneuvered by Lodge, now determined upon one last desperate effort, a cross-country speaking tour to rouse public support for the league to such a degree that the Senate would be forced to succumb.

The results were counterproductive. Not only did Wilson break his health in the process, but he ended up challenging the very senators he ought to have been courting by threatening them with electoral defeat in 1920. Clearly, Wilson had already settled on the all-or-nothing stance that characterized his actions on the treaty in the ensuing months. When in the course of his speaking tour he began to insult senators and to identify the peace settlement he had devised with God's will, and its opponents with Germanism or Bolshevism, he was already ruling out the possibility of a cooperative compromise with the Senate.[85]

The final disposition of the treaty in the Senate followed inevitably. It was defeated twice, initially on November 19, 1919, and again on March 19, 1920. There were never sufficient votes to ratify the treaty without the Lodge reservations, and Wilson did everything he could to prevent Democratic senators from supporting the treaty with the Lodge reservations attached. Though Wilson's ill health undoubtedly increased his rigidity, historian Arthur Link is probably claiming too much when he argues that, as mentioned earlier, "in his normal healthy state, Wilson would have found compromise with the large group of moderate Republicans."[86] Wilson's political style and especially his manner of dealing with Congress throughout the negotiation of the treaty and the fight over its ratification made a compromise unlikely.

Public Opinion and the Role of Interest Groups

On one occasion in Paris Wilson is alleged to have remarked that "senators do not know what the people are thinking. They are as far from the people, the great mass of the people, as I am from Mars."[87] That was a dangerous attitude, and one that probably derived from an earlier period before the passage of the constitutional amendment calling for the popular election of senators. One recent state study shows that New Jersey's two Republican senators ran little political risk in opposing Wilson on the league and concludes with the judgment that "what is remarkable is that Wilson, an experienced politician and himself a paragon of partisanship, ever thought that a strategy premised on an aroused public opinion forcing senators of the opposing party to vote his way could succeed."[88]

Wilson's strategy failed to take into account that two thirds of the Senate is insulated by not having to stand for reelection. The president also failed to appreciate that public opinion could change against him; Lodge's strategy was based on procrastination and education in the hope that the public's "calm second thought," once the American people really understood what the league entailed, would be against ratification.[89]

Even if reliable public opinion polling had been available during this period, a poll asking the American people whether they wanted to "join a world organization to preserve peace" could hardly have been enlightening to the policymakers of the day. This has not precluded some writers from making the categorical judgment that "all surveys of opinion in 1918 and 1919, even in 1920, showed that the American people wanted to join a world organization to preserve peace."[90]

There is more agreement with respect to the spring of 1919, the high-water mark of public support for the league. It is probably true, as historian Ruhl Bartlett alleges, that "in May, 1919 the majority of the American people favored ratification . . . with the Covenant as it was"![91] Even Lodge agreed with that judgment. In his account of the treaty fight, *The Senate and the League of Nations*, he wrote that as late as May 1, 1919, the great mass of the people "did not understand the treaty at all," though they tended to favor it because of a natural desire to see peace restored as quickly as possible. Moreover, he conceded that "what I may call the vocal classes of the community, most of the clergymen, the preachers of sermons, a large element in the teaching force of the universities, a large proportion of the newspaper editors, and finally the men and women who were in the habit of writing and speaking for publication, although by no means thoroughly informed, were friendly to the League as it stood and were advocating it."[92]

This situation is what dictated Lodge's strategy. The fact that the public's first thought was "probably against us" called for special tactics. As he wrote his friend Albert J. Beveridge:

> I have no doubt that a large majority of the people of the country are very naturally fascinated by the idea of eternal preservation of the world's peace and that there shall be no more war. They are told that that is what this league means. They have not examined it; they have not begun to think about it. Now I do not think it would be wise for us at this stage to make it a party issue, nor to confront it with a blank negative. I think what is necessary for us to do is to begin to discuss it and try to get what it involves and what it means before the American people. That will be done.[93]

Lodge set himself a formidable task. Thirty-two state legislatures were quick to pass resolutions in support of the league. Many women's groups, professional societies, and churches rushed to jump on the league bandwagon. A poll of the press published by the *Literary Digest* on April 5, 1919, showed that a majority of the nation's newspapers favored the league as it stood, though there was also considerable support for some sort of conditional ratification. To the question "Do you favor the proposed League of Nations?" 718 newspapers answered yes, 181, no, and 478 gave conditional replies. To make matters worse, senators seemed to be reacting to this ground swell of public support. On April 30 the League to Enforce Peace issued from Washington a tabulation of senators, which listed sixty-four, (or enough to ratify) as for the League Covenant, twelve as opposed, and twenty as doubtful.[94]

Despite such initial support for the league, Lodge's strategy worked both in the Senate and among the public at large. There were several reasons for this. First of all, the Versailles

Treaty had so many provisions and affected so many countries that it was rare to find someone who did not object to some of its provisions. Initially the American people were uninformed about many of those provisions, but the educational campaign mounted by Lodge and the irreconcilables, buttressed as it was by the defection of the liberals and the hyphenates, soon took a heavy toll. The more the public learned about the league the more they became disenchanted with it. Public opinion tended to shift from pro- to anti-league as the shimmering Wilsonian ideal took on definite form and began requiring specific American pledges and sacrifices, a shift not uncommon in the history of American opinion on issues of foreign policy.[95]

Hence, when Wilson took his message directly to the American people in September 1919, he was already too late. The battle in the Senate for the hearts of the mild reservationists had already been lost, and he could never rekindle among the public their avid initial support for the league. It is difficult to gauge how sharply opinion swung against Wilson and his league. His receptions on his speaking tour were mixed, tepid in the Midwest but more enthusiastic on the West Coast. Massachusetts was undoubtedly an extreme case, in that public opinion probably swung more sharply there than in any other state, but it is also a revealing case. In Massachusetts the Democratic state committee denounced the league, the American Federation of Labor announced its "bitter opposition," the Democratic state platform plank on the league issue was even more hostile than the Republican stand, and in the 1920 election James Cox, the Democratic presidential candidate, could poll only 28.9 percent of the votes. This was due only in small part to the efforts of Lodge; it was due primarily to the opposition of Irish-Americans who feared that the league might become an instrument for perpetuating British control over Ireland. Of course, the election of 1920 was not a referendum on the league issue such as Wilson once desired. There were too many other issues involved. Still, Warren G. Harding's landslide victory over Cox (16 million votes to 9 million) does indicate that the referendum was for isolation and that public opinion on "Wilson's League" had so changed that it was no longer the electoral asset it was once assumed to be.[96]

Pressure groups did not play a particularly prominent role in the treaty fight. Many labor organizations, churches, women's clubs, civic clubs, and professional societies did register individual favorable opinions of the league at an early stage, but there was never any umbrella organization to coordinate and focus pro-league sentiment. The League to Enforce Peace might have played such a role, but Wilson always kept his distance from it. There were probably several reasons for this. Though it had a few prominent Democratic members, such as former Democratic National Committee Chairman Vance McCormack and Senator William Gibbs McAdoo (D-Ga.), it was primarily an organization of prominent Republicans from the Northeast. It was not really either a national or a grass-roots organization. It had been pro-Ally when Wilson was still trying to arrange a "peace without victory," and though it contemplated the use of force, it was to be used to support a much more juridically based internationalism than that envisaged by Wilson.

Just like the mild reservationists, many members of the League to Enforce Peace were uncomfortable with Article 10, and on the eve of the first vote on the treaty the group's Executive Committee voted to accept the Lodge reservations. Its conclusion was announced on November 18 and read into the *Congressional Record* by Senator Charles McNary (R-Ore.), a prominent mild reservationist. Though the leadership of the League to Enforce Peace still thought that some of the reservations were not constructive, it had come to the conclusion that the reservations did not diminish the peacekeeping abilities of the League of Nations and that consequently ratification with the reservations was preferable to no ratification at all or even to a protracted political struggle. As their communiqué phrased it:

> The treaty, even with the reservations now adopted, can accomplish
> the purpose and should be ratified. There is no adequate reason
> why it should not be. The world waits. Delay is perilous. Any action
> which casts the covenant. . . . into the politics of a presidential
> election will delay peace and halt political reorganization and
> economic rehabilitation of nations sorely smitten by war, by winter,
> and by famine.[97]

Wilson, however, remained of a different opinion and wrote to Senator Hitchcock urging Democratic senators to oppose ratification with the Lodge reservations because ratification in that form would not be ratification at all but rather actually a nullification of the treaty.[98]

Though the role of the League to Enforce Peace was an important one, the role of a much less formally organized group of opponents of the League of Nations may have been even more significant. League opponents met quite regularly in the Washington homes of Senator Frank Brandegee (R-Conn.) and of Mrs. Nicholas Longworth, the former Alice Roosevelt. They organized anti-league speaking tours by prominent senators (especially Hiram Johnson) and supervised the distribution of anti-league propaganda at mass meetings, particularly in the Midwest. By enlisting the financial support of multimillionaires Henry Clay Frick and Andrew Mellon, they made sure that the anti-league movement would never suffer for lack of funds. Their anti-league propaganda campaign may not have actually been decisive, but it certainly did much to speed the public's changing image of "Wilson's League."[99]

Conclusion

Wilson made so many mistakes in his handling of the Versailles Treaty that his actions became something of a model for how not to proceed. Republican handling of the Washington Conference was meant to convey the message that the results both in Paris and in the Senate might have been totally different if Wilson had only shown Harding's good judgment in keeping out of the limelight himself and involving prominent senators. In planning for the United Nations during World War II, Franklin Roosevelt was haunted by Wilson's mistakes and determined not to repeat them at any cost.[100]

Yet, despite all of his mistakes, Wilson could have had his treaty and his league at any time had he been willing to compromise. In the end it was he, Wilson, who blocked ratification. He could not accept ratification with the Lodge reservations attached, perhaps because he could not bear to see Lodge's name attached to his handiwork, but primarily because he thought the Lodge reservation to Article 10 negated that article and in so doing "cut the heart out of the Covenant." His judgment remained faulty. Article 10 did not make the league an effective collective security organization. Virtually all well-informed commentators agreed that it hardly mattered whether Article 10 was in the treaty or not. Historian Robert M. Crunden states: "Leon Bourgeois, Elihu Root, and David H. Miller, one of Wilson's own experts, all shared that view. . . . Article X did not matter because a nation had to be willing to join the fight, and no outsider could force that act."[101] Throughout the history of the League of Nations most countries acted as if "the heart of the Covenant" carried no obligations at all. Canada tried to have Article 10 suppressed in 1920, and the League Council in 1923 could not even decide whether its advice was binding.[102]

The United States probably should have joined the League of Nations, but it is unreasonable to argue that U.S. membership would have transformed a flawed and experimental organization into a collective security organization truly capable of keeping the world's peace. Had Wilson been able to acknowledge this reality, much of the divisive debate over the league could have been avoided.

Notes

1. "International Peace," Roosevelt's Address before the Nobel Prize Committee, delivered at Christiana, Norway, May 5, 1910, and cited in *The Works of Theodore Roosevelt, XVIII*, ed. Hermann Hagedorn, (New York: Charles Scribner's Sons, 1923–26), 415. See also Warren F. Kuehl, *Seeking World Order: The United States and International Organization to 1920* (Nashville, Tenn.: Vanderbilt University Press, 1969).

2. *Enforced Peace*, Proceedings of the First Annual National Assemblage of the League to Enforce Peace, Washington, May 26–27, 1916 (New York: League to Enforce Peace, 1916), 159–61.

3. Robert Lansing, *The Peace Negotiations: A Personal Narrative* (Boston, Mass.: Houghton Mifflin Co., 1921), 34.

4. Review of Reviews, ed., *Messages and Papers of Woodrow Wilson* (New York: Review of Reviews Corp., 1924), 372–83.

5. Ibid., 464–72.

6. *World Peace: A Written Debate Between William Howard Taft and William Jennings Bryan* (New York: George H. Doran Co., 1917), 147.

7. Lawrence Lowell, "Win the War" (A Reference for Speakers on Behalf of the League to Enforce Peace), League to Enforce Peace Manuscripts, Widener Library, Harvard University.

8. *World Peace: A Written Debate Between Taft and Bryan*, 52–53.

9. *Congressional Record*, 65th Cong., 3d sess., 1918, 727.

10. Quoted in Roland Stromberg's "The Riddle of Collective Security, 1916–1920," in *Issues and Conflicts: Studies in Twentieth Century American Diplomacy*, ed., George L. Anderson (Lawrence: University of Kansas Press, 1959), 159.

11. Henry Cabot Lodge, ed., *Selections from the Correspondence of Theodore Roosevelt and Henry Cabot Lodge, 1884-1918*, vol. 1 (New York: Charles Scribner's Sons, 1925), 547.

12. The quotation is from the memorandum enclosed with Lodge to Henry White, December 2, 1918, Lodge Manuscripts, Massachusetts Historical Society (hereafter cited as Lodge MSS), but the same message is conveyed in Lodge to Arthur Balfour, November 25, 1918, Lodge MSS, and in Lodge's speech in the Senate on December 21, 1919 (*Congressional Record*, 65th Cong., 3d sess., 1918, 728).

13. Arthur Walworth, *America's Moment: 1918* (New York: W. W. Norton and Co., 1977).

14. Raymond J. Sontag, *A Broken World, 1919-1939* (New York: Harper & Row, 1971).

15. Ray Stannard Baker, *Woodrow Wilson and World Settlement*, vol. 1 (Garden City, N.Y.: Doubleday, Page and Co., 1923), 102.

16. Quoted in Walworth, *America's Moment*, 1.

17. Ibid., 138–41.

18. John Maynard Keynes, *The Economic Consequences of the Peace* (London: Macmillan & Co., 1920), 35.

19. Arthur Walworth, *Wilson and His Peacemakers: American Diplomacy at the Paris Peace Conference, 1919* (New York: W. W. Norton and Co., 1986), 278, 282.

20. Keynes, *The Economic Consequences of the Peace*, 32.

21. House quoted in Allan Nevins, *Henry White: Thirty Years of American Diplomacy* (New York: Harper and Brothers, 1930), 446.

22. Keynes, *The Economic Consequences of the Peace*, 37–50.

23. Harold Nicolson, *Peacemaking 1919: Being Reminiscences of the Paris Peace Conference* (New York: Harcourt, Brace & Co., 1939), 7, 15, 28, 36–37, 42, 52–53, 72, 146, 164, 170, 184, 196–199.

24. Walworth, *Wilson and His Peacemakers*, 181–86.

25. *New York Times*, October 8 and 14, 1918; *Congressional Record*, 65th Cong., 2d sess., 1918, 1170–71; *Boston Herald*, October 31, 1918; and Henry Cabot Lodge "The Necessary Guarantees of Peace," *Scribner's Magazine* 64 (November 1918): 471–72.

26. Wilson quoted in John Garraty, *Henry Cabot Lodge: A Biography* (New York: Alfred A. Knopf, 1953), 342, and in Walworth, *America's Moment*, 111.

27. Seward W. Livermore, *Politics is Adjourned: Woodrow Wilson and the War Congress, 1916-1918* (Middletown, Conn.: Wesleyan University Press, 1966), 206–47.

28. Lodge, *Selections from the Correspondence of Roosevelt and Lodge*, vol. 2, 547 (November 26, 1918).

29. Wilson to Mrs. Sayre, November 13, 1918, quoted in Walworth, *America's Moment*, 113. See also note 10 on the same page.

30. Robert M. Crunden, *Ministers of Reform: The Progressives' Achievement in American Civilization, 1889-1920* (Urbana: University of Illinois Press, 1984), 265.

31. *New Republic*, May 17, 1919; ibid., May 24, 1919.

32. Herbert F. Margulies, *The Mild Reservationists and the League of Nations Controversy in the Senate* (Columbia: University of Missouri Press, 1989), 100.

33. William C. Widenor, *Henry Cabot Lodge and the Search for an American Foreign Policy* (Berkeley: University of California Press, 1980) 306–7; John Chalmers Vinson, *Referendum for Isolation: The Defeat of Article Ten of the League of Nations Covenant* (Athens: University of Georgia Press, 1961), 36; and Thomas A. Bailey, *Woodrow Wilson and the Great Betrayal* (New York: Macmillan Co., 1945), 2.

34. Joseph Tumulty, *Woodrow Wilson As I Knew Him* (Garden City, N.Y.: Doubleday, Page and Co., 1921), 517.

35. Widenor, *Henry Cabot Lodge and the Search for an American Foreign Policy*, 308.

36. Albert J. Beveridge to Lodge, January 28, 1919, Beveridge Manuscripts, Library of Congress (hereafter cited as Beveridge MSS).

37. Lodge to Albert J. Beveridge, February 18, 1919, Beveridge MSS.

38. John McCook Roots, "The Treaty of Versailles in the U.S. Senate," 86, Widener Library, Harvard University.

39. Lodge to Charles G. Washburn, February 22, 1919, Lodge MSS, and *Congressional Record*, 66th Cong., 1st sess., 1919, 6128.

40. Henry Cabot Lodge, *The Senate of the United States* (New York: Charles Scribner's Sons, 1921), 16.

41. Lodge to Charles G. Washburn, February 22, 1919, and Lodge to George Trevelyan, December 27, 1918, Lodge MSS.

42. David Lloyd George, *Memoirs of the Peace Conference*, vol. 1 (New Haven, Conn.: Yale University Press, 1939), 146–47.

43. Henry F. Pringle, *The Life and Times of William Howard Taft*, vol. 1 (New York: Farrar and Rinehart, 1939), 932.

44. Denna Frank Fleming, *The United States and the League of Nations, 1918-1920* (1932, reprint, New York: Russell and Russell, 1968), 54, and Walworth, *America's Moment*, 121–24.

45. Quoted in Walworth, *America's Moment*, 122.

46. Ibid., 131.

47. Ibid., 132.

48. Alexander George and Juliette George, *Woodrow Wilson and Colonel*

House: A Personality Study (New York: J. Day Company, 1956), 114–21.

49. Walworth, *Wilson and His Peacemakers*, 277.

50. Walworth, *America's Moment*, 132.

51. Walworth, *Wilson and His Peacemakers*, 335–58.

52. Tumulty, *Woodrow Wilson As I Knew Him*, 435.

53. The important secondary treatments are Alfred W. Crosby, Jr., *Epidemic and Peace, 1918* (Westport, Conn.: Greenwood Press, 1976), and three works by Edwin A. Weinstein: "Woodrow Wilson's Neurological Illness," *The Journal of American History* 57, no. 2 (September 1970): 324–51; *Woodrow Wilson: A Medical and Psychological Biography* (Princeton, N.J.: Princeton University Press, 1981); and with James W. Anderson and Arthur Link, "Woodrow Wilson's Political Personality: A Reappraisal," *Political Science Quarterly*, 93, no. 4 (Winter 1978–79), 585–98. See also Cary Grayson to Joseph Tumulty, April 10, 1919, printed in Tumulty, *Woodrow Wilson As I Knew Him*, 350.

54. *Washington Post*, November 26, 1990, A7.

55. Crunden, *Ministers of Reform*, 269.

56. *Washington Post*, November 26, 1990, A7.

57. *Congressional Record*, 65th Cong., 3d sess., 1918, 724.

58. Colonel House diary, May 17, 1918, quoted in Walworth, *America's Moment*, 124.

59. Josephus Daniels, *The Wilson Era*, vol. 1 (Chapel Hill: University of North Carolina Press, 1944), 535.

60. Walworth, *America's Moment*, 125.

61. Nicholas Murray Butler, *Across the Busy Years*, vol. 2 (New York: Charles Scribner's Sons, 1939–40), 201.

62. W. Stull Holt, *Treaties Defeated by the Senate* (Baltimore, Md.: The Johns Hopkins University Press, 1933), 258.

63. Lodge, *The Senate of the United States*, 10.

64. Henry Cabot Lodge, *A Fighting Frigate and Other Essays and Addresses* (New York: Charles Scribner's Sons, 1902), 223, 245, 254–55.

65. *Congressional Record*, 65th Cong., 2d sess., 1918, 11170.

66. Lodge to Henry White, December 2, 1918, and Lodge to Arthur Balfour, November 25, 1918, Lodge MSS; *Congressional Record*, 65th Cong., 3d sess., 1918, 728.

67. Lodge to Arthur Balfour, November 25, 1918, Lodge MSS.

68. Quoted in Walworth, *America's Moment*, 127.

69. Sewell Thomas, *Silhouettes of Charles S. Thomas* (Caldwell, Idaho: Caxton Printers, 1959), 194–96.

70. *Congressional Record*, 66th Cong., 1st sess., March 3, 1919, 4974.

71. See, for example, Lodge to Frank B. Kellogg, May 28, 1919, and Kellogg to Lodge May 31, 1919, Lodge MSS.

72. Fleming, *The United States and the League of Nations*, 299, 366.

73. Lodge to Elihu Root, September 3, 1919, Root Manuscripts, Library of Congress (hereafter cited as Root MSS).

74. Lodge to Louis A. Coolidge, August 7, 1919, Lodge MSS. The best account of the role of the irreconcilables is Ralph Stone's *The Irreconcilables: The Fight Against the League of Nations* (Lexington: University Press of Kentucky, 1970). The mild reservationists receive their due in Margulies, *The Mild Reservationists*.

75. Lodge to Louis A. Coolidge, August 7, 1919, Lodge MSS.

76. Lodge to Albert J. Beveridge, August 4, 1919, Beveridge MSS.

77. *New York Times*, June 27, 1919.

78. Bailey, *Woodrow Wilson and the Great Betrayal*, 58, 171–72.

79. Jack E. Kendrick, "The League of Nations and the Republican Senate, 1918-1921" (Ph.D. diss., University of North Carolina, 1952), 211, 254, and Herbert F. Margulies, *Senator Lenroot of Wisconsin: A Political Biography, 1900-1929* (Columbia: University of Missouri Press, 1977), 276–77.

80. *Congressional Record*, 66th Cong., 1st sess., 1919, 8778–80.

81. Lodge to Elihu Root, September 3, 1919, Root MSS.

82. *New York Tribune*, August 16, 1919.

83. *New York Times* and *New York Tribune*, August 20, 1919, and Widenor, *Henry Cabot Lodge and the Search for an American Foreign Policy*, 337–39. For a full report of the conference, see *Congressional Record*, 66th Cong., 1st sess., 58, pt. 4: 4013–31.

84. *New York Times*, August 20, 1919.

85. Lloyd Ambrosius, *Woodrow Wilson and the American Diplomatic Tradition: The Treaty Fight in Perspective* (Cambridge: Cambridge University Press, 1987), 180.

86. *Washington Post*, November 26, 1990.

87. Arthur Walworth, *Woodrow Wilson* (New York: W. W. Norton and Co.,

1978), 338.

88. Ralph Levering, "Partisanship, Ideology, and Attitudes toward Woodrow Wilson: New Jersey's Republican Senators and the League of Nations Controversy, 1918–1920" (Paper presented at the American Historical Association Annual Meeting, 1989), 16.

89. Lodge to Charles G. Washburn, February 22, 1919, Lodge MSS.

90. Alan Cranston, *The Killing of the Peace* (New York: Viking Press, 1960), ix.

91. Ruhl Bartlett, *The League to Enforce Peace* (Chapel Hill: University of North Carolina Press, 1944), 130.

92. Henry Cabot Lodge, *The Senate and the League of Nations* (New York: Charles Scribner's Sons, 1925), 147–48.

93. Lodge to Albert J. Beveridge, February 18, 1919, Beveridge MSS.

94. Fleming, *The United States and the League of Nations*, pp. 199, 218–19.

95. See Widenor, *Henry Cabot Lodge and the Search for an American Foreign Policy*, 311–15.

96. J. Joseph Huthmacher, *Massachusetts People and Politics, 1919-1933* (Cambridge: Harvard University Press, 1959), 26, 30, 42; Charles Tansill, *America and the Fight for Irish Freedom, 1866-1922* (New York: Devin-Adair, 1957), 331; and Fleming, *The United States and the League of Nations*, 470.

97. The only study of the League to Enforce Peace is Ruhl Bartlett's *The League to Enforce Peace*. The league's communique is reprinted in Fleming, *The United States and the League of Nations*, 394-95.

98. Fleming, *The United States and the League of Nations*, 395.

99. Ibid., 208–11.

100. William C. Widenor, "American Planning for the United Nations: Have We Been Asking the Right Questions?" *Diplomatic History* (Summer 1982): 245-65.

101. Crunden, *Ministers of Reform*, 273.

102. Widenor, *Henry Cabot Lodge and the Search for an American Foreign Policy*, 337.

Selected Bibliography

Ambrosius, Lloyd. *Woodrow Wilson and the American Diplomatic Tradition: The Treaty Fight in Perspective.* Cambridge: Cambridge University Press, 1987.

Bailey, Thomas A. *Woodrow Wilson and the Great Betrayal.* New York: Macmillan Co., 1945.

———. *Woodrow Wilson and the Lost Peace.* New York: Macmillan Co., 1944.

Birdsall, Paul. *Versailles Twenty Years After.* New York: Reynal and Hitchcock, 1941.

Buehrig, Edward H., ed. *Wilson's Foreign Policy in Perspective.* Bloomington: Indiana University Press, 1957.

Crunden, Robert M. *Ministers of Reform: The Progressives' Achievement in American Civilization, 1889-1920.* Urbana: University of Illinois Press, 1984.

Floto, Inga. *Colonel House in Paris: A Study of American Policy at the Paris Peace Conference.* Princeton, N.J.: Princeton University Press, 1980.

Gelfand, Lawrence E. *The Inquiry: American Preparations for Peace, 1917-1919.* New Haven, Conn.: Yale University Press, 1963.

Huthmacher, J. Joseph, and Warren Susman, eds. *Wilson's Diplomacy: An International Symposium.* Cambridge: Harvard University Press, 1973.

Kennedy, David. *Over Here: The First World War and American Society.* New York: Oxford University Press, 1980.

Keynes, John Maynard. *The Economic Consequences of the Peace.* London: Macmillan & Co., 1920.

Kuehl, Warren F. *Seeking World Order: The United States and International Organization to 1920.* Nashville, Tenn.: Vanderbilt University Press, 1969.

Levin, N. Gordon, Jr. *Woodrow Wilson and World Politics: America's Response to War and Revolution.* New York: Oxford University Press, 1968.

Link, Arthur S. *Wilson the Diplomatist: A Look at His Major Foreign Policies*. Chicago: Quadrangle Books, 1965.

——. *The Higher Realism of Woodrow Wilson and Other Essays*. Nashville, Tenn.: Vanderbilt University Press, 1971.

Margulies, Herbert F. *The Mild Reservationists and the League of Nations Controversy in the Senate*. Columbia: University of Missouri Press, 1989.

Mayer, Arno. *Politics and Diplomacy of Peacemaking: Containment and Counterrevolution at Versailles, 1918-1919*. New York: Alfred A. Knopf, 1967.

Nicolson, Harold. *Peacemaking, 1919: Being Reminiscences of the Paris Peace Conference*. New York: Harcourt, Brace & Co., 1939.

Schwabe, Klaus. *Woodrow Wilson, Revolutionary Germany and Peacemaking, 1918-1919: Missionary Diplomacy and the Realities of Power*. Chapel Hill: University of North Carolina Press, 1985.

Smith, Daniel M. *The Great Departure: The United States and World War I, 1914-1920*. New York: John Wiley and Sons, 1965.

Stone, Ralph. *The Irreconcilables: The Fight Against the League of Nations*. Lexington: University Press of Kentucky, 1970.

Tillman, Seth P. *Anglo-American Relations at the Paris Peace Conference of 1919*. Princeton, N.J.: Princeton University Press, 1961.

Vinson, John Chalmers. *Referendum for Isolation: The Defeat of Article Ten of the League of Nations Covenant*. Athens: University of Georgia Press, 1961.

Walworth, Arthur. *America's Moment: 1918*. New York: W. W. Norton and Co., 1977.

——. *Wilson and His Peacemakers: American Diplomacy at the Paris Peace Conference, 1919*. New York: W. W. Norton and Co., 1986.

Widenor, William C. *Henry Cabot Lodge and the Search for an American Foreign Policy*. Berkeley: University of California Press, 1980.

Yates, Louis A. *The United States and French Security, 1917-1921: A Study in American Diplomatic History*. New York: Twayne Publishers, 1957.

2 The Washington Naval Treaties
Thomas H. Buckley

On November 11, 1921, President Warren G. Harding presided at a colorful ceremony in Arlington Cemetery at the burial of America's Unknown Soldier. The next day the Washington Conference on the Limitation of Armaments began. Harding welcomed the delegates and pointed out that the hopes of the world centered on Washington. Secretary of State Charles Evans Hughes, most expected, would make the same type of general welcoming address, but midway through his speech Hughes sternly called for the end of constant talking about disarmament and asked for action. He startled the delegates, and indeed the world, by listing 845,740 tons of warships (fifteen capital ships under construction and fifteen other battleships) that the United States would stop construction on or scrap. One can imagine the short-lived delight of the Japanese and the British. Hughes next asked the British to stop construction on 583,000 tons of capital ships (four ships under construction and nineteen existing ones). One British admiral leaned forward in his chair in the "manner of a bulldog, sleeping on a sunny doorstep, who had been poked in the stomach by the unwary foot of a traveling salesman seriously lacking in any sense of the most ordinary proprieties or considerations of personal safety."[1] Hughes then proposed that Japan scrap 448,000 tons of capital ships (by stopping construction on six capital ships and scrapping seventeen others).

Hughes's proposal to destroy a total of seventy-six ships planned, under construction, or already built would sink in half an hour more battleships than all the admirals of the world had sunk in centuries. He went on to call for a ten-year naval holiday in the construction of capital ships and for a strength ratio of 5–5–3 (roughly 500,000 tons each for the

United States and the United Kingdom, with 300,000 for Japan). He later suggested 175,000 tons each for France and Italy. Hughes, in perhaps the most dramatic proposal ever made by a U.S. diplomat, played his trump card at the very beginning of the conference. He captured the attention of America and the world.[2] The *New York Evening Post* rejoiced that "Hughes has injected into the work of international understanding and peace that touch of audacity, almost of ruthlessness, which has hitherto been associated with the business of war."[3]

Where had the plan come from? President Harding had appointed Elihu Root, former secretary of state and elder statesman of the Republican party; Oscar W. Underwood (D-Ala.), the Senate Democratic minority leader; and Henry Cabot Lodge (R-Mass.), chairman of the Senate Foreign Relations Committee, as delegates along with Hughes. Harding had apparently learned from Woodrow Wilson's experiences. The delegation, along with Theodore Roosevelt, Jr., the assistant secretary of the navy, very carefully developed proposals for the conference. The navy, of course, did not want to stop the construction program or scrap large numbers of capital ships and first proposed that the United States and the United Kingdom have navies of 1 million tons apiece. The U.S. delegation, however, supported by Harding, scaled the proposal down to half that size. Harding and Hughes had kept the final form secret; only eleven men knew the contents of the administration's proposal.[4]

After some difficult negotiations with the Japanese, who wanted a higher ratio of 70 rather than 60 percent, the addition of a clause prohibiting the further fortification of the Pacific Islands, and negotiations with the French, who forced the exclusion of all noncapital ships (light cruisers, destroyers, and submarines) from coverage, the five powers signed the naval arms control treaty. It provided for the scrapping of seventy-one ships, imposed a ten-year naval holiday on the construction of capital ships, set up a ratio of 5–5–3–1.75–1.75 among the five fleets (U.S., Britain,

Japanese, French, and Italian, respectively), and provided for no further fortification of stipulated Pacific Islands (Philippines, Guam, and Wake on the U.S. side and Formosa, the Pescadores, Amoni-Oshima, the Bonin Islands, and others on the Japanese side).[5] Many foreign delegates, expecting Hughes to make at the second open session of the conference a similarly comprehensive Pacific, however, and Asian proposal "were on tenterhooks and were relieved beyond expression" when he did not do so.[6] Other conference treaties dealing with the Pacific did form major links with the naval treaty and contributed to the overall settlement at the conference. First, the Four-Power Treaty (the United States, the United Kingdom, France, and Japan) ended the Anglo-Japanese Alliance and provided that the four powers would jointly confer if disputes among them arose or aggression from outside threatened the peace of the Pacific area.[7] This arrangement, rather than the arms control treaty, soon became the controversial center of the Senate ratification struggle.

Second, the Nine-Power Treaty (the United States, the United Kingdom, Japan, Italy, France, Portugal, the Netherlands, Belgium, and China) pledged the powers to respect the sovereignty, independence, and integrity of China. They also promised to give the Chinese a chance to establish a stable government and to uphold the open door of commercial opportunity in China. For the first time the leading world powers accepted the U.S. policy of the open door in treaty form.[8]

Third, the Submarine–Poison Gas Treaty regulated the use of submarines and gas warfare. Fourth, the Chinese Customs Treaty (signed by all nine powers) provided for an effective tariff rate that all the powers could follow. Finally, a group of agreements were concluded outside the formal confines of the conference, but these were not formal treaties and thus not subject to the U.S. ratification process: Japan agreed to restore Shantung to the Chinese and also to sell the

Japanese-owned Shantung railway to the Chinese. In addition, the Japanese agreed to withdraw their troops from Siberia. Hughes knew that the latter two settlements, on which Wilson had failed, would win wide support for the other treaties among Republican senators in the ratification debates.[9]

International Political Context

President Woodrow Wilson's attempt to have the United States join the League of Nations failed when the Senate refused to give its advice and consent to the ratification of the Treaty of Versailles. Wilson's final hope, that the election of 1920 would be a "solemn referendum" on the league issue, also floundered when the Republican candidate, Warren G. Harding, won by the greatest majority in American history up to that time and promptly announced that his administration would not attempt to take the United States into the league.[10]

Without a doubt, the shadow, writ large, of the Versailles Treaty debates and the arguments over the League of Nations had an enormous effect on the origins of the Washington Conference, actions taken during the conference, and the later strategies of ratification. The conference, designed, in part, to treat specific problems that had been left unresolved by the Versailles settlement, met on American soil, where the intrigues of Europe could not flourish: The United States would provide the world with an example of open diplomacy. In contrast with U.S. representation at Versailles, two major senators, Henry Cabot Lodge, the Republican majority leader, and Oscar W. Underwood, the Democratic minority leader, participated as important members of the U.S. delegation. References to the league are found in almost every major ratification speech on the floor of the Senate; anti-league senators actively sought to link, by any means, the conference treaties with the league.[11] Opposition senators, in particular, viewed the Four-Power Treaty as an indirect step toward the league. Lodge's advice to Harding, to defuse this concern by accepting a reservation to the Four-Power Treaty, and Harding's acceptance of that advice stand in stark contrast with Wilson and the league debate.

The memories of the league controversy, just two years before, remained strong and constant. Had the opponents of the conference treaties discovered any links with the league, links existing in fact rather than just in their allegations, the whole Washington Conference edifice, arms control measures and all, would have cracked and might well have collapsed. Harding, Hughes, and Lodge, however, gave the opposition no major openings on the league issue. Their skill attests to their political wisdom and ingenuity.

Harding, however, had suggested in several of his campaign pronouncements (or "bloviations," as he so aptly called them) that although he opposed any permanent world organizations or attachments, he did favor meetings of an "association of nations." This "association" could come together periodically, when necessary, to discuss and settle certain specific international issues that needed attention, without impairing either U.S. rights or sovereignty. Disarmament, he had suggested, could form an appropriate subject for one such future meeting. Harding, to his surprise, found that both international and domestic considerations hastened his proposal faster than he wished.

Congress in 1916 had passed a naval act calling for the construction of 156 vessels, of which 16 were capital ships—battleships and battle cruisers. Fifteen of the 16 still under construction, sat on building blocks in 1921.[12] President Wilson had threatened the building of even more ships, and Harding's reputation as a "big navy" senator had not passed unnoticed overseas. The British regarded the continuation of the U.S. plan as a direct challenge: in the words of the young Winston Churchill to his compatriots, "Nothing in the world, nothing that you may think of, or dream of, or any may tell you; no arguments, however strong, no appeals, however seductive, must lead you to abandon that naval supremacy on which the life of our country depends."[13] The United Kingdom in 1921 announced plans to build a navy "equal to, or superior to, any other navy." Further, the United Kingdom's ally, Japan, widely viewed in the United States as the most likely future foe in the event of war, in 1920 put into full effect its 8–8 plan, whereby the Japanese would also construct sixteen capital ships. It looked to many in the world as if another great naval race, on a far greater scale than the Anglo-German competition before World War I, might again lead to war.[14]

Linked to the naval race as a source of tension between the United States, the United Kingdom, and Japan, the Anglo-Japanese Alliance represented a potential threat to many Americans. First signed and directed against Russia in 1902, renewed in 1911, and then directed against Germany, it was to expire, unless renewed, in 1921. The Harding administration believed that since the threats of Russia and Germany had disappeared, the alliance must be envisioning action against the United States. In reality the U.S. government did not worry about having to fight the two powers. What really concerned the United States was that the existence of the alliance appeared to give the Japanese the support, albeit sometimes the unwilling support, of the British in carrying out Japan's aggressive plans in East Asia. In early 1921 the British held an imperial conference in London and suggested renewal of the alliance. When the Canadians registered strong opposition, the British, in unrealistic hopes of getting the Americans to become a part of the alliance, began to talk to the United States about holding a conference on Pacific problems.[15]

Distrust of the United Kingdom and Japan had permeated the League of Nations debates in the U.S. Senate. The British, accused of not paying back their war debts to the United States, of misruling Ireland, and of having led naive Americans into the World War I, found themselves pilloried in the general U.S. press and hung for high crimes in the

papers of William Randolph Hearst, who believed that
nothing good could emanate from London.

These comments were tepid in comparison with those
directed against Japan. Japanese actions—in annexing Korea
in 1910, in presenting various demands to China, in taking
over former German islands in the Pacific, in attempting to
restrict U.S. cable rights on the island of Yap, in taking over
German privileges in the Chinese province of Shantung, and
in marching Japanese troops into Siberia—and the presence
of Japanese immigrants in California, which challenged that
state's immigration and land ownership laws, all this and more
had caused many Americans to conclude that Japanese
aggression presented a threat. Senator William E. Borah (R-
Idaho) noted, "There are bureaucrats here, who expect to
wake up any morning and hear Japanese guns battering away
at the Capitol."[16] Another senator, Hiram Johnson (R-
Calif.), claimed that Harding told him that his intelligence
officers warned "that war with Japan was imminent."[17] The
London Times, however, shortly before the conference, quoted
the insurance odds against a U.S.-Japanese war as 19-1, while
the French *L'Oeuvre* predicted "the conflagration appears as
fatally certain as lightning which leaps from two clouds
charged with opposing currents."[18] Harding, sincerely
desirous of alleviating tensions with both the United Kingdom
and Japan, came to believe that arms control might offer him
the opportunity to address these problems.

The Harding administration thought of its national security
objectives largely in political terms, both domestic and
international, rather than in military terms. It had followed
the traditional American pattern of cutting back on U.S.
military forces after every war; naval disarmament clearly fit
within this tradition and was domestically popular.
Disenchantment with U.S. participation in World War I was
already setting in, and it was the rare American or member of
the administration who saw threats to U.S. security in events
in Europe. The Far East, however, presented a different
perspective. Despite the great imprecision of any definition of

U.S. security interests in the Far East, there was substantial agreement that Japan somehow or other threatened U.S. long-range interests in Asia. Senator Joseph Robinson (D-Ark.) expressed an almost universal sentiment when he said that although he opposed Japan and wanted to do nothing to help it, "I would not put my country at war to stop Japan's advances."[19] With the understanding that the use of military power was ruled out, U.S. interests had of necessity to be protected by diplomacy rather than warships.

Domestic Political Context

The British proposal on a Pacific conference merged with the U.S. interest in arms limitation. On December 14, 1920, Senator Borah had offered a resolution asking the president to work toward an understanding with Japan and the United Kingdom whereby the three powers would cut their *building* programs 50 percent.[20] One cannot be certain of Borah's motivations. Borah clearly recognized a strong public movement in support of either general disarmament or arms limitation. He did not create that movement, but he had, nonetheless, become its champion. Whether he did so because he truly believed in it or because he saw the opportunity to overcome a tarnished, negative reputation acquired as an "irreconcilable" in the League of Nations debate is unknown.[21] Historian Robert J. Maddox has suggested that Borah did not believe that either the United Kingdom or Japan would ever accept such a proposal, thereby proving their bad intentions, but instead believed that his proposal would gain him a more positive image.[22]

At first, both as president-elect and as president, Harding had opposed the resolution, but he eventually supported it as part of a compromise that gave the administration the right to continue naval construction until it reached a naval agreement. Republicans, in both the House and the Senate, from 1921 to 1932 supported navy and army bills more favorably than did Democrats.[23] Both the Republican Senate and the House, however, also strongly supported the Borah idea.[24]

Borah himself later said: "There has been much dispute about who was the author of the disarmament conference. The real author of the disarmament conference was public opinion."[25] C. Leonard Hoag, in his classic study on the Washington Conference and public opinion, argued: "It is not to be doubted that it was the pressure of public opinion which moved Congress to act and, through Congress, President Harding. . . . [It is] one of the most significant chapters in the history of public opinion."[26] Although there is substantial truth in both the Borah and Hoag statements, neither presents the whole story.

Harding and Hughes both followed, ignored, and led public opinion at different times before, during, and after the conference. Public opinion's greatest impact occurred during the origins of the conference, largely in the period between Harding's election in November 1920 and his inauguration in March 1921. Not yet in office, the Harding administration had limited ability to manipulate either public opinion or Congress. Nevertheless, Harding and Hughes both claimed that they had discussed arms limitation before the passage of the Borah resolution and that they disagreed with its timing more than with its content; both wanted a strong naval bill passed first.[27] Harding wanted both to achieve a reduction in arms and to gain a navy "second to none" to please all of his constituencies. Borah did not recognize the connection between Harding's goals. As the invitation to the conference in June and the agenda in July indicate, large differences existed between what Borah proposed, what organized public opinion wanted, and what Harding and Hughes finally did.

Organized public opinion centered on the broad belief that expenditure on armaments was far too high and must be reduced. Almost every group, with the exception of the pacifists, concentrated on that issue.[28] Very few stressed that fewer arms would bring greater chances of peace. The *New York World*, Chambers of Commerce, the Women's Committee for World Disarmament, the National League of Women's Voters, the National Council for the Limitation of Armaments, the World Peace Foundation, the General Committee on the Limitation of Armaments, and the National Student Committee led the way. Women's groups, churches, labor, and students formed the bulwark of the movement. All had slightly different agendas, but all agreed about lifting the burden of arms spending. The country, suffering a serious recession with much unemployment, could use tax cuts that citizens and companies could then apply to help themselves and the economy. No one can deny the yeoman service performed by these groups and the publicity that Borah gave to them and to himself.

Before receiving the British proposal on a Pacific conference, Secretary of State Hughes had sent a cable to London suggesting a disarmament conference in Washington. The two cables probably crossed in the middle of the Atlantic; they proposed, one should note, two different kinds of conferences. Hughes, when he received the British proposal, put the two proposals together and decided to have a conference that would deal with Pacific and Asian problems as well as with disarmament. The secretary of state was not optimistic about solving Asian concerns, but he believed that it was necessary to merge the two in order to solve the Anglo-Japanese problem.[29] After beating off another British proposal for a separate Pacific conference, Hughes invited the United Kingdom, Japan, France, and Italy to come to the disarmament conference. He then added Portugal, the Netherlands, Belgium, and China, all of which would attend only the Far Eastern part of the conference.[30]

Borah had proposed *only* a reduction in *naval building* programs. The conference invitation from Hughes said limitation of armaments, which clearly implied land armaments. The disarmament organizations, pleased by that broadening from naval to all arms, tried to conceal their unhappiness with the inclusion of Far Eastern issues. Harding and Hughes had thus gone considerably beyond the goals of both Borah and public opinion in setting the agenda of the conference.

Role of the President

President Harding enjoyed tremendous popularity in both the negotiation and ratification stages of the treaties. The overwhelming election victory of 1920 had not only secured Harding strong public support but also had dramatically increased the number of Republican senators and representatives who rode into office on his coattails.[31] Since he did not take office until March 1921, the preliminaries of the conference, the conference itself, and the ratification took place in the first fifteen months of his administration; the honeymoon period of his presidency, which lasted until late 1922, thus encompassed the entire Washington Conference process. His political popularity constituted the main asset of the administration. Neither the election nor his first year in office had fully revealed the limitations of his abilities and lack of judgment, which were to lead to major scandals. Those later incidents, however, should not obscure the fact that Harding did have significant political skills and that he used them with great success during both the election and his first year in office. Secretary of State Hughes effectively used that popularity both to negotiate and to gain ratification of the Washington treaties.

Harding created a Republican consensus in foreign policy with an accommodating approach that left the progressive-isolationists in the Republican camp (Johnson and Borah) without his open support and, more important, without fellow Republicans to follow them. Lodge, who was worried that Harding might become too internationalist, expressed his concerns in December 1920 to the president-elect. Harding replied that he was searching for "some common ground on which we ourselves may unite" in foreign policy. Further, in a line clearly meant as advice for Lodge to follow, he concluded that "I should venture upon no negotiation until I was reasonably assured of the ample support of the Senate in making the program effective."[32]

Harding also went out of his way to avoid partisanship on foreign policy. He did not attack Democrats and thus avoided the deep hatreds that had existed during the league debates, when Wilson lost almost all support among Republicans.[33] To the genial Harding, confrontation was to be avoided. His principles allowed much compromise, and all could enter his political tent. He proved difficult for the Democrats to pin down and attack. His nonpartisan approach became an important key to his success.

Historians are in dispute over whether President Harding or whether Secretary of State Hughes should have the title of primary architect of the Washington agreements. Roger Dingman makes a strong case for Harding, but he is the exception.[34] The preponderance of the evidence points to the secretary of state. His previous record as governor, associate justice of the Supreme Court and his subsequent record as secretary of state and chief justice of the Supreme Court demonstrated strong management skills. Harding had the political popularity; Hughes had the vision and the competence to carry out their plans. They were, in other words, a very effective team, with Harding the popular coach and Hughes the quarterback. Harding made the game possible, Hughes assured success.

Harding, particularly effective, led a united front in the administration in support of the treaties. Few civilian or military leaders broke ranks publicly to suggest that the treaties were less than perfect; indeed, almost all indulged in great exaggeration in praising the agreements. Seldom before, and especially since, has a president had such nearly unanimous support for arms control measures. (Perhaps the absence of copying machines, radio, and television made the task of controlling dissent somewhat more manageable.) He had, with the exception of a very few newspapers, total support. In addition, on several occasions when obstacles presented themselves, both during the conference and in the ratification fight, recalcitrant individuals called at the White House and talked to the president. During the conference Harding tended to let Hughes handle the problems; in the Senate, Lodge and, to a lesser but still important degree, Underwood led the ratification supporters. Harding's co-option of Underwood, the Democratic minority leader of the Senate, deprived Senate Democrats of the ability to make the treaties a partisan issue, as several of them clearly desired to do. The president's old colleagues in the Senate were, in general, extremely deferential to him during the honeymoon period. Few thought of him as a great leader, but many genuinely liked him personally, and all could follow the election returns.

The executive branch did attempt to link the treaties of the conference to the general cause of peace. Harding, as pointed out earlier, had suggested that conferences called to find solutions to specific, narrow issues could contribute to world peace and, not incidentally, allow the United States to operate outside the League of Nations structure. Pleased with the results of the Washington Conference, Harding offered his suggestion of a continuing series of conferences to the press on several occasions, both during the conference and after.[35] Some, unsure what he had in mind, suggested that they were classic Harding "bloviations" and that the president was deliberately trying to obscure the issue by his imprecision. Harding, it is clear, meant well and wanted to do something "becoming" for world peace. It is quite likely that he just was not sure what he wanted to do and preferred to let the course of events determine what steps he might take in the future. One cannot be certain. Nonetheless, the issue died and never became a part of the ratification debate.

The domestic political context favored the Harding administration. President Harding had carried large majorities with him into both the Senate and the House. His program of a return to "normalcy" found a popular response both in Congress and with the public. Wartime controls disappeared, perhaps too quickly, and the country began to suffer from both an economic recession and heightened unemployment. No new programs of major importance were developed to deal with these difficulties; government intervention in economic spheres, except in wartime, had not yet become an American tradition.

The economy, it was widely believed, would right itself in time. Indeed, with the exception of agriculture, it did. A new tax law provided for tax reductions, a tariff act was under consideration, and debate was in progress over the funding of a soldiers' bonus bill.[36]

The Harding administration, however, did not see itself as facing any key domestic issues in 1921 that would make it want to bargain for votes on the ratification by promising wavering senators support on domestic issues. In part, the apparent overwhelming support for the treaties made it unnecessary. Lodge, however, did use the greater senatorial interest in domestic legislation, which more directly impacted on senatorial reelection than did foreign affairs, to speed up the ratification debates so that more time could be spent on domestic affairs.[37] It was, moreover, a midterm election year, and the Republicans did not want to do anything that might cost them further gains in Congress, nor did they wish to make the treaties a partisan issue. In these two goals they were quite successful, and the nonpartisanship, in general, of the ratification debate is a remarkable feature. As it turned out, the Republicans worried far more about the progressive wing of their own party than they did about the Democrats.

If electoral politics did not play a key role in the ratification process, they had done so in the negotiations leading up to the conference. Borah's resolution calling for a cut of 50 percent in naval building programs stimulated public discussion that the Harding administration, preferring to move at its own pace on its own program, had not welcomed.

Harding clearly wanted to continue the naval building with congressional support before he made any approaches to other nations on naval arms limitations. His first priority to get the naval bill passed by Congress. He soon discovered, however, that Borah's proposal had struck not only a public chord but also a congressional one. Rather than let Borah retain control of a popular movement, Harding wisely decided to compromise and then take command of the movement himself by calling for an expanded conference. Borah soon found himself isolated and was certainly not surprised when he did not get an invitation from Harding to serve as a delegate to the conference.[38] Borah, at that point, appeared less dangerous outside the conference than inside.

Harding's greatest opposition to the arms control treaty did not come so much from Congress either during the negotiation or ratification stage as it did from the navy. The navy's General Board had called for twice as much capital ship tonnage as had the administration; Hughes and Harding had rejected the navy's proposals and called for deeper cuts.[39] The navy found itself in a difficult position. Nationally, disarmament was immensely popular, as it had traditionally been after every war. Although both the public and Congress expressed eagerness to cut back the military expenses of the United States to peacetime levels, both the army and navy budgets remained far higher in 1921 than in 1914, the last normal peacetime mark. Faced with no serious international threats, naval boosters found it almost impossible to arouse support outside of military circles.

The navy's leadership did not offer a clear rallying point around which naval officers could organize their opposition. Secretary of the Navy Edwin Denby did not play a key part in the evolution of the naval proposal.[40] Both he and his assistant secretary of the navy, Theodore Roosevelt, Jr., overpowered by Hughes and Harding, chose to side with the administration rather than with the naval establishment. When two key senior officers, Admiral Robert E. Coontz, the chief of naval operations, and Admiral-designate William V. Pratt supported the president, naval officers had no one to lead the fight.[41]

There is little question that few naval officers approved of the massive cuts that Hughes had proposed. There is also little doubt that civilian supremacy dominated the major decisions that brought forth the U.S. plan. Only a small number of officers spoke publicly about the naval treaty during the conference, and even then did so in extraordinarily cautious terms. Lodge's strategy of pushing the treaties through the Senate as fast as possible, without hearings or the testimony of naval officers, took away the last chance of the naval opponents to affect the outcome decisively. Their complaints became more public with each passing year and reached a crescendo during the hearings held at the London Naval Conference of 1930, but by then the Washington system had operated for eight years.[42] The Harding administration carefully avoided an acrimonious struggle with the navy and its congressional supporters.

Not accidentally, Harding and his colleagues handled the navy with great skill and made it clear that they viewed the arms treaty as a political question to be decided on the basis of political considerations. Military considerations fell into a secondary category. Military advice, therefore, did not become a major determinant of policy. Lodge, during the Senate ratification, strongly expressed the administration's view.

> It is not for technical experts to make this treaty any more than I regard it as the duty of technical experts to make the tariff bill . . . . The idea should be dismissed that the naval experts were to formulate the policy to be pursued or that we should ever have allowed them to do it. The policy, be it good or bad, was the policy of the government represented by the American delegates at the conference.[43]

The army, ignored even more than the navy in both the pre-conference planning and the conference negotiations, had no impact on the proceedings. General John J. Pershing, on the Advisory Committee, had favored reduction of arms for quite some time.[44] Army bureaucrats tried to offset Pershing by sending Hughes memoranda and letters with recommendations and also requests for closer liaison with the Department of State.[45] Hughes kept the political/diplomatic and the military branches of the government as widely separated as he could. Despite the fact that land limitation was at least implicitly on the agenda, Hughes presented no proposals at the conference. French lack of interest and antagonism killed Hughes's remaining interest in an area in which he could see slight chance for success. The army also had input on the poison gas issue, but the French refused to ratify the Submarine–Poison Gas Treaty, and it never went into effect. Despite great efforts, "The army proved to be impotent in its attempts to influence foreign policy."[46]

The Japanese, British, and French, in that order, had major critics and opponents in the United States. The Japanese had the most negative image—militaristic, imperialistic, clever, deceitful, and untrustworthy—and, as noted earlier, Japan was considered the most likely power that the United States might face in a future war. Such feelings were strongest on the West Coast, but also arose in other sections of the country. These suspicions, on occasion mixed with the threat of a "yellow peril" and often implicitly racist, appeared without apology in the speeches of a handful of senators. They came out the strongest in the Four-Power Treaty debates when opposition senators questioned why the Japanese would give up the benefits of the Anglo-Japanese Alliance to accept a treaty that the administration had attempted to sell as meaningless and not binding on anyone.[47] The proposed treaty must, since the other great villain, the United Kingdom, was a part of it, be just an enlarged alliance designed by these two worrisome nations to entangle the United States in their nefarious goals in the Far East. If the Japanese came to the conference with the worst reputation, they calmed, by their largely cooperative attitude, all but the most paranoid of American fears.

The British appeared slightly safer but certainly bore watching. No one doubted that the British protected their interests. Only the Irish-Americans and the Hearst press (and a handful of senators) publicly saw the United Kingdom as perfidious Albion. One senator believed that the award of the Order of the Garter to Arthur Balfour, immediately after he returned to London after serving as the chief British delegate at Washington, represented his reward for getting the United States into the Four-Power Treaty; he had duped the innocent U.S. delegates into an alliance.[48]

Suspicion of Japan and the United Kingdom was more rhetorical bombast than an effective tool used by the opponents of the treaties. France, because of its obstructionism at the conference, went home with diminished support from Americans. The opposition, never able to make an effective case on foreign entanglement, gathered almost no voting support in the Senate on these grounds except on the Yap and the Four-Power treaties.

The only direct attempt to link the conference with domestic issues occurred in the economic sphere. Gilbert Hitchcock (D-Nebr.) expressed a widely held belief that the United States had a recession because European nations could not buy U.S. goods. Why? Europeans were spending all of their money buying more arms; if they stopped, unemployment would disappear in the United States as Europeans purchased American-made products.[49] The administration did not argue at any time, as many peace groups did, that money not spent on armaments could be diverted to education or other social needs; indeed, both the executive and legislative branches preferred to lower taxes and spend as few funds as possible. Almost no one mentioned such issues during the ratification debate. Organized labor, however, which had supported the conference treaties strongly through the activities of Samuel Gompers, was shocked to find that the closing of naval construction yards would bring about even more unemployment.[50]

A favorable international context for the treaty ratification also helped the Harding administration. The British strongly favored the treaties, which they believed favorable to their interests. Opposition within the Royal Navy remained under the firm control of the Lloyd George government. The

Japanese government, which had survived the assassination of the pro-conference Prime Minister Hara Kei just days before the conference opened, continued to take a supportive line. Opposition from the Imperial Navy, however, was quite strong if not publicly vocal. Considerable resentment against the inferior ratio given Japan under the Five-Power Naval Treaty simmered for almost ten years before boiling over during the London Naval Conference of 1930. The French believed that they had been badly treated and unfairly singled out because of their demands for a higher ratio of capital ships and for the absence of any limits on auxiliary ships and because they were linked to the failure of attempts to secure the limitation of land armaments. They argued they were the front line against Germany. The Italians had cooperated almost completely with the U.S. proposals and had gained much respect in the United States as the strongest European supporters of the treaties.

Two of the major European powers, Germany and the Soviet Union, did not have navies of any importance. Both temporarily resided outside the pale of respectability, since the United States did not recognize the Soviet Union and the Versailles Treaty prohibited the Germans from constructing large naval vessels. Hughes had not invited the Soviets or the Germans to the conference. (Several senators believed this a mistake.) Europeans in general were largely wrapped up in reconstruction problems and with the exception of the British and the French did not attach major importance to the specifics of naval arms control.[51]

The Washington Conference ended on February 6, 1922, with a speech by Harding in which he concluded, "How simple it all has been."[52] From the president on down, the administration supported the treaties by praising them at every opportunity, even with some exaggeration. Hughes said that the Five-Power Naval Treaty "ends, absolutely ends," the naval race.[53] The report to the president by the U.S. delegation stated that "probably no more significant treaty was ever made."[54] Vice President Calvin Coolidge boasted that the Washington agreements "promised to be one of the achievements of history."[55] Only Secretary of the Interior Albert B. Fall failed to get on the bandwagon. He supported the naval treaty but withheld his approval of the Four-Power Treaty because of a lack of consultation with the cabinet before its public announcement.[56]

Executive-Congressional Relations

The major task of getting the treaties through the Senate fell to Henry Cabot Lodge. The wisdom of appointing Lodge to the delegation became apparent during the ratification debates. Lodge handled his task with experience and skill, and, it is important to reemphasize, with the cooperation of Underwood. The cabinet made declarations of support but did little active politicking of the senators themselves. The major numerical opposition, after all, was composed of Democrats (not overly susceptible to Republican blandishments) and Republicans like Borah and Johnson, whose lack of party regularity led no one to count on their approval. Hughes worked on senators through the press and attempted to arouse support through influential groups that he hoped in turn would influence the Senate. The key figure in the Senate itself, however, was Lodge.

The senior senator from Massachusetts was entering the twilight of his career, and of his life, in 1921 and 1922. Not just the Senate majority leader, or chairman of the Senate Foreign Relations Committee, he also represented the leadership of the Republican party. He had supported Harding and worked hard to elect him president; his closeness to Harding was a source of power every bit as important as his senatorial positions.[57] One could not say that Lodge, respected, and even feared by some of the fledgling Republican senators, was loved or popular within his own party. Democrats hated him with a vengeance. One, John Williams (D-Miss.), bragged that he had never agreed with Lodge and hoped he would die before such a catastrophe occurred.[58] Democrats threw many bitter and hateful words at Lodge during the ratification debates. Some were even his own, as the opposition delighted in citing speeches Lodge had made against the League of Nations in 1919 and 1920 to enhance their arguments against the Four-Power Treaty. Lodge demonstrated no public uneasiness at his change in position but did take to leaves of absence during some of the more vociferous debates. Nevertheless, although he won no friends in the Senate, he performed brilliantly in the ratification struggle.

There can be little doubt that the positive position of Oscar W. Underwood lent the Harding administration great strength. A friend of Harding's when the Ohio politician had served in the Senate, the Alabama Democrat offered to resign as minority leader when Harding appointed him to the U.S. delegation. Several leading Democrats, William Gibbs McAdoo (D-Ga.) and Carter Glass (D-Va.) among them, called upon him to do so, but the party failed to take a position and he remained. Underwood said: "The president and I are not playing party politics. We are out of the three-mile limit and are fighting the battles of American democracy."[59] He played an active role at the conference on the Chinese Customs Treaty and did very little on the Five-Power Treaty. During the ratification debates, Thaddeus Caraway (D-Ark.) accused him of ignoring Democrats who opposed the treaties and of spending all of his time with Lodge and Harding.[60] Underwood defended himself and the treaties in a three-hour speech on the Senate floor. Hughes wrote him that he had "never known a finer illustration of non-partisan statesmanship."[61] Harvard University gave him an honorary doctor of laws degree. Later offered a position on the Supreme Court by Harding, he declined. Underwood certainly hurt his credibility among his colleagues as Democratic Senate minority leader, and he resigned in 1923.[62]

Both Underwood *and* Lodge were attacked by fellow senators during the ratification debates for serving on the U.S. delegation. Hiram Johnson expressed a hope that "this is the last time that upon any such commission or conference senators will be appointed."[63] On the next day Senator Robinson, pointing to the appointments as an unwise mixture of executive and senatorial obligations, concluded that such appointments made biased senators who could not retain their objective independence in judging the treaties for ratification.[64]

A positive state of executive-congressional relations existed during the entire process of the Washington treaties. The results of the presidential election had changed a narrow senatorial margin of 49 Republicans and 47 Democrats in 1919 to 59 Republicans and 37 Democrats in 1921; those figures for the House of Representatives changed from 240 Republicans and 190 Democrats in 1919 to 301 Republicans and 131 Democrats in 1920. Harding had far more strength in Congress, and thus a much better position, than had Woodrow Wilson. Harding, as senator, had not made many enemies in the Senate, and his performance as president had not yet created divisive camps. Even the small group of progressive Republicans allowed Harding a respite until the announcement of the Four-Power Treaty.

The Senate Foreign Relations Committee, composed of ten Republicans and seven Democrats in 1919, changed to ten Republicans and six Democrats in 1921. Albert B. Fall (R-N.M.), Harding (R-Ohio), and Philander C. Knox (R-Pa.) were replaced by James W. Wadsworth, Jr. (R-N.Y.), Joseph Medill McCormick (R-Ill.), and Frank B. Kellogg (R-Minn.) on the Republican side. Marcus A. Smith (D-Ariz.) was not replaced in the Democratic ranks, despite protests from Democratic leaders. Lodge remained as chairman, and he made sure that the new members agreed far more with his foreign policy views than with those of the two mavericks of the committee, Borah and Johnson. With such strong majorities, the constitutional requirement for a two-thirds vote played no part at all in the popular arms control treaty and only a small role in the Four-Power Treaty. If the Republicans remained cohesive and followed Lodge, Harding would need just five Democratic votes. Lodge's task was to make sure that only a few Republicans would join Borah and that Underwood could deliver enough Democrats to offset those desertions.

The fight against the treaties was led by senators William Borah, Joseph France (R-Md.), Hiram Johnson, Robert M. La Follette (R-Wis.), James Reed (D-Mo.), and Joseph Robinson; the first four were Republicans, the last two Democrats. All had voted against the League of Nations (although Robinson had voted for the League of Nations with no reservations on one of the three key votes).[65] Almost all of the remaining irreconcilables from the league fight were to vote against the Four-Power Treaty; none but France voted against the naval treaty. All of the action centered on the Four-Power Treaty.

The Harding administration worked hard to prevent a major split within the Republican ranks. Hiram Johnson, after an hour's talk with Harding, wrote in disgust that Harding was "seeking in every possible way to unite every possible element. . . . He wants to move smoothly along the path of least resistance, and in order to do so, will make, I think, to us, as well as to others opposed to us, all sorts of concessions."[66] Few expected Borah, France, Johnson, or La Follette to vote for the Four-Power Treaty; Borah voted in favor of the Five-Power Naval Treaty, as did La Follette, Johnson did not cast a vote, and France voted against the naval treaty. These irreconcilable Republicans did not attract any other Republicans to their side. Many Democrats, however, gleefully joined them on the Four-Power Treaty fight, but not one voted against the Five-Power Naval Treaty. The Harding administration thus not only prevented a split within the Republican party that might cause difficulty in a future election but also prevented the treaties from becoming a partisan issue. The enormous popularity of the arms control treaty prevented such an occurrence.

Often overlooked is that the election of 1920, combined with retirements and deaths, brought twenty-three new senators (almost one fourth of the Senate) to the ratification debates in 1922. Eighteen Republicans and five Democrats made up the freshman class. Led by Lodge and conscious of Harding's popularity, the Republicans followed the party line to such an astounding degree that not a single new Republican cast so much as a vote against any of the treaties. Only two, Samuel Shortridge (R-Calif.) and Frank B. Willis (R-Ohio) even made major speeches. Lodge had them in his pocket. Four of the five new Democrats, however, argued strongly and voted against several of the treaties; one, Edwin Broussard (D-La.), voted for all of them.[67]

To open the Senate battle, the administration brought out its chief asset, President Harding, still basking in the honeymoon glow of his great election victory. Harding appeared personally before the Senate on February 10, 1922, and reminded the senators of their overwhelming support of the Borah resolution. He also again linked the treaties together in one package and boasted that he was submitting the "complete minutes of both plenary sessions and committee meetings," along with a report by the U.S. delegation. Here was open diplomacy at its finest. He noted that the treaties attempted to solve important problems without a sacrifice of national pride—"There were no punishments to inflict, no rewards to bestow." The president said he knew the sentiment against European entanglement. He pledged that the Four-Power Treaty had "no commitment to armed force, no alliance, no written or moral obligation to join in defense, no expressed or implied commitment to arrive at any agreement except in accordance with our constitutional methods." Aggression now became a "hazardous enterprise." In almost Wilsonian terms Harding argued that if the Senate did not approve the treaties, "We shall discredit the influence of the Republic, render future efforts futile or unlikely, and write discouragement where today the world is ready to acclaim new hope." He invited the Senate to approve all the treaties, since each depended upon the others.[68]

Even then, however, Harding made a mistake on the Four-Power Treaty that had the potential to jeopardize not only the

Four-Power Treaty but the naval treaty as well. When Harding inadvertently misinterpreted a clause in the Four-Power Treaty, over whether the Japanese main islands were included within its purview, he gave the impression of not knowing what his delegates had done.[69] The opponents of the treaties used this to suggest that the U.S. delegation had acted in such secrecy that not even the president had correct information. Only some very sharp footwork by Hughes and Lodge, and a correction by Harding, smoothed over the situation. Still, in the ratification debates it came up time and again.[70] Harding, thereafter, became very cautious in his comments.

The *Washington Post* had reported that Harding did not plan "to exert any pressure on the Senate in connection with the Washington conference treaties. . . . that the President would neither trade, lobby, admonish, or supplicate, but would expect the Senate, as the ratifying body to be the judge of its own actions."[71] Although, in general, Harding tried to keep that promise, within two weeks he had talked to two Democratic senators, Ellison Smith (D-S.C.) and John B. Kendrick (D-Wyo.), as well as John T. Adams of the Republican National Committee, Joseph Medill McCormick, who headed the Republican senatorial campaign, and Charles Curtis (R-Kans.), the Republican whip of the Senate.[72] He had constant talks with Lodge and Underwood. So many with the latter, in fact, that several Democratic senators publicly complained.

There is little evidence, with a few important exceptions, that once the battle lines were drawn, the president attempted to influence directly key opposition senators. He was on better personal terms with Johnson than he was with Borah and did talk on occasion with the former, but not with the latter, during the ratification debate. After the surprise announcement of the Four-Power Treaty on December 10, opposition had begun to form around Borah and a small group of Democratic senators, but it soon became apparent that Borah could neither lead nor organize the group. Borah, during most of his senatorial career, was a loner who did not attract followers in the sense that other senators lined up behind him. Johnson said Borah "is a most difficult person to keep in agreement. . . . a very strange and a very uncertain individual."[73] A large degree of unpredictability in Borah always made his leadership of any group problematical. Yet the fact that it was Borah, and not, for example, Lodge or Underwood, obviously made Harding's task so much easier.

It did not take the senators long to realize that the "complete record" promised by Harding did not include any of the Four-Power Treaty negotiations or any of the minutes of the subcommittees where much of the conference work had occurred.[74] The Senate on November 8, 1921, three days before the conference had begun, had passed a resolution asking the U.S. delegates to admit representatives of the press and to preserve a complete record.[75] Hiram Johnson had written that the "only hope for disarmament is that the public opinion of the world exerted by reason of open sessions upon the diplomats of the world will make them for the first time, act for peoples" rather than for governments.[76] Harding and Hughes had not completely fulfilled that request, so the Senate passed another resolution on February 16 requesting records, minutes, arguments, debates, and conversations relating to the Four-Power Treaty.[77]

Hughes drafted a tactful refusal, which Harding sent to the Senate. In this message the president denied the existence of any records, but then he went on to say that even if such documents had existed, he did not think it "compatible with public interest or consistent with the amenities of international negotiation" to reveal such information. He reported that "no concealed understandings, and no secret exchanges of notes, and . . . no commitments whatever" regarding the Four-Power Treaty existed.[78]

Lodge, then, began to run a blitzkrieg campaign. As the Senate majority leader, he was in a position to influence greatly the calendar of the Senate and thus to set the pace of treaty ratification. He first presented the treaties to the Senate Foreign Relations Committee on February 10; by February 27 all had acquired a favorable imprint after only eleven meetings of the committee. The printed record of the committee's deliberations on the Five-Power Naval Treaty reports that on February 25 "after discussion, Mr. Williams moved that the treaty be reported favorably. The roll was called, and the vote resulted—yeas 13, nays 0. So, by unanimous vote, a favorable report was ordered thereon." All ten Republicans, including Borah and Johnson, were present and voted yes; three Democrats (John Williams [D-Miss.], Atlee Pomerene [D-Ohio], and John Shields [D-Tenn.]) were present and voted yes, and three Democrats (Claude Swanson [D-Va.], Key Pittman [D-Nev.] and Gilbert Hitchcock) were absent. This was the only meeting at which the treaty was discussed, and then, only briefly; not a single objection, at least according to the published minutes, was raised.[79]

At all the other meetings, the opponents of the Four-Power Treaty were seeking more information from the president. The final result was a reservation stating that the Four-Power Treaty was not an alliance and did not envision the use of force. Hiram Johnson, confirmed in his beliefs, wrote, "The very fact that they will consent to this reservation demonstrates conclusively the Treaty is of the character I have denounced."[80] Even more amazing, not a single hearing on *any* of the treaties was held, not a single witness either in favor of or opposed to *any* of the treaties testified or, more correct, ever got the opportunity to do so. As one newspaper commented, "One great difference between the Four-Power Treaty and the League Covenant is that one was of Republican origin and the other of Democratic origin."[81]

The whole process stood in stark contrast with the League of Nations debates two years earlier. Committee records indicate no dissent to these procedures, but several senators in the full debate on the Senate floor indicated that they had argued in favor of having naval and military experts testify on the naval treaty. That no hearings were held is an indication of the weakness of the opposition and the strength of Harding and Lodge.

The steamroller continued at high speed when the treaties came before the full Senate. Senators found their mail stuffed with letters and petitions from virtually every organized church, women's, pacifist, and pro–arms control group in the country calling for the ratification of the naval arms control treaty. It was rare, indeed, that any opposition dared to poke up its head. Support for the other treaties ran almost as high; what little dissent existed centered, as expected, on the Four-Power Treaty.

Attempting to capitalize on the enormous support for the naval treaty, Harding and Lodge insisted that the defeat of the Four-Power Treaty would lead to the defeat of the naval treaty, since the treaties were so closely tied together. In strong terms Lodge argued that senators should remember that the "defeat of the Four-Power Treaty would endanger the treaty for the limitation of naval armament, and the failure of the naval treaty would shock and startle the world and bitterly disappoint the American people. We must not forget the close relationship between the two treaties. The defeat of the Four-Power Treaty would mean the failure of the conference."[82] Underwood also stated that the Four-Power Treaty "represents a political settlement which undoubtedly was necessary before the treaty providing for the limitation of armaments was signed."[83] Irvine Lenroot (R-Wis.) suggested that rejection of the quadruple arrangement probably would not in itself mean defeat of the naval arms treaty in the Senate but would lead to the same result if Japan and France then refused to ratify the Five-Power Naval Treaty.[84] The connection between the treaties represented a constant theme in the Senate by its supporters and may well have led several reluctant Democratic senators to vote for the Four-Power Treaty. Lodge presented first the two most controversial treaties, the Yap and the Four-Power treaties, in an attempt to put pressure on any wavering senator and create the impression that a vote against the Four-Power Treaty would lead to the crippling or rejection of the naval treaty.

Lodge also kept the treaties constantly before the Senate, so much so that opposition senators on both sides complained about the pressure.[85] Many remembered that Lodge in the debates over the league had insisted on slow, careful investigation of every word of the League Covenant. Frequent reminders of this did not cause Lodge to pause for a moment. Everyone recognized Lodge's strategy, but he had the troops and his opponents did not. They had little recourse as Lodge struck at the peak of public support, at the crest of a popular president's power, at a time when many Americans exhibited great pride over the fact that a successful diplomatic conference, held in their own country, directed by Americans, had attained major accomplishments toward world peace. In the Senate the Yap Treaty came first, widely regarded as a test for the more important treaties. Negotiated and signed with Japan just before the Washington Conference, it involved U.S. cable rights on Yap Island. Yap, in the Carolines Island group, given to the Japanese as a mandate by the League of Nations, had been selected by the General Board of the navy as a crucial communications point; Wilson had failed in his efforts to obtain satisfactory rights for the United States, but Hughes had persevered.[86]

Senators Johnson, Robinson, France, and Pittman led the opposition, contending that the treaty represented a victory for the Japanese, who now gained full title to the Pacific mandates. To Senator Reed's way of thinking, Lodge might have referred to them in a poetic quotation as " 'sprinkled isles, lily on lily that o'erlace the sea,' but if you lift up the lily pads you will find a Jap or Britisher under each of them. There they are by the thousands."[87] Hiram Johnson advised caution to his colleagues "because this treaty is the initial bluff and the first surrender" of the ratification fights.[88] Lodge replied that U.S. acquiescence in the league decision did not mean the islands would remain Japanese. Underwood even believed that the United States, having refused to join the League of Nations, had no rights on Yap; Japan did not have to give the United States any concessions.[89] After some attempts to amend the treaty, the final vote came on March 11—sixty-seven voted in favor, twenty-two voted against, and seven were absent.[90]

The Yap vote indicated that the Four-Power Treaty might run into serious difficulties and even jeopardize the naval arms control treaty. Of sixty Republican senators (counting the progressive senator, Hiram Johnson) fifty-seven had voted, with fifty-four favoring the Yap Treaty. Of thirty-six Democratic senators thirty-two had voted, with nineteen against and thirteen in favor.[91] A shift of four or five votes, even with the addition of the absent seven senators (four Democrats and three Republicans, one of whom, La Follette, had spoken against the treaty), could mean the defeat of the Four-Power Treaty.

The Republican-controlled Committee on Foreign Relations decided to resolve the difficulty by adding the Brandegee reservation on February 27: "No commitment to armed force, no alliance, no obligation to join in any defense" was intended by the treaty. Harding had felt any reservation useless, but if a "becoming reservation" would reassure some senator, he had no objection; Harding himself even drafted a reservation that duplicated the no-alliance statement of his February 10 speech. He would have preferred to thrash out with the Senate the question of whether the executive could negotiate treaties without fear of senatorial repudiation, but Hughes and Lodge advised him not to.[92]

When debate started, foes of the Four-Power Treaty expressed disbelief that Japan and the United Kingdom could give up the substantial advantages of the Anglo-Japanese Alliance for the quadruple agreement. There was more to the treaty than met the eye; the U.S. delegation must have secretly promised something. Lodge's evasive presentation at the surprise original announcement of the treaty had also aroused a suspicion that a cover-up existed in his fancy words. James Reed had said it reminded him of a "mother's blandishments when she is about to administer a dose of castor oil."[93] Harding's later press conference blunder of not including the Japanese islands, and his reversal, had brought comment by the Missouri senator, who told of a blacksmith and wheelwright deciding on a sign for their partnership that read, "All kinds of twisting and turning done here."[94] Harding's refusal to submit any conference records on the treaty added further suspicion.

Johnson and other opposition senators believed that the Harding administration had misled Americans by calling a disarmament conference, when the real intention, to find a replacement for the Anglo-Japanese Alliance, had not even appeared on the agenda.[95] Borah wrote that he favored the naval treaty but that the Four-Power Treaty concealed just another alliance. He declared that "even if every man, woman, and child in the United States were in favor of it, I should unhesitatingly defeat it if I could."[96]

Lodge pointed out that a question of war would not come before a conference: "if a fleet of Japan were to attack the Hawaiian islands, . . . an act of war," that would remove any need to confer, since a state of war would then exist. The responsibility under the treaty to consult if an outside power committed aggression against one of the treaty powers presented the only obligation. Moreover, any decision would take a unanimous vote. The key gain, he stressed, the termination of the Anglo-Japanese Alliance, had major importance.[97]

To defuse opposition, Hughes wrote to Underwood—who then read the letter to his senatorial colleagues—an argument that the treaty represented a "model regional agreement" that destroyed any reason for war between the four major sea powers of the Pacific. Bristling, Secretary of State Hughes had written that he resented implications that U.S. delegates had given in to the clever British and Japanese. The American delegation had negotiated with the clear understanding that the United States would join no alliances or obligations pertaining to the use of force. The treaty, he argued, was short, clear, and required no commentary. Hughes admitted authorship of the draft that had become the basis of the final agreement. He sternly warned that "its failure would be nothing short of a national calamity."[98] The Cincinnati *Times-Star* supported Hughes and complained that "our over important Senate" is scrutinizing the work of Harding and Hughes "a good deal as if the Beef Trust had done something off color."[99]

The first vote came on March 14 when an amendment offered by Senator Robinson requiring the four nations to refrain from aggression met defeat by a vote of 30–55, 11 members not voting. Two other attempts to amend the treaty met defeat, and on March 15 a unanimous consent agreement passed, which cut off voting until March 24, when the final treaty vote would come.[100] During this breather Thomas E.

Watson (D-Ga.) mounted a scathing attack on the treaty and Elihu Root. Behind the treaty, he charged, was the money trust represented by Boss Tweed, the Ryans, the Belmonts, and Root, the lawyer of predatory corporations. The senator accused Root of selling out Korea to the Japanese in 1905 by refusing to heed a Korean appeal for support. He declared that if the United States ratified the treaty, it would surrender its independence. "What sort of speeches," he asked, "will orators make on the Fourth of July hereafter? Spread eagleism will be out of date. You will have caged your eagle. He will not have the freedom to look into the eyes of the sun and beat the heavens with perfectly free wings. Ah, no."[101]

Then, as if to confirm the opposition's worst fears, an incident that seriously embarrassed the Harding administration occurred. New York lawyer Paul D. Cravath, seemingly in touch with leading Republicans, made a speech before the newly organized Council on Foreign Relations in which he said that the most important achievement of the Washington Conference did not appear in the written record or in any of the treaties; it consisted of an "understanding" between the Americans and British concerning the Far East. His view, he said, found the approval of "every member of the American delegation," who had told him that because of this understanding each nation could count on the other for "closest cooperation" in an emergency.[102] Borah read a stenographic report of the speech into the record and charged that an alliance now in fact existed. Underwood and Lodge denied they had made any such statement, and the latter became furious with those attacking the motives of the U.S. delegates. Root never denied having talked to Cravath, and Hughes wrote Cravath, "Of course I did not believe that you had said anything of the sort reported." However, a strong denial from Cravath, which Lodge presented the next day, did not convince the opponents who had pounced on the speech.[103]

Hughes again came to the defense of the treaty by writing an open letter to Lodge in which he denied an understanding with the British. "Any such statement," he declared, "is absolutely false." The secretary hoped that the U.S. delegates would not listen to "further aspersions upon their veracity and honor."[104]

March 24 and the vote on the treaty approached, and based on the response to the Yap Treaty and the obinson amendment, and close counting by observers, it looked as if the Harding administration had the votes. As long as Underwood could swing Democratic votes, the treaty would pass. Underwood called at the White House on the evening of March 21 and promised the president the treaty would pass by at least three votes.[105]

Voting on the Four-Power Treaty advanced article by article on March 24. Acceptance of Article 1 came by a vote of 74–15, 7 members not voting. Opposition, however, had centered on Article 2, which seemed to make, at least in the opinion of a small group of senators, the quadruple agreement into an alliance: "If the said rights are threatened by the aggressive action of any other Power, the High Contracting Powers shall communicate with one another fully and frankly in order to arrive at an understanding as to the most effective measure to be taken, jointly or separately, to meet the exigencies of the situation." Many pro-league Democrats thought this a duplication of Article 10 of the League Covenant. Hours went by as senators looked up the term "alliance" in dictionaries, encyclopedias, international law texts, even history books. Six attempts to amend the article failed. By a vote of 66–28, with 2 abstentions, the article passed.[106] Articles 3 and 4 passed by 67–26 and 73–8.[107]

This left the Brandegee reservation and the final treaty vote. Sixteen attempts by senators David I. Walsh (D-Mass.), Robinson, Pittman, La Follette, Johnson, Reed, and Pomerene to clarify further the meaning of the reservation failed, with 36 votes the highest number in favor of any proposal.[108] Lodge then offered the Brandegee reservation, which passed by a vote of 91–2.[109]

The Four-Power Treaty then passed by a vote of 67–27, with 2 abstentions. Fifty-five Republicans and 12 Democrats supported the treaty; while 23 Democrats and 4 Republicans did not.[110]

One cannot help but reflect on the League of Nations controversy. Harding's decision, strongly influenced by Lodge, to accept the crucial reservation, stood in stark contrast with Wilson's stance on the league. Wilson's stubbornness had prevented U.S. entrance into the league, but Harding and Lodge in a somewhat similar situation compromised. President Harding, still somewhat reluctant, wrote Ambassador George Harvey in London: "It would be very easy to defeat any reservation, but such course might endanger ratification so I prefer toleration of the reservation to endangering ratification. It will interest you to know that it is necessary for me to help the Brandegee forces secure the adoption of the reservation."[111] Along with Harding, Lodge also had the undoubtedly important cooperation of Underwood. Still, the old senator from Massachusetts had proved more practical, more successful, than the former president he so disliked.

Three days later the Senate adopted the supplementary Four-Power Treaty, which defined the islands included in the agreement. Key Pittman offered an amendment giving the United States the right to decide when a controversy in the islands fell within domestic jurisdiction. He claimed that this proposal was the same reservation Lodge had offered during the league debate. This move lost by a vote of 21–40, and Lodge voted against it with no apparent embarrassment. The final vote was 73–0, with 23 not voting.[112] The Four-Power Treaty fight had finally ended.

Resistance thereupon collapsed. There were only two big speeches against the Five-Power Naval Treaty. James Reed believed that in the event of war the Philippines would fall in three days and Guam in twenty-four hours. He had predicted that Japan would do as it had done against China and Russia, "Namely to attack at the time best suiting her purposes and without giving us any notice."[113] Reed quoted two unnamed naval experts who had found incorrect tonnage figures in the naval treaty.[114] He clearly would have voted against the treaty but was absent at the vote. Joseph France outlined his reason for voting against the naval treaty. He realized that he was in the minority (indeed, as noted earlier, he cast the only vote against the Five-Power Naval Treaty), but he believed that the American people loved the navy and did not want reductions.[115] In contrast with the controversy over the Four-Power Treaty, the naval treaty was the subject of short, superficial, and not particularly illuminating debate. At no time during the ratification process were the problems of the Five-Power Naval Treaty really raised. The administration clearly oversold and exaggerated the treaty's benefits. This is not to say that it was not a good treaty, for it was; it is to say that the Senate ignored its duties. The treaty was adopted, 74-1, with 21 abstentions.[116]

On the question of safeguards, the conference delegates relied on "good faith"—the belief that they and their countries were all honorable. Trust was the key word. With trust, no verification measures were necessary in the treaties. After all, who could hide the construction of a battleship? Indeed, that feat was impossible, but it was very possible to hide the details, such as gun elevations and additional tonnage. This possibility did allow the Japanese in particular to cheat on individual ship tonnages. A minor reportage requirement on the construction of replacement tonnage did not include any method to verify the accuracy of the reported information. No requirement for inspection of Pacific Islands fortifications marred the trust of the Five-Power Naval Treaty. The 1920s were an age of idealism and trust that only the harsh realities of the 1930s and 1940s would destroy.

Senatorial support for the Five-Power Naval Treaty allowed Republicans to combine popular support of arms limitation with party regularity. The only Republican vote cast against the Five-Power Naval Treaty, by Senator France, came about largely as a result of his distrust of the British and Japanese, combined with a belief that the United States could find greater safety in a large navy than it could ever find in a diplomatic treaty. Senator France had voted against the league on the three major votes; his vote certainly qualifies as a principled disagreement. No Democrat voted against the Five-Power Naval Treaty, but Reed would have had he been present. The popularity of the arms control treaty might have

100 The Washington Naval Treaties

prevented his casting a vote against it, but he was such a stubborn man and generally more against all kinds of proposals rather than for anything, that it would appear he would not have hesitated to vote against the treaty if the entire state of Missouri had favored it. Other doubters kept their opinions to themselves (and the national popularity of the treaty certainly could have contributed to that effect), but based on the evidence available, it appears that almost every senator favored the arms control treaty.

Here, of course, party regularity did not play a part. Popular support did, and most of the Democrats had, in fact, voted for the league and had previously supported other arms control proposals. Very little partisanship developed over the Five-Power Naval Treaty until several leading Republicans, including Vice-President Calvin Coolidge, began to claim it as a Republican achievement. This irritated several Democratic senators, who then pointed to the strong and continuing support of both the treaty and arms control by Democrats.[117]

Bitter partisanship had exploded over the Four-Power Treaty. Four Republicans (Borah, France, Johnson, and La Follette), all irreconcilables, deserted the party banner; all believed it an alliance, all had voted against the league for the very same reason. Twenty-three of the thirty-seven Democrats voted against the Four-Power Treaty, and thirteen voted in favor. Republicans who had voted against the league and Democrats who had voted for the league now changed sides. The great majority of the speeches mentioned the League of Nations in one context or another. Democrats in particular delighted in digging up speeches made against the league by Republicans and using their very words against the Four-Power Treaty. Again, it was the Four-Power Treaty and not the naval arms control treaty that drew the lightning, the flak, and the partisanship. There is little proof that this focusing of opposition was Lodge's intent; nevertheless, it did work in his favor.

Very early in the process, when it became apparent that the Four-Power Treaty must have a reservation to guarantee its passage, Lodge and Harding, as noted, proposed one. Harding announced that he did not think that it was necessary, but if it would calm the fears of those who sensed an alliance, he was willing to support a reservation that specifically said that the treaty was not. It is difficult to point to any specific Republican who changed his mind as a result of the reservation; the four irreconcilables needed far more than that to support the treaty. It may have brought as many as five Democrats or as few as two over to support, but this is impossible to determine from the available records. It might well have calmed more of the public's fears than those of the opposing senators.

Notable in the debates was a questioning of the intelligence, integrity, and truthfulness of the four U.S. delegates, Hughes, Root, Lodge, and Underwood. Suspicions of Hughes, because he had supported the league, surfaced early among the former opponents of the league. Questions about the authorship of the Four-Power Treaty arose until Hughes admitted that it had largely been based on his final draft, an admission that only deepened the antagonism of the irreconcilables. Hughes had also conveniently left town for Bermuda and was not present to answer questions during much of the Four-Power Treaty ratification debate. Several suggested that Hughes be called before the Senate Foreign Relations Committee, as former Secretary of State Robert Lansing had been during the league debates, to testify on both the Five-Power Naval Treaty and the Four-Power Treaty, but Lodge's tight control prevented this. Hughes did write several public letters to answer questions to which he chose to reply; Harding also followed that approach. Several senators attacked Root as an agent of the Japanese, British, and international money powers.

The most reproachful remarks, however, were aimed at Lodge and Underwood. Both were called upon to explain various aspects of the treaties, especially the Four-Power Treaty, and could not always come up with the answers in a way that illuminated rather than further obscured the discussion. The attacks on Lodge were largely shrugged off, but the questioning of Underwood visibly irritated the Senate minority leader. Despite his explanation that he had been absent from the conference, owing to the death of his mother, and therefore not in on all the negotiations of the treaties, he was severely pressed and did not like it. James Reed and Joseph Robinson had two of sharpest tongues in the Senate on the issue of the U.S. delegates and their neglect of duty. Both Hughes and Harding, as already noted, publicly came to the support of the delegates.

The Nine-Power Treaty (66–0) and the Submarine–Poison Gas Treaty (72–0) passed without recorded opposition; a single vote was cast against the Chinese Customs Treaty (58–1) by William H. King (D-Utah), who thought the treaty an infringement on China's integrity.[118]

The submarine issue, as mentioned, was also an arms control item at the conference. As the conference began the United States had the largest fleet of submarines. American public opinion, however, had strong feelings against the use of submarines in war. The 5–5–3 ratio proposed at the conference would have given 90,000 tons to the United States and the United Kingdom and 54,000 to Japan. Arthur Balfour of the United Kingdom called for abolition. When the French refused to accept any ratios for auxiliary ships, all chance of total tonnage or numerical limitations for submarines disappeared. The so-called Root resolutions attempted to limit the legal activities of submarines in wartime to traditional international laws and also to outlaw unrestricted submarine warfare. Root privately explained that the rules were designed to "meet public opinion with regard to [the] horrors and lawlessness of the Germans."[119] Submarines were combined with poison gas rules (described in chapter 3 of this volume) and included in a separate treaty on submarines and poison gas, which France refused to ratify and thus never went into effect.

The Washington treaties thus, with the exception of the Four-Power Treaty, went through the Senate with little difficulty. Hughes wrote Lodge and congratulated him on the passage of the Four-Power Treaty, saying that it destroyed any possible opposition to the rest of the treaties. With enormous pride Lodge wrote George Harvey: "I not only got two-thirds of the Senate, but I had thirteen to spare on the vote on the Four-Power Treaty where the fight centered, and all the other treaties passed unanimously, with the single exception of one vote by France against the naval treaty. I must say, speaking without regard to imputations of vanity, that it was on the whole pretty well done."[120]

Public Opinion and the Role of Interest Groups

Harding, in a politically skillful move, set up an Advisory Committee whose task before and during the conference was to sample American public opinion and report its state to the U.S. delegation. The members of the committee, however, saw themselves not as a conduit but as representing each in his or her own way American public opinion.[121] The administration used the committee to influence both foreign delegates and American opinion.

Headed by the former Republican senator from Utah, George Sutherland, whom Harding was to appoint to the Supreme Court within a few months after the end of the conference, the Advisory Committee played a prominent role in keeping the conference before the public and the Senate. It also included positions for all types of people whom Harding did not want on the official delegation but whose public support could be secured by their appointment to the committee. Among its twenty-one members were such luminaries as Secretary of Commerce Herbert Hoover, Undersecretary of State Henry P. Fletcher, Representative Stephen G. Porter (R-Pa.), chairman of the House Committee on Foreign Affairs, General John J. Pershing, Governor John B. Parker, and labor leaders John L. Lewis and Samuel Gompers. Four women, representing nongovernmental groups, Mrs. Charles Sumner Bird, Mrs. Thomas G. Winter, Katherine Phillips Edson, and Mrs. Eleanor Franklin Egan, were on the committee as well. The appointment of women, who had been completely left out by President Wilson at Versailles, reflected the wide support women voters had given Harding in the election of 1920 and brought him critical acclaim from women's groups throughout the country.[122]

Hughes, in acknowledgment of the importance he placed on the role of the Advisory Committee, met with its members three days before the conference began and said that the U.S. delegation wanted them to come up with "sound and well-informed opinion" made possible by the "representative character of the Committee."[123] The committee saw itself as the key link between the public and the delegates, and it clearly viewed that link as a two-way street. It would inform both the public and the delegation, but only with Hughes's approval. In the former role, because such members of the Advisory Committee as Theodore Roosevelt, Jr. and Henry P. Fletcher were also members of the official U.S. delegation, the administration was able to give the committee the correct interpretation.

The committee issued news summaries, editorial summaries, and periodical summaries chosen from newspapers and periodicals that had Washington correspondents. Approximately one hundred reports were distributed. While stressing the positive comments of the newspapers they also reported the negative ones to the U.S. delegation.[124] Few of these reports became public. Most did not differ greatly from the Department of State's summaries, although those condensations, of course, tended to concentrate more on newspaper reports from foreign countries.

The Advisory Committee also issued a series of special reports largely written by its subcommittees, which discussed specific conference agenda items. These reports were given to Hughes, who then decided whether to release them to the public. An important report, and one of the most widely reprinted—on the resolutions received by the U.S. delegation up to January 14, shortly before the conference closed—is indicative of general public opinion and revealing of the outlook of the Advisory Committee itself both in the phrasing of the categories and in the shifting emphasis of the questions. For example, the category "against alliances and ententes" saw its totals dramatically increase after the

December 10 announcement of the Four-Power Treaty. Another large change also occurred in the call for the abolition of submarines after the French refused to accept their abolition.[125]

The Advisory Committee, however, did not believe that it should just tabulate the information that it gathered through its Subcommittee on General Information; in fact, the Advisory Committee largely wrote its reports and recommendations without paying much attention to its subcommittee. That definitely was not the public perception or the perception of organized pressure groups, which had concluded that the administration was highly interested in their opinions and that they had a great deal of input at the conference negotiations as well as in the ratification process. This was not true. The Harding administration used that support but seldom obeyed its specific demands.[126]

The strategy and tactics of the administration in taking advantage of an already mobilized public opinion worked extremely well. Again and again, senators during the ratification debate mentioned the strong public support for the treaties. Although some of the irreconcilables argued that the support was based on false information, they recognized its power. It did matter. The arms control treaty would have passed without such strong support, but the Yap and Four-Power treaties, especially in the absence of further reservations, might well have failed. The prevailing beliefs in both disarmament and in the power of public opinion helped the administration and its senatorial supporters.

The role of public opinion was of great importance in bringing about the conference, in supporting the U.S. proposals at the conference, and in continuing pressure in support of the ratification of the treaties. There are those who argue that it played the key role, that the conference would not have come about and the outcome would not have been successful without the impact of public opinion. The Harding administration's position was that it had already made its plans before public opinion became highly organized and demanding. Harding and his colleagues then used this support to pressure the foreign delegates and senators to carry out the administration's proposals. Both of these interpretations are self-serving and, as usual, the truth is much more complex.

Public opinion favorable to the naval arms control treaty appears to have been overwhelming; most of that support then translated into gains for all of the conference treaties. "Appears" is the operative word, for this was a period in which there were no public opinion polls. Only the *Literary Digest*, the Department of State, and the Advisory Committee made any attempt to ascertain public opinion. All of them used surveys of editorial and news stories from newspapers as the foundation of their conclusions. Most of the newspapers, owned and operated by Republicans, had supportive editorial comment. News stories were often somewhat less enthusiastic but were nonetheless largely positive. Opposition stories were few.

Although the author believes that newspaper accounts probably did accurately reflect public opinion, especially on naval arms control, one cannot be confident in that type of survey. The *Literary Digest*, for example, predicted Alfred M. Landon over Franklin Delano Roosevelt in the presidential election of 1936. There is little direct evidence in the published record about how public opinion might have affected the votes of key "fence-sitting" senators; however, there were irreconcilables who voted against other treaties of the conference but did not vote against the arms control treaty.

The president, the secretary of state (as well as other cabinet members), and the U.S. delegation received daily press reports from both the Department of State and the Advisory Committee. The former continued prior to, during the conference, and during the ratification struggle; the latter published only during the conference. Executive branch officials also received letters, phone calls, and personal visits from proponents of the treaties. Almost all of what they read or heard was positive and pleasing. Public opinion encouraged the administration to use strong arguments to any questioning senator. It certainly helped to quiet opposition and prevent the opposition from getting much support.

Perhaps most surprising, and often overlooked, is that while American public opinion as represented in the newspapers strengthened the hand of the administration, it weakened the position of Japan. Edward Lawry of the *Washington Post* characterized the Japanese delegates as "wary, cautious, reticent, careful, not credulous, taking nothing for granted. . . . [making] concessions reluctantly, yielding always as little as possible," but there are strong indications in the telegrams sent from the Japanese delegates in Washington back to Tokyo that the delegates were strongly affected by the news stories in U.S. papers that criticized Japan.[127] The delegates advised Tokyo that Japan must compromise at several points in order to win a better public image for Japan.[128] Indeed, Japan did enjoy a more positive image with the American public as a result of their generally cooperative attitude at the conference. Hughes, because of the code-breaking activities of the secretive American "Black Chamber," headed by the famous cryptographer, Herbert Osborn Yardley, had access to almost all of the Japanese telegrams and on several occasions approached the Advisory Committee to suggest a particular emphasis or timing on the committee's reports.[129] Hughes also demonstrated great success in defending the administration's position in the public press, especially in the *Washington Post*, which was a major supporter of the Harding administration and which all the delegates were reading.

Newspapers urged ratification by a 9–1 margin in a poll taken by the *Literary Digest*, which concluded, "Reports of opposition are so negligible as to make it clear to us that the people are more significantly united on the proposals of the conference than they have been on any similar issue."[130] The Hearst press, however, was conspicuous in its opposition to the naval treaty. Hearst's *San Francisco Examiner* editorialized that the conference represented a plot to reduce the U.S.

Navy so that the British and Japanese fleets could crush it. One cartoon depicted two pigs, captioned "Rich and Natural Resources" and "Vast Wealth," running past a pack of wolves labeled "Hate," "Jealousy," "Envy," and "Treachery"; fortunately Uncle Sam guarded the pigs with a gun called "A Mighty Navy."[131]

Groups of Irish-Americans, opposed to British rule in Ireland, attacked the treaties so strongly that Senator John Sharp Williams retorted that they appeared more Irish than American. Shortly before the conference, Admiral William S. Sims, obviously not running for public office, said of the Irish-Americans: "They are like zebras, either black horses with white stripes, or white horses with black stripes. But we know they are not horses—they are asses, but each of these asses has a vote, and there are lots of them. . . . One inconvenience of a republic is that these Jackass votes must be catered to."[132] Large numbers of Irish-Americans, as well as other ethnic groups, who had abandoned the Democrats in 1920 to vote for Harding, were disappointed in the president's treaties with the United Kingdom.

The opposition, however, met a plethora of well-organized supporters. A national Committee for Treaty Ratification included such men as Stephen P. Duggan, John Foster Dulles, John H. Finley, A. Lawrence Lowell, and George W. Wickersham. After canvassing the United States to ascertain popular feeling toward the treaties, the committee reported to Congress that church, civic, and labor organizations, along with educational institutions and women's groups, overwhelmingly supported the ratification of the treaties.[133]

The support of the country's churches, perhaps intended in part as an atonement for their strong support of World War I, helped the administration. The Federal Council of Churches led the way. Others, such as the Church Peace Union, the Unitarian Layman's League, the Central Conference of American Rabbis, and the Quakers, joined. The Advisory Committee estimated that of 13,878,671 letters received by January 15, 1922, a total of 10,092,736 had some religious connotation.[134]

Steel manufacturers also approved the treaty. Charles M. Schwab, head of Bethlehem Steel, said he "would gladly see the war-making machinery" of his company "sink to the bottom of the ocean." Companies competed to prove their lack of dependence on arms manufacturing; they, too, had a bad reputation from World War I that needed refurbishing.[135]

Civic, educational, and pacifist groups joined in an ad hoc National Council for the Limitation of Armaments. It included representatives from forty-three organizations and claimed to speak for more than six million people. It had worked hard during the conference and promised to continue its work during the ratification fight.[136]

Labor, careful to point out that it did not support pacifism, rallied its members. Samuel Gompers had served on the Advisory Committee during the conference and had organized a General Committee on the Limitation of Armaments. Shocked, as noted earlier, when the government laid off 10,000 ship workers owing to the cutback in naval construction, Gompers appealed to Secretary of the Navy Edwin Denby, who replied that the government could not continue to pay men for needless employment.[137]

The Washington Conference, as previously noted, did arouse some opposition from U.S. naval officers, but they hesitated to criticize the Five-Power Naval Treaty openly because of its enormous popularity with both the public and the administration. Its popularity, as Admiral Hilary P. Jones noted, prevented immediate counterarguments.[138] By the time that they got themselves organized in late 1922, and began to attack the treaties, ratification had occurred.

World opinion, as distinct from American public opinion, appeared strongly to support the Washington treaties. Only in France was there an organized opposition, contributing to the widely held view among American newspapers and commentators that Paris was the chief villain of the conference. The French obsession with security against Germany was well known in the United States, and if French obstructionism was not liked, it was at least understood. It did not affect the ratification struggle at all. Americans liked to think that world opinion had been so captured by Hughes's opening address that European governments had to go along with the treaties in their ratification processes. There is no hard evidence to accept this supposition. There is also no evidence at all to suggest that world opinion affected the U.S. ratification process, either directly or indirectly.

Events abroad, with the exception of the very existence of the League of Nations, did not play an important role in the ratification of the treaties. The British role in Ireland assured the continuing opposition of Irish-American groups in the United States, but there is no evidence that the ratification debate increased that opposition among the already committed anti-British Irish-Americans. A great power meeting held at Genoa to discuss European problems that occurred during the ratification fight saw the United States decline an invitation; the Harding administration was not about to jeopardize the Washington agreements with any European complications. The Harding administration, at first, even went so far as to refuse to talk to the League of Nations or acknowledge receipt of its communications.

Governmental instability and chaos in China led to difficulties both during the conference, when the competing Chinese groups could not agree on their positions, and during ratification, when several senators questioned the soundness of any concessions to Chinese governments that could not control the country. The change of leadership in the Japanese government that took place during the conference appeared to promise a continuation of previous Japanese policies, which seemed supportive of the treaties. In sum, no specific contemporaneous event abroad affected the ratification debate, but the general existence of the league, as noted earlier, was portrayed by opponents of both the league and the treaties as a villain who was lurking over the horizon and with whom the United States should have no contact.

Conclusion

Several factors, working together, led to the successful negotiation and ratification of the Five-Power Naval Treaty. First, the timing of the conference was most opportune on both the international and domestic level. A great and bloody war had just ended. Governments, and their citizens, often for very different reasons, were tired of the sacrifices and chaos of war. With few exceptions, predictions of imminent war did not exist. There were those, like the French, who continued to see the German threat over the horizon, and a small group who held that an U.S.-Japanese clash was somewhere down the road, but few agreed with these pessimists. Peace between the major powers, at least for the foreseeable future, appeared to have broken out. Outside the United States there were hopes that the League of Nations would contribute to its continuation. War was out of fashion; it was time to return to normalcy. Among governments there was little altruism in this sentiment for peace; they had swung into war easily, they would return to peace in the same manner—it was all part of a life cycle in the history of nations. In sum, 1921 and 1922 internationally was a relatively peaceful period in which concerns about future wars between the major powers were placed on the back burner.

Domestically, there were demands from citizens for the lifting of the financial burden of higher taxes that the cost of armaments involved. Again, there was little altruism involved in that quest; few really believed that the "war to end all wars" from 1914 to 1919 had actually done so. It was peacetime, and in the United States there was a belief that the end of war should also bring the end of large armies and navies, that the world should return to normalcy. Peace, not war, was thought to be the normal condition of humanity. There can be absolutely no doubt that the major motivating force behind public demands for arms control in the United States came from citizens who wanted financial relief. The intensity of a short recession and high unemployment increased that demand. Special interest groups, sparked by the Borah resolution, organized and mobilized public opinion. Coupled with some uneasiness of conscience on the part of many Americans over the refusal of the United States to enter the League of Nations, and a desire to do something "becoming" for peace, this demand for financial relief through disarmament swept away all before it.

Timing also played a role. A new administration, eager to lead the nation on the correct Republican road to peace, as opposed to the obviously incorrect Democratic detour toward the league, had to produce some step toward peace. Harding had won the greatest election victory in American history to that point. He and Secretary of State Hughes seized on naval arms control as the ideal American solution. It would solve both international and domestic problems, and it would do so on American soil. No secret treaties here, no alliances could stand the attack of honest, open American diplomacy; the perfidy of Paris would become but a bad memory in the cleansing atmosphere of the citadel of American democracy. An American reporter expressed a widely shared American belief about the environment in Washington: "There is a sort of plainness and simplicity and lack of pretense that makes for understanding."[139] The Republicans would demonstrate to the world, and especially to Democrats, how a real peace conference, free of world intrigue, could operate in a manner that would not involve permanent American participation in the sordid problems of the world.

The timing, thus, could not have been better. The combination of an immediate postwar period, no serious threats of war among the major naval powers, strong public support for disarmament, a demand for tax relief, which arms control seemed to promise, and a new administration determined to make its contribution to world peace formed a nearly ideal situation for the Harding administration. Indeed, it leads one to ask if the administration could not have achieved even more. Harding and Hughes, however, had deliberately sought limited goals, and until they had actually carried out their negotiations, they did not make the mistake of promising more than they could actually deliver. They had feared failure and were thus willing to settle for less, to take a few steps toward peace rather than a leap into unknown waters such as Wilson had taken. Unfortunately, they later marred their record by claiming too much.

Hughes's dramatic presentation at the opening of the conference was both a negotiating and public relations stroke of genius. It put the other nations on the defensive and attracted world attention. Just as important, however, was that it was a clear, simple, and straight-forward proposal that Americans could understand: scrap battleships, build none for ten years, provide for U.S. equality with Britain and superiority over Japan, and refrain from further fortifying Pacific Islands. The treaty was actually much more complex, all of its implications were not clearly thought out, and many of the original proposals were not carried out; there were no verification and inspection provisions and there were loopholes big enough to steam a light cruiser through. But these problems were in the future. They did not surface until well after the negotiation and ratification of the treaty. The initial impulses carried all before them. The conference agenda, short, limited, and in general easily understandable, played an important part. Hughes argued that he believed "the conference had a certain definite and limited aim. . . . that is the reason why the conference succeeded."[140] The public's desire to see a cut in the spending of tax money on weapons of destruction coincided with the administration's desire to cut government expenditures. Everyone could believe that Hughes's dramatic proposal, the actual scrapping of ships and no battleship building for ten years, would accomplish that purpose.

The Harding administration made a major strategic decision when it tied all of the treaties together in one political-military package. It used the enormous popularity of the arms control treaty to carry five other treaties through both negotiation and ratification. During the conference itself the United States clearly indicated to both the United Kingdom and Japan that the United States would not ratify the arms control treaty until the two powers gave up the Anglo-Japanese Alliance and until Japan relaxed its aggressive attitude in the Pacific and on the mainland of Asia. Unwillingness by either Japan or the United Kingdom would lead the United States to go ahead and build its navy "second to none." Since that was a race that neither Japan nor the United Kingdom could win without serious stress and strain in both their political and economic polities, both accepted the U.S. positions, but not without gains for themselves. The decision to tie the arms control treaty to political arrangements in Asia was *the* major decision of the conference and made both the arms control treaty and the other treaties possible.

That same strategy pushed the treaties through the U.S. Senate. Lodge deliberately did not schedule the vote on the Five-Power Naval Treaty until after the votes on the controversial treaties of the Washington system. Almost all of the public supporters of the arms control treaty fell into line and demanded the ratification of all the treaties. This was a tremendous source of strength for Lodge in the ratification debates, and he used it for all it was worth. Many commentators and senators argued that the Five-Power Naval Treaty be in serious difficulty if the Four-Power Treaty were defeated. This conclusion, it appears, was an erroneous one, but the persistent repetition of the threat leads one to conclude that a number of senators had at least a modicum of belief in the prospect.

The Harding administration made few errors in the ratification process. Hughes, Lodge, and Underwood were towers of strength. The arms control treaty, never in trouble at any time, sailed through the Senate. Since the Four-Power Treaty attracted all of the attention and fire, the Five-Power Naval Treaty was not given the attention that it deserved. This, of course, was an advantage for the administration; a better strategy could not have been designed. There is no evidence, however, that the procedure and problems of the Four-Power Treaty were designed to take the pressure off of the naval treaty. Lodge would certainly have claimed that credit.

The Harding administration had succeeded in securing the advice and consent of the Senate. Hughes coolly wrote a few years later that the main American achievement, clearly a limited one in his eyes, was "that for the next fifteen years we should not do what everyone knew we would not do," that is, not build capital ships or fortify the Pacific Islands. Harding, however, stated, "'The success or failure of this administration depends on the ratification of these treaties . . . . If these treaties are ratified by the Senate, then this administration's name is secure in history.'"[141] Strong popular support for the limitation of armaments (aroused and mobilized by Hughes's opening speech) coupled with astute parliamentary tactics had secured ratification.

In the history of twentieth century arms limitation, if politics is indeed the art of the possible, then the Washington Conference of 1921–22 represents the peak of political impressionism. Bold in conception, a daring break with the past, it was to be a model, its originators hoped, for the restriction of weapons that future statesmen could emulate. Bright but powerful facets of domestic and international politics flowed together on a canvas in a form that captured momentary reality and reflected both the hopes and ambiguities that have always marked the pursuit of arms control. Repetition of this stunning, hugely popular performance proved unattainable. Sixty-five years later one reviewer wrote that unlike the Strategic Arms Limitation Talks, the Washington Conference "involved serious arms reduction; indeed, it is the only historical example of reductions of this magnitude."[142] Later imitators neither

forgot nor ignored the achievements of the Washington
Conference, but they failed to understand the foundation of
political craftsmanship that made the success of the
conference possible.

Notes

1. Mark Sullivan, *The Great Adventure at Washington* (New York:
Doubleday, Page and Co., 1922), 27.

2. Thomas H. Buckley, *The United States and the Washington Conference,
1921-1922* (Knoxville: University of Tennessee Press, 1970), 63–74.

3. *New York Evening Post*, November 26, 1921.

4. Buckley, *Washington Conference*, 49–62.

5. Ibid., 75–125. See also U.S. Department of State, *Conference on the
Limitation of Armament* (Washington D.C., Government Printing Office,
1922) and *Conference on the Limitation of Armament: Subcommittees*
(Washington, D.C.: GPO, 1922).

6. *Washington Post*, December 11, 1921.

7. Buckley, *Washington Conference*, 127–44.

8. Ibid., 145–46.

9. Ibid., 157–71.

10. William C. Widenor, *Henry Cabot Lodge and the Search for an American
Foreign Policy* (Berkeley: University of California Press, 1980), 221–348.

11. For example, Senator Thomas E. Watson (D-Ga.) on February 25, 1922,
said: "The nations with whom we are going into a four power treaty are
members of the League of Nations and we are not. What will be the
relationship between the League of Nations and ourselves after we shall
have ratified the four power treaty?" *Congressional Record*, 3050.

12. Buckley, *Washington Conference*, 14–15. See also *Congressional Record*,
April 12, 1921, 169–73.

13. Speech of November 1918, as quoted in Benjamin H. Williams, *The
United States and Disarmament* (New York: McGraw-Hill, 1931), 137.

14. The naval background can best be found in Harold Sprout and Margaret
Sprout, *Toward a New Order of Sea Power: American Naval Policy and the
World Scene, 1918-1922* (Princeton, N.J., Princeton University Press, 1943)
and Buckley, *Washington Conference*, 6–26.

15. Buckley, *Washington Conference*, 26–32.

16. As quoted in Robert J. Maddox, *William E. Borah and American Foreign Policy* (Baton Rouge: Louisiana State University Press, 1969), 109.

17. Hiram Johnson to his sons, October 21, 1921, in *The Diary Letters of Hiram Johnson*, vol. 3 (New York: Garland, 1983).

18. *Washington Post*, October 25, 1921, and *Literary Digest*, November 21, 1921.

19. *Congressional Record*, February 27, 1922, 3103.

20. Ibid.

21. Claudius O. Johnson, *Borah of Idaho* (New York: Longmans, Green, and Co., 1936), 268. The author claims that the senator did it for reasons of economy and peace.

22. Maddox, *Borah and American Foreign Policy*, 87–89.

23. George L. Grassmuck, *Sectional Biases in Congress on Foreign Policy* (Baltimore, Md.: The Johns Hopkins University Press, 1951), 32.

24. It passed the Senate on May 25, 1921, by a vote of 74–0, *Congressional Record*, 1758, and the House on July 11, 1921, by a vote of 332–4, *ibid.*, 3526, 3569.

25. Ibid., March 29, 1922, 4704.

26. Hoag's volume remains the classic study some fifty years after its publication. C. Leonard Hoag, *Preface to Preparedness: The Washington Disarmament Conference and Public Opinion* (Washington, D.C.: American Council on Public Affairs, 1941), 69–70.

27. Harding to Frank W. Mondell, June 25, 1921, as reprinted in the *Congressional Record*, June 29, 1921, 3223–27. See also Harding to Raymond Robins, May 19, 1921, and Nicholas Butler to Harding, July 13, 1921, in the Harding Manuscripts, Ohio Historical Society (hereafter cited as Harding MSS), and Hughes to the Sprouts, August 5, 1940, as cited in Sprout and Sprout, *Toward a New Order of Sea Power*, 129.

28. Hoag, *Preface to Preparedness*, 73.

29. Hughes to Harding, July 6, 1921, Harding MSS.

30. Hughes to George Harvey, telegram to London, July 8, 1921, in U.S. Department of State, *Papers Relating to the Foreign Relations of the United States, 1921*, vol. 1 (Washington, D.C.: GPO, 1936), 18, and the same on July 9, 1921, ibid., 23. See also Beerits to Hughes, memorandum, "Calling the Conference," Charles Evans Hughes MSS, Library of Congress.

31. Donald R. McCoy, ed., "Election of 1920," in *History of American Presidential Elections*, ed. Arthur Schlesinger, Jr., vol. 3 (New York: McGraw-Hill, 1971), 2384.

32. Harding to Henry Cabot Lodge, December 29, 1920, Harding MSS.

33. Thomas N. Guinsburg, *The Pursuit of Isolationism in the United States Senate from Versailles to Pearl Harbor* (New York: Garland, 1982), 75.

34. Roger Dingman, *Power in the Pacific, The Origins of Naval Arms Limitation, 1914-1922* (Chicago: University of Chicago Press, 1976).

35. *Washington Post*, November 25, 1921.

36. Ibid., February 6, 1922.

37. Ibid.

38. Borah wrote his brother that Harding had not asked him, at least "not loud enough for me to hear it, although I wasn't expecting to hear anything of that kind and I might have overlooked it." Borah to Frank Borah, August 23, 1921, Borah Manuscripts, Library of Congress (hereafter cited as Borah MSS).

39. Buckley, *Washington Conference*, 50-54.

40. Ibid. See also Gerald Wheeler, "Edwin Denby," in *American Secretaries of the Navy*, ed. Paolo E. Coletta, vol. 2 (Annapolis, Md.: Naval Institute Press, 1980), 584-87.

41. Lawrence Douglas, "Robert Edward Coontz," in *The Chiefs of Naval Operations*, ed. Robert William Love, Jr. (Annapolis, Md.: Naval Institute Press, 1980), 29-30.

42. U.S. Congress, Senate Committee on Naval Affairs, *London Naval Treaty of 1930, Hearings*, 71st Cong., 2d sess., May 1930 (Washington, D.C.: GPO, 1930).

43. *Congressional Record*, March 28, 1922, 1677.

44. Thomas Lynwood Powers, "The United States Army and the Washington Conference, 1921-1922" (Ph.D. diss., University of Georgia, 1978), 172.

45. Ibid., 188.

46. Ibid., 231.

47. *Congressional Record*, December 16, 1921, 438.

48. Ibid.

49. Ibid., March 28, 1922, 4692-93.

50. Gompers to Denby, February 15, 1922, and Denby to Gompers, February 22, 1922, Gompers Manuscripts, American Federation of Labor Archives.

51. For an excellent survey, see Christopher Hall, *Britain, America, and Arms Control, 1921-1937* (New York: St. Martin's Press, 1987).

52. U.S. Department of State, *Conference on the Limitation of Armament*, 396–404.

53. Buckley, *Washington Conference*, 172.

54. "Report of the American Delegation, February 9, 1922," in U.S. Department of State, *Papers Relating to the Foreign Relations of the United States [FRUS], 1922*, vol. 2 (Washington, D.C.: GPO, 1938), 328.

55. *Congressional Record*, March 26, 1922, 4723.

56. Theodore Roosevelt, Jr., diary, January 30, 1922, Roosevelt Manuscripts, Library of Congress.

57. John M. Carroll, "Henry Cabot Lodge's Contributions to the Shaping of Republican European Diplomacy, 1920–24," *Capitol Studies* 3 (1975), 153ff.

58. *Congressional Record*, March 15, 1922, 3908.

59. Evans C. Johnson, *Oscar W. Underwood, A Political Biography* (Baton Rouge: Louisiana State University Press, 1980), 314–15.

60. *Congressional Record*, March 23, 1922, 4310.

61. Hughes to Underwood, April 1, 1922, quoted in Johnson, *Oscar W. Underwood*, 322–23.

62. Ibid., 323, 334–35.

63. *Congressional Record*, March 21, 1922, 4190.

64. Ibid., March 22, 1922, 3242.

65. Ralph Stone, *The Irreconcilables: The Fight Against the League of Nations* (Lexington: University Press of Kentucky, 1970), 183–88, describes the league's opponents.

66. Johnson to his sons, December 7, 1920, *The Diary Letters of Hiram Johnson*, vol. 3.

67. See senatorial voting chart.

68. "Message of the President, February 10, 1922," in U.S. Department of State, *FRUS, 1922*, vol. 1, 298–306.

69. *New York Times*, December 21, 1921.

70. Henry Cabot Lodge diary, December 20, 1921, Lodge Manuscripts, Massachusetts Historical Society (hereafter cited as Lodge MSS), and December 23, 1921, ibid.

71. *Washington Post*, March 8, 1921.

72. Ibid., March 21, 1921.

73. Johnson to Archibald Johnson, September 23, 1921, *The Diary Letters of Hiram Johnson*, vol. 3.

74. The documents submitted to the Senate are printed in S. Doc. 126, 67th Cong., 2d sess.

75. *Congressional Record*, November 8, 1921, 7537.

76. Johnson to Archibald Johnson, August 13, 1921, *The Diary Letter of Hiram Johnson*, vol. 3.

77. *Congressional Record*, February 16, 1922, 2640.

78. Harding to Hughes, February 18, 1922, and Hughes to Harding, February 19, 1922, and Hughes to Harding, February 19, 1922, in U.S. Department of State, Index File 500.A4A/1, National Archives; copy of Harding letter to Senate, February 20, 1922, ibid., 500.A4A/17 1/2.

79. *Proceedings of the Committee on Foreign Relations, United States Senate, from April 7, 1913 to March 3, 1923* (New York: Garland, 1979), 331.

80. Johnson to Hiram Johnson, Jr., February 23, 1922, *The Diary Letter of Hiram Johnson*, vol. 4.

81. *The Brooklyn Eagle* as quoted in Thomas A. Bailey, *The Man in the Street* (New York, 1948), 93.

82. *Congressional Record*, March 8, 1922, 3552. See also Frank B. Kellogg, *Congressional Record*, March 6, 1922, 3408.

83. Ibid., March 11, 1922, 3710.

84. Ibid., March 14, 1922, 3839–40.

85. Ibid.

86. Buckley, *Washington Conference*, 141–43.

87. *Congressional Record*, December 16, 1922, 438.

88. Ibid., February 27, 1922, 3093.

89. Ibid., February 22, 1922, 2881, and March 1, 1922, 3183.

90. Ibid., March 1, 1922, 3193.

91. Ibid.

92. A longhand draft of Harding's reservation is in the Lodge MSS, and *New York Times*, February 26, 1922, Lodge MSS.

93. *Congressional Record*, December 16, 1922, 438.

94. Ibid., December 21, 1921, 629.

95. Ibid., March 13, 1922, 3777.

96. Borah to James Barton, March 6, 1922, Borah MSS.

97. *Congressional Record*, March 8, 1922, 3547–54.

98. Ibid., March 11, 1922, 3711.

99. *Literary Digest*, March 11, 1922.

100. *Congressional Record*, March 14, 1922, 3854, 3859; March 15, 1922, 3893, 3915.

101. Ibid., March 17, 1922, 4013–16.

102. Ibid., March 20, 1922, 4119.

103. Buckley, *Washington Conference*, 181.

104. Hughes to Henry Cabot Lodge, March 21, 1922, as printed in the *Congressional Record*, March 21, 1922, 4158.

105. *New York Times*, March 22, 1922.

106. *Congressional Record*, March 24, 1922, 4487.

107. Ibid., 4490.

108. Ibid., 4491–96.

109. Ibid., 4496.

110. Ibid., 4497.

111. Harding to George Harvey, March 22, 1922, Harding MSS.

112. *Congressional Record*, March 27, 1922, 4621.

113. Ibid., February 28, 1922, 3154.

114. Ibid., March 15, 1922, 3944–57.

115. Ibid., March 29, 1922, 4708–10.

116. Ibid., March 29, 1922, 4718–19.

117. Ibid.

118. Ibid., March 30, 1922, 4784; March 29, 1922, 4730; March 30, 1922, 4791.

119. Lawrence Douglas, "The Submarine and the Washington Conference of 1921," *Naval War College Review* 26 (1974), 96.

120. Lodge to George Harvey, April 15, 1922, Lodge MSS. Lodge's arithmetic was incorrect. He did not have thirteen votes to spare on any of votes taken on the Four-Power Treaty.

121. Hoag, *Preface to Preparedness*, 136.

122. *Literary Digest*, November 26, 1921.

123. Minutes of the Advisory Committee to the Delegation, November 9, 1921, in Record Group 43, U.S. Department of State, *Conference on the Limitation of Armament, 1921-1922*, National Archives.

124. Copies of all the reports can be found in Special Reports Prepared by the Advisory Committee, 1921-1922, ibid.

125. See report number one, ibid.

126. Rosemary Rainbolt, "Arms Reduction versus Arms Modernization: U.S. Nongovernmental Organizations and Arms Conferences, 1920-1935" (Ph.D. diss., Carnegie-Mellon University, 1988), 92ff.

127. *Washington Post*, December 25, 1921.

128. Japanese Ministry of Foreign Affairs, Tokyo, Japan, 1868-1945, microfilmed for the Library of Congress, 1949-1951, reels MT 306, 312-319, and UD 29-30, 131.

129. Manuscript on Herbert O. Yardley in preparation by author.

130. *Literary Digest*, April 8, 1922.

131. Hoag, *Preface to Preparedness*, 152, 153-54, 159.

132. *New York Times*, June 8, 1921.

133. *Congressional Record*, March 22, 1922, 4226-27.

134. See report number one, U.S. Department of State, *Conference on the Limitation of Armament, 1921-1922*.

135. Hoag, *Preface to Preparedness*, 143-44.

136. Buckley, *Washington Conference*, 175.

137. See note 50.

138. Admiral Jones to Vice-Admiral Daniel McDonald, March 10, 1922, Papers of the Naval Historical Foundation, Library of Congress.

139. *Washington Post*, December 11, 1921.

140. *Washington Post*, February 9, 1922.

141. As quoted in Maddox, *Borah and American Foreign Policy*, 118; as quoted in Francis Russell, *The Shadow of Blooming Grove: Warren G. Harding in His Times* (New York: McGraw-Hill, 1968), 485.

142. Charles Fairbanks, Jr., and Abram N. Shulsky, "From 'Arms Control' to Arms Reduction: The Historical Experience," *Washington Quarterly* (Summer 1987), 65.

Selected Bibliography

Books

Braisted, William R. *The United States Navy in the Pacific, 1909-1922*. Austin: University of Texas Press, 1971.

Buckley, Thomas H. *The United States and the Washington Conference, 1921-1922*. Knoxville: University of Tennessee Press, 1970.

Burns, Richard Dean. *Arms Control and Disarmament, A Bibliography*. Santa Barbara,Calif.: ABC-Clio, 1977.

Burns, Richard Dean, and Donald Urquidi. *Disarmament in Perspective: An Analysis of Selected Arms Control and Disarmament Agreements Between the World Wars, 1919-1939*. Washington, D.C.: U.S. Arms Control and Disarmament Agency, 1968.

Coletta, Paolo E., ed. *American Secretaries of the Navy*. Annapolis, Md.: Naval Institute Press, 1980.

Dingman, Roger. *Power in the Pacific, The Origins of Naval Arms Limitation, 1914-1922*. Chicago: University of Chicago Press, 1976.

Grassmuck, George L. *Sectional Biases in Congress on Foreign Policy*. Baltimore, Md.: The Johns Hopkins University Press, 1951.

Guinsburg, Thomas N. *The Pursuit of Isolationism in the United States Senate from Versailles to Pearl Harbor*. New York: Garland, 1982.

Hall, Christopher. *Britain, America, and Arms Control, 1921-37*. New York: St. Martin Press, 1987.

Hill, J.R. *Arms Control At Sea*. Annapolis, Md.: Naval Institute Press, 1989.

Hoag, C. Leonard. *Preface to Preparedness: The Washington Disarmament Conference and Public Opinion*. Washington, D.C.: American Council on Public Affairs, 1941.

Hyde, Harlow A. *Scraps of Paper: The Disarmament Treaties Between the World Wars*. Lincoln, Nebr.: Media Publishing, 1988.

Kaufman, Robert Gordon. *Arms Control During the Pre-Nuclear Era: The United States and Naval Limitation Between the Two World Wars*. New York: Columbia University Press, 1990.

Love, Robert William, Jr., ed. *The Chiefs of Naval Operations*. Annapolis, Md.: Naval Institute Press, 1980.

Sprout, Harold, and Margaret Sprout. *Toward a New Order of Sea Power: American Naval Policy and the World Scene, 1918-1922*. Princeton, N.J.: Princeton University Press, 1943.

Vinson, John Chalmers. *The Parchment Peace, The United States Senate and the Washington Conference, 1921-1922.* Athens: University of Georgia Press, 1955.
Widenor, William C. *Henry Cabot Lodge and the Search for an American Foreign Policy.* Berkeley: University of California Press, 1980.

Government Publications

U.S. Congress. *Congressional Record.* Washington, D.C., 1919–1921.
U.S. Congress. *Congressional Record.* Washington, D.C., 1921–1923.
U.S. Department of State, *Papers Relating to the Foreign Relations of the United States, 1921.* Washington, D.C.: GPO, 1936.
U.S. Department of State, *Papers Relating to the Foreign Relations of the United States, 1922.* Washington, D.C.: GPO, 1938.
——. *Conference on the Limitation of Armament, 1921-22.* Washington,D.C.: GPO, 1922.
——. *Conference on the Limitation of Armament, 1921-1922: Subcommittees.* Washington, D.C.: GPO, 1922.

Unpublished Works

Goldman, Emily Oppenheimer. "The Washington Treaty System: Arms Racing and Arms Control in the Interwar Period." Ph.D diss., Stanford University, 1989.
Powers, Thomas Lynwood. "The United States Army and the Washington Conference, 1921-1922." Ph.D diss., University of Georgia, 1978.
Rainbolt, Rosemary. "Arms Reduction versus Arms Modernization: U.S. Nongovernmental Organizations and Arms Conferences, 1920-1935." Ph.D diss., Carnegie-Mellon University, 1988.

3 The Geneva Protocol of 1925

Rodney J. McElroy

When President Gerald Ford signed the instruments of ratification for the Geneva Protocol of 1925 on January 22, 1975, a tortured, half-century-long chapter in U.S. arms control policy was brought to a close. Fifty years earlier, at the Geneva Conference for the Control of the International Trade in Arms, Munitions and Implements of War, the United States had played a key role in drafting and reaching agreement on the Protocol for the Prohibition of the Use in War of Asphyxiating, Poisonous or Other Gases and of Bacteriological Methods of Warfare. The protocol, signed by thirty nations, including the United States, on June 17, 1925, prohibits "the use in war of asphyxiating, poisonous or other gases, and of all analogous liquids, materials or devices" as well as "the use of bacteriological methods of warfare." Despite the unreserved support of the Coolidge administration for the protocol, after heavy lobbying by the U.S. Army's Chemical Warfare Service (CWS), the chemical industry, and veterans organizations, the Senate declined action on the treaty without a formal vote. It would be approximately forty-five years before the Senate had another opportunity to advise and consent to ratification of the protocol.

The Geneva Protocol was not the first effort to control the use of chemical or biological weapons in warfare through international treaties. The 1868 Declaration of St. Petersburg prohibited the use of weapons that caused unnecessary suffering. The 1874 Brussels Declaration, though never formally adopted, sought to forbid the use of "poison and poisoned weapons." Inspired by these earlier efforts, the Hague Gas Declaration of 1899 attempted to ban "the use of

The author wishes to thank Elisa Harris, for her many contributions to this study and for her special friendship; Susan Schweik, for her close reading and loving support; and Emma Montana McElroy, for her peaceful spirit.

projectiles the sole object of which is the diffusion of asphyxiating or deleterious gases." The United States rejected the Hague Gas Declaration, arguing against prohibiting newweapons before they had been developed and without proofthat they wereless humane than other arms.[1]

These efforts to ban poison gas were overtaken by widespread use of chemical weapons during World War I by all the major belligerents. Gas injured well over a million soldiers during the war, killing more than 90,000. The collective memory of the use of poison gas put chemical weapons firmly on the postwar disarmament agenda.

The 1919 Treaty of Versailles forbade Germany from producing, importing, or using "asphyxiating, poisonous or other gases and all analogous liquids, materials or devices." Other postwar peace treaties with Austria and Hungary used similar language to prohibit chemical warfare activities.[2] This language, despite its vagueness and ambiguity, became a model for future agreements to control chemical and biological weapons.

In 1921 the United States convened the Washington Conference on the Limitation of Armaments in an effort to curb the global naval arms race and promote peaceful relations in the Pacific. As the result of U.S. leadership, one of the treaties that emerged from the conference prohibited the use of chemical weapons in war and set limits on the use of submarines. The Treaty Relating to the Use of Submarines and Noxious Gases in Warfare, signed by the United States, the United Kingdom, Japan, France, and Italy on February 6, 1922, borrowed some of its language from Article 171 of the Treaty of Versailles. The new treaty on chemical and submarine warfare was approved by the Senate on March 29, 1922, by a vote of 72-0, with 24 senators not voting. Twenty of the nonvoting senators indicated that if they had been present they would have voted for the treaty. The treaty did not enter into force, however, because France, objecting to the provisions on submarines, failed to ratify it.[3]

Subsequent multilateral efforts toward the banning of

chemical warfare reflected a growing body of international opinion against gas. In 1923 five Central American states signed a convention forbidding the use of gas in war. The following year, the Fifth International Conference of American States, which included the United States, agreed to "reiterate the prohibition . . . indicated in the Treaty of Washington."[4]

By 1922 the executive branch had begun a gradual process of increased involvement with the League of Nations that expanded throughout the Harding and Coolidge administrations, especially with respect to league-sponsored conferences on the limitation of armaments.[5] The 1925 Geneva Conference was seen by the Department of State as another chance to pursue chemical disarmament. The United States placed the restriction of trade in commercial chemicals with potential military applications on the conference agenda, though this step met stiff resistance. The U.S. delegation then proposed a new draft convention that was intended to make universal the prohibition on chemical warfare contained in Article 5 of the Treaty Relating to the Use of Submarines and Noxious Gases in Warfare, and that would use similar language. At Poland's suggestion the ban was extended to cover biological warfare, and the revised draft was accepted by the conference.[6] The Coolidge administration sent the Geneva Protocol to the Senate for its advice and consent in January 1926. Debate began in December of that year.

International Political Context

President Calvin Coolidge believed in arms control as a way to prevent war. He also thought that the public money saved through disarmament would stimulate economies, that prosperous nations were less likely to resort to war, and that countries that owed the United States war debts would be more likely to repay them if their economies were healthy.[7] These beliefs were translated into increased U.S. participation in international affairs, including arms control conferences. The Coolidge administration's efforts to lead the United States into formal international security structures sometimes collided with the powerful movement against U.S. entanglement with the League of Nations. This movement was spearheaded by a disparate group of senators, sometimes called the "bitter-enders" or "Battalion of Death," but best known at the time as the "irreconcilables"—senators irreconcilably opposed to participation in the League of Nations.[8] Coolidge, except for his advocacy of joining the league-sanctioned World Court, carefully avoided any treaty commitments that would tie the United States into the league structure. The Geneva Protocol, for instance, did not include any monitoring mechanisms or enforcement structures, relying instead on the good behavior of individual nations.

Despite the fact that the Washington Treaty had never entered into force, interest in a global ban on gas warfare remained. President Coolidge and Secretary of State Frank B. Kellogg saw in the Geneva Protocol a way to preclude any future move toward international control of chemical warfare under the league's auspices.[9] The momentum behind the banning of gas warfare suggested by the earlier treaties seems to have led Coolidge and Kellogg to assume that ratification of the protocol by the Senate would go smoothly. As it turned out, however, the protective shadow of the Washington Conference was not nearly long enough to save the protocol from defeat.

Two significant international issues provided the broader backdrop to the debate over the Geneva Protocol: U.S. membership in the World Court and U.S. participation in the League of Nations–sponsored Preparatory Commission for a Conference for the Reduction and Limitation of Armaments. Neither of these issues was directly linked to the protocol's ratification by its proponents or opponents, but both were surely on the minds of senators most actively involved in the ratification debate.

During the year preceding Senate floor consideration of the protocol in December 1926, debate over whether or not to join the League of Nations–affiliated World Court raged throughout the country and Congress. William E. Borah (R-

Idaho), the new chairman of the Senate Foreign Relations Committee and the man who would make the Coolidge administration's case for ratification of the Geneva Protocol in December, led a successful Senate fight in January 1926 to add a damaging reservation to U.S. adherence to the World Court. The reservation, which would have given the United States a veto over advisory opinions related to U.S. concerns, was rejected by the league after Coolidge refused league requests to discuss the matter, thus preventing the membership of the United States on its own terms. Kellogg and Coolidge publicly declined to press the Senate to alter its position, conceding defeat to Borah and others who had opposed the World Court.[10]

For six months before the December Senate debate on the protocol, the United States participated in the first session of the League of Nations-sponsored preparatory commission to the League of Nations disarmament conference. The U.S. contribution was minimal, reflecting the belief that the limitation of land armaments was best handled in a regional context and that naval arms limitation should follow the 1922 Washington Conference approach of involving the powers most directly concerned.[11] In his State of the Union message to Congress two days before the Senate began debating ratification of the Geneva Protocol, Coolidge expressed interest in further naval arms limitation but failed to call upon the Senate to ratify the protocol.[12]

Coolidge made a point of separating discussions about the limitation of armaments from those about the repayment of wartime debts incurred by European nations.[13] Other international issues unrelated to the debate on the protocol may have had a more direct influence on its outcome. Crises in relations with China, Mexico, and Nicaragua had been building throughout the latter half of 1926 and occupied much of Kellogg's attention. A rebel government in Nicaragua was established just days before the Senate debate (a step that eventually led to renewed U.S. military intervention). When the Senate deliberations began, both Coolidge and Kellogg were undoubtedly preoccupied with developments in Central America. In addition, Kellogg's physical and mental health had been severely strained by these crises.[14] These factors may have distracted the president and the Department of State from more closely attending to ratification of the protocol, although there is no evidence to suggest that the administration was planning a concerted campaign for ratification before these distractions occurred.

Representative Theodore Burton (R-Ohio), chairman of the House Committee on Foreign Affairs, was chosen by Coolidge to be head of the U.S. delegation to the Geneva Conference. His report to the secretary of state, which accompanied President Coolidge's submission of the Geneva Protocol to the Senate, stated that the protocol was intended "to bring about the general recognition" of a ban on the use of chemical weapons. So that national defense would not be jeopardized, however, Burton recommended that if the Senate approved the protocol, final U.S. ratification should await the willingness of enough nations to ratify "sufficient to make the Convention generally effective" and also suggested simultaneous ratification by the five nations that signed the 1922 Washington Treaty.[15]

Domestic Political Context

The nineteen months spanning the negotiation of the protocol and Senate deliberations came during a time of economic expansion, often called by Republicans the "Coolidge Prosperity." By the time the protocol was debated in the Senate, the Teapot Dome and other scandals concerning high-level appointees in the Harding administration, which soured relations between the executive and legislative branches, had receded. The 1924 election returning Coolidge to the White House also gave him significant Republican majorities in both houses of Congress. During the year when the protocol resided in the Senate, Coolidge succeeded with much of his domestic legislative agenda—most important, reduction of taxes, increased appropriations for civil aviation, and prevention of subsidized dumping of agricultural surpluses abroad. Nevertheless, Coolidge's reluctance to campaign for his party's candidates during the 1926 election campaign contributed to serious losses for the Republican party.[16] Though the debate took place while Coolidge still had a strong majority in the Senate, the election results surely had a disturbing effect on an already fragile party unity.

Coolidge and Kellogg selected a surprisingly low-ranking delegation to attend the Geneva Conference. Representative Burton was joined by Hugh Gibson, minister to Switzerland, Allen Dulles, chief of the Department of State's Division of Near Eastern Affairs, and two military officers representing the army and navy. The presence of an influential senator who could organize a pro-treaty coalition in the Senate would have significantly helped the protocol's chances. No satisfactory explanation about why this was not done has been found in the historical record. It can probably best be understood as the result of the administration's ambivalent relationship with the League of Nations, which sponsored the conference.

The Coolidge administration's decision to negotiate a complete ban on the use of chemical weapons was apparently made with minimal consultation with the War Department, headed by John W. Weeks. Although the military representatives on the U.S. delegation strongly opposed any ban, approval for a reaffirmation of the Washington Treaty prohibition was obtained from the acting chief of staff, General Dennis E. Nolan, and from Admiral Hilary P. Jones of the navy's General Board. Chemical officers in the War Department's War Plans Division adamantly objected to the protocol's ratification and briefed Senator Lawrence Tyson (D-Tenn.), a member of the Military Affairs Committee, before the Senate debate.

On the day the debate opened, Secretary of War Dwight F. Davis barred department officials from speaking about the purported lack of coordination during the negotiations. Tyson articulated the concerns of the protocol's critics on the Senate floor and engaged in an extended colloquy with Borah about the degree of coordination with the War Department during the negotiations. Borah probably got the best of this skirmish for the pro-ratification side by quoting Kellogg's description of the consultations with the designated departmental representatives and by citing the report to the Washington

Conference of then-General of the Armies John J. Pershing as follows: "Chemical warfare should be abolished among nations as abhorrent to civilization. It is a cruel, unfair, and improper use of science. It is fraught with gravest danger to noncombatants and demoralizing to the better instincts of humanity."[17]

Groups that were so vocally opposed to the use of chemical weapons after World War I were mostly quiet during the 1926 debate, as were the protocol's supporters in the Senate. With the exception of Senator Borah, who was floor manager of the protocol and who recommended its ratification in the most restrained manner possible, only one senator and one representative were heard in support of ratification.

The protocol was linked to two domestic issues during the Senate ratification debate. One concerned the impact of the protocol on the CWS and continuing preparations for chemical warfare. Senator James W. Wadsworth, Jr. (R-N.Y.) feared that under the protocol preparedness would inevitably slip to the point that the country would become vulnerable to an aggressor using chemical weapons. Borah maintained that the treaty did not interfere with the development of chemical weapons and defenses.[18] The truth of the matter was somewhere in between. Nevertheless, Wadsworth expressed an anxiety that underlay the movement against the protocol.

The other issue, raised by Senator Joseph E. Ransdell (D-La.), involved the protocol's potential impact on the domestic chemical industry. Although recognizing that "along with the development of innumerable useful things comes the manufacture of material which can be readily converted into weapons of war," he praised organic chemistry—"a wonderful science"—as the most important in the United States and the world. Ransdell wanted to encourage the chemical industry and its leaders "in every way," and he claimed that it "would discourage them if we should ratify any such protocol as this."[19] He presented the case of the American Chemical Society (ACS) by placing in the record an exchange of letters, which the ACS had made public on the first day of debate, between ACS Secretary Charles L. Parsons and Secretary of

State Kellogg in which Parsons argued against passage of the protocol.[20]

Role of the President

Coolidge inherited a 51–43 Senate Republican majority in the Sixty-eighth Congress, and that majority increased by 5 after the 1924 elections, when the incumbent president was handily elected using the slogan "Keep Cool with Coolidge." For the next two years, during which the Geneva Protocol was negotiated by the administration and debated by the Senate, Coolidge enjoyed modest popularity with the American people.[21] The 1926 legislative year was Coolidge's most successful in getting his domestic programs through Congress.[22] There is no evidence to indicate, however, that the president's standing with the public or Congress had any significant influence on either his negotiation or ratification strategy.

Despite his prior legislative and executive experience as a Massachusetts state senator, as lieutenant governor and governor, and then in his vice presidential role as president of the Senate, Coolidge displayed remarkably little interest in working with the Congress to get what he wanted. He generally trusted Congress to fulfill its legislative duties responsibly and independently as the Constitution prescribed.[23] His lack of interaction with Congress, however, can also be attributed to his aloof leadership style.

Coolidge was an exceptionally restrained administrator, and it showed during both the negotiations at the Geneva Conference and Senate deliberations over ratification. He is quoted in Herbert Hoover's memoirs as having once said, "If you see ten troubles coming down the road you can be sure that nine will run into the ditch before they reach you and you have to battle with only one of them."[24] For the most part, Coolidge ignored the troubles bearing down on the

Geneva Protocol, while Kellogg made some effort to stand in their way.

The desire for further limitation of armaments was a recurring theme in the president's public statements throughout his administration. For instance, in a January 1926, message to Congress he said, "The general policy of this Government in favor of disarmament and limitation of armament can not be emphasized too frequently or too strongly."[25] Specific references to the Geneva Protocol, however, were rare. In his December 1925 State of the Union message to Congress Coolidge briefly mentioned that the Geneva Protocol would be sent to the Senate for ratification.[26] During a press conference the following July, he noted that the protocol had not yet come up for final consideration in the Senate.[27]

Coolidge was not a manager who closely supervised details (except in domestic White House affairs), preferring to delegate responsibility to his subordinates—in this case, Kellogg. Coolidge did play a part in selecting the delegates to the Geneva Conference, but his direct involvement in negotiating the protocol was limited. He participated in a meeting with Kellogg, Burton, and Secretary of Commerce Herbert Hoover at which the instructions to the delegates were made final, and he agreed with the suggestion, thought to have been Burton's, that the trade in poison gas be addressed at the Geneva Conference.[28] During the negotiations, Burton also sought and received Coolidge's agreement to call a separate conference, if necessary, to deal with chemical warfare.[29]

The failure to appoint a U.S. delegation of sufficient stature that included a senator able to steer the resulting treaties through the Senate effectively was the first, and perhaps the most serious, error Coolidge made.[30] Senator Borah, who, as noted earlier, had recently assumed the chairmanship of the Senate Foreign Relations Committee, was approached, but he declined the offer to head the delegation.[31] Even if Borah had accepted the job, it is uncertain whether he would have been able to deliver the Senate, given his problematic leadership abilities. No evidence has been found that another senator was asked.[32]

Coolidge relied heavily on Kellogg and Burton to negotiate the protocol and to maneuver it through the Senate ratification process. He never made a public appeal for ratification, not even when he transmitted the protocol to the Senate, nor did he try to persuade individual senators of the treaty's merits. Coolidge's behavior is probably explained by a combination of factors: his personality, management style, belief in public and Senate antipathy toward poison gas, and underestimation of the strength of the opposition. In addition, when the protocol was debated in the Senate in December 1926, Coolidge was preoccupied with the domestic issues of taxation and farm relief and with the mounting crises in China, Mexico, and Nicaragua.[33] Combined with the error of not appointing a higher-level delegation that included an influential senator, these elements weakened the administration's position and allowed the forces against ratification to seize the initiative.

Executive-Congressional Relations

When President Coolidge submitted the Geneva Protocol to the Senate for advice and consent to ratification in January 1926, he and his administration felt confident of a favorable outcome. After all, less than four years earlier President Harding had received overwhelming Senate support for one of the Washington treaties containing much the same language.

Coolidge's relationship with Congress reached its zenith in 1926; the result was a fairly positive political context for the protocol's ratification debate. Coolidge enjoyed especially good relations with Senator Borah, who frequently visited the White House.[34] Secretary of State Kellogg, who had served one term in the Senate and a short time on the Foreign Relations Committee, maintained a working—if not close—relationship with Borah.[35] But Coolidge and Kellogg were unable or unwilling to translate those assets into political capital that could be spent in pushing the protocol through the Senate.

Borah had a well-deserved reputation as an inspired individualist who stood on principle. Borah, "the original irreconcilable" against U.S. membership in the League of Nations and the World Court, and, according to one biographer, "without any question [the Senate's] most commanding figure,"[36] reconciled himself to the Geneva Protocol, but without much enthusiasm. Borah's responsibility for the protocol's passage came during "a time when he experienced a growing indifference toward external matters."[37] His demeanor during the debate did not demonstrate the impassioned oratory for which he was known. Biographer Claudius O. Johnson noted, "Men listen to Borah because he is Borah; in fact they cripple each other to get seats near him . . . but they hope he will not persuade them to follow him."[38]

As chairman of the Senate Foreign Relations Committee, Borah was in the key position to lead the administration's ratification effort. Unfortunately, despite his considerable charisma and powers of oratory, Borah had difficulty working with his colleagues.[39] His reputation was such that Coolidge, having seen Borah on horseback in Rock Creek Park, reportedly said, "Must bother the Senator to be going in the same direction as his horse."[40] Borah "became a nay-sayer par excellence, more constructive in the negative . . . than in the positive."[41] He so despised political coalition-building that "he knew and all others who understood him knew that he would be about the last Republican in the Senate to entrust with a program."[42] Fellow irreconcilable Senator Hiram Johnson (R-Calif.), in a letter to his sons at the very

time the protocol was being debated, criticized Borah
stingingly.

> Take men like Borah, for instance. He will do no detail work. He
> attends the sessions when he wishes to make a speech, or wishes
> to go into the press, and because he devotes himself exclusively to
> publicity, and because of the unique position he occupies, due in
> great part to his ability, his share of publicity exceeds that
> practically of all other members. He has reduced advertising to an
> art, and is to be congratulated upon his success. In doing this,
> however, he has reduced his usefulness to a minimum, and his
> influence in the body is nil.[43]

When his conspicuous lack of fervor over the protocol was
combined with his modest ability to lead even in the best of
circumstances, it is not surprising that Borah failed to muster
the requisite support among his colleagues.

In contrast, there seemed to be no lack of senators willing
to voice their objections to the treaty. Led by Senator James
Wadsworth, chairman of the Military Affairs Committee and
a good friend of the cws, the vocal opposition was an
amorphous group of both political parties with both pro- and
anti-League of Nations inclinations. Not one was an
acknowledged irreconcilable, although four of the six who
spoke against the protocol sat on the Military Affairs
Committee. Wadsworth, though not a hard-core irreconcilable, was strongly opposed to involvement with the League of
Nations or the World Court.[44] His voice was the only one
heard arguing against a ban on chemical warfare during
Senate debate in 1922 on the Submarine–Poison Gas
Treaty.[45] Senator Ransdell, also a member of the Military
Affairs Committee, was an impassioned advocate of the
league.[46] Also speaking forcefully and at length against the
protocol were Senator Tyson and Senator David Reed (R-
Pa.); the two Republican senators from Connecticut, Hiram
Bingham and George McLean, registered their opposition in
less adamant terms. Ransdell and McLean were both recent
converts to the fight against chemical arms control; in 1922
they had supported the Washington Treaty's ban on chemical

warfare.[47] Of the four who spoke at any length, two were southern Democrats.

The proponents of ratification must have seemed, to some, hopelessly and dangerously naive about international affairs, especially in light of the unfolding record of German noncompliance with the Treaty of Versailles.[48] The Geneva Protocol did not contain any enforcement provisions or sanctions against violators (not that the protocol's opponents would have wanted any). Instead, as Secretary of State Kellogg—future coauthor of the 1928 Kellogg-Briand Pact to outlaw international war—remarked, the United States would have to depend upon "the good faith of nations" with respect to those nations' honoring their treaty commitments: "The execution of any international agreement for the limitation of armaments must depend in so far as the United States is concerned upon international good faith and respect for treaties. The United States will not tolerate the supervision of any outside body in this matter nor be subject to inspection or supervision by foreign agencies or individuals."[49]

The historical record provides no evidence of a coherent administration strategy adopted to secure ratification of the Geneva Protocol in light of the level of opposition that had developed. Representative Burton was the principal spokesman of the administration's case, with Kellogg available to reinforce him. Burton appeared before the Senate Foreign Relations Committee in May 1926. He testified that the protocol was "in accordance with our settled policy," referring to the Washington Treaty and two subsequent conferences in the Americas. He also argued against those who claimed that poison gas was more humane than other weapons. Nevertheless, Burton acknowledged the necessity of maintaining the cws for a time "to carry on experiments and make adequate preparation in case of war with a nonsignatory power."[50]

The following week Senator Wadsworth appeared before the Senate Foreign Relations Committee in opposition to ratification.[51] Wadsworth's testimony centered on alleged lack of consultation with the War Department during the Geneva negotiations and on possible French refusal to ratify. Kellogg immediately responded with a letter to Borah in which he explained how the Pentagon *had* been consulted and in which he stated that the French had already ratified the protocol.[52] He noted that positive French action toward the protocol was important because earlier the French had blocked entry into force of the Washington treaty prohibiting chemical warfare. French approval of the Geneva Protocol meant, for Kellogg, that the United States "could not consistently withhold its ratification." Kellogg concluded by pointing out that "in order to give further proof at this time of our genuine interest in the cause of disarmament, I think it highly important that the two instruments concluded at Geneva . . . should receive the advice and consent of the Senate for ratification as soon as possible."[53] In June 1926 the Senate Foreign Relations Committee favorably reported the protocol to the Senate by a vote of 8–1. Senator George Moses (R-N.H.) dissented, stating his intention to file a minority report.[54]

Kellogg met with a committee of the ACS in November in an effort to curtail the society's activities against the protocol. This resulted in a spirited exchange of correspondence just before the Senate ratification debate.[55] It does not appear that Kellogg's intervention had any effect on ACS lobbying.

The role of shepherding the protocol through the Senate fell to Senator Borah, who opened the floor debate with a summary of the protocol's historical antecedents, building a case for the treaty as conforming to well-established U.S. policy. He characterized the protocol as "nothing new," essentially "the same proposition" as that found in the 1922 Washington Treaty that the Senate had swiftly ratified. His statement did not respond to the criticisms that had been raised in the earlier closed committee hearings.[56] Borah did argue strenuously, however, with Wadsworth and others as they challenged the protocol.

Opponents of the Geneva Protocol based their case

primarily on four beliefs, conceived as follows: First, World War I had shown chemical weapons to be "one of the most effective military weapons ever known." Second, "we shall never be able to prevent in war the use of a weapon which is militarily effective. When a nation is fighting for its life, like an individual, it will seize any weapon which will save its life." Third, "compared with other weapons used in warfare, gas is the least cruel, not only in its effect at the time of its use but in its after effects." Fourth, ratification would lead to abandonment of an offensive and defensive chemical warfare capability with which to deter aggressors or fight them if necessary.

The first and third beliefs were reinforced by statistics on World War I casualties from a report of the U.S. Army surgeon general. Chemical weapons, the report said, produced nearly 30 percent of all American casualties; of these, only 2 percent had died. In comparison, 24 percent of the casualties from all other weapons had died. Of all American, British, and German gas casualties, nearly 3 percent had died, compared with more than 40 percent for all other weapons. These statistics were used to make the case not only that gas was the most effective single weapon of the war—causing approximately 30 percent of all casualties—but that it was the most humane of all the weapons because so few casualties had died or became permanently disabled.[57]

The second idea, that it was impossible to prohibit the use of an effective weapon of war, was presented as a kind of natural law. As Senator Wadsworth said, "It is inherent in human nature to use whatever weapon may save the life of the person using it." He argued that "when war breaks out treaties and conventions perish, and a perfect example of that was the fact that one of the parties to The Hague convention of 1907 [Germany] resorted to the use of a weapon forbidden in that convention." He even suggested that the United States "would violate this treaty if put to it."[58]

The final and most important contention was that even though the Geneva Protocol did not prohibit the production of chemical weapons and other preparations for chemical warfare, adherence to the treaty would inevitably result in the gradual abandonment of a military capability to use chemical weapons. This would leave the United States vulnerable to other nations that had not forsaken their chemical warfare programs.[59]

The most compelling oratory against the Geneva Protocol and for chemical warfare came from Senator David Reed, who later distinguished himself as a negotiator of the 1930 London Naval Treaty. He called for the use of tear gas and incapacitating agents as the way to achieve war without death.

> The whole purpose of a weapon is not to kill your adversary; it is to make him ineffective from a military standpoint so that the battle may be won. . . . If in our next war we can anesthetize or temporarily blind our adversary, he may be as good as new the next day, but we have accomplished the same military advantage as if we put him underground with a little wooden cross over him. . . .
>
> Are we, then, to go against an inferior antagonist, with all the abundance of artillery that the World War has left us, to blow out of existence a lot of peasants who scarcely know what the war is about? Or are we to take advantage of this great chemical opportunity which we, as a manufacturing nation, have open to us? Would it not be more merciful, assuming that we were at war with some Central American country, to win our battles by the temporary disabling of our enemies than to blow them all over their cactus plants . . . ?[60]

The only senator to speak for ratification on the crucial first day was Senator Borah. He was followed by four senators who called for rejection of the treaty, three of them speaking at some length and with considerable force. Despite the opposition's domination of the first day's debate, friends of the protocol had almost nothing to say the following day. Senator Borah introduced a letter from General Pershing into the record reconfirming his support for the abolition of chemical warfare. Pershing stated:

> I can not think it possible that our country should fail to ratify the protocol. . . . Scientific research may discover a gas so deadly that

it will produce instant death. To sanction the use of gas in any form would be to open the way for the use of the most deadly gases and the possible poisoning of whole populations of noncombatant men, women, and children. The contemplation of such a result is shocking to the senses. It is unthinkable that civilization should deliberately decide upon such a course.[61]

The strength and effectiveness of the military and veterans lobby against ratification became apparent during the first two days of debate. A number of resolutions against the protocol from these groups were read on the Senate floor, as was a widely distributed American Legion pamphlet attacking the protocol.[62] By the end of the second day, the intensity of opposition to ratification both from within the Senate and from without prompted the protocol's supporters to consider referring the treaty to committee before a vote.[63]

Although the decision had already been made to withdraw the protocol after the second day of debate, a brief discussion took place after a weekend break. Senator Ransdell rose to champion the views of the ACS and to express his hope that the protocol be "buried so deep it would never appear before us again."[64]

The very last senator to speak, Thomas Heflin (D-Ala.), was the first to support the protocol since Borah had opened the debate four days before. Responding to all of the previous testimony about the relative humanity of chemical weapons, and perhaps especially to the suggestion that exposure to poison gas might "tend to prevent" tuberculosis, Heflin commented with ironic levity (too late to influence action on the protocol) as follows:

> When I sit here and listen to the eulogies pronounced on poison gas, and hear its interested friends tell how delightful it is, I have been surprised that they have not suggested that it should take the place of perfume. [Laughter.] I have thought about what the children miss in the springtime, when they wander out into the woods among the wild flowers, blooming and sweetening the air with their perfume. How much more delightful these Senators think it would be if they could have mingled with the fragrance of the flowers a little poison gas. [Laughter.]
> Oh, Mr. President, this delightful stuff! We have here in the

Senate an old-fashioned snuffbox which Senators used in days gone by. They would take a little pinch of snuff and sneeze when they had a cold. If this poison gas is such a delightful thing, why not throw the old snuffbox away and bring some of this mild-mannered poison gas here for Senators to inhale? [Laughter.][65]

The only other evidence of congressional support came in the form of a letter from Representative Hamilton Fish, Jr. (R-N.Y.), which was entered into the record.

When the Department of State realized that there was little chance of attaining the support of two thirds of the Senate, the protocol was withdrawn before a vote. Proponents characterized this move as a strategic retreat until conditions were more favorable for ratification. Consideration was given to amending or perhaps accepting reservations to the protocol to undercut its critics. Nothing came of this idea, however, and the protocol would languish in the Senate Foreign Relations Committee for many years.[66]

The Coolidge administration's expectation of ratification as a mere formality constituted a major error in judgment. The administration had clearly expected a repeat of the 1922 ratification experience; it had grossly and inexplicably underestimated the strength of the anti-ratification lobby and its ability to influence the Senate.

Public Opinion and the Role of Interest Groups

Throughout the post–World War I period up until at least 1925 when the Geneva Protocol was negotiated, public sentiment in the United States was decidedly against chemical warfare. During this time, the U.S. chemical industry waged a "virulent and effective" propaganda campaign about the threat of chemical warfare in order to help secure protective tariffs and an embargo on chemical imports. This crusade focused on the future threat to a United States without a strong chemical industry. The example of German use of poison gas during World War I was used to illustrate the menace the country might face. By 1925, when the U.S. delegation to the Geneva Conference proposed an international treaty to ban the use of chemical weapons based upon the Washington Treaty, it was with the unqualified belief that the American people were behind it.[67]

The chemical industry's campaign emphasizing the threat of chemical warfare was supported by the CWS as a way of helping justify its continued existence to Congress. Although the effort was successful in obtaining protectionist policies for the industry, it also had unintended and undesired consequences, especially for the CWS. It helped single out gas, among all the new weapons developed during World War I, for special public concern. According to Frederic J. Brown: "Thanks to the determined efforts of the chemical industries, aided by the CWS, gas was no longer considered one among many hardships of war. By 1921, it had become the bête noire of World War I, a symbol of the inhumanity of modern war." Consequently, when the Washington Conference was held, "chemical warfare was a sure candidate for inclusion on the agenda." In fact, "the driving force behind the poison gas negotiations" at the conference had been public opinion.[68]

The American people's aversion to gas warfare and their desire for chemical disarmament were fueled by forces in addition to the propaganda campaigns of the CWS and the chemical industry. After World War I popular representations of how a future war might be fought found a wide audience. Probably the most influential of these, especially for the disarmament movement, was Will Irwin's book *"The Next War": An Appeal to Common Sense.* Irwin warned that the military technology and tactics of World War I could be further developed, combined, and applied for mass destruction of civilian populations in the next war between industrial nations. He characterized gas as "a killing instrument . . . of a power beyond the dream of a madman." The next war he envisioned thus:

[It] will be, in one phase, a war of aeroplanes loaded with gas shells. And professional military men in all lands are remarking among themselves that the new warfare may—some say must—strike not only at armies but at the heart of the matter—peoples. . . . They see that even with the known gases, the existing aeroplanes, Paris, Rome or London could in one night be changed from a metropolis to a necropolis.[69]

When Elihu Root, at the Washington Conference, introduced the U.S. proposal to ban the use of gas based upon Article 171 of the Treaty of Versailles, he said that the Versailles provisions "presented the most extraordinary consensus of opinion one could well find upon any international subject."[70] A national public opinion poll carried out by the Advisory Committee for the U.S. delegation to the Washington Conference had found overwhelming public support for the abolition of chemical warfare, with 366,975 people favoring a complete ban on gas and only 19 in favor of retaining restricted use of gas.[71]

The League of Nations also played a minor role in steering public opinion toward favoring a prohibition of chemical warfare. In September 1924 the assembly adopted a resolution to request publication of a report on chemical and biological warfare by the Temporary Mixed Commission and "to encourage the work of making the information on this subject generally accessible to the public." The report expressed special concern about the possibility of dropping gas on cities from airplanes in a future war, concluding that "It is . . . essential that all nations should realize to the full the terrible nature of the danger which threatens them."[72]

An organization that could have been expected to support ratification of the protocol actively was the American Red Cross, as the International Red Cross had protested vigorously the use of poison gas during World War I. In 1921 the International Red Cross called for an "absolute prohibition of the use of gas," and in 1925 it urged quick ratification of the protocol by states that had not yet done so.

The American Red Cross, however, adopted a detached view and made no attempt to muster public support for the treaty.[73]

The peace and disarmament movement, especially women's groups, agitated against the CWS and for chemical disarmament throughout the 1920s. Especially active in the fight against poison gas before and after the Washington Conference were the National Council for the Prevention of War and the Women's International League for Peace and Freedom (WILPF), the latter of which made the abolition of chemical warfare one of its central goals in 1924. At the 1925 Geneva Conference WILPF distributed a pamphlet by Gertrud Woker entitled "Poison Gas: The War of the Future."[74]

Opponents of chemical arms control had been caught by surprise by the 1922 Washington Treaty, which was approved by the Senate less than two months after signing. (See chapter 2 of this volume.) They had too little time to mobilize and their efforts had been "unorganized" and "ineffective."[75] In 1926 the situation was reversed: proponents of chemical arms control were surprised by and unable to respond to the anti-protocol movement. During the year and a half that separated the signing of the Geneva Protocol and the final Senate floor debate, the CWS enlisted the chemical industry and veterans organizations in an extensive and ultimately successful lobbying campaign against ratification. Their combined effort, in the absence of any coherent executive branch or public strategy, was one of the most significant factors determining the outcome of the debate.

The CWS considered the Geneva Protocol to be a serious threat to its existence and to represent a further shift in U.S. policy toward the non-use of chemical weapons. Surely with considerable justification, it feared that U.S. adherence to the treaty would jeopardize continued investment in preparations for chemical warfare. As it was, the CWS had been fighting for its life since the demobilization at the end of World War I.

The CWS originated in September 1917, as the wartime Gas Service, American Expeditionary Forces, under the command of Colonel Amos Fries. An expanded CWS was established the following June. Faced with the imminent dissolution of the CWS by the army in 1919, Fries "embarked on an extraordinary sales campaign in direct violation of Army customs and regulations" in an effort to win permanent establishment of a separate CWS organization.[76] He appealed to powerful friends in Congress, especially Senator George Chamberlain (D-Ore.), chairman of the Senate Military Affairs Committee, and Representative Julius Kahn (R-Calif.), chairman of the House Military Affairs Committee. He also enlisted the aid of chemists who had served in the CWS during World War I, professional chemical societies, and the other army specialized service chiefs. Articles by Fries were distributed widely throughout the chemical industry, which, in turn, lobbied the War Department on behalf of the CWS. Despite "the near unanimous opposition of the military establishment," the tireless efforts of Fries, by now a brigadier general, resulted in a stunning victory in 1920 when Congress approved the CWS as a distinct service.[77]

The experience gained and the connections established during the postwar fights to save the CWS and strengthen the chemical industry provided Fries and his friends a solid base from which to oppose the Geneva Protocol by the time it came up for ratification.[78] Fries also enlisted the help of the major veterans organizations and other military groups, including the American Legion, the Veterans of Foreign Wars, the Spanish-American War Veterans, the Military Order of the World War, the Reserve Officers' Association of the United States, and the Association of Military Surgeons. These groups passed resolutions opposing ratification at their national conventions and informed Congress of their views. Many local chapters and posts of these organizations did similarly. The protocol's opponents made much of these resolutions during the Senate deliberations, reading some on the floor and entering all of them into the record.[79]

The most active and influential of these groups was the American Legion. General Fries served as the legion's department commander for the District of Columbia at the time of the Senate debate over the protocol. The legion's campaign was spearheaded by the vice chairman of its National Legislative Committee, John Thomas Taylor, who was a close friend of Fries's and a reserve officer in the CWS.[80] He sent a letter to every legion department commander, announcing that "there is apparently a determined effort on the part of a selective few gentlemen here in Washington who took no personal part in the War to regulate the kind and use of weapons during the next emergency. Their enthusiasm seems to be fostered mostly by the group of pacifists who have as their ultimate objective the elimination of war entirely.[81] Taylor authored and distributed 25,000 copies of an influential pamphlet entitled "The Truth About the Geneva Gas Protocol—America Should Reject It—Preparedness Essential to Our National Security," which was widely used by senators who spoke against ratification of the protocol and which was entered into the *Congressional Record*. He also wrote every senator a personal letter asking them to reject the treaty.[82]

Taylor's activities were roundly criticized, first in the *Washington Post* a week and a half before the Senate debate commenced. He was accused of a conflict of interest, of using his positions with the American Legion and as treasurer of the National Association for Chemical Defense (an organization of industrial chemists that financed the anti-protocol lobbying campaign) to misrepresent the opinions of the legion rank and file membership.[83] Later, after the Senate debate was concluded, supporters of the protocol in the House of Representatives also condemned Taylor. Representative John Rankin (D-Miss.) announced that Taylor was given the unusual promotion from captain to lieutenant colonel in the CWS reserves (skipping one rank entirely) after the American Legion had passed the anti–Geneva Protocol resolution.[84] One of the founders of the American Legion, Representative Hamilton Fish, Jr., charged Taylor with having used his official position in the Legion to pull the wires and to railroad the resolution through two Legion Conventions. . . . With carrying on a tremendous propaganda, financed by the chemical industries to defeat the poison gas treaty in the Senate. . . . With having attempted to bamboozle [the Senate]. . . . With misrepresenting the views of the rank and file of the veterans and misleading our colleagues in the other body into believing that they will incur the wrath of the legionaires [*sic*] if they vote for the gas treaty. . . . With being the treasurer of an association of chemical officials whose aim is to defeat the pending treaty prohibiting the use of poison gas.[85]

The ACS led the chemical industry's efforts to prevent ratification of the Geneva Protocol. Resolutions passed at its national convention, and editorials in its journal opposed the treaty. A committee of the ACS met with Kellogg in early November 1926 "to protest against the misinformation that was being given to the American people."[86] As noted earlier, this meeting led to an exchange of letters between Charles L. Parsons, secretary of the ACS, and Kellogg debating U.S. chemical weapons policy. A week before the Senate took up the Geneva Protocol, Parsons sent a letter to all 15,000 members of the ACS in which he argued that the provisions of the protocol "were born of hysteria and are fostered by ignorance" and in which he urged them to lobby their senators against ratification.[87] The ACS then released to the press the Parsons-Kellogg letters on the first day of the Senate debate in an effort to undercut the administration's position.

Another element in the anti-ratification campaign was an unattributed and undated pamphlet entitled "Disarming America," which was distributed to senators. Probably produced by the National Association for Chemical Defense, a chemical industry organization with strong ties to the CWS, this tract charged the peace movement with attempting to disarm and destroy the United States as part of an international communist conspiracy. It began with the statement, "Humanity and National Safety Demand that the Geneva Protocol . . . be not ratified by the United States

Senate."[88] According to the author, "the Communist" feared and fought against chemical warfare "because he cannot cope with it. Tear gas or irritating gases . . . turned loose down a street filled with Communists will make every last one of them helpless and open to capture by a few soldiers with gas masks." The capability of gas to "rout any group of Communists in any city," the pamphlet continued, was the real reason that the CWS opposed ratification of the Geneva Protocol. In fact, "The very safety of civilization may finally depend on just this one thing."[89] The influence of this pamphlet on the Senate is impossible to measure, but it was undoubtedly diminished by its atrocious grammar and confused organization.

In contrast with the impressive array of forces assaulting the Geneva Protocol at the crucial time, the friendly trenches were nearly empty. The only exception seems to have been a group of women's organizations that happened to be meeting for a conference in Washington on "the cause and cure of war" at the time of the Senate debate. While their concerns were far-ranging and prominently included an appeal for U.S. participation in the World Court, the women's groups also lobbied senators in behalf of the protocol.[90] This minimal effort did not come close to counterbalancing the powerful anti-protocol lobby. In this way "the peace groups forfeited the opportunity to influence the most significant debate on chemical warfare during the interwar period."[91]

Anti-ratification lobbying mattered less in convincing senators to oppose the protocol actively than in silencing those who might have otherwise spoken in favor of ratification. Those senators who stood in opposition would probably have done so had there been no anti-protocol campaign. In addition, the anti-protocol campaign probably influenced some swing votes and raised doubts in the minds of others who were inclined to support the treaty. All of these factors led Borah, when he took an informal tally of senators to ascertain their positions, to conclude that the protocol was unlikely to attain the two-thirds vote required for ratification.

The following day the *Washington Post* suggested in an editorial that "more than two-thirds of the senators doubtless feel that the United States would be merely concurring in a hypocritical act if it should ratify a treaty pretending to outlaw the use of gas in warfare." There is no evidence in the historical record, however, to suggest that fully two thirds of the Senate were persuaded by the anti-ratification argument. The *Washington Post* applauded the Senate's rejection of the protocol, calling the characterization of the use of gas as inhumane "arrant humbug."[92]

The *Washington Post*'s position, considering its strong anti–League of Nations editorial stance, was not surprising. Other newspapers, however, supported the Geneva protocol. The Syracuse *Post-Standard*, for instance, editorialized, "Whatever the chemists may think, it would be a startling development, indeed, if the United States should refuse to give its assent to a declaration of nearly all the other great nations of the earth against the employment of weapons of warfare that would wipe out whole communities of non-combatants."[93]

Conclusion

The primary responsibility for the Coolidge administration's failure to secure Senate consent to ratification of the Geneva Protocol rests squarely on the president's shoulders. A U.S. president—at least one neither wracked by scandal nor totally out of touch with the political environment—who uses his constitutional powers wisely and creatively can, with rare exceptions, get his most important foreign policy programs through Congress. Coolidge did not win Senate approval for the Geneva Protocol primarily because he failed to exercise some of his most basic presidential powers from the start of the negotiations to the final Senate floor debate, and not because of the strength of the anti-ratification campaign.

The administration's mistakes began even before the Geneva Conference was convened, when Coolidge and Kellogg selected a congressional representative instead of a senator to lead the U.S. delegation. An influential senator committed to the protocol would have been much more effective in countering the anti-protocol lobby and in persuading his colleagues to favor ratification. Coolidge and Kellogg also failed to follow the lead of President Warren G. Harding and Secretary of State Charles Evan Hughes at the Washington Conference in that they did not establish an advisory committee of distinguished Americans to represent public opinion and ease the ratification process and in that they did not enlist active military support.

This behavior is difficult to explain solely by appealing to Coolidge's detached management style. It also bears the imprint of a profoundly ambivalent attitude toward involvement with the League of Nations, sponsor of the Geneva Conference. That ambivalence led the administration to insist on a treaty without provisions for ensuring compliance. It relied instead on the good faith of nations. The administration, however, never admitted to, or adequately reconciled the contradiction of, trusting other nations to honor the protocol while distrusting them too much to join the League of Nations. With the memory of Germany's shattering of treaties during World War I—including the Hague Gas Declaration—so fresh, and with Germany's record of noncompliance with the Treaty of Versailles so evident, Senate skepticism about the ability of the protocol to prevent the use of gas in future wars should not have surprised Coolidge or Kellogg. This lack of confidence in the treaty to accomplish its goals—a lack of confidence even, to some extent, shared by the administration—was one of the most damaging elements of the case against the protocol. The potentially catastrophic consequences foreseen for U.S. national security if chemical warfare preparedness lapsed, in the absence of adequate administration moves to address this concern, undermined confidence in the protocol even further.

Compounding these fundamental problems, the administration also seems to have both overestimated the ability of public opinion against chemical warfare to carry the protocol through the Senate and underestimated the strength of the forces attempting to block the protocol. The peace movement made similar miscalculations. Yet even after all of the earlier errors made by the administration, and after the full weight of the opposition became apparent as the Senate floor debate approached, an eleventh-hour effort by the president or the secretary of state to persuade senators to support the protocol might have succeeded. Kellogg might have intervened more strenuously if he had not been distracted by crises in other parts of the world and hampered by his mental and physical exhaustion. Coolidge delivered his State of the Union address only two days before the final Senate floor debate opened but failed even to mention the protocol. He chose, instead, to follow his well-worn pattern of restraint as an important foreign policy initiative collapsed around him.

Although the bulk of the blame for non-ratification of the protocol rests at the door of Coolidge, the sophisticated and well-organized campaigns against ratification waged by the ACS, the CWS, and such veterans organizations as the American Legion heavily influenced the outcome of the Senate debate. These groups filled the vacuum left by the administration's overconfidence and neglect, and they joined forces with sympathetic senators. Together they effectively persuaded enough senators to derail the protocol.

Borah's unenthusiastic handling of the protocol on the Senate floor also contributed to its disapproval. Although he more than held his own in debate with Wadsworth over some of the latter's arguments, his performance was so lackluster compared with what his colleagues had come to expect that they must have questioned his own commitment to the treaty. More important, Borah failed to rally a group of protocol proponents to counter the opposition directly. Because of this, the protocol's opponents dominated the debate and defeated a prominent part of the administration's arms control agenda.

The withdrawal of the Geneva Protocol from Senate consideration in December 1926 marked a significant shift in U.S. policy, from a reliance on public opinion as the main sanction against gas warfare to a reliance on preparedness for offensive use of chemical weapons as the primary deterrent to gas warfare. Nearly half a century would pass before the Senate again had the opportunity to consent to ratification of the Geneva Protocol. The Department of State apparently contemplated making another appeal for ratification of the protocol in April 1937, following Italy's use of poison gas in Ethiopia, but it did not do so.[94] In April 1947 President Harry S. Truman withdrew the Geneva Protocol and eighteen other "obsolete" treaties from the Senate "with a view to placing the treaty calendar on a current basis."[95]

Not until the United States started using vast quantities of herbicides and "riot control agents" (irritant agents or tear gas) during the Vietnam War, claiming that they were not chemical weapons and that their use in war was not prohibited by the Geneva Protocol, did renewed calls arise for U.S. ratification of the protocol. Several factors led the Nixon administration to reassess U.S. chemical and biological warfare policy in 1969: public opposition, especially among academic scientists, to United States' use of herbicides and tear gas in Vietnam; concern about the safety of the U.S. chemical and biological weapons program; and pressure from Congress and the international diplomatic community on the United States to join the large community of nations that had already formally acceded to the protocol.[96]

In November 1969, as part of a major decision regarding U.S. chemical and biological warfare policy, President Richard M. Nixon announced that he would resubmit the Geneva Protocol to the Senate for advice and consent to ratification. He did so nine months later, insisting, however, as President Lyndon B. Johnson had done before him and in defiance of nearly universal opinion to the contrary, that the Senate agree that the use of herbicides and tear gas was not a violation of the protocol.[97]

After a series of hearings in March 1971, the Senate Foreign Relations Committee, under the chairmanship of J. William Fulbright (D-Ark.), strongly endorsed the protocol's objectives but asked Nixon to reconsider the administration's restrictive interpretation. Nixon's refusal to do so stalled ratification not only of the Geneva Protocol but also of the 1972 Biological and Toxin Weapons Convention, which outlawed the production and possession of such weapons.[98]

Only after direct U.S. military participation in the Vietnam War had ended and President Nixon had resigned did the executive branch and the Senate Foreign Relations Committee reach a compromise that made ratification possible. At the initiative of the director of the U.S. Arms Control and Disarmament Agency (ACDA), Fred Iklé, and with the approval of President Gerald Ford, during the latter half of 1974 ACDA staffers brokered an agreement between the Department of Defense and the Senate Foreign Relations Committee.[99] This compromise allowed the U.S. government to retain its interpretation of the protocol as not prohibiting the use in war of tear gas and herbicides while requiring that the U.S. renounce, as a matter of national policy, first use of these agents in war except in a few narrowly defined defensive situations "in order to save lives."[100] The Senate voted unanimously to approve the Geneva Protocol in December 1974, clearing the way for the United States to become the last industrial nation to adhere to the treaty. The Biological and Toxin Weapons Convention was also approved unanimously at the same time.[101]

The Geneva Protocol outlawing the use of all chemical and biological weapons in war has become, owing to reservations by many nations, including the United States, essentially a no-first-use prohibition. The protocol does not address the production or stockpiling of chemical weapons. Nevertheless, despite a handful of serious violations, the protocol has contributed to limiting the use of chemical weapons for more than sixty years. A truly global ban on the development, production, and stockpiling of all chemical weapons to complement the Geneva Protocol's prohibition on use awaits a successful conclusion to the Chemical Weapons Convention negotiations in Geneva.

Notes

1. Ann Van Wynen Thomas and A. J. Thomas, Jr., *Legal Limits on the Use of Chemical and Biological Weapons* (Dallas, Tex.: Southern Methodist University Press, 1970), 44–47.

2. Ibid., 58–62.

3. *Congressional Record*, 67th Cong., 2d sess., 1922, vol. 62, pt. 5, 4723–30; Augustin M. Prentiss and George J. B. Fisher, *Chemicals in War: A Treatise on Chemical Warfare* (New York: McGraw-Hill, 1937), 690–91; Frederic J. Brown, *Chemical Warfare: A Study in Restraints* (Princeton, N.J.: Princeton University Press, 1968), 61–67; and Thomas and Thomas, *Legal Limits*, 62–67. For a detailed analysis of U.S. ratification of the several Washington treaties, see Thomas Buckley's study, chapter 2 of the present volume.

4. United Nations, *Treatment of the Question of Chemical and Bacteriological Warfare in the League of Nations: Review by the United Nations Secretariat*, August 3, 1951, U.N. Document A/AC.50/3, 26–51, reproduced in U.S. Congress, Senate Committee on Foreign Relations, Subcommittee on Disarmament, *Disarmament and Security: A Collection of Documents, 1919-55*, 84th Cong., 2d sess., 1956, Committee Print, 170–88.

5. Donald R. McCoy, *Coming of Age: The United States During the 1920's and 1930's* (Baltimore, Md.: Penguin, 1973), 44–45.

6. *Congressional Record*, 69th Cong., 2d sess., 1926, vol. 68, pt. 1, 141, and Brown, *Chemical Warfare*, 98–102.

7. See Coolidge's Memorial Day speech, "Ways to Peace," at Arlington, Virginia, May 31, 1926, in Calvin Coolidge, *Foundations of the Republic: Speeches and Addresses* (New York: Charles Scribner's Sons, 1926), 433–35. See also Donald R. McCoy, *Calvin Coolidge: The Quiet President* (New York: Macmillan Co., 1967), 186, 363.

8. For a detailed study of the fight against U.S. ratification of the Treaty of Versailles and membership in the League of Nations, see Ralph Stone, *The Irreconcilables: The Fight Against the League of Nations* (Lexington: University Press of Kentucky, 1970), and William C. Widenor's study, chapter 1 of this volume.

9. U.S. Department of State, *Papers Relating to the Foreign Relations of the United States [FRUS], 1925*, vol. 1, (Washington, D.C.: GPO, 1940), 55–59.

10. Robert H. Ferrell, *Peace in Their Time: The Origins of the Kellogg-Briand Pact* (1952; reprint, New York: W. W. Norton and Co., 1969), 44; Ethan L. Ellis, *Frank B. Kellogg and American Foreign Policy, 1925-1929* (New Brunswick, N.J.: Rutgers University Press, 1961), 226–29, and Ethan L. Ellis, *Republican Foreign Policy, 1921-1933* (New Brunswick, N.J.: Rutgers University Press, 1968), 71–73; McCoy, *Calvin Coolidge*, 359–63; Robert J. Maddox, *William E. Borah and American Foreign Policy* (Baton Rouge: Louisiana State University Press, 1969), 168–70; Thomas N. Guinsburg, *The Pursuit of Isolationism in the United States Senate from Versailles to Pearl Harbor* (New York: Garland, 1982), 79–109; and Thomas H. Buckley and Edwin B. Strong, Jr., *American Foreign and National Security Policies, 1914-1945* (Knoxville: University of Tennessee Press, 1987), 81–82.

11. Ellis, *Frank B. Kellogg*, 159–62.

12. *Washington Post*, December 8, 1926, A1, A14–15.

13. Howard H. Quint and Robert H. Ferrell, eds., *The Talkative President: The Off-the-Record Press Conferences of Calvin Coolidge* (Amherst: University of Massachusetts Press, 1964), 157.

14. Ellis, *Frank B. Kellogg*, 9, 38, 65–69, 123–24, 233–34, and McCoy, *Calvin Coolidge*, 351–52, 417.

15. U.S. Congress, Senate, *Prohibiting Use of Gases in War: Message from the President of the United States*, 69th Cong., 1st sess., January 12, 1926, Executive G, 6.

16. *New York Times*, November 5, 1924, and November 6, 1924, and McCoy, *Calvin Coolidge*, 222–23, 301–14, 320.

17. Brown, *Chemical Warfare*, 99, 101, 105; U.S. Congress, Senate, *Prohibiting Use of Gases in Warfare: Report from Senator Borah*, 69th Cong., 1st sess., June 26, 1926, calendar no. 16, report no. 1, 5; and *Congressional Record*, 1926, 151–52.

18. *Congressional Record*, 1926, 146–47.

19. Ibid., 364.

20. Ibid., 364–67; *New York Times*, December 10, 1926, A2.

21. One of Coolidge's early biographers even claimed that "few Presidents of the United States have been as popular." Claude M. Fuess, *Calvin Coolidge: The Man from Vermont* (Boston: Little, Brown & Co., 1940), 359.

22. See Coolidge's comments to the press in Quint and Ferrell, *The Talkative President*, 99–100, and McCoy, *Calvin Coolidge*, 310.

23. Quint and Ferrell, *The Talkative President*, 89–90, 96–97, 99, and McCoy, *Calvin Coolidge*, pp. 193–94, 266–67.

24. Cited in McCoy, *Calvin Coolidge*, 193.

25. U.S. Department of State, *Papers Relating to the Foreign Relations of the United States [FRUS], 1926*, vol. 1 (Washington, D.C.: GPO, 1941), 44.

26. U.S. Department of State, *FRUS, 1925*, vol. 1, xiii-xiv.

27. Quint and Ferrell, *The Talkative President*, 99.

28. Brown, *Chemical Warfare*, 99.

29. U.S. Department of State, *FRUS, 1925*, vol. 1, 55–57.

30. The Coolidge administration's approach to delegate selection handicapped its other arms control efforts. Ellis made the following comment regarding delegate selection during the winter of 1926–27 to the 1927 Geneva naval limitation conference:

> Coolidge and Kellogg adopted an approach which minimized the political and maximized the technical side of the negotiations. Whether for reasons of economy, because they were too much concerned with other matters (this was the winter when Kellogg was under great strain over Nicaraguan affairs), or from sheer ineptitude in estimating the complexity of the problem, they failed to match Hughes's perspicacity in the choice of delegates and the balance within the delegation. Instead of choosing a group carefully for the particular occasion, they assigned the added chore of discussing naval disarmament to a delegation appointed to attend the League's Preparatory Commission on the Disarmament Conference. (*Republican Foreign Policy*, 141–42)

It is also interesting to note that Coolidge was asked by the American Legion to name a legionnaire to the preparatory commission delegation. On the March 25, 1926, letter from National Commander John R. McQuigg, Coolidge handwrote the following note: "Have only 1 rep. Gibson who reps. us in Switz. All the mil. advisers served in the war. At the final conference this can be considered." Series 1, 2758A, Calvin Coolidge Manuscripts, Library of Congress (hereafter cited as Coolidge MSS).

31. Kellogg to Coolidge, memorandum, March 24, 1925, Series 1, 3002, Coolidge MSS.

32. There is some reason to believe that non-ratification of the two Geneva Conference treaties had more of an impact on the Coolidge administration than the lack of official public comment might suggest. Memoranda from Kellogg to Coolidge on May 24 and 27, 1927, discuss the importance of sending a delegation of sufficient stature to the 1927 Geneva naval

limitation conference. See Series 1, 2758A, Coolidge MSS. According to Ellis, however, Coolidge and Kellogg did not follow through, relying instead on the delegation already in Geneva for the preparatory commission discussions. *Frank B. Kellogg*, 7.

33. For Coolidge's domestic preoccupations, see his State of the Union message of December 7, 1926, in *Washington Post*, December 8, 1926. For his foreign concerns, see Ellis, *Frank B. Kellogg*, 38, 65–69, 123–24, and McCoy, *Calvin Coolidge*, 343, 351–52.

34. Ellis, *Republican Foreign Policy*, 54.

35. Ellis, *Frank B. Kellogg*, 14. Although Kellogg had been a leader of the mild reservationists in the Senate struggle over the League of Nations, he eventually came closer to Borah's irreconcilable opposition to any U.S. participation. Ibid., 7. For Kellogg's role as a leader of the mild reservationists, see Herbert F. Margulies, *The Mild Reservationists and the League of Nations Controversy in the Senate* (Columbia: University of Missouri Press, 1989).

36. Claudius O. Johnson, *Borah of Idaho* (1936; reprint, Seattle: University of Washington Press, 1967), 315.

37. Maddox, *William E. Borah*, 170.

38. Johnson, *Borah of Idaho*, 312.

39. This negative assessment of Borah, however, was not shared by all who knew him. A colleague of Salmon O. Levinson, champion of the outlawry-of-war movement, wrote in 1925 that "no American public man has a larger personal following throughout the country than Senator Borah." John Chalmers Vinson, *William E. Borah and the Outlawry of War* (Athens: University of Georgia Press, 1957), 95. Former Senator Gerald Nye recalled in 1965 that when he became a senator in 1926, "Borah was the man I looked to more than any other. . . . The younger senators couldn't help being impressed by the way he followed his principles." Guinsburg, *The Pursuit of Isolationism*, 112.

40. John Hiram McKee, *Coolidge Wit and Wisdom* (New York: Frederick A. Stokes, 1933), 2.

41. Ellis, *Republican Foreign Policy*, 54.

42. Johnson, *Borah of Idaho*, 315.

43. Hiram Johnson to Hiram Johnson, Jr., and Archibald Johnson, December 11, 1926, in *The Diary Letters of Hiram Johnson*, vol. 4 (New York: Garland, 1983).

44. Denna Frank Fleming, *The United States and the League of Nations, 1918-1920* (New York: G. P. Putnam's Sons, 1932), 377-78, and McCoy, *Calvin Coolidge*, 185.

45. *Congressional Record*, 1922, 4727-30.

46. Fleming, *The United States and the League of Nations*, 288-90, and Stone, *The Irreconcilables*, 169.

47. *Congressional Record*, 1922, 4730.

48. E. J. Gumbel, "Disarmament and Clandestine Rearmament Under the Weimer Republic," in *Inspection for Disarmament*, ed., Seymour Melman (New York: Columbia University Press, 1958), 203-19; and Walter H. Nelson, *Germany Rearmed* (New York: Simon and Schuster, 1972).

49. Kellogg cables in February and April 1926 to U.S. diplomats in Europe setting out the U.S. negotiating principles for the preparatory commission. U.S. Department of State, *FRUS, 1926*, vol. 1, 54, 88.

50. U.S. Congress, Senate, *Prohibiting Use of Gases in Warfare*, report. no. 1, 2-4, and Richard D. Challener, *Proceedings of the Committee on Foreign Relations, United States Senate, from December 3, 1923, to March 3, 1933*, vol. 2 of *The Legislative Origins of American Foreign Policy* (New York: Garland, 1979), 93-94, and, for reproduction of Borah's statement, 95-97.

51. Challener, *Proceedings*, 94.

52. France ratified the Geneva Protocol on May 9, 1926.

53. U.S. Congress, Senate, *Prohibiting Use of Gases in Warfare*, report no. 1, 5-6, and reprinted in Challener, *Proceedings*, 97-99.

54. Challener, *Proceedings*, 94. No evidence that he ever did submit a minority report has been found.

55. *Congressional Record*, 1926, 364-67.

56. Ibid., 141-43.

57. There is still considerable uncertainty about the number of casualties caused by chemical weapons during World War I, as well as their relative lethality. The figures provided by the surgeon general after the war are at variance with the statistics usually mentioned in contemporary historical accounts, such as those mentioned earlier in this chapter.

58. *Congressional Record*, 1926, 146.

59. Ibid., 144-51.

60. Ibid., 148, 150.

61. Ibid., 226.

62. Ibid., 152-54, 226-29.

63. *Washington Post*, December 11, 1926, A9.

64. *Congressional Record*, 1926, 363-64.

65. Ibid., 145-46, 367.

66. *Washington Post*, December 14, 1926, A1; *New York Times*, December 14, 1926, A16; and Stockholm International Peace Research Institute (SIPRI), *The Rise of CB Weapons*, vol. 1 of *The Problem of Chemical and Biological Warfare* (New York: Humanities Press, 1971), 250.

67. Brown, *Chemical Warfare*, 56-61.

68. Ibid., 58-61, 68.

69. Will Irwin, *"The Next War": An Appeal to Common Sense* (New York: E. P. Dutton & Co., 1921), 44, 46.

70. Brown, *Chemical Warfare*, 66-67.

71. Ibid., 69.

72. United Nations, *Treatment of the Question of Chemical and Bacteriological Warfare in the League of Nations*, and SIPRI, *CB Disarmament Negotiations, 1920-1970*, vol. 4 of *The Problem of Chemical and Biological Warfare*, 55.

73. Buckingham, Clyde E., "The Geneva Convention Outlawing Poisonous Gases and Bacteriological Warfare," unpublished paper, August 22, 1957, 9; and International Red Cross, Proceedings of the Twelfth International Red Cross Conference, Geneva, October, 1925, Report of Commission V on Chemical Warfare, pp. 101-108, separate translation by Leon Gilbert, August 1957, 2, 14; both in American Red Cross Library, Washington, D.C.

74. "Disarming America," n.p. [1925], 4, 18, 79, 83-84.

75. *Congressional Record*, 1926, 364.

76. Brown, *Chemical Warfare*, 78.

77. Ibid., 73-82, and Leo P. Brophy and George J. B. Fisher, *The Chemical Warfare Service: Organizing for War*, vol. 1 of *The United States Army in World War II: The Technical Services*, History of the Chemical Warfare Service Series (Washington, D.C.: GPO, 1959), 3-17.

78. Cooperation between the CWS and the ACS was very strong. Many members of ACS had served in the CWS during the Great War and maintained contact, some even as reserve officers, afterward. The CWS even adopted the ACS's colors, cobalt blue and gold. During 1919 and 1920 when the CWS's future was threatened by War Department demobilization plans, the ACS lobbied Congress for a separate chemical service. In June 1920 the

ACS Committee Advisory to the Chemical Warfare Service was formed to advise the chief chemical officer on policies and procedures of the CWS's research and development program. Soon after, the ACS "pledged the active aid of its 15,000 civilian members in the successful development and prosecution of the work of the Chemical Warfare Service." It was not long before the ACS 'mounted the platform' to discourage the ratification of what it considered to be "unhealthy treaties against the use of chemical warfare." See Carl B. Marquand, "American Chemical Society Committee Advisory to the Chemical Corps," in *Armed Forces Chemical Journal* 12, no. 5 (September-October 1958): 18, 22, 30–33; Walter J. Murphy, "The American Chemical Society and the Chemical Corps," in *Armed Forces Chemical Journal* 11, no. 2 (March-April 1957), 20–21, 23; and Brophy and Fisher, *The Chemical Warfare Service: Organizing for War*, 28.

79. *Congressional Record*, 1926, 152–54, 226.

80. Brown, *Chemical Warfare*, 103–4.

81. Marcus Duffield, *King Legion* (New York: Jonathan Cape & Harrison Smith, 1931), 153. See also, Roscoe Baker, *The American Legion and American Foreign Policy* (New York: Bookman Associates, 1954), 137.

82. Brown, *Chemical Warfare*, 103–4; Duffield, *King Legion*, 153. The pamphlet was printed in the *Congressional Record*, 1926, 226–29.

83. *Washington Post*, November 28, 1926.

84. *Congressional Record*, 69th Cong., 2d sess., 1927, vol. 68, pt. 2, 2089. Such a promotion would have been highly unusual, since it would have meant skipping over the intermediary rank of major, an uncommon action in wartime and certainly an exceedingly rare occurrence for a reserve officer in peacetime. When World War II began, Taylor reportedly went on to head public relations for the army and to a promotion to brigadier general. Buckingham, "The Geneva Convention," 7.

85. *Congressional Record*, 1927, 2090.

86. Charles L. Parsons to members of the ACS, November 29, 1926, quoted in *New York Times*, December 10, 1926, A2.

87. Ibid.

88. "Disarming America," 1.

89. Ibid., 47.

90. Baker, *The American Legion*, 136.

91. Brown, *Chemical Warfare*, 105–6.

92. *Washington Post*, December 14, 1926, 6. The editorial writer's assertion about two thirds of senators opposing ratification was probably a result of confusion over the two-thirds requirement. At least one third of the Senate may have felt as the editorial suggested.

93. Quoted in *Literary Digest*, December 25, 1926, 8.

94. Brown, *Chemical Warfare*, 145.

95. Harry S. Truman, "Message of the President to the Senate, April 8, 1947," *Department of State Bulletin* 16, no. 407, April 20, 1947, 726–27. The treaties were marked "unperfected" at the Department of State and sent to the National Archives.

96. See U.S. National Security Council, National Security Study Memorandum 59, May 28, 1969, and National Security Decision Memorandum 35, November 25, 1969, NNMM Collection of NSC Documents, folder "National Security Decision Memoranda," National Archives.

97. See U.S. Congress, Senate, *Message from the President of the United States transmitting the Protocol for the Prohibition of the Use in War of Asphyxiating, Poisonous, or Other Gases, and of Bacteriological Methods of Warfare, signed at Geneva June 17, 1925*, 91st Cong., 2d sess., August 19, 1970, Executive J.

98. See U.S. Congress, Senate Committee on Foreign Relations, *Hearings on the Geneva Protocol of 1925* (1971), 92d Cong., 1st sess, 1972.

99. Fred Iklé, telephone interview with author, September 27, 1990; Thomas Graham, telephone interview with author, October 2, 1990; and Richard Moose, interview with author, Washington, D.C., October 4, 1990.

100. See U.S. Congress, Senate Committee on Foreign Relations, *Hearings on Prohibition of Chemical and Biological Weapons*, 93d Cong., 2d sess., 1974, and *The Geneva Protocol of 1925*, 93d. Cong., 2d sess., 1974, Executive Report, no. 93-35; Gerald Ford, Executive Order 11850, "Renunciation of Certain Uses in War of Chemical Herbicides and Riot Control Agents," April 8, 1975, *Federal Register* 40, no. 70 (April 10, 1975): 16187.

101. *Congressional Record*, 93d Cong. 2d sess., December 16, 1974, vol. 120, pt. 30, December 16, 1974, 40067–68.

Selected Bibliography

Books

Baker, Roscoe. *The American Legion and American Foreign Policy*. New York: Bookman Associates, 1954.

Brophy, Leo P., and George J. B. Fisher. *The Chemical Warfare Service: Organizing for War*, Vol. 1 of *The United States Army in World War II: The Technical Services*. History of the Chemical Warfare Service Series. Washington, D.C.: GPO, 1959.

Brown, Frederic J. *Chemical Warfare: A Study in Restraints*. Princeton, N.J.: Princeton University Press, 1968.

Buckley, Thomas H. *The United States and the Washington Conference, 1921-1922*. Knoxville: University of Tennessee Press, 1970.

Buckley, Thomas H., and Edwin B. Strong, Jr. *American Foreign and National Security Policies, 1914-1945*. Knoxville: University of Tennessee Press, 1987.

Buell, Raymond L. *The Washington Conference*. New York: D. Appleton and Co., 1922.

Challener, Richard D. Proceedings of the Committee on Foreign Relations, United States Senate, from December 3, 1923 to March 3, 1933. Vol. 2 of *The Legislative Origins of American Foreign Policy*. New York: Garland, 1979.

Coolidge, Calvin. *Foundations of the Republic: Speeches and Addresses*. New York: Charles Scribner's Sons, 1926.

Duffield, Marcus. *King Legion*. New York: Jonathan Cape & Harrison Smith, 1931.

Ellis, Ethan L. *Frank B. Kellogg and American Foreign Relations, 1925-1929*. New Brunswick, NJ: Rutgers University Press, 1961.

———. *Republican Foreign Policy, 1921-1933*. New Brunswick, N.J.: Rutgers University Press, 1968.

Ferrell, Robert H. *Peace in Their Time: The Origins of the Kellogg-Briand Pact*. 1952. Reprint. New York: W. W. Norton and Co., 1969.

Fleming, Denna Frank. *The United States and the League of Nations, 1918-1920*. New York: G. P. Putnam, 1932.

Fuess, Claude M. *Calvin Coolidge: The Man from Vermont*. Boston, Mass.: Little, Brown & Co., 1940.

Guinsburg, Thomas N. *The Pursuit of Isolationism in the United States Senate from Versailles to Pearl Harbor*. New York: Garland, 1982.

Gumbel, E. J. "Disarmament and Clandestine Rearmament Under the Weimer Republic." In *Inspection for Disarmament*, edited by Seymour Melman. New York: Columbia University Press, 1958.

Hoag, C. Leonard. *Preface to Preparedness: The Washington Disarmament Conference and Public Opinion*. Washington, D.C.: American Council on Public Affairs, 1941.

Irwin, Will. *"The Next War": An Appeal to Common Sense*. New York: E. P. Dutton & Co., 1921.

Johnson, Claudius O. *Borah of Idaho*. 1936. Reprint. Seattle: University of Washington Press, 1967.

Johnson, Hiram. *The Diary Letters of Hiram Johnson*, vol. 4. New York: Garland, 1983.

Maddox, Robert J. *William E. Borah and American Foreign Policy*. Baton Rouge: Louisiana State University Press, 1969.

Margulies, Herbert F. *The Mild Reservationists and the League of Nations Controversy in the Senate*. Columbia: University of Missouri Press, 1989.

McCoy, Donald R. *Calvin Coolidge: The Quiet President*. New York: Macmillan Co., 1967.

——. *Coming of Age: The United States During the 1920's and 1930's*. Baltimore, Md.: Penguin, 1973.

McKee, John Hiram. *Coolidge Wit and Wisdom*. New York: Frederick P. Stokes, 1933.

Nelson, Walter H. *Germany Rearmed*. New York: Simon and Schuster, 1972.

Prentiss, Augustin M., and George J. B. Fisher. *Chemicals in War: A Treatise on Chemical Warfare*. New York: McGraw-Hill, 1937.

Quint, Howard H., and Robert H. Ferrell, eds. *The Talkative President: The Off-the-Record Press Conferences of Calvin Coolidge*. Amherst: University of Massachusetts Press, 1964.

Stockholm International Peace Research Institute. *The Problem of Chemical and Biological Warfare*. Vol. 4 of *CB Disarmament Negotiations, 1920-1970*. New York: Humanities Press, 1971.

Stone, Ralph. *The Irreconcilables: The Fight Against the League of Nations*. Lexington: University Press of Kentucky, 1970.

Thomas, Ann Van Wynen, and A. J. Thomas, Jr. *Legal Limits on the Use of Chemical and Biological Weapons*. Dallas, Tex.: Southern Methodist University Press, 1970.

Government Publications

Coolidge, Calvin. *Message to the Senate*. January 12, 1926. Record Group 46. Treaty Files. Sen 80B-B26, 8E4/16/2, Tray 88. National Archives.

Ford, Gerald. Executive Order 11850, "Renunciation of Certain Uses in War of Chemical Herbicides and Riot Control Agents," April 8, 1975. *Federal Register* 40, no. 70 (April 10, 1975): 16187.

Truman, Harry S. "Message of the President to the Senate, April 8, 1947." *Department of State Bulletin* 16, no. 407 (April 20, 1947): 726-27.

United Nations. *Treatment of the Question of Chemical and Bacteriological Warfare in the League of Nations: Review by the United Nations Secretariat*. U.N. Document A/AC.50/3 (August 3, 1951): 26-51. Reproduced in U.S. Congress. Senate. Committee on Foreign Relations. Subcommittee on Disarmament. *Disarmament and Security:*

A Collection of Documents, 1919-55. 84th Cong., 2d sess., 1956. Committee Print, 170-88.

U.S. Congress. *Congressional Record.* Washington, D.C., 1922-27.

U.S. Congress. Senate. *Conference on the Limitation of Armament.* 67th Cong., 2d sess., 1922. S. Doc. 126.

————. *Message from the President of the United States transmitting the Protocol for the Prohibition of the Use in War of Asphyxiating, Poisonous, or Other Gases, and of Bacteriological Methods of Warfare, signed at Geneva June 17, 1925.* 91st Cong., 2d sess. August 19, Executive J.

————. *Prohibiting Use of Gases in War: Message from the President of the United States.* 69th Cong., 1st sess., 1926. Executive G. Record Group 46. Treaty Files. Sen 80B-B26, 8E4/16/2, Tray 88. National Archives.

————. *Prohibiting Use of Gases in Warfare: Report from Senator Borah, Committee on Foreign Relations.* 69th Cong., 1st sess., June 26, 1926. Calendar No. 16. Report No. 1. Record Group 46. Treaty Files. Sen 80B-B26, 8E4/16/2, Tray 88. National Archives. Reproduced in U.S. Congress. Senate. Committee on Foreign Relations. Subcommittee on Disarmament. *Disarmament and Security: A Collection of Documents, 1919-55.* 84th Cong., 2d sess., 1956. Committee Print, 700-704.

U.S. Congress. Senate. Committee on Foreign Relations. *The Geneva Protocol of 1925.* 93d Cong., 2d sess., 1974. Executive Rept. No. 93-35.

————. *Hearings on the Geneva Protocol of 1925 (1971).* 92d Cong., 1st sess., 1972.

————. *Hearings on Prohibition of Chemical and Biological Weapons.* 93d Cong., 2d sess., 1974.

U.S. Congress. Senate. Committee on Foreign Relations. Subcommittee on Disarmament. *Disarmament and Security: A Collection of Documents, 1919-55.* 84th Cong., 2d sess., 1956. Committee Print.

U.S. Department of State. *Papers Relating to the Foreign Relations of the United States, 1925,* vol. 1. Washington, D.C.: GPO, 1940.

————. *Papers Relating to the Foreign Relations of the United States, 1926,* vol. 1. Washington, D.C.: GPO, 1941.

U.S. National Security Council. National Security Decision Memorandum 35. November 25, 1969. NNMM Collection of NSC Documents. Folder "National Security Decision Memoranda." National Archives.

————. National Security Study Memorandum 59. May 28, 1969. NNMM Collection of NSC Documents. Folder "National Security Decision Memoranda." National Archives.

Unpublished Works:

"Disarming America." N.p. [1925].

4 The Limited Test Ban Treaty

Benjamin S. Loeb

The Limited Test Ban Treaty came at the end of nearly five years of frustrated efforts to obtain a comprehensive test ban. Negotiations toward that end had begun in October 1958. At the same time a voluntary, informal moratorium on tests was initiated. The negotiations soon stalled over the Soviet Union's resistance to internationally supervised inspections on its soil. This problem mostly concerned underground tests, which were difficult to distinguish from earthquakes with monitoring equipment located far from the test site. To overcome the problem, President Dwight D. Eisenhower proposed in April 1959 a phased ban that was to be limited at first to atmospheric tests conducted below an altitude of 50 kilometers. Such tests were thought to be easily verifiable. The Soviets rejected this idea and continued to insist that a complete test ban need not require numerous inspections. The two sides nevertheless appeared to be nearing agreement on a treaty to ban all but relatively small underground tests when, in May 1960, an U.S. U-2 reconnaissance plane was shot down over Soviet territory. The bitter recriminations against Eisenhower that followed made it impossible to progress further toward a test ban while he was president.[1]

After a thorough review of the U.S. position, the Kennedy administration proposed in April 1961 a draft treaty that made several concessions toward the Soviet position. Nevertheless, the Soviets, still disagreeing with the provisions for verification and with the makeup of the control

The author wishes to thank George Bunn, Frederick G. Dutton, John E. Rielly, and John G. Stewart for very helpful comments offered after reviewing a first draft of this chapter.

organization, rejected it.

In September 1961 the Soviets suddenly broke the voluntary moratorium that had been established in October 1958 by conducting a massive and obviously long-prepared series of atmospheric tests. The U.S. response was to resume testing underground and, beginning in April 1962, in the atmosphere. Under pressure of world opinion, negotiations for a test ban treaty nevertheless resumed after March 1962 at a newly established Eighteen Nation Disarmament Committee, in which eight nonaligned nations played an active part. On August 27, 1962, the United States and the United Kingdom jointly unveiled two new treaty proposals, one covering testing in all environments, the other limited to tests in the atmosphere, under water, and in outer space. The Soviets rejected both treaties, the comprehensive one because of its inspection requirements, the limited one because it permitted underground testing to continue.

In October 1962 the world was shaken by the Cuban missile crisis. This searing experience, which made it clear to both sides that a nuclear war could indeed happen, seemed to draw President John F. Kennedy and Soviet Premier Nikita Khrushchev into a closer relationship in which they corresponded and exchanged ideas more frequently, with greater mutual sympathy, and with what seemed to be a shared desire to make progress toward a test ban treaty. The main stumbling block still appeared to be the number of on-site inspections, with the United States now publicly offering to accept an annual quota of seven (down from the previous demand of twenty), the Soviets maintaining an offer of three, and then, in pique over an apparent misunderstanding, withdrawing even that offer.

To break the deadlock, the United States and the British suggested in April 1963 that they send senior representatives to talk directly with Khrushchev in Moscow. The latter assented, though in a disagreeable tone that offered little encouragement. To improve the atmosphere, Kennedy delivered on June 10 a masterfully wrought, conciliatory speech at The American University in Washington. The speech had its desired effect, and, after the small Western delegations (the U.S. one headed by W. Averell Harriman)[2] arrived in Moscow on July 15, it proved possible in ten days to agree on the Treaty Banning Nuclear Weapon Tests in the Atmosphere, in Outer Space and Under Water, which differed very little from the U.S.-U.K. draft of the previous August. The treaty was initialed on July 25, 1963, signed in Moscow in an atmosphere of celebration on August 5, and transmitted to the Senate by President Kennedy on August 8.

International Political Context

Although President Kennedy would have preferred a comprehensive test ban treaty, he was highly pleased with the treaty signed in Moscow. "No other accomplishment in the White House," wrote Theodore C. Sorensen, "ever gave Kennedy greater satisfaction."[3]

The president was frank in acknowledging the treaty's limitations. "This treaty is not the millennium," he told the nation the day after it was initialed. "It will not resolve all conflicts, or cause the Communists to forgo their ambitions, or eliminate the dangers of war. It will not reduce our need for arms or allies or programs of assistance to others." At the same time Kennedy emphasized the treaty's value as a step toward highly significant objectives, saying, "It is an important first step—a step toward peace—a step toward reason—a step away from war."

Symptomatic of the hope engendered by the treaty was the fact that the "doomsday clock" on the cover of the *Bulletin of the Atomic Scientists*, which had stood at seven minutes to midnight, was set back after the treaty was signed to twelve minutes to midnight, its most optimistic reading since the clock was first published in 1947. Nevertheless, there were those who warned that optimism about the treaty's political effects was itself a danger. Indeed, Joint Chiefs of Staff (JCS) Chairman Maxwell Taylor testified that the chiefs' most serious reservation about the treaty was that it might give rise to a state of euphoria "which will eventually reduce our vigilance and the willingness of our country and of our allies to expend continued effort on our collective security."[4] Secretary of Defense Robert McNamara acknowledged that the possibility of undue euphoria was his chief concern also.[5] Treaty proponents, however, pointed to the military safeguards being adopted at the behest of the joint chiefs (discussed below in the section on domestic political context) as evidence that the nation's readiness would be maintained at a high level.

A second benefit that Kennedy emphasized in espousing the treaty, in addition to its value as a first step, was its likely effect in stemming the spread of nuclear weapons capability to additional countries. This seems to have been Kennedy's principal motive in his pursuit of a comprehensive test ban. Thus, Atomic Energy Commission (AEC) Chairman Glenn T. Seaborg, with reference to a National Security Council meeting on February 8, 1963, recorded in his diary: "The president said that, in his opinion, the principal reason for having a test ban was its possible effect in arresting or preventing the nuclear development of other nations, particularly China. If it weren't for this possible gain, it wouldn't be worth the internal disruption, fighting with Congress, and so forth."[6]

A month later Kennedy said to reporters: "I am haunted by the feeling that by 1970, unless we are successful [in achieving a test ban treaty], there may be ten nuclear powers instead of four, and by 1975, fifteen or twenty. I regard that as the greatest possible danger."[7]

It was acknowledged that a comprehensive test ban would be a more effective anti-proliferation measure than the signed limited treaty. Still, the latter was thought to introduce some inhibitions to proliferation in that underground testing was more difficult, costly, and time-consuming than atmospheric testing.[8] Furthermore, the international climate following widespread adherence to the treaty was thought likely to increase the political costs for any nation intent on acquiring nuclear weapons.

A third benefit of the treaty adduced by the president was that it would reduce contamination of the world's atmosphere by radioactive fallout. Here Kennedy was playing into an area of known public sensitivity. As the ratification debate proceeded, the treaty's benefit in curtailing fallout turned out to be the leading basis for its popular support.

Overhanging the test ban negotiations and the ratification debate in 1963 were several dramatic and momentous events. The previous year's Cuban missile crisis, when, as Secretary of State Dean Rusk testified, "men had a chance to peer into the pit of the inferno,"[9] had injected several new ingredients into the situation. These included (1) an improvement in the president's standing in the country and with Congress, particularly as regards confidence in his willingness and ability to stand up to the Soviet Union; (2) greater public awareness of the fearful dangers of nuclear confrontation; (3) a clearer awareness within the Soviet leadership of President Kennedy's willingness to use force, even nuclear force, in defense of vital U.S. interests; and (4) an increase in the intensity of the president's pursuit of a test ban.

Another past event influencing the ratification debate was the Soviet Union's sudden resumption of testing in September 1961. Within sixty days the Soviets conducted fifty tests, exceeding in megatonnage all preceding tests by all nations. They followed these 1961 tests with a further extensive series in late 1962. The two series were widely believed to have given the Soviets a lead in the knowledge and technology of high-yield and high-altitude weapons and their effects, and this was thought to constitute a substantial military advantage.[10] It was argued, for example, that being behind in these areas prevented the United States from acquiring the ability to penetrate hardened Soviet targets, from knowing how vulnerable its own missile silos were to enemy attacks, how vulnerable its own missile silos were to enemy attacks, from learning about weapons effects such as the blackout of radar electronics by high-altitude bursts,[11] and from acquiring an effective antiballistic missile (ABM).

Treaty opponents argued further that whereas the treaty prevented the United States from catching up with the Soviets in these fields where they were ahead, it permitted the Soviets, by testing underground, to catch up in areas where the United States was ahead, in weapons of low and medium yield. Such arguments were made most impressively by Edward Teller, then an associate director of the Livermore weapons laboratory, who testified before the Senate Foreign Relations Committee (SFRC) for a full day, having previously testified before the Senate Armed Services Committee's Preparedness Investigating Subcommittee. Senate supporters of the treaty, concerned about the impression left by Teller, believed it necessary to mount a scientific refutation. The witnesses used for this purpose included George Kistiakowsky, who had been Eisenhower's science adviser; Harold Brown, director of defense research and engineering; and Herbert L. York, who had occupied that post under Eisenhower. A telling point made about Brown's testimony was that whereas he had all the information available to Teller, the reverse was not true. Regarding the alleged military disadvantages of the treaty, pro-treaty witnesses made, in summary, the following points:

● There was much doubt about the utility of high-yield weapons. The United States had previously considered and rejected their use.[12]

● There were no strong indications that as a result of their high-yield tests, the Soviets had superior knowledge about weapons effects.

● The numbers, separation, and hardening of the projected U.S. Minuteman force would provide an adequate margin to assure its survival, despite uncertainties about the effects of hostile attacks.

• There was no evidence that the Soviets were ahead of the United States in ABM development. Moreover, nuclear testing was not required to solve the major problems in this field.

• No matter what progress might be made on missile defense, indications were that offense would continue to prevail over defense.

• Although the Soviets could conceivably catch up with the United States by testing underground, it would be at higher cost and slower pace than if both sides could continue to test in the atmosphere. The treaty would therefore actually prolong U.S. military superiority.

Some opponents of the treaty argued that it would sow dissension with the United States' allies, particularly France and West Germany. It was evident from the first that French President Charles de Gaulle did not intend to have France sign the treaty. Kennedy tried to persuade de Gaulle to change his mind, offering to share with France nuclear weapons information previously made available only to the British. De Gaulle, however, haughtily refused, arguing that nuclear cooperation with the United States would violate French sovereignty.

The administration gave up on the French as a lost cause and then turned toward West Germany. The government of Konrad Adenauer was nervous that secret superpower understandings compromising the future of Germany might have been reached during the Moscow negotiations. The administration went to elaborate lengths to reassure the Germans that nothing of the kind had occurred. The U.S. embassy in Bonn briefed the Germans daily during the negotiations, and Secretary of State Dean Rusk spent seven hours with Adenauer on his way home from the signing ceremonies. These assurances were buttressed by the credibility Kennedy had established through his resolute behavior during the Berlin crisis of 1961. U.S. diplomatic efforts bore fruit on August 18, 1963, when West Germany became the sixty-seventh nation to sign the treaty.

A further West German concern was that the East Germany might gain de facto diplomatic recognition through its expected adherence to the treaty. The Soviets had a matching concern about Taiwan, a regime whose existence they did not acknowledge.[13] Both sides were reluctant to call world attention to this awkward problem, so it was not addressed in the language of the treaty. An explicit oral understanding was reached, however, whereby any of the three depositary governments (the United States, the United Kingdom, and the Soviet Union) could receive the ratification of any government not recognized by all three. The receiving country would then notify the other two, and the ratification would be considered valid without affecting recognition status. During his visit in Bonn, Rusk explained this agreement to the West Germans. In transmitting the treaty to the Senate, President Kennedy specifically stated that it did not "alter the status of unrecognized regimes." His assurance was supplemented later by Department of State testimony and legal opinions.[14] Despite all assurances, some nervousness on this point persisted.

An important factor overhanging the ratification debate was the mounting evidence that the split between the Soviets and the Chinese was deep and lasting. An indication of this was provided by the failed attempt at fence-mending by a high-ranking Chinese delegation that visited Moscow for prolonged negotiations beginning in late June 1963. Senator Robert Byrd (D-W.Va.) argued on the Senate floor that the split was a sham and that Soviet tests in violation of the treaty might be conducted in the People's Republic of China.[15] Few senators, however, shared this view, and it was considered an argument for the treaty that the treaty might exacerbate relations between the communist giants.

There was considerable speculation about why Khrushchev was willing in 1963 to accept a treaty not significantly different from ones he had previously rejected. Some, like Edward Teller and U.S. Air Force Chief of Staff Curtis LeMay, viewed this change of mind with deep suspicion, speculating that the Soviets might have achieved some important breakthrough in technology in their recent tests and wanted to foreclose the possibility that the United States would make a similar advance.[16] But Secretary Rusk, among others, pointed to the possibility that what was in the Soviet interest was not necessarily contrary to that of the United States, that "there are many agreements from which both sides take away advantage."[17] The Senate Foreign Relations Committee's report, based on testimony the committee had received, concluded that the Soviet's acceptance of the treaty arose from their confidence that they had achieved rough technical parity with the United States; the sobering implications of the Cuban missile crisis; a desire to isolate the Chinese within the communist world by showing a tangible benefit of the Soviet policy of coexistence; a need to divert resources from the burdens of the arms race to the area of consumer goods; and a desire to inhibit the proliferation of nuclear weapons.[18]

A strong influence on both the negotiation and ratification processes was a steady pressure from world opinion. A Department of State survey in early August 1963 indicated that sixty-four governments were rated as being highly favorable to the treaty, twenty-nine favorable, two noncommittal, sixteen undecided, and only three opposed.[19] At the Eighteen Nation Disarmament Committee in Geneva the eight nonaligned nations—Brazil, Burma, Ethiopia, India, Mexico, Nigeria, Sweden, and the United Arab Republic— consistently brought pressure on the nuclear powers to reach agreement on a comprehensive test ban. At times, the eight, under the goading leadership of Sweden's Alva Myrdal, advanced challenging proposals of their own. The superpowers were well aware that the nonaligned nations would not be satisfied by the retreat from a comprehensive to a limited test ban, and it was largely to placate this sentiment that the preamble to the treaty included, as a statement of future intent, the following words: "Seeking to achieve the discontinuance of all test explosions of nuclear weapons for all time, [and] determined to continue negotiations to this end. . . ."

An additional source of pressure on the Senate was the provision of the treaty that threw it "open to all States for signature." As of August 5, 1963, the date when the three "original parties" signed the treaty in Moscow, thirty-three nations had already indicated their intention to accede to it. By September 9, the date when the Senate began its floor debate, ninety nations had signed. To have rejected a treaty so widely endorsed, and one that the United States had itself sponsored, would have been a heavy responsibility for the Senate, tending to discredit the country's moral leadership in international affairs. Several senators indicated on the floor that this was a factor in their support of the treaty. Some expressed resentment that a gun was being placed to their heads in this manner. Karl Mundt (R-S.Dak.) argued, for example, that the procedure amounted to a downgrading of the constitutional rights of the Senate.[20] Richard Russell (D-Ga.) complained that although it was desirable for other nations to think well of the United States, the concern about world opinion had become "almost a national disease."[21]

Domestic Political Context

To maximize the treaty's impact as a "first step" toward further agreements and an improved international atmosphere, President Kennedy instructed his administration to seek in the Senate not mere approval but an overwhelming vote. As he noted in a news conference, "If we are to give it now only grudging support, if this small, clearly beneficial step cannot be approved by the widest possible margin in the Senate, then the Nation cannot offer much leadership or hope for the future."[22]

As the ratification contest drew near, the administration had only rough indications of what senatorial opinion was likely to be. There had previously been indications that a *comprehensive* treaty would fail in the Senate. Senator John O. Pastore (D-R.I.), chairman of the Joint Committee on Atomic Energy (JCAE), had written the president in March 1963 that ratification of the comprehensive treaty then being proposed by the United States "could only be obtained with the greatest difficulty."[23] Two months later a private poll conducted by Senator Joseph S. Clark (D-Pa.), an enthusiastic test ban supporter, indicated that the same treaty would fall ten votes short in the Senate.[24]

Indications concerning a limited test ban treaty were more hopeful. One came from a resolution introduced on May 27, 1963, by Hubert H. Humphrey (D-Minn.) and Thomas J. Dodd (D-Conn.), and endorsed by thirty-two other senators, declaring it the sense of the Senate that the United States should again offer the Soviets a limited treaty. Although this resolution was never brought to a vote, it strongly suggested that some opponents of a comprehensive test ban, such as Dodd himself, would not be hostile to a limited treaty.

A second straw in the wind was an "Estimate of Senate Vote" on the already initialed Limited Test Ban Treaty put together by the Federation of American Scientists (F.A.S.) early in August 1963. It listed twenty senators as "Probable No's" and an additional twenty-four in the category "Need Encouragement."[25] This left only fifty-five relatively sure votes for the treaty. The F.A.S. noted, however, that the large "Need Encouragement" group had been "drawn up by erring on the side of caution, [including] all senators about whom there [was] the slightest doubt."

Another head count was put together at about the same time by the U.S. Arms Control and Disarmament Agency (ACDA). It rated only eleven senators as "Against" and seventeen as "Probably Against," thus indicating a comfortable margin of approval even if all those "Probably Against" were lost.[26] This accorded with speculation in the media that the treaty was fairly certain to be approved. *Time*, for example, quoted "an influential Republican senator" as predicting a vote "at least 80 to 20 in favor."[27] President Kennedy, on the other hand, who had been pessimistic about his quest for a test ban from the beginning,[28] was, in the observation of George Bunn, then ACDA general counsel, "running scared."[29] On August 7, Kennedy told a group of administration officials and private citizens that if a vote was held right then it would fall far short of the necessary two-thirds.[30]

In truth, none of these early estimates, including that by President Kennedy, represented much more than an educated guess.[31] In advance of the committee hearings most senators appear simply not to have made up their minds. As minority whip Thomas H. Kuchel (R-Calif.) observed: "We have got some senators who said they were for this treaty almost immediately. We have got some others who said they were against it almost immediately. I think the rest of us are the great majority."[32] Similarly, Dodd commented at the end of Teller's testimony, "I haven't made up my mind despite the fact that I offered that resolution with my colleague from Minnesota [Humphrey], and I am not ashamed or afraid to say that I may change my mind, and I think we should all wait until we hear all the testimony."[33]

One of the prominent themes in the ratification debate was the perception of the Soviet Union as a negotiating partner that could not be trusted. This view had been reinforced by the Soviet resumption of testing in 1961, which had seemed to be an abrogation of an agreement between the powers, albeit an informal one.[34] It became one of the underlying assumptions of the debate that the Soviets would violate the test ban treaty if they could get away with it and might suddenly abrogate it at any time if that seemed to their advantage. President Kennedy and others in the administration did not challenge this assumption, even though Secretary Rusk introduced evidence that the Soviet Union had satisfactorily observed some twenty-seven multilateral and bilateral agreements to which the United States was a party.[35] Instead, treaty supporters contented themselves with arguing that what little the Soviets might accomplish by clandestine tests in violation of the treaty would be too inconsequential to affect the military balance and that, as Kennedy observed in transmitting the treaty to the Senate, "the risk to the United States from such violation is outweighed by the risk of a continued unlimited arms race."

Nor did the administration contest treaty opponents' estimates of Soviet intentions. In the words of Senator Strom Thurmond (R-S.C.) these were, quite simply, to "dominate and enslave the world."[36] Against such extreme characterizations, members of the administration argued that the treaty would make it more, rather than less, difficult for the Soviets to accomplish any sinister aims they might harbor.

Negative perceptions of the Soviet Union became an important factor in a running debate on what was militarily necessary for U.S. national security. Many critics of the treaty maintained that, granted Soviet ambitions and perfidy, the United States would not be secure unless it continued to possess "a substantial margin of superiority."[37] A typical expression was that by U.S. Air Force Chief of Staff LeMay: "I would never be happy with a situation where we had parity with our enemies."[38] (Some twenty senators expressed similar views during the floor debate.)[39]

The argument then proceeded that the desired substantial superiority could be obtained only by equipping the armed services with the best weapons attainable and that this in turn could be done only if there were no restrictions on nuclear testing. Defenders of the treaty, on the other hand, argued that the arms race itself was inexorably weakening U.S. national security even as the nation's military power increased. Thus, Herbert L. York observed that in the early 1950s the Soviets could have attacked the United States with bombers and killed several millions; that in the late 1950s they could have attacked with bombers carrying hydrogen bombs and killed tens of millions; and that in the mid-1960s they could attack with bombers and intercontinental ballistic missiles and kill 100 million.[40] It was noteworthy, however, that, when pressed on the question, treaty supporters tended to agree with opponents that at least some superiority in nuclear weapons was important for U.S. security and the maintenance of peace.

The most stalwart senatorial support for the treaty centered in the Senate Foreign Relations Committee, particularly in Chairman J. William Fulbright (D-Ark.) and Hubert H. Humphrey. Through hearings extending back to 1958 before the committee's Disarmament Subcommittee, which Humphrey created and chaired, the senator from Minnesota had been tireless in drumming up support for disarmament in general and a test ban in particular.[41] The subcommittee had provided a forum to keep the arguments for arms control before the public even during periods of rising U.S.-Soviet tensions, such as in the aftermath of the U-2 incident. It also provided a rallying place for groups committed to arms control, such as A Citizen's Organization for a SANE World (SANE), the F.A.S., and United World Federalists. Humphrey had also been perhaps the single person most instrumental in obtaining passage in 1961 of the legislation establishing ACDA. A net effect of the senator's activity and that of his subcommittee was to help create a solid "infrastructure of support" that the administration was able to build on in seeking ratification of the test ban treaty.[42]

The SFRC's hearings on the treaty were well planned and conducted to make a strong case for ratification. It was in these hearings and in the committee's report, adopted by a vote of 15-1,[43] that the political arguments for the treaty achieved some of their most eloquent expression. At the same time, the hearings and report aimed to blunt criticisms of the treaty as having adverse national security effects. Fulbright and Humphrey were most skillful, for example, in leading scientific witnesses through the points that had been raised by Edward Teller so as to refute them, one by one.

Three potential sources of opposition were of foremost concern to the administration. These were the Republican minority in the Senate, particularly the more conservative among them; the membership of, and those strongly influenced by, the Senate Armed Services Committee, as led by senators Richard Russell and Henry M. ("Scoop") Jackson (D-Wash.); and the Joint Chiefs of Staff. Estimates were that opposition from any of these quarters, if intense enough, could deprive the president of the wide margin he sought and in one case, the joint chiefs, could probably defeat the treaty outright. It was sobering to realize that all three groups had opposed the test ban proposals the United States had been making in Geneva during the first six months of 1963.[44] A central task of the pro-treaty forces was, therefore, to win the support, or at worst to minimize the opposition, of these three groups. Two other important, if less worrisome, sources of opposition were the atomic energy establishment, particularly the weapons laboratories, and southern Democrats embittered by the struggle over civil rights. The situation with respect to each of the potential opposition groups, as it appeared to be at the outset of the debate on the treaty, is reviewed below.

Republicans

Simple arithmetic indicated that some Republican votes would be needed to achieve even a minimum two-thirds vote. There were sixty-six Democrats in the Senate (not counting Clair Engle [D-Calif.], who was gravely ill), versus thirty-three Republicans, and several southern Democrats were considered virtually certain to vote against the treaty. The likelihood of generalized Republican opposition was enhanced by the forthcoming presidential election, in which Kennedy's opponent was expected to be Senator Barry Goldwater (R-

Ariz.), one of the most vehement opponents of the treaty. Republican senators might well have been reluctant to repudiate the position of their colleague and prospective candidate on an issue so central to his way of thinking.

Given the initial uncertainty of most senators on this very complex issue, as described above by Senator Kuchel, it seemed likely that the attitude of many Republicans might be influenced by the positions of such recognized leaders of their party as former President Eisenhower and Senate minority leader Everett Dirksen (R-Ill.). Eisenhower's initial reaction to the treaty was cautious. On July 31 he indicated that he was "not ready to come out radically on either side because we still have to hear military and scientific opinion."[45] On August 23, however, he wrote to SFRC Chairman Fulbright and expressed his view that "with one specific reservation, the ratification of the treaty is desirable." (As to the reservation, see the section below on executive-congressional relations.)

Dirksen, on the other hand, seemed at first hostile toward the treaty. Immediately following Kennedy's announcement in his American University speech that negotiations were to take place in Moscow, Dirksen asked on the Senate floor whether this would be "another case of concession and more concession to Khrushchev." As the negotiations were about to begin a month later, he predicted that they might "end in our virtual surrender."[46] On July 30 he warned that the newly initialed treaty might open the way for recognition of East Germany and that it might lead to "underground development of nuclear warheads by Cuba."[47] He also declined an invitation to be a member of the delegation that went to Moscow for the signing ceremonies, stating that he wanted to preserve his freedom of action.

To minimize partisan divisions over his arms control efforts, Kennedy had appointed John J. McCloy, a prominent Republican attorney, as his disarmament adviser; William Foster, a Republican business executive, as the first director of ACDA; and another Republican attorney, Arthur H. Dean, as principal U.S. negotiator at the test ban talks in Geneva. In making these appointments, Kennedy seems to have been acknowledging a special burden assumed by Democratic administrations in the arms control field, the stock prejudice that they might be "soft on Communism."[48]

In the same vein Frederick G. Dutton, assistant secretary of state for congressional relations, who managed the administration's planning for the Senate vote on the treaty, believed that the hope for wide support was threatened not only by right-wing groups but by "supporters of the treaty like World Federalists, SANE, the Friends Committee, and other ban-the-bomb types." He suggested a discreet campaign to assure that such groups "do not get out in front."[49] When, at Dutton's suggestion and with the president's encouragement, a Citizens' Committee for a Nuclear Test Ban was formed to drum up support for the treaty, Kennedy persuaded James J. Wadsworth to head it. Wadsworth, a former Republican congressman, had been Eisenhower's chief test ban negotiator. In addition, the SFRC heard testimony from six witnesses who had held responsible positions in the Eisenhower administration. Five of these supported the treaty, the only exception being former AEC Chairman Lewis Strauss.

To attract Republican votes, there was also an attempt to associate the treaty with the agreement offered by Eisenhower in 1959 for a ban on tests in the atmosphere up to fifty kilometers. Kennedy's formulation was that the treaty "grew out of" Eisenhower's proposal.[50] Treaty supporters also called attention to the 1960 Republican platform, which quite unequivocally said, "We advocate an early agreement by all nations to forgo nuclear testing in the atmosphere."

The Armed Services Committee and Its Leaders

When President Kennedy transmitted the treaty to the Senate on August 8, 1963, "with a view to receiving the Senate's advice and consent to ratification," it was routinely referred to the Senate Foreign Relations Committee. It was pursuant to the SFRC's review that the treaty would or would not be referred to the whole Senate for formal action. Two other congressional committees had also interested themselves in the matter over the five years of test ban negotiations, however. These were the Senate Armed Services Committee, particularly its Preparedness Investigating Subcommittee, and the Joint Committee on Atomic Energy. Both of these committees had held hearings on several aspects of the test ban issue, and senators could be expected to look to them for guidance as well as to the SFRC.

Kennedy and Fulbright were especially concerned about the Preparedness Investigating Subcommittee as a competing center of influence. In addition to its chairman, John Stennis (D-Miss.), the group included among its seven members such influential senators as Jackson, Goldwater, and Thurmond. The subcommittee had begun hearings on the military and technical implications of various test ban proposals in September 1962. Initially the focus had been on the comprehensive test ban then being negotiated in Geneva, but it quickly shifted after the Moscow negotiations to a consideration of the Limited Test Ban Treaty. In eleven days of closed hearings on the treaty the subcommittee collected 2,800 pages of testimony from twenty-four witnesses before submitting its report on September 9, 1963, the day that debate began on the Senate floor. Consistent with the subcommittee's intention to confine itself to military and technical aspects, sixteen of the witnesses were from the Department of Defense or the armed services, including all of the joint chiefs, but not including Secretary of Defense McNamara. Although the subcommittee's hearings were not open to the public, the highlights of each day's testimony were selectively made available. Based on this testimony, the subcommittee concluded that "serious—perhaps even formidable—military and technical disadvantages [would] flow from the ratification of the treaty."[51] The report spelled out in some detail the reasons for this conclusion, primarily those summarized in the section above on international political context.

President Kennedy was greatly concerned over what the Preparedness Investigating Subcommittee's activity might portend as to the attitude of Scoop Jackson. Probably the Senate's most authoritative member on matters dealing with nuclear weapons, Jackson was in constant touch with scientists at the Livermore weapons laboratory, and he was very much in tune with their objections to any test ban agreement. From time to time Jackson called Livermore experts in to testify before the JCAE's Subcommittee on Nuclear Weapons, of which he was chairman. At the time the treaty was initialed, Jackson indicated that he was "cautiously skeptical" about the effect it would have on U.S. security.[52] So concerned was the administration about Jackson that, on the day the treaty was initialed, Harriman sent the senator the following cable from Moscow, "I am convinced this is a good agreement for us in itself and may lead to others outside test ban field. Hope you will support it. Anyway, don't commit yourself until we have a full talk. Will be in Washington late Sunday. Warm regards. Harriman."[53]

Notwithstanding what Harriman may have told him when they talked, Jackson emphasized some of the treaty's adverse military effects during the Preparedness Investigating Subcommittee's hearings. For example, he asked each key witness virtually the same question, "Can the United States afford a position of parity or equality with the Soviet Union in nuclear weapons techniques and systems?" eliciting uniformly negative responses.[54] In an August 1963 phone conversation the president asked Fulbright how he thought Jackson would vote. Fulbright acknowledged that he could not tell. What worried him particularly was that Jackson was "such an advocate of Teller . . . so devoted to him. . . . " At the least, he thought Jackson might introduce some crippling amendment.[55]

There was similar uncertainty about Richard Russell, of whom Dean Rusk has written, "One of the most skillful parliamentarians the Senate has ever seen, Russell had

eighteen or twenty votes in his back pocket, mostly fellow
Southern senators, that he could deliver on any vote."[56]
Russell had said on "Meet the Press" (August 11, 1963) that
he hoped he could support the treaty, but he had also given
contrary indications.

The seriousness of the apparent threat from leaders of the
Armed Services Committee and their adherents played a large
part in determining the administration's overall strategy in the
ratification debate. Thus, even though much of Kennedy's
enthusiasm for the treaty was based on hopes that it would be
a first step toward further arms control agreements and a
more peaceful world, the administration downplayed such
notions during the debate. Instead, it concentrated on allaying
concerns that the treaty might have an adverse effect on the
military balance. The decision not to dispute negative
perceptions of the Soviet Union was consistent with this
strategy.

Certain tactical ploys were adopted to diminish the
importance of the Preparedness Investigating Subcommittee
as a competing source of influence to the SFRC. Thus, at the
opening of the SFRC's hearings on the treaty, Chairman
Fulbright announced that members of the Armed Services
Committee and the JCAE were being invited to sit on the dais
and ask questions of the witnesses along with SFRC members.
This was by way of implying that all important military or
technical issues could be fully dealt with at the SFRC hearings,
that there was no need for other committees to get involved.
At another point President Kennedy intervened in delicate
senatorial protocol in order to ensure that the joint chiefs
would publicly announce their support of the treaty through
the SFRC before being heard in private by the Preparedness
Investigating Subcommittee.[57]

The Joint Chiefs of Staff

Dean Rusk has observed that members of Congress tend
to be "hypnotized by the sight of a man in uniform."[58] This

has applied in particular to the joint chiefs of staff. The presumption has grown that the chiefs can generally muster the needed votes—one third of the Senate plus one—to defeat any arms control treaty they do not like. Thus, President Kennedy was only being realistic when he said, in an August 12, 1963, phone conversation with majority leader Mike Mansfield (D-Mont.): "I regard the Chiefs as key to this thing. . . . If we don't get the Chiefs just right, we can . . . get blown."[59]

The chiefs had been opposed to the comprehensive test ban proposals being discussed at Geneva over the previous five years. Their major objection, as stated by Chairman Maxwell Taylor was that in a situation where the United States could not test, the Soviets might do so clandestinely underground or in deep space and possibly achieve some important breakthrough in technology.[60] The chiefs had not bothered, however, to make their opposition known within the administration, largely because they did not take the test ban negotiations seriously. As General LeMay later testified, the chiefs were "caught a little bit by surprise at the seriousness of the administration trying to get a treaty signed" when the Moscow negotiations were announced.[61] Because they had said nothing to the contrary, it was assumed, when the Department of Defense formally signed off on the August 1962 proposals before they were presented at Geneva, that the chiefs were on board. As George Bunn, who was ACDA general counsel at the time, writes, "I could not imagine a DOD [Department of Defense] clearance that didn't include at least some review by the Chiefs."[62]

Matters came to a head at an interagency meeting on June 14, 1963, four days after Kennedy's American University speech.[63] The purpose of the meeting had been to make final the U.S. position in the upcoming negotiations. At the very start of the meeting, General Taylor stated that the chiefs were not ready to approve the current U.S. position regarding a comprehensive test ban. This brought an uncharacteristic outburst from the usually reticent Dean Rusk. He pointed out that the position had been thoroughly reviewed within the government and approved by the president. Unless changed by the president, it would be the position represented by Harriman in Moscow. Rusk added, pointedly, that he would not dare take a foreign policy position that differed from that of the president. McNamara attempted a mediating role. He indicated that the chiefs' opposition was based on some technical findings by AEC's weapons laboratories that he, McNamara, thought were inaccurate. Until these findings were refuted, however, the chiefs, who relied on the laboratories for technical guidance, were in a difficult position. The findings were under review, McNamara said.[64]

The review failed to resolve the doubts of the chiefs regarding a comprehensive treaty. Then, just two days before Harriman's departure, General Taylor dropped another bombshell. At a National Security Council meeting attended by the president, Taylor said he thought there should be further study on whether even a *limited* test ban was to the advantage of the United States. Kennedy promptly ruled against such a study at that late hour. He fully appreciated, however, the difficulty of facing a ratification debate without having the chiefs on board. Accordingly, he began a renewed quest for their support while the Moscow negotiations were still in progress.

On July 23 Kennedy talked with the chiefs as a group, having discussed the pending limited treaty with each service chief individually the week before. It is probable that it was in these conversations that the president made his pivotal commitment to support four military "safeguards" advocated by the chiefs. As announced by General Taylor in his testimony to the SFRC, these were (1) an "aggressive" underground test program, (2) maintenance of "modern" weapons laboratories, (3) readiness to resume atmospheric testing promptly, and (4) improvement of the U.S. capability to monitor Sino-Soviet nuclear activity. At the SFRC hearings Taylor testified that if these safeguards were established, the chiefs would favor accepting the military risks inherent in the treaty in order to seek its political benefits. Under questioning, he and each of the other chiefs assured senators that this position represented their "agreed views" and that no pressure had been put on any of them to adopt it. To underscore the importance of the safeguards, each of the four service chiefs stated specifically that in the absence of safeguards he would have recommended disapproval of the treaty.[65] Indeed, Goldwater elicited from LeMay an acknowledgment that if the treaty had not already been initialed, he might have been against it even with the safeguards.[66]

Whatever may have been their lack of enthusiasm, the chiefs supported the treaty on the record, and none of them broke ranks publicly. Thus, a major threat to the treaty in the Senate was averted.[67]

The Atomic Energy Establishment

As already indicated, the views of the AEC's weapons laboratories were frequently represented on Capitol Hill by members of the JCAE, especially Senator Jackson. Even more important, however, was the influence that the laboratories had on the joint chiefs of staff. The chiefs repeatedly made it clear that they relied on the laboratories for technical advice. Because of this tie to the chiefs, the laboratories may have exercised more influence on the ratification debate than did the AEC commissioners, who, in the testimony of Chairman Seaborg and Commissioner Lee Haworth, loyally supported the treaty.

The atomic energy establishment (defined here as including the AEC, the weapons laboratories, and the JCAE) also had an important parochial interest that affected its attitude toward the treaty: the AEC's program for peaceful nuclear explosions, which was called the Plowshare program. The Western draft treaty of August 27, 1962, which provided the basis for the signed treaty, proposed an exemption for peaceful nuclear explosions under certain conditions. This provision was deleted in the Moscow negotiations in response to Soviet arguments that it would diminish the treaty's international appeal.[68] Instead, Article 1 of the treaty took direct aim at peaceful nuclear explosions by forbidding in the prohibited environments (atmosphere, under water, and space) not only a "nuclear weapons test explosion" but also "any other nuclear explosion." This action in Moscow, taken without the prior knowledge of anyone in Congress, embittered several members of the JCAE who were ardent supporters of Plowshare.[69] In particular, it was feared that it would rule out important excavation experiments that were preliminary to some major projects around the world, such as the excavation by nuclear means of a second Panama Canal.

In assessing how much damage the treaty would do to the Plowshare program, much depended on the interpretation given several undefined words in the treaty's provisions regarding underground explosions. These were considered to be atmospheric explosions, and therefore prohibited, if they caused "radioactive debris to be present" outside the exploding nation's territory. AEC Chairman Seaborg, adopting a "commonsense" interpretation of the words "radioactive debris" as meaning a significant amount having some conceivable relation to human health, testified that this provision would allow those Plowshare excavation experiments that had a "downwind distance of several hundred miles from the project site to a territorial limit."[70] Based principally on Seaborg's testimony, the SFRC reported to the Senate its understanding that "the Plowshare program . . . will not be seriously inhibited by the treaty." Seaborg believes that his testimony and the resulting SFRC conclusion had a strong influence in moving Senator Clinton Anderson (D-N.Mex.), Jackson, and perhaps others from a doubtful to a favorable position on the treaty's ratification.

By April 1964, however, the ACDA had begun to argue for a much stricter interpretation of the treaty's language, one that would consider as a violation the escape across a U.S.

border of *any* measurable radioactivity from an underground explosion, even a minute amount. ACDA argued that to adopt any other standard would injure the reputation of the United States as a country that took arms control agreements seriously. This interpretation, which clearly outlawed virtually all excavation experiments, prevailed within the government and contributed to Plowshare's final decline. Years later, still contending that his interpretation of the treaty was the only one that made sense, Seaborg worried that he may unintentionally have misled some senators by his optimistic testimony.[71]

Southern Democrats

A principal concern of President Kennedy when the Senate began its consideration of the signed treaty was that there might be a wholesale defection of southern Democrats angered over the wide-ranging civil rights bill he had submitted to Congress on June 19, 1963.[72] Submission of the legislation had followed some exceedingly bitter confrontations in the South. This danger was made the more acute because many southern senators had habitually conservative views on defense issues, often following the lead of Richard Russell on such matters.

Role of the President

While in the Senate John F. Kennedy made the need for a nuclear test ban agreement a principal personal theme. In November 1959, during the nuclear testing moratorium, he opposed pressures for resumption of testing by the United States. He proposed instead redoubled U.S. efforts to achieve a "comprehensive and effective" test ban, saying "Both sides in this fateful struggle must come to know, sooner or later, that the price of running this arms race to the end is death—for both. . . . Our job is to bring the peaceful processes of history into play quickly, even though the ultimate resolution may take generations—or even centuries. . . . We should not let our fears hold us back from pursuing our hopes."[73]

Kennedy's interest in seeking a test ban seems to have grown even stronger after he became president. He mentioned it frequently in his public utterances. Thus, in a May 1961 address to Congress on "urgent national needs," the president called for a test ban as part of the "the creation of an orderly world where disarmament will be possible."[74]

Kennedy resisted pressures within his administration to resume testing in the spring of 1961, apparently unconvinced that there was any military necessity to do so.[75] He was highly skeptical about the value of most nuclear tests. His skepticism was increased by the meager results achieved in the mishap-filled 1962 atmospheric series and by instances in which U.S. underground tests vented into the atmosphere.[76]

Jerome Wiesner, Kennedy's science adviser, reported that the president "spent hundreds and hundreds of hours" studying the nuclear testing issue.[77] After the Cuban missile crisis he began to focus his energy and attention on it beyond probably any other activity. The president's dedication to the test ban treaty, once it was signed, was such that he confided to associates his readiness, if necessary, to forfeit his reelection for its sake.[78]

During Kennedy's first two years in office, there was a widespread feeling that he was too naive and unsure of himself to deal effectively with the Soviets. This feeling had been nurtured by the Bay of Pigs fiasco, the unsuccessful summit meeting with Khrushchev in Vienna in June 1961, and the administration's passive reaction to construction of the Berlin Wall. Kennedy's firm handling of the Berlin crisis of 1961, however, helped to diminish these doubts about him, and they were all but erased by the manner in which he faced down Khrushchev in the Cuban missile crisis.

An important factor in the drive for a test ban was the degree of unity achieved within the Kennedy administration. At its top levels the administration harbored very little of the internal feuding and backbiting that have characterized some others. Rusk, McNamara, and National Security Adviser McGeorge Bundy, for example, worked together in excellent harmony, despite the many opportunities for friction that existed among their operations. They were united on the desirability of a test ban.

Below the cabinet level there was some resistance to a test ban by agency officials concerned about its possible effect on departmental missions. Some in the Department of State believed that the treaty unduly disturbed interallied relations, particularly with West Germany. The AEC's weapons laboratories worried about their ability to recruit and retain quality professionals if the opportunity to experiment was curtailed. Within the Department of Defense, the air force was especially resistant, protesting that its mission and the nation's defenses, particularly the ability to deploy an effective ballistic missile defense, would be weakened in the absence of atmospheric testing. Dissension of this nature, although not silenced, was effectively bottled up by agency heads sympathetic to the president's objectives. When the critical decisions were made in the spring and summer of 1963, Kennedy tended to restrict information and consultation to a very few top officials and thereby to limit the potential for objections and delay from within the bureaucracy.

To the extent that there were differences among agencies, these were often worked out in the Committee of Principals, a group established by President Eisenhower specifically to coordinate administration review of arms control policy. Under Eisenhower the group consisted of the secretary of state (chairman), the secretary of defense, the national security adviser, the director of central intelligence, and the chairman of the AEC. Kennedy enlarged the group by adding the director of the U.S. Information Agency,[79] the director of ACDA, and the chairman of the Joint Chiefs. Backstopping the Committee of Principals was a Committee of Deputies, composed of second-echelon officials of the same organizations and chaired, in Kennedy's time, by Adrian Fisher, deputy director of ACDA and a consummate arms control professional.

Disappointed by his failure to gain a comprehensive test ban, Kennedy believed, as already indicated, that a limited treaty might still have significant benefit if momentum could be imparted by an overwhelming Senate vote, and he decided to exert maximum effort in quest of such a margin. As Assistant Secretary Dutton wrote to Secretary Rusk on August 8, 1963, Kennedy instructed Dutton to mount a public campaign that was "to be carried on with more directness than has been undertaken thus far in the administration in relation to any other piece of pending legislation."[80]

In the final drive for a test ban Kennedy assumed personal command of the process to an extent unusual for a president, attending not only to broad strategy but also to tactical details. He did this despite other important demands on his time.[81] Kennedy's personal involvement included the following activities:

● During the negotiations in Moscow, Kennedy insisted that Harriman send a detailed account, not a summary, of each day's discussion. The president then closeted himself each evening at the White House with a handful of advisers and personally supervised the drafting of an answering cable containing instructions for the next day's negotiations.[82]

● The president participated actively in coordinating the testimony of pro-treaty witnesses at congressional hearings.[83]

● Kennedy used the "bully pulpit" of the presidency to full advantage in behalf of the treaty's ratification. The day the treaty was initialed in Moscow he went on national television to announce the event and to call on the nation to support its ratification, calling it "a shaft of light cut into the darkness."[84] He followed with an eloquent transmittal message to the Senate, three press conferences and two television interviews while the treaty was before the Senate, and a letter to the majority and minority leaders conveying important reassurances. (See the section below on executive-congressional relations.)

● Kennedy encouraged the formation of a Citizens' Committee for a Nuclear Test Ban and personally advised its officers on how best to conduct an effective campaign. As Norman Cousins, one of the committee's directors, wrote:

> He reiterated the need for important business support and suggested a dozen names. . . . He felt that religious leaders, farmers, educators, and labor leaders all had key roles to play and he mentioned a half dozen or more names in each category. Then he went down the list of states in which he felt extra effort was required. He was confident that [various liberal organizations] were going to continue to give full support . . . but he wanted to be sure that they did not make the test ban appear to be solely a liberal cause.[85]

Then, according to Cousins, the president added:

> You must not hesitate to use me in any situation where you think I can help. If there's any person you want me to communicate with personally, I'll do it. I want you to stay in close touch with me. I'd like to receive regular reports on your efforts and to know of problems as they develop.[86]

● Kennedy personally sought the public support of former President Harry S. Truman and saw to it that others did the same with Eisenhower. Both wrote letters of support.[87]

• The president personally screened the names of senators who were to be invited to attend the signing in Moscow. He even participated in deciding on who should invite each senator and the manner in which it was to be done.[88]

• As discussed above, Kennedy personally negotiated for, and won the essential support of, the joint chiefs of staff.

• He spoke privately to a number of senators. His meeting with majority leader Mike Mansfield and minority leader Everett Dirksen on September 9, 1963, may have been pivotal in gaining the support of Dirksen.

The fact that the test ban treaty was approved by a wide margin in the Senate may give the impression that the result was preordained. Such a conclusion overlooks the fact that votes on this issue tended to move in clusters. But for Kennedy's vigorous and skillful personal participation, more than one cluster might well have moved the other way.

Executive-Congressional Relations

President Kennedy started early and worked hard to put the Senate in a favorable frame of mind toward a test ban treaty. Having himself been a senator so recently, Kennedy was acutely aware of the sensitivities of the Senate as a whole and of individuals whom he knew well. He and leading members of the administration therefore treated the Senate with elaborate consideration, scrupulously informing and consulting with senators at every important turn in the road. Before presenting his first test ban proposal in Geneva in March 1961, Kennedy hosted a large White House luncheon at which the questions of congressional leaders were fully addressed. There was another such get-together to consider the U.S.

response when the Soviets suddenly resumed testing in September 1961.[89] Just before to the negotiations in Moscow, Secretary Rusk and ACDA Deputy Director Adrian Fisher each briefed the Senate Foreign Relations and Armed Services committees, as well as the Joint Committee on Atomic Energy.[90] While the negotiations were in progress Rusk again briefed the same three committees. At a meeting with the Senate Foreign Relations Committee two days before the treaty was initialed, the secretary showed the senators the current draft and invited their comments.[91] Rusk, Harriman, and Fisher then conducted a further series of briefings after the treaty was signed.[92] These were in addition to the continuing liaison maintained by ACDA officials with the three committees and with the House Foreign Relations Committee.

Remembering in particular Woodrow Wilson's triumphal but counterproductive tour of Europe in connection with the signing of the Treaty of Versailles, President Kennedy was determined to keep the spotlight off himself and, instead, to maximize the ceremonial role of the Senate. He therefore instructed Harriman to resist the known desire of both Harold Macmillan, British prime minister, and Khrushchev to have the treaty signed by heads of government at a summit conference. Harriman was instructed instead to "advise Soviets that for formalizing of treaty we expect perhaps as many as, but not more than, six senators to travel to Moscow with Secretary Rusk. It should be left open that the senators may, repeat may, wish to sign the treaty."[93] The next day Soviet Foreign Minister Andrey Gromyko announced that he had discussed the U.S. idea with Khrushchev and that the Soviet government would be pleased to welcome the senators.

The six senators were chosen with a view to having a maximum impact on their colleagues. From the Democratic side there were JCAE Chairman John O. Pastore and the three ranking Democrats on the SFRC: Fulbright, Humphrey, and John Sparkman (D-Ala.). Presaging the hostility of the Armed Services Committee toward the treaty, not one of its

Democratic members was willing to attend. The administration's first choices among Republicans were minority leader Dirksen and Bourke Hickenlooper (R-Iowa), ranking member on the Armed Services Committee. Both declined, saying they wished to preserve their freedom of action. The administration thereupon selected Leverett Saltonstall (R-Mass.) of the Armed Services Committee and George Aiken (R-Vt.) of the Foreign Relations Committee. The senators did not sign the treaty; the idea was not pursued by the U.S. side.

As the congressional hearings and floor debate proceeded, administration forces working for ratification maintained the closest liaison with pro-ratification forces in the Senate. The point man in this exercise was undoubtedly Hubert H. Humphrey. As the Senate's majority whip, and the body's most vocal and committed advocate of ratification, he readily assumed command of day-to-day operations. To quote John Stewart, Humphrey's legislative assistant at the time, "Humphrey and other pro-ratification senators, such as Clark, Pastore, and Fulbright, met almost daily with administration representatives such as Larry O'Brien, Fred Dutton, or Adrian Fisher, and representatives of external groups, to count votes and develop approaches for winning the support of undecided or wavering senators."[94]

Much of the opposition to the treaty seems to have been based on genuine concerns about its effects on national security. As discussed earlier, these concerns were based largely on fears about what the Soviets might have learned in their 1961–62 tests. By and large, the debate on the treaty was impressively bipartisan. Whatever the temptation, Republicans did not choose to make it a partisan issue. Support of the treaty by their floor leader, Dirksen, was undoubtedly important in preventing such a course. Dirksen made his declaration on September 11, the third day of the floor debate, before a crowded chamber.[95] Two days before, he, along with majority leader Mansfield, had met with President Kennedy. At the meeting Dirksen suggested that

Kennedy write the two Senate leaders a letter conveying various assurances. This the president readily agreed to do. Then, in a masterful political stroke, Kennedy asked Dirksen, not Mansfield, to read this letter to his colleagues.

The president's letter, a very strong document, picked up on the principal national security misgivings that had been raised, giving several "unqualified and unequivocal assurances." Kennedy repeated the pledges he had made to the joint chiefs: the United States would conduct a vigorous program of underground testing, remain ready to resume testing in the atmosphere, maintain strong weapons laboratories, and improve in its ability to detect violations of the treaty. It had become politically necessary to reaffirm these pledges because a number of senators had raised questions about the genuineness of the administration's commitment. It was one thing to affirm the four safeguards in principle. But when it came to actual implementation, would programs be prepared, would budgetary authority be sought, would expenditures actually be made for what could be very costly activities?[96] Senators appeared to have their doubts, and President Kennedy's letter was important in helping put these doubts to rest.[97] As if to underline the president's assurances, the AEC, two days after his letter was written, conducted two underground tests in Nevada, one of them yielding about a megaton.

In addition to implementing the four safeguards, the president wrote, the United States would retain the right to resume atmospheric testing *at once* if the Soviets violated the treaty—not in three months, as specified by the treaty's withdrawal clause. He stated that the treaty would not limit use of nuclear weapons for defense. Furthermore, the United States would take action if Cuba was used to circumvent or nullify the treaty. Nor would East German accession to the treaty change the U.S. policy of nonrecognition. Finally, international agreement would be sought to conduct aboveground Plowshare explosions when technical progress in the program made constructive uses of such explosions possible.

After reading the president's letter to the Senate, Dirksen, speaking without notes as was his wont, announced his support of the treaty. He pointed out that the 1960 Republican platform had advocated such a pact. He noted that "preponderant evidence" from the "most competent" scientific, military, and diplomatic leaders favored the treaty and that failure to ratify it would "place us in an awkward and difficult position with other nations." Referring to his age (sixty-seven), Dirksen then said: "I should not like to have written on my tombstone: 'He knew what happened at Hiroshima but he did not take a first step.' . . . If there be risks, I am willing to assume them for my country."[98]

Another eagerly awaited statement was that by Scoop Jackson. As noted earlier, he had given some indications that he was opposed to the treaty. Yet, when Jackson took the floor on September 13, it was to announce that "in the light of testimony given and understandings reached with respect to the policy of the administration in safeguarding the national interest," and of other considerations that he listed, he believed that the Senate might prudently give its advice and consent to ratification. The efficacy of the administration's strategy in meeting the opposition on its own terms was shown by two of the items on Senator Jackson's list of six considerations that led him to support the treaty. These two were (1) "no responsible official had based his recommendation on the view that basic Soviet purposes had changed" and (2) "no responsible official had based his case for the treaty on the belief that the Soviets could be trusted." The "other considerations" on Jackson's list were (3) no responsible official had disputed the view that national security depended on a favorable military position; (4) the secretary of defense and the joint chiefs had testified that the military balance favored the United States; (5) in Jackson's belief, men like Teller would devote their energies to overcoming the treaty's military disadvantages; and (6) hoped-for political gains from the treaty, although difficult to specify, could still be significant.

There were other noteworthy moments in the debate. On September 10 JCAE Chairman Pastore appealed dramatically to the undecided: "I want them to open their hearts and look into their consciences. . . . If by their vote they . . . kill the treaty, God help us, God help us!" Also on September 10 Hubert H. Humphrey held the floor for three and one-half hours. Acknowledging that the treaty had risks for the United States, he concluded that there would be far greater risks without the treaty. He noted that the treaty reduced the chance for war, minimized fallout, inhibited proliferation, and weakened the Communist bloc.[99] In the closing hours of the debate on September 23 Humphrey rose again and, in a remarkable tour de force, summarized thirty arguments that had been made against the treaty and briefly refuted each one "so that both proponents and opponents may have one more opportunity to reflect on this question."[100]

On September 13 John Stennis declared that he opposed the treaty because of what he had learned from the testimony presented to his Preparedness Investigating Subcommittee. He lingered somewhat bitterly over the part played by the joint chiefs in the debate. He insisted that an impartial jury would find that the chiefs were opposed to the treaty on military grounds, "their real field of competence," and that they had been "driven into . . . foreign policy" in order to find a basis for supporting it. Both Fulbright and Mansfield at this point vigorously disputed any insinuation that the chiefs had been pressured into giving their support, Fulbright noting that each one of them had denied this under oath.[101]

On September 17 Richard Russell announced his opposition. He said that the treaty would handicap U.S. efforts to develop an ABM and that it might be the first of a series of disarmament measures that would favor the Soviets. He added that he would favor a comprehensive test ban if it had adequate inspection. It is noteworthy, however, that Russell, in George Bunn's characterization, "did not play hardball" in that he made no visible effort to use his parliamentary talents to deliver the votes of other senators.[102]

In all, seventy-nine senators rose to state their positions during the two weeks of floor debate on the treaty. One reason for this extraordinarily high participation may have been a cooperative effort between Senator Humphrey's office and ACDA. Early in September, Humphrey requested ACDA to prepare fifteen short draft speeches for presentation by senators who had not previously been involved in the issue. They were to stress the treaty's political advantages. Humphrey hoped that once these senators "got their feet wet," they "might be prepared for some greater immersion in the future."[103] ACDA and Department of State staff also regularly attended the floor debate and were waved down from the gallery to the cloakroom to answer difficult questions as they arose.[104]

A potential hazard faced by the treaty during the ratification process was the introduction of various reservations. Only a majority vote was needed to pass a reservation. Legal authorities, among them former chief negotiator Arthur H. Dean, pointed out that if any reservation was attached to the treaty by the Senate, the entire document would have to be renegotiated with the Soviets and the British and resubmitted to all the other nations that had signed.[105] It was apparent that several reservations were introduced with malice aforethought by foes of the treaty who hoped to kill it through the achievement of a majority vote for some popular goal.

On the last day of floor debate various proposed reservations were voted on. One, introduced by Goldwater, would have delayed the effectiveness of the treaty until all Soviet forces were removed from Cuba under international inspection. It was rejected, 75–17. John Tower (R-Tex.) introduced two reservations providing, respectively, that the U.S. instrument of ratification not be deposited until (1) the USSR paid all its assessments for financing the peacekeeping operations of the United Nations (defeated 82–11) and (2) the treaty was revised to provide for on-site inspection (defeated 76–16).

Former President Eisenhower had at first urged a reservation stating that the treaty would not prevent U.S. use of nuclear weapons to repel aggression. His concern on this point arose from the cryptic language of Article 1 forbidding "any nuclear weapons test explosion, *or any other nuclear explosion*," in the prohibited environments (emphasis added). As explained earlier, the italicized words had been added to exclude peaceful explosions, but on their face they seemed unclear regarding the use of weapons in war.[106] Despite repeated reassurances by Secretary Rusk, the Department of State's legal adviser, and others, this question kept surfacing in the debate. At one point, Senator Humphrey burst out in exasperation that the right to use nuclear weapons in war "has been stated about twenty-five times today, and about a hundred times in the last week and a half in executive and public session."[107] The concern seemed to be finally put to rest by Kennedy's letter to Mansfield and Dirksen, in which the president said unequivocally:

> In response to the suggestion made by President Eisenhower, . . . and in conformity with the opinion of the legal adviser of the Department of State, . . . I am glad to emphasize again that the treaty in no way limits the authority of the Commander in Chief to use nuclear weapons for the defense of the United States and its allies, if a situation should arise requiring such a grave decision.[108]

In his speech endorsing the treaty, Dirksen explained that he had contacted Eisenhower at his home in Gettysburg to ascertain whether the latter really wanted a reservation, with all that word's legal ramifications. Eisenhower answered that what he really wanted was "ironclad assurance." In answer to a question from Fulbright, as to whether Kennedy's letter "entirely satisfies the view of General Eisenhower," Dirksen answered, "Exactly."[109]

When he talked to President Kennedy about the

reservation worry, Fulbright mentioned that he was working with Dutton to find a technique whereby he could offer "something of an innocuous nature that would give these boys a little face saving . . . to let them feel that they had done something."[110] It was decided to fall in behind an amendment to the Senate's resolution of ratification (not a reservation to the treaty) introduced by Russell and providing that "any future amendments to this treaty must be submitted to the Senate for its advice and consent." In transmitting the treaty to the Senate, President Kennedy had specifically stated that it could not be amended "without the consent of the United States, including the consent of the Senate." Secretary Rusk had later written two letters, one citing legal authority to the effect that the Russell proposal was constitutionally unnecessary, the other stating that the amendment "would not be in the best interests of the United States." Nevertheless, with support on the floor by Fulbright, Mansfield, Dirksen, and several others, Russell's amendment was adopted by a vote of 79–9. Accepting this amendment had several advantages in addition to the one mentioned by Fulbright (to "give these boys a little face saving"): it could assuage the feelings of members of Russell's Armed Services Committee; it provided a relatively harmless vehicle for the expression of senatorial outrage that so many other countries had been allowed to sign the treaty before the Senate had given its advice and consent; and it was a personal concession to Russell, who had been fairly restrained in his opposition to the treaty.

All in all, the administration and pro-treaty forces in the Senate appear to have handled the matter of reservations and amendments with skill and sensitivity.

Public Opinion and the Role of Interest Groups

In his address to the nation the day after the initialing of the treaty in Moscow, President Kennedy urged his listeners to take part in the legislative process by making their opinions known. "It is my hope," the president said, "that all of you will take part in this debate, for this treaty is for all of us. . . . This debate will involve military, scientific, and political experts, but it must not be left to them alone. The right and responsibility are yours."

Thus, the president played, right at the start, one of the trump cards in the administration's strategy for ratification—an attempt to bring a favorable public opinion to bear as an influence on the Senate. A Louis Harris poll published two days after the president's speech gave support to this tactic. It showed that 53 percent of those questioned gave unqualified approval to the treaty, 29 percent gave qualified approval,[111] and only 17 percent were opposed. Congressional mail at this time also was reported generally to support the treaty, although by a lesser margin.[112]

Throughout the period of the cold war there was always a small percentage of the public at the poles of opinion about arms control, one group advocating a hard line toward the Soviet Union and maximization of armaments, another group a more aggressive pursuit of disarmament. The vast majority of Americans appear to have fallen between these extremes, desiring both peace and military security. This large middle group tended to be influenced by the swings in government policy and by the views of opinion leaders with whom they identified on other issues.[113] This helps to explain why opinion about nuclear testing was subject to mercurial swings in the 1950s and 1960s.[114]

Kennedy wanted a vigorous effort to create an avalanche of favorable opinion toward the treaty. Following the president's instructions, Dutton mounted an intensive three-week effort beginning early in August, timed to take maximum effect at the time the Senate floor debate began. Government officials activated labor unions and other influential friends and constituents in the private sector, including Dr. Spock, who issued a statement "aimed at the mothers' vote."[115] A massive letter-writing campaign was organized in behalf of the treaty. It was perhaps overdone, because it stimulated some resentment. Thus, Senator Hickenlooper observed to the Foreign Relations Committee, "If the letters I get each Tuesday and Wednesday, which is about enough time for letters to reach Washington after the Sunday sermons . . . mean anything, the people are being told that this treaty will end war."[116]

Whether because of the administration's efforts or merely because of increased exposure to the issue, public support for the treaty seems to have increased over the summer. A Harris poll taken in September showed that the proportion of respondents giving it unqualified approval had increased since July from 52 percent to 81 percent. A Gallup poll published September 1 on the question "Do you think the Senate should vote approval of this ban or not?" showed 63 percent for approval, 17 percent opposed, and 20 percent with no opinion. Support was lowest in the South, but even there more than twice as many favored ratification as opposed it. Republicans were 58 percent for approval versus 67 percent for Democrats.[117]

Congressional mail and other public expressions made it clear that the fallout question was probably the most important factor in popular support of the treaty.[118] The emphasis on fallout probably lessened the influence of public opinion on the Senate, since both pro-treaty and anti-treaty witnesses, although acknowledging that there could be some risk from fallout, attributed relatively little importance to it.[119] Stennis, for example, stated that he would have attached more weight to the letters he received had they shown more understanding of the issues.[120]

Although President Kennedy, as the instigator of a drive to influence public opinion, was undoubtedly very well informed about the latest polling data and other indicators of popular sentiment, he appears to have had some skepticism about at least one of the indicators. Thus, Arthur M. Schlesinger, Jr., narrates that, the week after the American University speech, the president's mail report showed some 900 letters about the speech and more than 28,000 about a freight rate bill. "The President, tossing the report aside, said, with disgust, 'That is why I tell people in Congress that they're crazy if they take their mail seriously.'"[121] Later, he had reason to think he might have underestimated the true popularity of the treaty. This occurred on a trip to the western United States that began the day of the Senate vote. The trip traversed eleven states, the ostensible purpose being to observe efforts at, and to preach, conservation of natural resources. In reality, with the 1964 election approaching, there was little doubt that Kennedy had presidential politics on his mind in this foray into Republican territory. During the trip the president noted that while his references to conservation drew mild applause, references to the test ban treaty were greeted with what seemed like genuine enthusiasm. On his return to Washington Kennedy told Jerome Wiesner that he would have been firmer in the search for a comprehensive test ban treaty had he known how much support there was among U.S. citizens.[122]

There was extensive coverage of the treaty in the mass media. A survey in the *Columbia Journalism Review* found it to be the fifth most covered news story of 1963, trailing the assassination of Kennedy, tensions over civil rights, the death of Pope John XXIII, and the mounting hostilities in Vietnam.[123] Because of the complexity of the test ban issue, the explanations and argumentation in print media, including both newspapers and periodicals, may have played a more than usually significant role in helping members of the public reach opinions of their own. A majority of the papers opposing the treaty were located in the South and West. Support for the treaty tended to be greater among papers with larger circulation. Some 90 percent of papers with circulation over 250,000 endorsed the treaty.[124]

There is no indication that senators were strongly influenced in their votes by newspaper columns and editorials, although a fairly large number of these pieces were inserted in the *Congressional Record* as support for senators' own points of view. Hubert Humphrey, in particular, flooded the *Record* with favorable editorials; on September 19 alone he inserted fifty-nine from newspapers large and small across the country.[125]

Among mass circulation magazines in the summer of 1963, *Life, Saturday Evening Post,* and *Newsweek* clearly favored the treaty, *Time* seemed moderately favorable, *Reader's Digest* and *Look* were noncommittal, and only *U.S. News & World Report* was clearly opposed. Most magazines of opinion with smaller circulation supported the treaty, a notable exception being the conservative *National Review*.[126] A meeting was arranged between the president and the editors of leading women's magazines, representing a total reading audience of some 70 million. A transcript of the meeting was then published in all the magazines represented, an unprecedented joint publishing endeavor.[127]

Coverage of the news on broadcast networks appeared to favor the treaty just by the way news events associated with it tended to happen. Thus, the initialing and signing in Moscow, the messages and press conferences of the president, and the accessions by other countries all received wide coverage. The committee appearances by Edward Teller also received extensive publicity. Conservative broadcast commentators like Fulton Lewis, Jr., attacked the treaty vigorously, but often in tones so strident that few beyond their core constituencies paid heed.

A very large number of public interest groups took a position regarding the treaty. Ronald J. Terchek polled 110 groups believed likely to be interested. Of the 67 that replied to his inquiry, 42 said they did indeed become involved. All of these informed their members about the issue, and about 30 urged their members to play a part, at least to the extent of writing their senators. Leaders of most of the organizations, as well as key constituents among their members, contacted senators in writing, by telephone, and, in some cases, by personal visits.[128] The daily vote-counting operation led by Senator Humphrey helped to pinpoint senators for whom such special attention was most necessary.[129]

The attention of many interest groups was diluted by the fact that sweeping civil rights legislation was pending at the same time as the treaty. Liberty Lobby, which opposed the treaty, was so involved in opposing the civil rights bill that it devoted little attention to the treaty. The massive March on Washington led by Martin Luther King in behalf of civil rights took place on August 28, and this also diverted much interest-group attention and energy. A variety of groups whose main interests were in the economic field gave only secondary attention to the treaty. On the other hand, for peace groups such as SANE, the Women's Strike for Peace, the Friends Committee on National Legislation, and United World Federalists, the treaty was a main order of business, and they devoted vigorous attention to it. Several religious groups supported the treaty, interpreting the quest for peace as a moral issue. Trade unions supported the treaty also, but with varying degrees of enthusiasm. President George Meany of the AFL-CIO (American Federation of Labor–Congress of Industrial Organizations), for example, who was specifically asked by President Kennedy to endorse the treaty, tempered his support in congressional testimony with warnings about the Soviet Union's evil intentions.[130] In all, some nineteen groups supporting the treaty either presented testimony or submitted statements during the SFRC's hearings. By contrast, only three groups opposing the treaty made such presentations.[131]

The administration made special efforts to court veterans groups, but with scant success. Statements by the American

Legion and Veterans of Foreign Wars both alluded to the dangers in disarmament deals with the Soviets, the former ending up with a conditional endorsement, the latter with an outright condemnation, of the treaty. Right-wing groups such as the John Birch Society condemned the treaty in very shrill tones, questioning the patriotism of its sponsors.[132]

President Kennedy's role in the establishment of a Citizens' Committee for a Nuclear Test Ban has already been discussed. One of the committee's missions was to emphasize the bipartisan and respectable nature of the treaty undertaking. Hence, it was headed by a Republican, Wadsworth, and numbered among its members, or obtained the support of, former Eisenhower cabinet members, civic leaders, thirty-four college presidents, business leaders, scientists, and distinguished people in the arts. Under the committee's leadership, some twenty groups supporting the treaty met periodically to coordinate strategy. The group engaged professional public relations assistance and mounted a very active and sophisticated campaign, following, in general, suggestions made by President Kennedy himself.[133] By contrast, the efforts of a rival National Committee Against the Treaty of Moscow were relatively feeble. Organized at an August 16, 1963, breakfast meeting in the apartment of William F. Buckley, editor of the *National Review*, it attempted without notable effect to "encourage the scientific, military and public figures who already oppose the treaty to speak up frankly about their reservations."[134] Its most visible effort was a full-page ad in the *Washington Post* for September 5, 1963, that Senator Strom Thurmond inserted in the *Congressional Record*. By and large, groups favoring the treaty were more numerous, more active, and better organized than those opposing it.

Measuring what impact interest groups in general may have had on the Senate vote is very difficult. What impact there was probably came indirectly through the effect of the groups' efforts on public opinion, as this may have been reflected in polls and senatorial mail. Nor, for that matter, is there a reliable way of knowing how much senators were influenced by public opinion in general. The treaty was not so salient an issue that senators had to fear mass retaliation at the polls if their votes were contrary to the preference of their constituents. Despite the president's admonition that the issue should not be left to experts alone, there were indications that senators were influenced more by the views of experts than by those of the public. To give but one example, Everett Dirksen, in his speech endorsing the treaty, let it be known that he was doing so despite having been "drenched" by an overwhelming volume of mail from his home state urging him to do the opposite.[135]

Conclusion

On September 24, all reservations and amendments having been disposed of, and all senators who wished to do so having explained their positions, it was time to vote. The treaty was approved, 80–19.[136] The president gained what he had sought—approval by a sizable majority. The treaty entered into force on October 10, 1963, having been ratified, as required, by the three "original parties."

Eleven of the negative votes were cast by Democrats, eight by Republicans—the feared split along party lines had not developed. Nor was there a wholesale defection of southern Democrats based on the civil rights issue. It is true that ten of the eleven Democrats who voted against the treaty were from the South, the only non-southerner being Frank J. Lausche (D-Ohio).[137] They appear to have done so, however, more because of their conservative views on defense issues than because of any linkage to civil rights. In fact, eight southern Democrats voted for the treaty. Of the Republicans who voted Nay, all but one—Margaret Chase Smith (R-Maine)—were from west of the Mississippi. Senator Smith's vote may well have been influenced by the testimony she heard as a member of the preparedness Investigating Subcommittee. Four of the subcommittee's seven members voted to reject the treaty, whereas only two of the Senate Foreign Relations Committee's sixteen members did so. An analysis of the vote indicates that those who voted against the treaty tended to support the conservative coalition in Congress on most votes; also that they opposed administration foreign policy more than half of the time.[138]

Six factors appear to have been mainly responsible for the favorable end result.

• The energy, dedication, and skill of President Kennedy—it now seems axiomatic that significant progress in arms control cannot be obtained without affirmative presidential leadership.

• The president's credibility, gained largely through his resolute stands in the Berlin and Cuban missile crises, as a national leader who was willing to stand up to the Soviet Union.

• Endorsements of the treaty by senators Jackson and Dirksen and by former President Eisenhower;

• The influence of public opinion, as expressed in polls, congressional mail, and the activities of interest groups.

• The early efforts, led principally by Hubert Humphrey, at building an infrastructure of opinion and organization favorable to arms control.

• Perhaps most important, Kennedy's decision to accept the four military safeguards, and the consequent endorsement of the treaty by the JCS.

Without the joint chiefs' endorsement Jackson's support would very likely have been lost, and with it those of other senators who followed his lead on nuclear matters. With slightly less confidence, one can say the same of Dirksen and those who followed him. Add to this the lack of enthusiasm with which several senators announced their support, and one sees a distinct likelihood that but for the acquiescence of the joint chiefs, the treaty would have lost the fifteen additional votes needed to defeat it. The joint chiefs' endorsement was of course won at a price, this being the president's acceptance of the four national security safeguards. By agreeing to these concessions, with their emphasis on military preparedness, the president may largely have forfeited the momentum toward further arms control steps he hoped would result from the treaty.

It is true that for a while after the treaty was signed the diplomatic atmosphere seemed to improve. In the words of one observer the treaty seemed to "codify" the improvement in relations brought about by the peaceful resolution of the Cuban missile crisis.[139] On the treaty's first anniversary Nikita Khrushchev spoke of a certain "fund of confidence" it had engendered.[140]

The improvement in atmosphere did not, however, carry over into the arms race; the pace of testing actually increased. From 1964 to 1968 there were 346 announced tests, more than for any prior five-year period.[141] In time, moreover, both sides increased their capabilities in underground testing, learning to do underground almost all of the things for which they had previously depended on atmospheric testing. The arms race accelerated in other respects as well. Between 1962 and 1972 the number of U.S. strategic ballistic missiles (intercontinental and submarine-launched) increased from 222 to 1,710; those of the Soviet Union from 60 to 1,950.[142] At the same time there were marked improvements in delivery systems, most particularly in the accuracy of missiles and in the introduction of multiple independently targeted reentry vehicles, which made possible a large increase in the number of warheads deployed on both sides.

These deployments took place in the absence of any strong

momentum toward arms limitations. Within the U.S. government the value of the test ban treaty as a first step toward a more peaceful world appears to have been discounted. President Lyndon B. Johnson, like Khrushchev, issued a statement on the treaty's first anniversary but with a wholly different emphasis. After a passing mention that "a year without atmospheric testing has left our air cleaner," Johnson's statement placed greatest emphasis on the fact that, because of the safeguards programs, the treaty had not impaired the nation's military strength. The president was careful to point out that the joint chiefs of staff were satisfied with the military progress being made. In December 1966 Johnson talked with AEC Chairman Seaborg about the treaty. As recorded in Seaborg's diary: "He said that he questioned the value of the treaty and asked me to give him some arguments in defense of it. I explained the hopes that the treaty would lead to a decrease in international tensions and to a slowing of nuclear weapons proliferation. The president seemed not at all impressed by these arguments."[143]

A similar lack of enthusiasm was later expressed by President Richard M. Nixon. At a National Security Council meeting on April 30, 1969, he recalled that it had been a close call with him to come out in favor of the Limited Test Ban Treaty and stated that he still was not sure this had been the correct decision. He said this in the context of doubting that the Soviet Union was really interested in arms control.[144]

Nor was there any strong push from American public opinion. By forcing tests underground the treaty eliminated what had been the public's principal objection to testing, the fallout hazard. The public's apathy may also have been due in part to the emphasis placed on military matters during the ratification debate. There were some who perceived that the opportunity to enlist public support for further steps was being lost in the debate and who protested about this at the time. Hubert Humphrey, for example, commented:

It would appear to me that it might be well to bring out in these hearings that not only does this treaty permit us to develop bigger and better weapons—which has been made quite clear—but also this treaty gives the people an opportunity to give some thoughtful consideration to . . . the processes of peace. . . . I would not want the whole world to think that all we were primarily concerned about was whether or not we had enough leeway within this treaty to create bigger and better weapons.[145]

Humphrey's view, however, did not prevail. Members of the administration, from President Kennedy on down, obviously believed that the surest path to the overwhelming vote they sought was to allay national security concerns and to play down anything that smacked of disarmament. It is hard to argue with the short-run political wisdom of this tactic. It was a key factor, for example, in enlisting the support of Jackson, as explained in his own testimony, and it may have been necessary to obtain the backing of the joint chiefs. The irony is that what was necessary to gain the victory in the short run may have contributed to denying, or at least delaying, the fruits of the victory in the long run.

Notes

1. Eisenhower later said that his greatest regret about his presidency was the failure to achieve a test ban treaty.

2. At the time, Harriman was undersecretary of state for political affairs. He had been ambassador to the Soviet Union during World War II and was highly regarded by the Soviets.

3. Theodore C. Sorensen, *Kennedy* (New York: Harper & Row, 1965), 740.

4. Quoted in Michael Krepon, *Strategic Stalemate: Nuclear Weapons and Arms Control in American Politics* (New York: St. Martin's Press, 1984), 71.

5. U.S. Congress, Senate Committee on Foreign Relations, *Nuclear Test Ban Treaty, Hearings,* 88th Cong., 1st sess., August 12–27, 1963, 109.

6. Glenn T. Seaborg with the assistance of Benjamin S. Loeb, *Kennedy, Khrushchev and the Test Ban* (Berkeley: University of California Press, 1981), 88.

7. Quoted in Arthur M. Schlesinger, Jr., *One Thousand Days: John F. Kennedy in the White House* (Boston, Mass.: Houghton Mifflin Co., 1965), 897.

8. On the other hand, it had to be recognized that most of the nations thought to be candidates for the nuclear club had insufficient territory even to consider atmospheric testing as an option.

9. U.S. Congress, Senate Committee on Foreign Relations, *Nuclear Test Ban, Hearings,* 33.

10. In this context "high yield" was defined by Secretary McNamara as meaning "in the tens of megatons." U.S. Air Force Chief of Staff Curtis LeMay defined it as meaning fifty megatons or more.

11. The Foreign Relations Committee conceded in its report to the Senate that the United States inability through atmospheric tests to acquire knowledge of such weapons effects was perhaps the most serious inhibition imposed by the treaty.

12. Secretary McNamara indicated that two or three smaller weapons gave a higher probability of kill than one large one; also that it was much more difficult and costly to make the high-yield weapons survivable. U.S. Congress, Senate Committee on Foreign Relations, *Nuclear Test Ban, Hearings,* 101. General LeMay dissented from this view, stating that the U.S. Air Force had been asking for a fifty-megaton bomb since 1954. Ibid., 350. Senator John Stennis (D-Miss.) said on the Senate floor that whereas unclassified testimony had been presented to the effect that a high-yield bomb was not needed, classified testimony had been presented that said the reverse. Franklin Pierce Huddle, "The Limited Test Ban Treaty and the United States Senate" (Thesis, The American University, 1965), A-48.

13. As reported by Harriman, Soviet Foreign Minister Andrey Gromyko said: "We don't recognize Spain but we acknowledge that it exists. As far as we are concerned, the Republic of China doesn't exist." At another point Gromyko called Chiang Kai-shek's regime "empty space." Seaborg and Loeb, *Kennedy, Khrushchev and the Test Ban,* 249–50.

14. Under well-established principles of international law, recognition is not accorded to an unrecognized regime merely by its becoming party to a multilateral agreement. As Secretary Rusk testified, "The governing criterion in determining recognition is intent . . . we do not intend to recognize the Soviet occupation zone of East Germany as a state." U.S. Congress, Senate Committee on Foreign Relations, *Nuclear Test Ban, Hearings,* 14.

15. *Congressional Record,* 17507.

16. U.S. Congress, Senate Committee on Foreign Relations, *Nuclear Test Ban, Hearings*, 392, 453.

17. Ibid., 32.

18. U.S. Congress, Senate Committee on Foreign Relations, *The Nuclear Test Ban Treaty, Report,* September 3, 1963, 2–3.

19. *New York Times*, August 4, 1963, p. 1. The three nations reported as opposed were Albania, the People's Republic of China, and France.

20. *Congressional Record*, September 23, 1963, 16829.

21. Quoted in Ronald J. Terchek, *The Making of the Test Ban Treaty* (The Hague: Martinus Nijhoff, 1970), 175.

22. Quoted in Huddle, "The Limited Test Ban Treaty and the United States Senate," VI-12f.

23. Seaborg and Loeb, *Kennedy, Khrushchev and the Test Ban*, 195.

24. Ibid., 227.

25. *F.A.S. Newsletter* 16, no. 6, June 1963, 4.

26. U.S. Department of State, Office of the Historian, Bureau of Public Affairs, *Administration Strategy Toward Congress on Three Nuclear Arms Issues (Limited Test Ban Treaty, Nonproliferation Treaty, SALT I Agreements)*, research project no. 1189, March 1978, 3–4.

27. *Time*, August 9, 1963, 14.

28. In his press conference on March 21, 1963, when asked whether he hoped to arrive at a test ban agreement, Kennedy answered, "Well, my hopes are somewhat dimmed, but nevertheless I hope." Two months later, in his May 20 news conference, the president began his answer to a similar question by saying, "No, I'm not hopeful, I'm not hopeful." He concluded this answer by saying, "If we don't get an agreement this year . . . perhaps the genie is out of the bottle and we'll never get him back in again."

29. George Bunn to author, August 17, 1990.

30. Norman Cousins, *The Improbable Triumvirate: John F. Kennedy, Pope John XXIII, Nikita Khrushchev* (New York: W. W. Norton and Co., 1972), 128–29.

31. George Bunn, who was responsible for the ACDA head count, freely acknowledges that it was little more than a "guesstimate," those senators being cast in opposition "who would, based on past votes and contemporary statements, likely oppose almost any limitation on U.S. weapons development in a U.S.-Soviet arms control treaty because they so distrusted the Soviets." George Bunn to Michael Krepon, October 10, 1990.

32. U.S. Congress, Senate Committee on Foreign Relations, *Nuclear Test Ban, Hearings*, 394.

33. Ibid., 463.

34. Some take a less harsh view of the Soviet action. They note that the U.S. pledge not to test had been for a one-year period ending December 31, 1959, and that President Eisenhower had announced that the United States would feel free to test thereafter. Eisenhower's announcement was said to have been interpreted by the Soviets as indicating that the United States intended to resume testing. When Eisenhower made his announcement, moreover, the Soviet Union's response had been to repeat its pledge not to resume testing unless "the Western nations" did so. The Soviets had said more than once that if France continued to test they might feel compelled to resume testing. Seaborg and Loeb, *Kennedy, Khrushchev and the Test Ban*, 84. There were several French tests during the moratorium.

35. U.S. Congress, Senate Committee on Foreign Relations, *Nuclear Test Ban, Hearings*, 967.

36. Ibid., 375

37. U.S. Congress, Senate Committee on Armed Services, Preparedness Investigating Subcommittee, *Military Implications of the Proposed Limited Nuclear Test Ban Treaty, Interim Report*, September 9, 1963, 12.

38. U.S. Congress, Senate Committee on Foreign Relations, *Nuclear Test Ban, Hearings*, 388.

39. Terchek, *The Making of the Test Ban Treaty*, 172.

40. U.S. Congress, Senate Committee on Foreign Relations, *Nuclear Test Ban, Hearings*, 761.

41. Richard G. Hewlett and Jack M. Holl, *Atoms for Peace and War, 1953-1961: Eisenhower and the Atomic Energy Commission* (Berkeley: University of California Press, 1989), 473.

42. John G. Stewart, former legislative assistant to Hubert H. Humphrey, to Amy Smithson, October 29, 1990.

43. The only negative vote was cast by Russell B. Long (D-La.).

44. Huddle, "The Limited Test Ban Treaty and the United States Senate," II-16n.

45. *Congressional Quarterly Almanac, 1963* (Washington, D.C.: Congressional Quarterly Press, 1964), 251.

46. Ibid.

47. *Facts on File Yearbook 1963* (New York: Facts on File, 1963), 273.

48. Because Republicans have not had to bear this burden, it is often observed that it was easier for Eisenhower to make peace in Korea than it would have been for Adlai Stevenson; and easier for Richard M. Nixon, with his impeccable anticommunist credentials, to make the opening to the People's Republic of China than it would have been for Humphrey. One can speculate also that a Democratic president would have been unlikely to obtain the 88–2 margin in the Senate that Nixon achieved for the ABM Treaty.

49. U.S. Department of State, *Administration Strategy*, 7.

50. U.S. Congress, Senate, *Message from the President Transmitting the Treaty Banning Nuclear Weapon Tests in the Atmosphere,* 88th Cong., 1st sess., August 8, 1963, 4. Eisenhower himself resisted this linkage. He pointed out that his proposal had been made when the United States was well ahead of the USSR in nuclear armaments, whereas—because of the Soviet tests of 1961–62—that situation might no longer prevail. U.S. Congress, Senate Committee on Foreign Relations, *Nuclear Test Ban, Hearings*, 848.

51. U.S. Congress, Senate Committee on Armed Services, Preparedness Investigating Subcommittee, *Interim Report*, 2. Leverett Saltonstall (R-Mass.) declined to sign the report, finding its conclusions "unduly pessimistic." Stuart Symington (D-Mo.) signed the report but noted in an accompanying statement that, although the report's factual data were accurate, he planned to vote for the treaty based on testimony he had heard before the Foreign Relations Committee, of which he was also a member.

52. Sorensen, *Kennedy*, 830.

53. W. Averell Harriman, information conveyed privately to the author, February 22, 1980.

54. Krepon, *Strategic Stalemate*, 31.

55. John F. Kennedy Library, Presidential Recordings, Transcripts, *Winning Support for the Nuclear Test Ban Treaty, 1963,* opened for research use October 6, 1988, Item 26C1.

56. Dean Rusk, as told to Richard Rusk, *As I Saw It* (New York: W. W. Norton and Co., 1990), 588.

57. JCS Chairman Maxwell Taylor had apparently made an agreement with Stennis that he and other chiefs would appear first before Stennis's subcommittee. Kennedy feared, however, that if Stennis heard the chiefs first, the "secret" testimony would be selectively leaked so as to emphasize negative aspects. In a phone conversation with the president majority leader Mike Mansfield (D-Mont.) appeared reluctant to ride roughshod

over Stennis, who he said had been "most patient and considerate."
Kennedy insisted that, as a matter of jurisdiction, this being a treaty
correctly before the Foreign Relations Committee, an Armed Services
subcommittee had no right to prior testimony. Presidential Recordings,
Transcripts, Item 25B2.

58. Dean Rusk, conversation with author, March 13, 1986.

59. Presidential Recordings, Transcripts, Item 25B2.

60. U.S. Congress, Senate Committee on Foreign Relations, *Nuclear Test Ban, Hearings*, 309.

61. Ibid., 382.

62. George Bunn to Michael Krepon, October 10, 1990.

63. A detailed account of this meeting is found in Seaborg and Loeb, *Kennedy, Khrushchev and the Test Ban*, 220–23.

64. Most of the technical controversy that disturbed the chiefs concerned
the ability of the Soviets to conduct undetected, clandestine tests in
violation of the proposed treaty. Paul H. Nitze has written that there were
some fifty technical issues on which he, acting for McNamara, listened to
conflicting arguments and made tentative findings, successfully resolving
most of the controversies. See Paul H. Nitze with Ann M. Smith and Steven
L. Rearden, *From Hiroshima to Glasnost: At the Center of Decision* (New
York: Grove Weidenfeld, 1989), 191ff.

65. U.S. Congress, Senate Committee on Foreign Relations, *Nuclear Test Ban, Hearings*, pp. 348-9.

66. Ibid., 372.

67. Senior military commanders in the echelon below the chiefs also
generally lined up in support of the treaty. Notable exceptions were
General Thomas S. Power, commander-in-chief of the Strategic Air
Command, and General Bernard A. Schriever, commander of the U.S. Air
Force Systems Command.

68. Harriman, who agreed with the Soviet contention, obtained President
Kennedy's permission to abandon the Plowshare exemption in exchange for
a clause that would in effect have allowed the United States to withdraw
from the treaty in the event of a Chinese nuclear test. It was thought that
the absence of such a withdrawal provision might hurt the treaty's chances
in the Senate. This was evidently a misjudgment, because when the first
Chinese test occurred in October 1964, not a single senatorial voice was
raised suggesting withdrawal from the treaty.

69. Seaborg and Loeb, *Kennedy, Khrushchev and the Test Ban*, 244ff.

70. U.S. Congress, Senate Committee on Foreign Relations, *Nuclear Test Ban, Hearings,* 211.

71. Seaborg and Loeb, *Kennedy, Khrushchev and the Test Ban,* 268. Seaborg points out that the ACDA interpretation caused the meaning of the treaty to change with every improvement in techniques for detecting radioactivity.

72. Sorensen, *Kennedy,* 830.

73. Quoted in Seaborg and Loeb, *Kennedy, Khrushchev and the Test Ban,* 32–33.

74. Quoted in Huddle, "The Limited Test Ban Treaty and the United States Senate," VI-5.

75. Seaborg and Loeb, *Kennedy, Khrushchev and the Test Ban,* 63–66.

76. Ibid., chapter 12.

77. Huddle, "The Limited Test Ban Treaty and the United States Senate," II-1.

78. Sorensen, *Kennedy,* 745.

79. The addition of the USIA head bespoke Kennedy's recognition of the importance of world opinion in arms control matters.

80. U.S. Department of State, *Administration Strategy,* 6–7.

81. In the summer of 1963 there were, for example, a threatened nationwide rail strike, the raging controversy about civil rights, and a grievous personal distraction—the death on August 8 of Kennedy's infant son.

82. According to Benjamin Read, then executive secretary of the Department of State and one of the participants in the nightly sessions: "The president showed a devouring interest in the . . . negotiations. He'd delve into the subject with gusto and in considerable detail." Benjamin Read, interview for Kennedy Library oral history program.

83. Sorensen, *Kennedy,* 38.

84. Rusk had advised that Kennedy delay this speech until Harriman had returned and briefed Senate committees, but the president thought otherwise, saying: "We got to hit the country while the country's hot. That's the only thing that makes an impression to [sic] these goddamned Senators." Presidential Recordings, Transcripts, Item 23C1.

85. Cousins, *The Improbable Triumvirate,* 135.

86. Ibid., 135.

87. Eisenhower was visited first by Rusk and then by Central Intelligence Agency Director John McCone. Truman's letter was not made public, reportedly because his "remarks about dealing with the Soviets were too tart to be released." *U.S. News & World Report*, September 16, 1963, 26.

88. Presidential Recordings, Transcripts, Item 24vB1.

89. Detailed accounts of these meetings appear in Seaborg and Loeb, *Kennedy, Khrushchev and the Test Ban*, 45–48, 83–84.

90. U.S. Department of State, *Administration Strategy*, 4.

91. The arrangement for finessing the unrecognized regimes problem by depositing instruments of ratification in any one of the capitals of the three original parties reportedly emanated from senatorial suggestions at this meeting. Terchek, *The Making of the Test Ban Treaty*, 144.

92. Harriman was reported to have antagonized senators by the patronizing and impatient way in which he answered their questions. The administration thereupon decided not to use him as a witness in the SFRC hearings. Ibid., 144.

93. State Department cable released to author pursuant to Freedom of Information Act.

94. John G. Stewart to Amy Smithson, October 29, 1990.

95. Fulbright helped to assure full attendance by staging a quorum call just before Dirksen spoke. Attendance on the floor had been meager to that point. When the debate opened on September 9, for example, there had been only eight senators present. *Time*, September 20, 1963, 25.

96. The Preparedness Investigating Subcommittee asked the joint chiefs to state what steps should be taken to implement the safeguards. General LeMay testified that the chiefs would comply but that the request was a very difficult one because conditions were in constant flux.

97. After the treaty was ratified, conservative members of Congress kept up relentless pressure for specific measures to implement the safeguards. Representative Craig Hosmer (R-Calif.) put forward a list of specifics estimated to cost $1 billion in capital outlays and $250 million annually in operating costs. These amounts were far in excess of any the administration was prepared to spend. The pressure continued into the Johnson administration. In March 1964 the joint Senate-House Republican leadership issued a statement requesting Johnson to reaffirm Kennedy's commitments and questioning whether sufficient funds were being expended on the safeguards. Dirksen personalized the request by pointing out that it was he who had read Kennedy's letter pledging the safeguards on the Senate floor and that he had done so at the president's request. See Glenn

T. Seaborg with Benjamin S. Loeb, *Stemming the Tide: Arms Control in the Johnson Years* (Lexington, Mass.: Lexington Books, 1987), 206.

98. *Congressional Record*, September 11, 1963, 16790–91.

99. Ibid., September 10, 1963, 15745ff.

100. Ibid., September 23, 1963, 16890.

101. Ibid., September 13, 1963, 16092ff.

102. George Bunn, telephone conversation with author, August 17, 1990.

103. U.S. Department of State, *Administrative Strategy*, 11.

104. Terchek, *The Making of the Test Ban Treaty*, 174.

105. U.S. Congress, Senate Committee on Foreign Relations, *Nuclear Test Ban, Hearings*, 821.

106. Harriman had been made aware of senatorial worries about this while in Moscow and raised the question of adding language to cover the matter. Gromyko, however, would have none of it, stating that by its terms the treaty related only to nuclear tests and that specifically authorizing the use of nuclear weapons in war in such a treaty was unnecessary and likely to create a bad impression. Harriman tended to agree, and the matter was dropped.

107. U.S. Congress, Senate Committee on Foreign Relations, *Nuclear Test Ban, Hearings*, 502.

108. *Congressional Record*, August 11, 1963, 15915.

109. Ibid., 15918.

110. Presidential Recordings, Transcripts, Item 26C1.

111. Terchek, *The Making of the Test Ban Treaty*, 121. Other caveats and accordant approvals were as follows: "if Russia keeps word" 12 percent; "only with inspection" 12 percent; "if on our terms" 5 percent.

112. *Facts on File Yearbook 1963*, 275. It is important to remember that congressional mail on a controversial issue can be an unreliable barometer of public opinion because of the possibility that organized mass-mailing campaigns may be in progress.

113. Samuel Lubell, Remarks to Research Conference on Disarmament, Columbia University, 1961. Lubell cited a poll taken in December 1961 on the resumption of testing. Those who had voted for Kennedy in 1960 adopted his stance of opposing testing, whereas those who had voted for Nixon followed his lead in advocating resumed testing.

114. Terchek, *The Making of the Test Ban Treaty*, 107ff.

115. Ibid, 8.

116. U.S. Congress, Senate Committee on Foreign Relations, *Nuclear Test Ban, Hearings*, 413.

117. Seaborg and Loeb, *Kennedy, Khrushchev and the Test Ban*, 268.

118. Terchek, *The Making of the Test Ban Treaty*, 119ff.

119. Perhaps the most authoritative testimony on this question was by AEC Chairman Seaborg, who, in answer to a question   by Senator Mundt, testified that pollution of the atmosphere from nonradioactive sources was "clearly more dangerous" to health than fallout and that he did not think that fallout was "one of the major reasons for the treaty." U.S. Congress, Senate Committee on Foreign Relations, *Nuclear Test Ban, Hearings*, 243.

120. Huddle, "The Limited Test Ban Treaty and the United States Senate," I-11.   This experience tends to emphasize the difficulty of involving the public in as intellectually demanding a subject matter as nuclear testing and is a sobering reminder of the limitations of democratic government.

121. Schlesinger, *One Thousand Days*, 910.

122. Jerome Wiesner to author, January 4, 1990.

123. Terchek, *The Making of the Test Ban Treaty*, 53.

124. Ibid., 49ff.

125. One can conjecture that these editorials were supplied to Humphrey by the Citizens' Committee for a Nuclear Test Ban or the public relations firm the committee had engaged.   Many of the editorials that appeared in smaller newspapers may, in fact, have been written and placed in the newspapers by the PR firm.

126. Terchek, *The Making of the Test Ban Treaty*, 70–71.

127. Cousins, *The Improbable Triumvirate*, 136-37.

128. Terchek, *The Making of the Test Ban Treaty*, 78ff.

129. John G. Stewart to Amy Smithson, October 29, 1990.

130. U.S. Congress, Senate Committee on Foreign Relations, *Nuclear Test Ban, Hearings*, 879ff.

131. The three were Americans for National Security, International Council of Christian Churches, and Young Americans for Freedom.

132. Terchek, *The Making of the Test Ban Treaty*, 92–93.

133. Cousins, *The Improbable Triumvirate*, 138-44.

134. U.S. Department of State, *Administration Strategy*, 1978, 8.

135. *Congressional Record*, September 11, 1963, 15912.

136. The absent Clair Engle (D-Calif.) sent word from his hospital bed that, had he been present, he would have cast an eighty-first vote for the treaty.

137. Lausche's vote was a strange one in that he had voted in favor of the Senate Foreign Relations Committee report recommending the treaty to the Senate.

138. Terchek, *The Making of the Test Ban Treaty*, 181.

139. George Bunn to Michael Krepon, October 10, 1990.

140. Seaborg and Loeb, *Stemming the Tide*, 6.

141. Data from the Natural Resources Defense Council, *Bulletin of the Atomic Scientists*, vol. 24 (March 1968): 56.

142. Paul P. Craig and John A. Jungerman, *Nuclear Arms Race: Technology and Society* (New York: McGraw-Hill, 1986), 6.

143. Seaborg and Loeb, *Stemming the Tide*, 214.

144. Glenn T. Seaborg, memoirs of his service as chairman of the Atomic Energy Commission under Nixon, in manuscript.

145. U.S. Congress, Senate Committee on Foreign Relations, *Nuclear Test Ban, Hearings*, 312-3.

Selected Bibliography

Books and Articles

Bundy, McGeorge. *Danger and Survival: Choices About the Bomb in the First Fifty Years*. New York: Random House, 1988.

Chang, Gordon H. *Friends and Enemies: The United States, China, and the Soviet Union, 1948-1972*. Stanford, Calif.: Stanford University Press, 1990.

Cousins, Norman. *The Improbable Triumvirate: John F. Kennedy, Pope John XXIII, Nikita Khrushchev*, New York: W. W. Norton and Co., 1972.

Fetter, Steve. *Toward a Comprehensive Test Ban*. Cambridge, Mass.: Ballinger, 1988.

Hewlett, Richard G., and Jack M. Holl. *Atoms for Peace and War, 1953-1961: Eisenhower and the Atomic Energy Commission*. Berkeley: University of California Press, 1989.

Jacobson, Harold Karan, and Eric Stein. *Diplomats, Scientists and Politicians: The United States and the Nuclear Test Ban Negotiations*. Ann Arbor: University of Michigan Press, 1966.

Krepon, Michael. *Strategic Stalemate: Nuclear Weapons and Arms Control in American Politics.* New York: St. Martins Press, 1985.
National Academy of Sciences. "Nuclear Test Bans." Chapter 7 in *Nuclear Arms Control: Background and Issues.* Washington, D.C.: National Academy Press, 1985.
Nitze, Paul H., with Ann M. Smith and Steven L. Rearden. *From Hiroshima to Glasnost: At the Center of Decision.* New York: Grove Weidenfeld, 1989.
Rovere, Richard. "Letter from Washington." *The New Yorker,* October 4, 1963, 149–56.
Rusk, Dean, as told to Richard Rusk. *As I Saw It.* New York: W. W. Norton and Co., 1990.
Schlesinger, Arthur M., Jr. *One Thousand Days: John F. Kennedy in the White House.* Boston: Houghton Mifflin Co., 1965.
Seaborg, Glenn T., with the assistance of Benjamin S. Loeb. *Kennedy, Khrushchev and the Test Ban.* Berkeley: University of California Press, 1981.
———. with Benjamin S. Loeb. *Stemming the Tide: Arms Control in the Johnson Years.* Lexington, Mass.: Lexington Books, 1987.
Sorensen, Theodore C. *Decision-Making in the White House: The Olive Branch or the Arrows.* New York: Columbia University Press, 1963.
———. *Kennedy.* New York: Harper & Row, 1965.
Terchek, Ronald J. *The Making of the Test Ban Treaty.* The Hague: Martinus Nijhoff, 1970.

Government Publications

John F. Kennedy Library. Presidential Recordings, Transcripts, *Winning Support for the Nuclear Test Ban Treaty, 1963.* Opened for research use October 6, 1988.
U.S. Congress. Senate. *Message from the President Transmitting the Treaty Banning Nuclear Weapon Tests in the Atmosphere.* 88th Cong., 1st sess., August 8, 1963.
U.S. Congress. Senate. Committee on Armed Services. Preparedness Investigating Subcommittee. *Military Implications of the Proposed Limited Nuclear Test Ban Treaty, Interim Report.* 88th Cong., 1st sess., September 9, 1963.
U.S. Congress. Senate. Committee on Foreign Relations. *Nuclear Test Ban Treaty, Hearings.* 88th Cong., 1st sess., August 12–27, 1963.
———. *The Nuclear Test Ban Treaty, Report.* 88th Cong., 1st sess., September 3, 1963.
———. *Test Ban Negotiations and Disarmament, Hearings.* 88th Cong., 1st sess., March 11, 1963.

——. *To Promote Negotiations for a Comprehensive Test Ban Treaty, Hearings.* 93d Cong., 1st sess., May 1, 1973.
U.S. Department of State. Office of the Historian. Bureau of Public Affairs. *Administration Strategy Toward Congress on Three Nuclear Arms Issues (Limited Test Ban Treaty, Nonproliferation Treaty, SALT I Agreements).* Research project no. 1189. March 1978.

Unpublished Works

Bunn, George. "Finding a Test Ban Formula." Draft chapter from "Too Many Cooks? Bargaining by Committee for Nuclear Arms Control." Unpublished manuscript.
Heckrotte, Warren. "The Debate on the Comprehensive Test Ban at the Geneva Disarmament Conference, 1962 to Present." Internal Atomic Energy Commission memorandum, October 20, 1970.
Huddle, Franklin Pierce. "The Limited Test Ban Treaty and the United States Senate." Thesis, The American University, 1965.

5 The Anti-Ballistic Missile Treaty

Alan Platt

In late May 1972 former President Richard M. Nixon went to Moscow and signed, among other documents, a Treaty to Limit Anti-Ballistic Missile (ABM) Systems. Under this agreement, both the United States and the Soviet Union made a commitment not to build nationwide ABM defenses against the other's intercontinental and submarine-launched ballistic missiles. They agreed to limit ABM deployments to a maximum of two sites, with no more than 100 launchers per site. Thirteen of the treaty's sixteen articles are intended to prevent any deviation from this. In addition, a joint Standing Consultative Commission to monitor compliance was created. "National technical means"—sophisticated monitoring devices on land, sea, and in space—were to be the primary instruments used to monitor compliance with the treaty.

The ABM Treaty was signed in conjunction with an Interim Agreement to Limit Strategic Offensive Arms. In this accord both superpowers pledged, inter alia, not to start construction of additional land-based intercontinental ballistic missiles (ICBMS) after July 1, 1972, and to limit their submarine-launched ballistic missiles (SLBMS) and modern ballistic missile submarines to the numbers operational and under construction on the date the agreement was signed. In signing these two landmark strategic arms control accords, the United States and the Soviet Union placed important limits on both defensive and offensive strategic weapons, paving the way for a range of future U.S.-Soviet arms control negotiations. On

The author is deeply grateful to Dan Caldwell, Al Carnesale, I. M. Destler, Pat Holt, and, most especially, Michael Krepon for their helpful comments on this chapter.

June 13, 1972, the president submitted the ABM Treaty to the Senate for ratification. He submitted the Interim Agreement as an executive agreement to both houses of Congress, requiring a majority vote for entry into force. In early August, less than two months later, the Senate decisively approved the treaty by a 88–2 vote, and it subsequently approved the Interim Agreement by an equal 88–2 vote. Two years later, President Nixon and General Secretary Leonid Brezhnev signed a protocol to the ABM Treaty, which reduced the number of permitted ABM sites from two to one.

While the ABM Treaty's substantive significance has taken on ever greater importance in the period since its conclusion, particularly with the Reagan administration's enthusiastic approach to strategic defenses, relatively little has been written about the politics associated with the ratification of this ground-breaking arms control treaty. President Nixon's success in convincing the Senate to consent to ratification in overwhelming numbers is worth reviewing, particularly considering the difficulties faced by his immediate successors in the treaty ratification process.

International Political Context

President Nixon and his assistant for national security affairs, Henry Kissinger, came into office believing in the principle of linkage, arguing that new arms control agreements with the Soviet Union could play a valuable role in helping bring about détente, that is, a relaxation of tensions between the superpowers. In pursuing arms control agreements with the Soviets, Nixon and Kissinger hoped to further the construction of a "seamless web of interrelationships" between the United States and the Soviet Union, a web, they hoped, that could lead to the end of the war in Vietnam and an easing of tensions in the Middle East. In Nixon's first press conference as president he noted that strategic arms limitation talks (SALT) with the Soviet Union would be more productive if they were conducted "in a way and at a time that will promote, if possible, progress on outstanding political problems at the same time."[1] Three and one-half years later, in a White House briefing to congressional leaders immediately after the signing of new arms control accords with the Soviets, Kissinger succinctly summed up the international context in which the SALT I accords were negotiated and concluded.

> The SALT agreement does not stand alone, isolated and incongruous in the relationship of hostility, vulnerable at any moment to the shock of some sudden crisis. It stands, rather linked organically, to a chain of agreements and to a broad understanding about international conduct appropriate to the dangers of the nuclear age. The agreement on the limitation of strategic arms is, thus, not merely a technical accomplishment, although it is that in part, but it must be seen as a political event of some magnitude.[2]

Along with the ABM Treaty and the Interim Agreement a number of other accords were signed by Nixon and Brezhnev at the 1972 Moscow summit meeting. This cluster of accords involved new arrangements concerning trade, space, health, the environment, and science and technology. In addition, there was a Basic Principles Agreement, which enumerated a set of broad political principles intended to be a "road map," denoting "the path that both sides should take if peace was to be lasting."[3] The Basic Principles Agreement formalized certain guidelines on which détente between the superpowers was to be based (that is, mutually advantageous commercial relations, avoidance of threats to each other's primary security interests, noninterference in internal affairs, and the need to prevent confrontations). However, as political scientist George Breslauer has pointed out, the Basic Principles Agreement of 1972 "did little to define realistic rules of competition in the Third World." This shortcoming led to the ultimate downfall of détente policy as the leaders of the two superpowers "fashioned strategies of detente [to] . . . maximize their overall comparative advantage in the competitive game."[4]

The SALT I accords were seen as being integral to creating a détente relationship with the Soviet Union and as a key part of the Nixon-Kissinger approach to foreign relations. Accordingly, the administration made the ratification of the ABM Treaty a very high priority goal. If this treaty was not ratified, the administration thought, U.S. foreign policy—as well as U.S. credibility in the international arena—would be in shambles. On the other hand, with the conclusion of this treaty and its successful ratification, the Nixon administration hoped to expand its web of interlocking ties with the Soviets, building on the Basic Principles Agreement of 1972.

Another element in the Nixon administration's approach to the Soviet Union involved the People's Republic of China. In the early 1970s Nixon and Kissinger conceived of a form of triangular diplomacy to pursue vis-à-vis the Soviets and the Chinese. Because the United States had better relations with these two countries than they enjoyed with one another, the Nixon administration endeavored to "exert maximum leverage on each of its principal adversaries." This triangular diplomatic approach, which had a positive impact on arms control with the Soviets, produced mixed overall results for the United States. As Peter Tarnoff has observed, "[Triangular diplomacy] created a favorable climate for significant strategic arms control and normalization with China on terms acceptable to the United States, but it failed . . . in Vietnam [and] . . . in regional disputes."[5]

The ongoing fighting in Vietnam threatened to affect the conclusion of the ABM Treaty as well as its ratification. This was clearly a consideration in the spring of 1972, as Henry Kissinger almost had to postpone his presummit trip to Moscow because of increased U.S. military activity in Vietnam. In addition, just before the summit, there was great concern at the highest levels of the Nixon administration that the Soviets would employ linkage themselves and tie progress in Vietnam to the conclusion of the SALT I accords. On May 8, 1972, in what Richard Nixon has since called his "most difficult foreign policy decision,"[6] the United States opted to mine several North Vietnamese ports, including Haiphong harbor. Most senior specialists in the Department of State and the Central Intelligence Agency (CIA) warned the White House that if this mining went forward, the Soviet Union, notwithstanding increased North Vietnamese military activities, would cancel the planned late May summit meeting. Former chief arms control negotiator Gerard C. Smith has recalled in his book on SALT I that after the United States announced its bombing and mining of Haiphong and several other North Vietnamese port cities, his "first sleepy thought was, 'Here goes the ball game' [the SALT I accords]."[7] In the end, these fears proved groundless, as the summit meeting and the strategic arms control agreements went forward as anticipated.

One set of continuing concerns to the Nixon White House were the views of the NATO (North Atlantic Treaty Organization) allies. As a result, during the period in which the ABM Treaty was being negotiated, there were countless discussions with Western European states at the upper echelons of government. In fact, both Nixon and Kissinger made a concerted effort to keep the most key European heads of state (Edward Heath of the UK, Willy Brandt of West Germany, and Georges-Jean-Raymond Pompidou of France, for example) and their immediate aides highly conversant with the direction of the ongoing strategic arms talks with the Soviets. Indeed, SALT was discussed more regularly with European leaders than with members of Congress, or at least that was the stated perception of some key congressional figures, including Senate Foreign Relations Committee Chairman J. William Fulbright (D-Ark.).[8]

Overall, European leaders were enthusiastically supportive of the ongoing strategic arms limitation talks with the Soviet Union, although they were lukewarm about linkage. European leaders generally felt that the Nixon administration had been slow in its efforts to improve relations with Moscow and were eager to get on with both SALT and conventional arms control discussions in Europe. Although generally supportive of a new strategic arms control agreement with the Soviet Union, European leaders periodically expressed concern to the Nixon administration about several specific issues under negotiation as well as a more general concern about a possible U.S.-Soviet condominium. Among specific European concerns three issues were of primary importance and represented consensus views: (1) British and French national nuclear forces should be excluded from the superpower arms talks and any ensuing arms control agreements; (2) U.S. forward-based systems in Europe, mostly dual-capable aircraft, should not be covered by a strategic arms agreement; and (3) the Soviet Union should not be free to deploy antiballistic missile systems in an unconstrained manner. In the end these European positions, which had considerable support within the Nixon administration, prevailed in the negotiations and were embodied in the SALT I accords.[9]

Although America's European allies were fairly active in making their views known in the course of the SALT negotiations, their efforts were not of great consequence in the ratification process. NATO governments openly backed the agreements, as did virtually all of the other countries in the world. Yet although worldwide support undoubtedly increased confidence on Capitol Hill in the wisdom of ratifying SALT I, arguments expressed by foreigners were not central to the ratification debate. If the accords had been widely criticized, rather than hailed, by America's NATO allies, arguments expressed abroad would have been more influential during the ratification process. Being supportive, these arguments carried useful but modest weight.

Moreover, it was not by accident that the NATO allies supported the new SALT accords, but as the result of extensive consultation. As Gerard C. Smith has since observed in his memoirs:

> At the start it was not at all clear how America's allies, especially in Europe, would react to Soviet-American arrangements affecting their strategic relations. . . . It was a significant but underappreciated SALT accomplishment that all countries of the

North Atlantic alliance gave clear endorsement to the SALT
agreements. It reflected the deep and continuous consultations
which the SALT delegation had maintained . . . with the North
Atlantic Council. . . . This unique consultation record went a long
way to meet the allies' inherent sensitivities about the United
States negotiating alone with the Soviet Union on matters of the
highest importance for their national security.[10]

Domestic Political Context

The 1972 presidential elections set the backdrop for the
conclusion and ratification of the ABM Treaty. Within the six
months before the 1972 elections, President Nixon went to
Moscow for a summit meeting, signed the ABM Treaty and
other wide-ranging documents with the Soviets, and pushed
forward with a ratification effort on a treaty. The domestic
political context in which the final SALT negotiations were
concluded was clear: that of a president seeking reelection.
Through the successful conclusion and ratification of the ABM
Treaty President Nixon hoped to focus domestic political
attention on his administration's accomplishments with the
Soviets and to gain domestically from his statesman-like
image. At the same time, these efforts were also driven by a
Nixon administration interest in keeping the political spotlight
away from the nettlesome issue of Vietnam and a variety of
troublesome issues at home, including growing inflationary
problems and the beginning investigation of the break-in at
the Democratic party's headquarters in the Watergate Hotel.
In short, ratification of the ABM Treaty was viewed by the
Nixon administration as being important for both foreign and
domestic political reasons in 1972, a presidential election year.

To make sure that the ABM Treaty ratification effort went
successfully, a widerange of prominent political figures and
constituencies were enlisted in the process. Not one of these
was more important than Henry Kissinger. As assistant to the
president for national security affairs during 1969–72,
Kissinger had avoided consulting with Congress on arms
control issues, invoking executive privilege as necessary.

Nevertheless, during this period, Kissinger, as all knew, was the central U.S. government figure in formulating and carrying out U.S. SALT policy. He was also the key figure in setting administration foreign policy across a wide range of issues and enjoyed enormous credibility in Congress and in the country.

Immediately after the treaty was signed and sent to Congress for ratification, Kissinger's role changed significantly. In the weeks and months during the ratification debate on the ABM Treaty, Kissinger led the effort to "sell" the SALT I accords to Congress, describing them at one point as "without precedent in the nuclear age; indeed in all relevant modern history."[11] Kissinger and his key aides also consulted frequently with individual senators on SALT, being as available during these few months as he had been unavailable during the previous three and one-half years.

Two other prominent political figures central to the ratification debate were Senator John Sherman Cooper (R-Ky.), the ranking Republican member of the Foreign Relations Committee, and Senator Henry M. ("Scoop") Jackson (D-Wa.), a senior Democratic member of the Armed Services Committee. A former ambassador to India and longtime advocate of arms control, Senator Cooper was convinced that it was the constitutional responsibility of the Senate—particularly members of the Foreign Relations Committee—to play an active role during the SALT negotiating process. Others in the Senate, including Foreign Relations Committee Chairman J. William Fulbright, were more inclined to offer their advice and consent largely after the Nixon administration concluded a SALT treaty and sent it to Capitol Hill for ratification.

Favoring a more activist approach during the negotiations, Cooper frequently met with executive branch officials, both formally and informally, to discuss strategic arms control issues. In the Foreign Relations Committee, Cooper, more than any other member, played a key role in initiating SALT-related legislation. On a number of occasions Cooper worked

Alan Platt   237

tirelessly with the administration to help speed the SALT talks to a successful, early conclusion. On a few occasions, on his own initiative, Cooper even traveled to Vienna and Helsinki to receive firsthand impressions of the nature and direction of the talks; however, the Kentucky senator was highly limited in what he could do or learn, both in Washington and on his visits abroad. Before the conclusion of the SALT I accords in May 1972, U.S. officials shared information with him and other Committee members very selectively. During negotiating rounds, he was accorded no official connection with the U.S. SALT delegation and was not even allowed to attend SALT plenary sessions as an observer.

During the early days of SALT, Cooper, unhappy with the administration's approach to consultation on strategic arms control policy matters, tried to persuade the White House to allow senators to participate directly in the SALT negotiations, either as official members of the U.S. delegation or as part of an official observer group. Citing constitutional and pragmatic grounds, Cooper noted that the administration ultimately would have to submit any SALT treaty to the Senate for ratification. He further argued that favorable Senate action on any such accord would be far more likely if senators were brought into the policy process at an early date. In these arguments Cooper and like-minded senators were largely rebuffed by the White House in the period before the submission of the ABM Treaty to the Senate for ratification.[12]

One former National Security Council (NSC) staff member has since admitted that several executive branch officials, including chief SALT negotiator Gerard C. Smith, were sympathetic to the idea of having Cooper and other interested senators participate in the SALT negotiations as members of the U.S. delegation, particularly during the last six months preceding the May 1972 summit in Moscow.[13]   Henry Kissinger strongly opposed such congressional participation in the talks, however, and his views were decisive on this matter. Consistent with this, Kissinger even vetoed the idea of having Senator Cooper, along with Senate majority leader Mike

Mansfield (D-Mont.) and Senate minority leader Hugh Scott (R-Pa.), accompany the president and his entourage to Moscow for the May summit meeting.

Because of his initiative, Cooper was an important voice on arms control policy during the negotiation of the SALT I accords. After the ABM Treaty was signed and sent to Capitol Hill, he and Chairman Fulbright were key allies of the Nixon administration as it tried to ensure favorable committee action and the Senate's consent to ratification. In part because of the administration's continuing, determined prosecution of the war in Vietnam, its domestic political interest in such liberal international objectives as arms control and in ties with such senators as John Sherman Cooper were heightened. As I. M. Destler has noted, it was "through such breakthroughs that he [Nixon] could make his stubbornness come across as statesmanship, broaden his political base and undercut his liberal adversaries."[14]

One of the other senators most strongly interested in U.S. strategic arms control policy was Scoop Jackson. A long-time student of defense and arms control issues and a key administration ally on Vietnam, Jackson had declined Nixon's offer in 1968 to be secretary of defense. As a senior member of the Armed Services Committee and chairman of the Government Operations Subcommittee on Investigations, Jackson had been initially cool to the establishment of the Arms Control and Disarmament Agency (ACDA) in 1961 and to the Limited Test Ban Treaty of 1963, although ultimately he supported both.

Aided by staff assistants Dorothy Fosdick and Richard Perle, Jackson, as the chairman of a newly created Subcommittee on SALT, took the lead within the Armed Services Committee in overseeing the strategic arms negotiations during the 1969–72 period. During this period, with the encouragement of Armed Services Committee Chairman John Stennis (D-Miss.), who was focused on other issues, Jackson periodically held oversight hearings and regularly offered advice to the executive branch officials testifying before his SALT subcommittee. In addition, he regularly met privately with knowledgeable CIA and Defense officials, including Lieutenant General Edward Rowny, then of NATO's Military Committee, to discuss the course of the negotiations. In the Armed Services Committee and on the Senate floor, he vigorously backed 1969–70 legislative efforts supporting the Nixon administration's Safeguard ABM system while he opposed congressional efforts to limit the development of multiple independently targeted reentry vehicles (MIRVs).

In late 1971, relations between Jackson and the Nixon administration deteriorated in a way that carried over to the ABM Treaty ratification debate. At that time, with Safeguard ABM funding seemingly secure and the administration considering ABM proposals for less than four sites, the Nixon White House, led by Henry Kissinger, purposefully attempted to limit the Washington senator's knowledge of the details of the emerging U.S. SALT policy, at one point even refusing to discuss what data the executive branch had used to estimate future Soviet force levels. This infuriated Jackson and aide Richard Perle. Referring to the months leading up to the conclusion of the ABM Treaty, Perle has since commented that "Kissinger never felt a responsibility to engage in what you might call real consultation."[15]

Jackson's bad feelings about what he considered the Nixon administration's mishanding of the consultative process and about the substance of SALT I were exacerbated by his perception that the executive branch had unwisely rushed the final stages of the negotiations. Having set a deadline for the conclusion of the ABM Treaty—the May date of the summit meeting in Moscow—the Nixon administration went to Moscow without having worked out some of the final details of the SALT I accords. These details were resolved in Moscow. However, given the nature of these meetings, there was no complete written record of the discussions, as there had also not been for some of the "back-channel" negotiations between Kissinger and Soviet Ambassador Anatoly Dobrynin.

Not surprisingly, when the ABM Treaty reached the Senate, Jackson led the forces that had serious concerns about the SALT I accords.

In 1972 the Nixon administration was wary of providing any ammunition to Senator Jackson and the Democratic party in the face of an ongoing presidential election campaign. Early in 1972, there was concern in the Nixon White House that Jackson might emerge as the Democratic presidential nominee and that he would attack Nixon on his handling of SALT. By mid-1972 Jackson had been eliminated in the presidential primaries, and Senator George McGovern (D-S.Dak.) was the Democratic nominee. At that time there was concern that McGovern, a long-time arms control advocate and noted dove on Vietnam, might become critical of the SALT I accords in an effort to "toughen" his image for the campaign.[16] Accordingly, the Nixon administration made a concerted effort during the ratification debate to allay the concerns of Jackson, and others with his views in the Democratic party, to ensure that the SALT I accords were considered on grounds of national interest, rather than on partisan grounds.

In making its arguments to the Senate and to public audiences, the Nixon administration emphasized that it was imperative for Congress to approve the SALT I accords in the course of the summer. In a White House briefing for members of Congress on June 15, 1972, President Nixon argued that it was important to go forward with a second round of negotiations in October. This meant, he noted, that Congress needed to act "sometime in the summer months," preferably before the first of September.[17] What the president failed to mention was that if Congress acted on this timetable and consented to the agreements by the beginning of September, Richard M. Nixon would enter the fall electoral campaign as a statesman who had concluded and had had Congress approve landmark arms control agreements with the Soviets. There is no way to measure exactly how helpful these arms control agreements proved to be for Nixon's reelection campaign. It is indisputable, however, that electoral politics played a role in the eagerness of the Nixon White House to accelerate the ratification process and that Nixon's reelection was helped by his image of being a president who could successfully manage relations with the Soviet Union, and not just a "war" president focused on carrying on hostilities in Vietnam.

The absence of great divisions within the executive branch helped the Nixon administration secure quick congressional action on the ABM Treaty. This was due in no small part to the centralization of the arms control negotiation process under Henry Kissinger. On January 21, 1969, the day after Nixon's inauguration, Kissinger issued a National Security Study Memorandum (NSSM #3), which assigned the executive branch bureaucracy the task of identifying and defining the criteria against which U.S. military needs were to be measured. Approximately two months later, Kissinger issued another National Security Study Memorandum, NSSM #28. This directed the bureaucracy to propose various options for future strategic arms control negotiations, including analysis of the verifiability of different negotiating options. These two efforts were closely interrelated, as NSSM #28 was designed to show what limitations the United States could accept or propose that did not intrude upon the needs of the military, as laid out in NSSM #3. As John Newhouse has summarily noted, in theory, "NSSM #3 was the root, NSSM #28 the stem."[18]

The terms of reference for both interagency studies were drawn up by Henry Kissinger, and both efforts were guided on a day-to-day basis by his staff. Nevertheless, the implementation of these two studies brought emerging differences of opinion within the executive branch out into the open. Differences concerning NSSM #28 were particularly sharp, especially those pertaining to verification issues. On June 25, 1969, a draft of NSSM #28 was aired at a meeting of the National Security Council. The U.S. Arms Control and Disarmament Agency had played a lead role in preparing the sections on verification. At the NSC meeting, the chairman of the Joint Chiefs of Staff (JCS), General Earle ("Bus") Wheeler, took strong exception to the analysis that bore the imprint of ACDA staffers. In an unusually blunt, frontal assault, Wheeler explained in detail "his serious doubt" about the study's verification analyses and stressed the importance of verification to any prospective strategic arms control agreement.[19]

Gerard C. Smith, director of ACDA and chief SALT negotiator, reacted strongly to General Wheeler's comments, defending ACDA's work on verification. Near the end of the meeting Smith suggested that a higher-level verification review panel be established within the executive branch in order to give the issue the special treatment that it deserved. This suggestion gave Kissinger the political opportunity that he had been looking for to create the same mode of closed, centralized operation for SALT issues that he had established for a range of other foreign policy issues.

Kissinger had been a longtime advocate of secrecy and centralization in foreign affairs decision-making, believing that the bureaucracy, if left to its own devices, would produce "set agency positions instead of dispassionate analysis." In his memoirs Kissinger subsequently expanded on this point.

A President should not leave the presentation of his options to one of the Cabinet departments or agencies. Since the views of departments are often in conflict, to place one in charge of presenting the options will be perceived by the others as giving it an unfair advantage. Moreover, the strong inclination of all departments is to narrow the scope for Presidential decision, not to expand it. They are organized to develop a preferred policy, not a range of choices.[20]

In the case of SALT, transferring control over key decisions from the executive branch bureaucracy to the White House meant having the president institutionalize the NSC's central role in the policy process. This was formally done in July 1969 when the president issued a directive establishing a SALT Verification Panel and associated working group. The designated members of the panel were presidential assistant Kissinger, who served as chairman, ACDA Director Smith, Undersecretary of State Elliot Richardson, Deputy Secretary of Defense David Packard, JCS Chairman Wheeler, CIA Director Richard Helms, and Attorney General John Mitchell. Laurence Lynn, a senior Kissinger aide for SALT matters on the NSC staff, was selected as chief staff member.

The SALT Verification Panel and its associated decision-making machinery allowed Henry Kissinger to dominate the strategic arms control policy-making process. It allowed Kissinger to define the shape of the broad range of SALT issues being considered by the government; to constrain the different agency viewpoints that could be presented to the president; to lay out "viable" alternatives; to limit and purposefully manipulate differences of opinion within the executive branch; and, ultimately, to present choices to the president for "his" decision. Contrary to previous administrations' practice, these decisions were taken by the president, with Kissinger's counsel, before or following the NSC's meetings. After a presidential decision, Kissinger's staff would draft the guidelines—National Security Decision Memoranda—for the different executive agencies and for the SALT delegation. Thus, on the substance of key SALT issues, the terms of the discussion were narrowly established and controlled by the president's national security adviser. As a result, there were few opportunities for major policy disagreements within the executive branch or for knowledgeable executive leaks to congressional committees or the press.

In the course of the two and one-half years during which the ABM Treaty was being negotiated, from November 1969 until May 1972, differences of opinion emerged within the executive branch around two issues: (1) the extent of the limits to be placed on U.S. ABM deployments and (2) whether and in what ways an ABM treaty should be tied to an agreement to limit strategic offensive arms. Here, the most contentious issue concerned the matter of whether or not to consider a total U.S. ban on ABM deployments, a position strongly opposed both by the Department of Defense and by the Soviet Union, which would have had to dismantle its already deployed ABM system around Moscow. This issue, which had slowed progress at the SALT negotiations for months and about which there were important divisions within the U.S. government, was the subject of a May 18, 1971, meeting of the SALT Verification Panel. At that session some elements of the Department of State and ACDA favored having the United States press for a zero ABM option at the SALT talks. Other Department of State and ACDA representatives wanted the United States to accept a proposal limiting U.S. ABM sites to one around Washington, thereby scrapping more extensive U.S. ABM plans in the hope that Moscow would accept some limits on offensive weapons. Still other elements, particularly in the Department of Defense, favored extensive ABM deployments in the United States, not limiting the country to either no site or one.[21]

It is now known that this meeting of the SALT Verification Panel, chaired by Kissinger, was in fact something of a charade. Negotiating privately with Dobrynin, Kissinger had within the previous few weeks reached agreement with the Soviets on both this issue and the defense-offense linkage issue. Using the so-called "back channel" for negotiating, Kissinger had reached an agreement with Dobrynin that embodied the national security adviser's preference for "equality" in ABMs. It also stipulated that the superpowers, "together with concluding an agreement to limit ABMs, would agree on certain measures with respect to the limitation of offensive strategic weapons."[22]

At the time, this agreement was known only to Kissinger and, presumably, President Nixon. Others in the executive branch, including chief arms control negotiator Smith, and the entire Congress were ignorant of it. Two days later on May 20, 1971, President Nixon read a brief statement over television and radio, outlining and hailing this "breakthrough" in SALT. He observed that this accord was "a major step in breaking the stalemate on nuclear arms talks," which, he noted, "have been deadlocked for over a year."[23] In a publicly released letter on that day Nixon indicated that the United States would reluctantly set aside its goal of banning all ABMs for the purpose of reaching an early agreement on defensive and offensive arms in the first round of the SALT negotiations. He went on to express the hope that in SALT II it would be possible to achieve a total ABM ban.

During the next year, the two SALT delegations, in essence, worked out the details of the general agreement announced on May 20, 1971.[24] Most of the discussions took place through normal channels—interagency discussions in the SALT Verification Panel in Washington and negotiations with the Soviets in Europe, alternating between Vienna and Helsinki. Just as he had done before the May 1971 "breakthrough," Kissinger continued to use the "back channel" to help "resolve" certain key differences in the negotiations. In late April 1972, roughly one month before the scheduled Moscow summit, Kissinger secretly traveled to Moscow for meetings with General Secretary Brezhnev and his top aides. Although Vietnam and other non–arms control issues were supposed to be the agenda, both defensive and offensive limitations were discussed in these private meetings in Moscow. When Kissinger returned to Washington in late April, he brought with him some new SALT negotiating papers from the Kremlin. These papers were stealthily moved from the "back channel" to the "front channel" by Kissinger and his closest aides and then tirelessly pursued in both Washington and Helsinki until President Nixon left for the summit meeting in Moscow in late May.

The final details of the SALT I accords were subsequently worked out in Moscow by Nixon and Kissinger. Concerning the ABM Treaty, one relatively minor issue that was resolved in Moscow by the heads of state concerned the minimum distance between the two allowed ABM locations. This issue was of some importance in order to "prevent overlapping radar and interceptor coverage having some area defense potential."[25] As with other issues resolved at the very last minute in Moscow, there is an incomplete written record of the details of the final negotiating sessions.

Since Kissinger's NSC system so centralized the SALT policy process, differences between agencies over negotiating the ABM Treaty had a limited overall impact on both the course of the negotiations and the subsequent ratification debate. To be sure, on some SALT issues there were significant differences of opinion within the executive branch. For example, important elements within the Department of State and the ACDA argued internally for a "stop where we are" approach to ABMS and MIRVS. Others in those agencies, supported by both Democrats and liberal Republicans on Capitol Hill, favored a ban on ABMS and MIRVS. The Department of Defense internally opposed any such prohibitions or limitations. Yet when President Nixon announced the terms of the "breakthrough" on the ABM Treaty on May 20, 1971, or when he signed the ABM Treaty in Moscow roughly one year later, there was no significant dissent within the executive branch. It would seem that, on both of these occasions and in the intervening twelve months, would-be critics—inside and outside the government—were limited in what they could do or say by their lack of detailed information and access to closely guarded policy developments. Further, to the extent that there was widespread and deep executive branch concern about the details of the SALT I accords, the focus was much more on the Interim Agreement to Limit Strategic Offensive Arms than on the ABM Treaty. The Department of Defense and the Senate Armed Services Committee were particularly concerned about signing an agreement that gave the Soviets, inter alia, approximately a 3–2 numerical superiority in ICBM and SLBM launchers, with significantly greater throw-weight than that possessed by the United States. In the end, however, these concerns were assuaged by a series of initiatives undertaken by the Nixon administration to ensure congressional approval of the SALT I accords.

Role of the President

Ultimately, the political management responsibility for concluding and ratifying the SALT I accords lay with President Nixon. Although Nixon was highly popular during his first year in office—presidential approval ratings hovered around 70 percent during much of 1969—his popularity seriously dropped after that. In June 1971 his approval levels had plunged to below the 50 percent level for the first time, with disapproval ratings at 39 percent.[26] Later in 1971 President Nixon actually ran behind his leading Democratic challenger, Senator Edmund Muskie (D-Maine). In the Harris poll taken in the first week of January 1972, Nixon and Muskie were tied, with the two men at 42 percent each and Alabama Governor George Wallace a distant third at 11 percent.[27] In part, President Nixon's falling popularity was due to the unpopularity of the war in Vietnam. Notwithstanding steady troop withdrawals and suggestions of future summit meetings, the war continued to drag on, with mounting casualties, frequent negative television coverage, and seeming stalemate on the military front. In part, too, President Nixon's falling popularity seemed traceable to the administration's domestic economic problems, in particular growing inflationary pressures.

With the SALT negotiations reaching a climactic phase, President Nixon seems to have been in serious political trouble, and he and his key aides, watching the polls carefully, sensed this. As part of a calculated strategy to shore up President Nixon's image as an accomplished international statesman, the White House opted in early 1972 to move forward publicly on several international fronts. Concerning Vietnam, President Nixon decided to take a gamble and disclosed publicly that his administration was actively engaged in forward-moving peace negotiations in Paris. Concerning the People's Republic of China, President Nixon and Henry Kissinger dramatically flew to Peking in February and concluded the Shanghai Communiqué, a joint statement reflecting complementary Sino-American interests. Concerning SALT, President Nixon exhorted the SALT delegation and his NSC staff to move forward as quickly as prudently possible to conclude an agreement. Despite the urging of those in the executive branch who feared that the United States would be seen as negotiating against a deadline, President Nixon also publicly announced a date with the Soviet leadership for a summit meeting in Moscow in late May.

Subsequently, when President Nixon and his entourage returned from Moscow with a landmark arms control agreement, the president's popularity was considerably bolstered. This change was clearly reflected in the polls, as presidential approval ratings jumped from the low 50 percent level in early 1972 to 61 percent at the end of May. President Nixon's performance at the Moscow summit won the approval of 82 percent of the American people, and the SALT I accords won an 80 percent approval rating.[28] Seymour Hersh, an often critical chronicler of the Nixon-Kissinger years, has summarily observed, "Richard Nixon came home from the May summit in Moscow with reelection in hand and his reputation as a peacemaker assured."[29]

While the presidential party had been in Moscow Representative John Ashbrook (R-Ohio), a conservative challenger for the Republican presidential nomination, took to the House floor to denounce the emerging SALT I accords. Ashbrook charged that the agreements would "lock the Soviet Union into unchallengeable superiority" and "plunge the United States and its allies into a decade of danger." He also inserted into the *Congressional Record* a detailed story that had appeared in *Newsday* to show how the proposed summit agreements "would doom the United States to nuclear inferiority."[30]

On the plane back to Washington from Moscow President Nixon mused to his aides about Representative Ashbrook's anti-SALT charges and his conservative challenge to the president's reelection campaign. A well-known anticommunist, Nixon observed to his staff that the accords could potentially jeopardize his reelection chances if they were not "sold" properly and ratified speedily and decisively by Congress. With these considerations in mind and hoping to capitalize on the public's support for the summit, the president addressed a joint session of Congress immediately upon his return to Washington. In his address Nixon patently oversold the accord to help underscore his role as world statesman and peacemaker, triumphantly noting that SALT I "witnessed the beginning of the end of that era [of the nuclear arms race]." He then went on to urge speedy action on the ABM Treaty as well as the Interim Agreement, suggesting that congressional approval would "forestall a major spiralling of the arms race." Finally, the president made it clear that administration officials would be willing to spend as much time briefing Congress as necessary to clarify the nature of the recently signed arms control agreements.[31]

President Nixon's promise of an accommodating approach in his briefing of Congress marked a major change from his administration's dealings with Capitol Hill up to that point. During the entire period of negotiation, the Nixon administration had not engaged in serious consultation with the legislative branch on the details of SALT policy. Instead, the executive branch repeatedly paid lip service to the idea of keeping Congress fully informed, typically briefing members in a pro forma manner. Executive branch witnesses were not fully conversant with the details of the ongoing negotiations, and Henry Kissinger invoked executive privilege when asked to testify or meet with members of Congress. Although numerous briefings were held—thirty-seven congressional briefings were conducted by ACDA alone during the period from June 1970 to January 1972—the consultative process was by no means substantive, a fact reflected in increasingly low congressional attendance at committee sessions.[32]

President Nixon had shown open contempt for consultation with Congress on the details of the SALT talks or for even taking into account congressional advice about the proper U.S. negotiating posture. For example, in mid-March 1970, the Senate Foreign Relations Committee, spurred by Senator Cooper and others, held a series of hearings to examine U.S. policy on ABMS and MIRVs and to analyze their relationship to SALT and the nuclear arms race. After the hearings, the committee unanimously approved a nonbinding resolution, jointly initiated by Senator Cooper and Senator Edward Brooke (R-Mass.), calling on the president to propose to the Soviet Union that both sides "immediately suspend deployment of all defensive and offensive nuclear weapons."[33] The day after the committee passed this resolution, President Nixon was asked at a press conference about the significance of the action, which reflected a viewpoint advocated by ACDA within the executive branch. Nixon responded in categorical terms, "I think the Resolution really is irrelevant to what we are trying to do."[34]

To the extent that President Nixon and Henry Kissinger truly engaged in consultation with Congress on SALT matters during the negotiation period, it was on an ad hoc, highly selective basis, usually to further a specific administration goal. For example, in the spring of 1970, Nixon and Kissinger decided that it was desirable to hold a bipartisan briefing of congressional leaders on the SALT negotiations because they feared that the administration's ABM budget request would be rejected by Congress. Accordingly, Kissinger's staff telephoned a small number of senators and representatives to invite them to a top-level SALT briefing. The meeting was set for July 23, 1970, the same day that Smith was presenting the latest U.S. ABM proposal to the Soviet delegation. Making a rare trip to Capitol Hill, Kissinger met secretly with the invited members of Congress in a room just off the Senate floor. Among the attendees were senators George Aiken (R-Vt.), Cooper, Fulbright, and Stennis, and House leaders John W. McCormack (D-Mass.) and Carl B. Albert (D-Okla.).

Kissinger selectively presented an overview of the administration's thinking about some of the key issues under negotiation with the Soviets in Vienna, arguing that full funding of the fiscal year 1971 Safeguard ABM budget request was critical to the success of the U.S. SALT negotiating effort. To the consternation of several members of Congress present, who wanted to be in on foreign policy "take-offs" as well as "landings," Kissinger incidentally noted that on that very same day Smith was proposing a new package of detailed U.S. SALT proposals to the Soviets. Overall, this rare, Kissinger-led briefing, interrupted by several roll-call votes, was not as comprehensive as members of Congress desired or as supportive as the administration had anticipated. On the following day Senator Clifford Case (R-N.J.), an ABM critic, requested a more detailed briefing on the exact course of the SALT negotiations as well as on the specifics of the new package of proposals. His request for such a briefing was subsequently denied by the White House.[35]

In the weeks following his address to the joint session of Congress, President Nixon led a concerted effort to ensure maximal legislative and public support for the SALT I accords. Nixon played a key role in this effort, personally participating where he deemed appropriate and delegating as he saw fit. In his many public comments on the accords the president consistently spoke in glowing terms in support of the agreements, language befitting that of a president seeking reelection as a statesman and peacemaker. In public speeches and in private meetings with members of Congress Nixon purposefully oversold the ABM Treaty in an effort to ensure its decisive approval, making arguments to the Left and to the Right to serve his tactical purposes.

President Nixon also drew on his previous experience in the legislative branch to engage in logrolling and horse trading with Congress and the military services. After the ABM Treaty and the Interim Agreement were signed and sent to Congress, Jackson and his supporters had a number of questions about the details of the agreement, especially in light of the seemingly rushed endgame to the negotiations in Moscow. Specific concerns were raised about the limitations on submarines in the Interim Agreement, the limits in the ABM Treaty, and associated documents on the testing and development of mobile or space-based ABM systems. Jackson was particularly interested in pursuing the distinction between the engineering development and testing of fixed, land-based ABMS, which were permitted by the treaty, and the engineering development and testing of mobile or space-based ABMS, which were seemingly prohibited. His detailed questions about this distinction were subsequently widely aired in the Senate Armed Services Committee's hearings on the treaty.

However, the absence of a complete negotiating record, in combination with a virtual absence of serious pre-summit consultation with the Congress, limited what Jackson could do at the time.[36]

In the subsequent ratification hearings and immediately afterward Jackson chose to focus his energies on the substance of the Interim Agreement rather than on the ABM Treaty or on the way both agreements had been negotiated. Jackson had two major problems with the SALT I Interim Agreement. First, he objected to an agreement that froze the United States at a numerical inferiority in both ICBM launchers and SLBMS. Second, he believed that the SALT I accords insufficiently addressed the possibility that the Soviet Union might be able to threaten the survivability of U.S. land-based forces by exploiting its asymmetrical advantage in throw-weight against a minimally defended United States. Jackson reasoned that America's resulting inferior strategic position might lead the Soviet Union to attack the Atlantic alliance's forward-based systems or even "intervene militarily in the affairs of China."[37]

Before formally introducing legislation that would amend the resolution of consent to the ratification of the SALT I accords, Senator Jackson met with President Nixon at the White House. Jackson explained to Nixon his misgivings about the SALT I agreements and discussed his proposed amendment. Calling for numerical equality in future strategic arms control agreements, this amendment was intended to limit the damage resulting from the asymmetries that Jackson worried about in the SALT I agreements. The amendment was intended to provide concrete policy guidance from Congress for subsequent SALT negotiations. In response President Nixon assured Senator Jackson of the administration's support, saying, according to one account, that "I am with you all the way through [on the amendment]."[38]

Following the Nixon-Jackson meeting at the White House, the precise language of the amendment was worked out by Jackson aide Richard Perle and John Lehman of the NSC staff. Jackson's amendment was advisory rather than binding in its effect. Directed toward the resolution of consent to ratification of the Interim Agreement, it represented an implicit criticism of the unequal freeze arrangements in the SALT I Interim Agreement, and called for numerical equality in future accords, just as the Soviets had insisted on in the ABM Treaty. During floor debate on his amendment, Senator Jackson characterized equality in different ways, sometimes referring to the numbers of ICBM and SLBM launchers deployed by each superpower, other times emphasizing the number of bombers and the missile throw-weight on each side, categories not included in the SALT I accords. The amendment also called for "the maintenance of a vigorous research and development program" in support of a "prudent strategic posture."[39] From President Nixon's point of view, agreeing to Senator Jackson's amendment made sense both substantively and politically, as it would strengthen his hand in subsequent negotiations and ensure congressional approval of the SALT I accords.

Concurrent with President Nixon's efforts to win Senator Jackson's support for the ABM Treaty was an effort to win the support of the Pentagon for the SALT I accords. It was widely believed in the White House that without JCS support, these arms control accords might run into serious opposition in the Senate. Conversely, Nixon believed that with military backing these accords would be overwhelmingly approved by Congress.

Accordingly, President Nixon agreed to link congressional approval of the accords with an aggressive weapons modernization program within the constraints of the SALT I agreements, an idea broached on August 19, 1970, when the president had met with the SALT delegation to hear a report on the Vienna phase of the negotiations. At that meeting the delegation discussed with Nixon the possibility of a supplemental defense request tied to a new arms control agreement. According to the account of former Chief of Naval Operations Elmo Zumwalt, Jr., Nixon noted at this meeting that this possibility of safeguards was "important" and needed to be given proper consideration at the appropriate time.[40]

During the spring of 1972, JCS Chairman Thomas Moorer, Secretary of Defense Melvin Laird, and Senate Armed Services Committee Chairman John Stennis, among others, had all become concerned that U.S. adherence to the emerging SALT I accords would leave the United States in an inferior military position vis-à-vis the Soviet Union. This was especially troubling after General Secretary Brezhnev had made it "absolutely clear" to President Nixon at the summit meeting that the Soviets planned to go forward with their weapons modernization plans in "those areas not controlled" by the SALT I accords. Subsequently, at a June 23 press conference, President Nixon announced that "for us not to [do the same] would seriously jeopardize the security of the United States and jeopardize the cause of world peace."[41]

During the same week as Nixon's press conference, Secretary Laird and Admiral Moorer testified to Congress that legislative approval of the SALT I accords should be tied to the passage of a defense supplemental budget request. They specifically requested increased authorizations to accelerate the development of the Trident submarine, the B-1 bomber, strategic cruise missiles, and improved intelligence and verification capabilities. On June 20, 1972, in testimony on the ABM Treaty before the Senate Armed Services Committee, Secretary Laird explicitly noted that as secretary of defense he could not support the SALT I agreements "without the assurance that these follow-on programs would go forward." He added, "I would certainly recommend that we not go forward with this treaty if we are going to abandon the programs that have been outlined in the strategic weapons field." Laird defended these additional monies as necessary to maintain U.S. "technical superiority" over the Soviet Union. Along with President Nixon, Secretary Laird endorsed a bargaining chip strategy for future strategic arms negotiations with the Soviets.[42]

Given the linkage between these additional arms requests and ratification, it was of some consequence whether the Senate vote on the ABM Treaty preceded or followed the vote on the Fiscal Year 1973 Defense Department Authorization Bill, the legislation containing the funds for Trident, B-1, and cruise missile development. If the vote on the ABM Treaty came first, the accord would be considered on its own merits rather than held hostage to the authorization for additional monies. The administration, however, with the concurrence of the Democratic majority in the Senate, engineered consideration of the authorization bill first. Amendments to the legislation to delete supplementary monies for the Trident and the B-1 were subsequently defeated, and on August 2, 1972, the authorization bill passed the Senate by a vote of 92–5.[43] On the very next day the ABM Treaty was brought up on the Senate floor for a vote.

Executive-Congressional Relations

It was far from predetermined that the Senate would overwhelmingly vote to approve the ABM Treaty. As the Department of State's Office of the Historian has observed, "The SALT I accords involved more difficult issues than either the Limited Test Ban Treaty or the Nuclear Proliferation Treaty. In addition, President Nixon faced a much more delicate public relations problem than did either Kennedy or Johnson,"[44] in large part owing to prior controversies over ABM deployments.

President Lyndon B. Johnson's September 1967 decision to deploy the Sentinel ABM system had provoked a national debate on the future of U.S. deployments of antiballistic missile systems. After years of debate about the feasibility and desirability of ABMs, the Johnson administration had finally given the go-ahead for actual deployment of Sentinel, a system designed to provide a "thin" shield for the total population of the United States.

This debate was far from over when the Nixon administration took office in early 1969. Nor did it end when the Nixon White House chose to go forward in March 1969 with a modified ABM plan called Safeguard, designed primarily to protect U.S. strategic offensive missiles from surprise enemy attack. Many in Congress believed that neither the Johnson nor the Nixon administration had persuasively made the case for its particular ABM deployment plan. In each of the three years of the Nixon administration before the signing of the ABM Treaty, congressional majorities in favor of ballistic missile defenses were uncomfortably narrow. Indeed, with the fiscal year 1969 defense authorization bill, the Safeguard program passed on a 50–50 vote.

Congressional divisions regarding ABM deployments—"a babble of discordant voices," in Kissinger's words[45]—were set against the general backdrop of decreasing willingness on the part of Congress to accept the primacy of the executive branch in making foreign policy.[46] In significant part owing to Vietnam, Congress was becoming increasingly assertive on a wide range of foreign affairs issues. No longer was it possible, as it had been during much of the 1960s, for the executive branch to hope to pass the annual Department of Defense appropriations bill by voice vote. No longer was it possible to disregard legislative requests for detailed information about various national security subjects as well as weapons systems.

Following the controversial ABM debate in mid-1969, which lasted for more than five weeks and which ended in a 50–50 tie vote, many senators publicly expressed the view that Congress was entering a new era of heightened involvement in the formulation of U.S. defense and arms control policy. Murray Marder, veteran diplomatic correspondent of the *Washington Post*, wrote about the first session of the Ninety-first Congress in the following dramatic way:

> Groundwork for a non-violent rebellion inside the American Establishment was begun during the session of Congress that

ended Tuesday. . . . Historians . . . will watch with scholarly fascination to see if the decade of the 70s produces only a sham revolt or a reapportionment of power between the executive and legislative branches on matters of war and peace. . . . The challengers of unquestioned executive branch primacy went on to question intended actions they never dreamed of seriously disputing in years past. They contested and lost by only one vote, the decision to develop an anti-ballistic missile system.[47]

Thomas Halsted, then chief lobbyist for the anti-ABM Council for a Livable World, summarized the new situation more tersely: "The ABM debates have brought about some permanent changes. The public has become involved to an important degree in national security decision-making. The days of congressional rubber-stamping may be over."[48]

In the face of serious divisions in Congress on ABM deployments and increasing distrust of the executive branch on Capitol Hill, the Nixon administration purposefully pursued a multipronged strategy to win Senate support for the ABM Treaty. Extensive consultation with Congress during the ratification process was at the center of this strategy, involving all the senior members of the Nixon administration, prominently including National Security Adviser Henry Kissinger. For example, on June 15, 1972, Kissinger held a two-hour, wide-ranging, bipartisan question-and-answer session with roughly 120 senators and representatives. In introducing Kissinger to the members of Congress assembled for the White House briefing, President Nixon noted that he had to decline previous suggestions that his national security adviser appear before committees of Congress on the SALT accords because "executive privilege had to prevail." He added, however, that since this was "really an unprecedented situation," he had asked Kissinger to appear before the members of the different committees in this format and on the record. He further promised that all members of Congress would be given a "total transcript" of what Kissinger said, and he noted that the presidential assistant would "be available to answer other questions in his office . . . as time goes on, during the course of the [ratification] hearings."[49]

At the White House briefing Kissinger glowingly described the details of the SALT I agreements and answered a range of questions that several senators had in mind to ask him for years. At one point during the question-and-answer session, Senator Claiborne Pell (D-R.I.), a senior member of the Foreign Relations Committee, pointedly inquired, "Why, in this set of negotiations, was the constitutionally normal course of congressional consultation, advice as well as consent, not engaged in?" Kissinger clearly had no good answer to this question. In reply, he observed, "As for the process of consultation, this is not my specialty, but it has been my understanding that Mr. Smith and the appropriate Secretaries have been in close consultation and we have tried from here to be . . . in contact with key Senators."[50]

Secretary of State William Rogers, Secretary of Defense Laird, chief SALT negotiator Smith, and Admiral Moorer, reiterating many of the same substantive arguments that Henry Kissinger made in his June 15 White House briefing, subsequently testified at length on the ABM Treaty before the Senate Foreign Relations Committee. Additional testimony on the ABM Treaty and the Interim Agreement was taken by the Senate Armed Services Committee. The key lieutenants in the Nixon administration had never been so available to testify before Congress and to meet with individual members to share information and answer questions as they were during the two months of the SALT I ratification debate.

The Nixon administration undertook a number of other steps to help ensure ratification of the ABM Treaty. The Senate leadership of both parties, influential members of Congress, relevant committees, and key constituencies were all carefully watched, listened to, and negotiated with. Ultimately, Senate approval of the ABM Treaty was tied, directly and indirectly, to other issues of concern to members of Congress. Two measures taken directly by President Nixon have already been discussed: tying approval of the ABM Treaty to supplemental authorizations for new weapons modernization programs and accepting the Jackson amendment to the

Interim Agreement. Several other "facilitating" steps were
subsequently taken by the Nixon administration, including a
linkage, never directly acknowledged by members of the
executive or legislative branch, between congressional
approval of the SALT I accords and the future orientation and
operation of the U.S. Arms Control and Disarmament
Agency.

A number of conservative senators favored the separation
of the job of ACDA director from that of chief SALT negotiator
and the replacement of the key SALT personnel in the
executive branch with more "hardheaded" negotiators.
Senators Jackson and Gordon Allott (R-Colo.) held
particularly strong beliefs about the "toughness" of the U.S.
negotiating team. In Gerard C. Smith's view, "Jackson
apparently believed that the unequal freeze arrangements
were the result of undue influence of 'arms controllers' in
ACDA and the State Department—against whom he believed
the military representative on the delegation had not stood
firmly enough."[51]

Soon after his reelection in November 1972, President
Nixon asked for the resignations of all appointed officials in
the executive branch. In some agencies the resignations were
formally submitted and subsequently rejected. At ACDA,
however, the resignation of virtually every top official was
accepted. In an earlier private conversation with President
Nixon, Smith had made it clear that he intended to leave
government service after the SALT I accords were ratified.
Several of Smith's chief assistants, however, were in fact
"purged" from the leadership ranks of ACDA. By early 1974
only four of ACDA's top seventeen officials were still with the
agency. In addition, Lieutenant General Royal Allison, the JCS
representative on the SALT I delegation, who was a frequent
target of conservatives in the Senate, also abruptly resigned
from government service. He was replaced by Lieutenant
General Edward Rowny, a man in whom Senator Jackson had
confidence.

In addition, the decision was made to make separate

appointments to the directorship of ACDA and to leadership of the SALT negotiating team. U. Alexis Johnson, a career foreign service officer, was subsequently chosen as chief of the SALT delegation, and soon thereafter Fred Iklé of the RAND Corporation was selected to be director of ACDA. Not coincidentally, during the 1960s, Iklé had completed several studies for Senator Jackson's Government Operations Subcommittee on National Security Affairs. After Congress had completed consideration of the SALT I accords, SALT I participant Joseph Kruzel observed, "It is a poorly kept secret in Washington that a mini-purge was conducted by the White House, at Senator Jackson's urging, in a deliberate attempt to start SALT II with a new team of officials unsullied by association with SALT I."[52]

The size and character of ACDA were also affected by the linkage forged during congressional approval of the SALT I accords. In late 1972 ACDA was directed by the White House and the Office of Management and Budget to cut its annual budget request by one third and to focus on research rather than negotiations. By the time the Senate had confirmed Iklé to be head of ACDA in July 1973, the number of Agency employees had fallen from 219 in December 1972 to 162. In addition, 15 military officers and 13 foreign service officers on temporary assignment to ACDA were released from the agency. Seemingly with Nixon administration assent, conservatives in the Senate, led by Senator Jackson, had not only played a central role in providing guidance to future arms control negotiators but also in forcing institutional changes based on their criticisms of how the first round of SALT had been conducted.[53]

Besides tying approval of the SALT I accords to these arms control personnel matters, the Nixon administration indirectly linked these arms control agreements to large, new U.S. grain sales to the Soviet Union. At the Moscow summit meeting in late May 1972 the two superpowers appeared to be entering a new era of commercial relations. The new arms control agreements, if approved by Congress, were to be the linchpin for new types of mutually beneficial economic accords. On July 8, 1972, while the Senate was holding hearings on the ABM Treaty, the Nixon administration announced its intention to go forward with one such accord: a historic superpower grain deal. At the time, the White House announced that it had extended a $500 million line of credit to the Kremlin in exchange for Soviet agreement to buy $750 million worth of U.S. grain over the next three years. Of great interest to farm state senators, the agreement further stipulated that at least $200 million of these grain purchases would be made during the first year, not coincidentally a presidential election year in the United States.

On September 9, 1972, roughly one month after the ABM Treaty was approved by the Senate, Secretary of Agriculture Earl Butz announced that Soviet purchases of wheat alone would amount to roughly 400 million bushels in 1972, representing more than one fourth the total U.S. crop. Butz added that total U.S. grain sales to Moscow would approach $1 billion for the year, considerably more than the total amount envisaged over the entire three-year life of the agreement.[54]

The Nixon administration's efforts to link ratification of SALT I to all of these other issues proved to be highly successful: the final vote tallied 88–2 in the Senate for both the ABM Treaty and the Interim Agreement, and 329–7 in the House in favor of the Interim Agreement. Senate support for the ABM Treaty proved to be strong and bipartisan. Several Democratic members of the Foreign Relations Committee, led by Chairman Fulbright and Stuart Symington (D-Mo.), raised doubts about whether larger defense authorizations were consistent with the spirit of SALT, which was intended to reduce tensions. The committee's report recommending approval of the ABM Treaty noted that although this was "an important first step toward arms limitation, a number of committee members believe there were serious questions as to the political wisdom of proceeding full steam ahead with some of the various systems now proposed." The report added, "It would be ironic indeed if what is purportedly an agreement on arms limitation might become a spur to further an arms buildup."[55]

Senators most supportive of arms control, like Chairman Fulbright and ranking Republican Cooper, publicly and privately groused about some of the tactics employed by the Nixon administration to gain conservative support for SALT, but, ultimately, they backed the treaty unanimously. Those more skeptical of arms control, a group spearheaded by Senator Jackson, also ended up supporting the treaty, although tying their approval to increased authorizations for strategic weapons modernization and passage of the Jackson amendment to the Interim Agreement. Some in this group, particularly Republican senators, might still have opposed SALT I but feared that a vote against the Nixon administration on SALT could seriously undermine both the U.S. effort in Vietnam and Richard Nixon's reelection chances.

The two senators who voted against the ABM Treaty—James Allen (D-Ala.) and James L. Buckley (R-N.Y.)—argued that it would expose civilian populations to destruction in the event of nuclear war by limiting each nation to only two ABM sites. In testimony before the Foreign Relations Committee, Buckley cast his opposition in terms of both prudence and morality. He noted that, as a matter of prudence, he was opposed to any arms control treaty that required the United States to "dismantle" its defenses "before agreement is reached on dismantling the weapons of mass destruction." He added that while the United States did not currently have "the technical means" to protect its civilian population, he was not comfortable with "the morality of precluding the possibility of developing at some future date new approaches to anti-ballistic missile defenses which could offer protection to substantial numbers of our people."[56]

When pressed by Senator Cooper in the course of the ratification hearing, Senator Buckley also expressed strong opposition to concluding arms control agreements with the Soviet Union. Cooper queried Buckley about whether ratifying the ABM Treaty, thus limiting the superpowers to two ABM sites, was not preferable to a situation where "one country deployed an areawide ABM system and gave the impression it was trying to protect its population." This latter situation, Cooper argued, "would cause such instability that one nation might launch a first strike in the belief that it would protect its population and, in fact, achieve the destruction of the other country, by a first strike." In response Buckley noted the wisdom of Cooper's reasoning, as long as both sides were "playing by the same concepts." In the case of the Soviet Union, the reasoning was faulty, Buckley added, because "the Soviet Union does not believe in the doctrine of mutually assured destruction," and Moscow would inevitably develop and enhance its nuclear capabilities for the purpose of influencing "diplomatic developments which ultimately affect the security of the free world."[57]

Senator Buckley ultimately offered an amendment to the resolution of ratification, adding an "understanding" by the Senate that failure to negotiate a satisfactory follow-on agreement to the Interim Agreement would be grounds for abrogating the ABM Treaty. Buckley envisaged that the conclusion of such a follow-on agreement would assure superpower parity in strategic offensive weapons and that this accord would be concluded before the Interim Agreement expired in 1977. Buckley added that this understanding merely would incorporate the U.S. position in SALT, as laid out by chief negotiator Gerard Smith in his testimony to the Senate in behalf of the SALT I accords.

After consulting with senior administration officials and senators Fulbright and Cooper, among others, Buckley subsequently withdrew his amendment. Before doing so, however, Buckley and Fulbright reached a compromise, jointly declaring on the Senate floor that "the legislative history of the treaty would establish congressional support for the U.S. position."[58] Although a number of amendments were subsequently offered in September to the Interim Agreement, including the Jackson amendment discussed earlier, no other amendments were offered to the ABM Treaty. So, without amendment or reservation, the ABM Treaty was passed by an 88–2 vote on August 3, 1972, after a mere few hours of debate on the Senate floor. Owing in significant part to the Nixon administration's strategy and tactics, which successfully accommodated or co-opted potential opponents across the political spectrum, the resolution of ratification was passed overwhelmingly.

Public Opinion and the Role of Interest Groups

In significant part due to severe restrictions by the Nixon administration on the amount of information made available publicly during the negotiation of the ABM Treaty, public opinion was not a significant factor in the making of SALT policy. Judging by polling data, the American public was generally uninformed and largely disinterested in the Nixon administration's SALT negotiating efforts. Support grew toward the conclusion of the negotiations, as more information was made public by the White House, and polling data were overwhelmingly supportive of the accords after the summit meeting in Moscow in May 1972, continuing to reflect high levels of support throughout the ratification debate.[59]

The one ABM-related issue that did arouse heated public concern involved the potential sites of ABM deployments. When the proposed listing for ABM deployments was released by the Department of Defense in early 1969, there was a serious public outcry at the grass-roots level. The loudest complaints came from those cities slated to be defended by the first deployments—Boston, Chicago, and Seattle—where communities were vociferous in their opposition to having antiballistic missile systems as neighbors. Residents of these communities and others interested in arms control lobbied locally and in Washington to prevent the deployment of any ABM systems, arguing that there were technical problems with deploying these systems; that the systems were too expensive and that "the United States could best serve its long-term security interests through attempts to negotiate a standstill in the strategic arms race."[60]

This grass-roots lobbying effort against ABM deployments came to a head during the summer of 1969 when the Senate voted to approve the Nixon administration's ABM budget request by a margin of one vote. A clear message, though, was sent to the White House: it would be very difficult to go forward with widespread ABM deployments in the United States.

Following the close Senate vote in 1969, a number of senators and representatives offered amendments in 1970-1971 aimed at modifying or ending the administration's ABM plans. Ultimately, these efforts all failed, although there is no question but that legislative opposition to the administration's annual ABM budget requests helped to shape the executive branch's ABM plans.

Grassroots community lobbying against ABM deployments was bolstered and supplemented by a notable and outspoken segment of the scientific community that tended to enthusiastically support arms control and that had been activated by the Johnson and Nixon administrations' proposals to deploy ballistic missile defenses. The scientific community had long been split about the technical feasibility of deploying ABMs.[61] Those favoring ballistic missile defenses were heartened by the Nixon administration's reorientation of the old Sentinel proposal, although some wanted more extensive deployments than the new administration envisaged.[62] Scientists opposed to ABM deployments swung into high gear, however, seeking to defeat the executive branch's ABM budget requests in Congress and to pressure the United States government to negotiate with the Soviet Union a mutual ban on ABMS. Convinced that ABMS were neither necessary nor reliable, these scientists were regularly invited to Washington to testify against administration plans, and they gave many public speeches around the country. The technical and political arguments against deploying ABMS were compiled in a book edited by Abram Chayes of Harvard Law School and Jerome Wiesner, provost of the Massachusetts Institute of Technology (MIT).[63] It contained chapters by a number of notable scientists (such as Hans Bethe and Bernard Feld) and raised serious and detailed doubts about the future effectiveness of ballistic missile defenses, becoming a standard reference for those in Congress opposed to ABM deployments. During the initial years of Senate consideration of ABMS, as Alton Frye has noted, "The game of 'pick your scientist' proceeded apace."[64]

After the ABM Treaty was signed in May 1972, the Nixon administration actively worked to ensure the backing of those against ballistic missile defenses, as it did not wish to risk losing the votes of those senators most committed to arms control and most involved in opposing any ABM deployments. The White House feared that elements of the arms control community and their allies in the Senate, including Foreign Relations Committee Chairman Fulbright, might actually work to defeat the ratification of the ABM Treaty. Opposition from the Left could be based on the grounds that rejection of the ABM Treaty might lead, ultimately, to zero ABM deployments in the United States, whereas approval of the treaty might ensure that two sites would be built within the United States. There was also concern in the White House that Senate consideration of the ABM Treaty would be tied to approval of the Interim Agreement. Given its modest and interim character compared with the permanent ABM Treaty, the Interim Agreement was relatively unpopular among arms control enthusiasts, especially when the passage of the SALT I accords was linked to new authorizations for weapons modernization programs.

At the end of a concerted executive branch lobbying effort the arms control community generally supported the ABM Treaty. Many in this community, like former Senator Joseph S. Clark (D-Pa.), chairman of the Coalition on National Priorities and Military Policy, held the opinion that the ABM

Treaty was a "fraud and an exceptionally ridiculous agreement." Clark and others believed that since "military leaders know that the ABM will in all likelihood not work under battle conditions," no sites should be built.[65] The Nixon administration combatted and undercut this sentiment by arguing that passage of the ABM Treaty heightened strategic stability. The administration also argued that the ABM Treaty, while perhaps generating some new authorizations would, overall, save the United States roughly $500 million in the next fiscal year alone.[66] Perhaps most tellingly, the administration argued that the ABM Treaty was a first step toward global disarmament and wide-ranging détente with the Soviet Union. MIT Professor George Rathjens, testifying on behalf of the Council for a Livable World before the Senate Foreign Relations Committee, summed up majority sentiment in the arms control community when he observed:

> The ABM Treaty, although not the best that could have been negotiated, is a notable agreement of perhaps lasting importance which should be supported. . . . The ABM Treaty can be faulted in that it has been more delayed than it need have been and because it permits too much. . . . But the delay and the wasted dollars pale into insignificance when measured against the importance of the treaty. It should allay concerns that either the Soviet Union or the United States may in the foreseeable future find it advantageous to attack the other; it codifies the legitimacy of verification by national means; and it [weakens] the case that is being made for developing and expanding strategic offensive forces. . . . In summary, the ABM Treaty should be supported enthusiastically.[67]

In contrast with the Interim Agreement, which generated some opposition across the political spectrum, the only formal opposition to the ABM Treaty came from such right-wing organizations as the Liberty Lobby and the National Association of Pro America. Representatives of these organizations testified against the ABM Treaty, calling it "dangerous, disadvantageous and devious,"[68] but their efforts in Washington and around the country were of very marginal significance. In the final analysis, Senate consideration of the

ABM Treaty took place without great regard to interest groups on either side of the agreement.

Conclusion

The broad support for the ABM Treaty when it was considered and voted on by the Senate is a testament to both the substance of the accord and to the successful tactics and strategy employed by the Nixon administration. The Nixon-Kissinger closed system of national security decision making severely limited the amount of public information available regarding the ABM Treaty before its conclusion in May 1972. This had the effect of stifling wide-ranging, serious debate within executive branch agencies, Congress, the press, and among outside experts and the public at large. When the treaty was ultimately signed and sent to Capitol Hill for consent to ratification, potential protagonists on different sides of the issues were, in essence, presented with a fait accompli. Their perceived choice was between this agreement and nothing at all.

To those most favorably disposed to arms control, the ABM Treaty clearly did not go far enough: it did not ban all ABMS. Nevertheless, the treaty, by prohibiting superpower ABM deployments save for two sites, was a major step forward for arms control. It was also seen, owing in part to the Nixon administration's purposeful overselling of the treaty, as a first step toward global disarmament. Accordingly, arms control enthusiasts inside and outside the government ultimately embraced the treaty, especially when they considered the consequences of its defeat in the Senate. If the Senate had not voted to ratify the treaty, NATO countries as well as the Soviet Union could have perceived the United States as an unsuitable partner for serious arms control negotiations. Moreover, a relaxation of superpower tensions could have been placed in jeopardy.

The Nixon administration persuaded not just arms control enthusiasts but also many skeptics of arms control to support the ABM Treaty. Relying heavily on Nixon's longtime, staunch anticommunist record, the administration effectively convinced the Pentagon and the large majority of conservative senators that this treaty was far preferable to a situation wherein the Soviet Union pursued nationwide ABM deployments and the United States, hampered by legislative and budgetary restrictions, was severely constrained in its ABM efforts. The administration also argued that this agreement was the best that the United States could achieve at this time and that its defeat in the Senate would seriously undermine the president's military efforts in Vietnam and his chances for reelection. Finally, by linking the treaty to new weapons authorizations and to tight guidelines for future strategic arms control negotiations, the Nixon administration mollified the concerns of most conservatives inside and outside the Senate. In the end, except for senators Allen and Buckley, who had moral reservations about an ABM Treaty, the Nixon administration managed to achieve a remarkable consensus on an issue that was previously the source of great divisiveness in the Senate and in the country.

Although the Nixon administration's secretive and pragmatic tactics in handling the ABM Treaty negotiations and ratification debate were highly successful in the nearterm, there may well have been important longer-term costs. The Nixon administration did not lay the groundwork for a consensus on future negotiated arms control efforts. Indeed, as one scholar has observed, the Nixon administration's use of linkage, its lack of consultation with Congress, and its "exploiting the process as a tool of presidential politics" may have confused Congress's and the American public's thinking about arms control.[69] There is undoubtedly some truth in this, as evidenced by the increasing numbers of MIRVs and strategic offensive weapons generally in subsequent years and by the historical record of unsuccessful U.S. efforts in the strategic arms control area during the remainder of the 1970s.

The failure of subsequent arms control efforts may also be attributed to a number of other factors, however, including the posture and behavior of the Soviet Union, the unattractiveness of key elements in U.S. strategic arms control initiatives, and the overall political ineptness of the Carter administration.[70]

The Nixon administration's handling of the ABM Treaty negotiations and ratification debate took place in an unusually closed, secretive environment. Given the significantly enhanced role of Congress and the media in the shaping of contemporary U.S. foreign policy, it is hard to believe that any future strategic arms control efforts will take place in a similar environment. Nevertheless, all future presidents and administration aides faced with the responsibility of ensuring legislative support for negotiated arms control agreements would do well to study the central role of President Nixon in the ratification of the ABM Treaty and the tactics and strategy employed so successfully by his administration in this case.

Notes

1. *New York Times*, January 28, 1969. For further discussion of the Nixon administration's view of the relationship between arms control and the overall U.S.-Soviet relationship, see Alan Platt, *The U.S. Senate and Strategic Arms Policy, 1969-1977* (Boulder, Colo.: Westview Press, 1978), 22–24. At various points, as indicated, this chapter draws heavily on this book.

2. "The White House–Congressional Briefing by Dr. Henry Kissinger, Assistant to the President for National Security Affairs," *White House Press Release*, June 15, 1972.

3. Henry Kissinger, *White House Years* (Boston, Mass.: Little, Brown & Co., 1979), 1253.

4. George Breslauer, "Why Détente Failed: An Interpretation," in *Managing U.S.-Soviet Rivalry: Problems of Crisis Prevention*, ed. Alexander L. George (Boulder, Colo.: Westview Press, 1983), 325–26. See also Richard M. Nixon, *RN: The Memoirs of Richard Nixon* (New York: Grosset and Dunlap, 1978), 940–43.

5. Peter Tarnoff, "America's Special Relationships," *Foreign Affairs* 69, no.3 (Summer 1990): 75. On the triangular element in the Nixon administration's diplomacy, see Raymond L. Garthoff, *Detente and Confrontation: American-Soviet Relations from Nixon to Reagan* (Washington, D.C.: The Brookings Institution, 1985), 199–247. Kissinger, *White House Years*, 163–71.

6. Richard M. Nixon, *In the Arena* (New York: Simon and Schuster, 1990), 334–35. See also Kissinger, *White House Years*, 1121–23.

7. Gerard C. Smith, *Doubletalk: The Story of the First Strategic Arms Limitation Talks* (Garden City, N.Y.: Doubleday & Co., 1980), 382.

8. U.S. Department of State, Office of the Historian, Bureau of Public Affairs, Memorandum from Torbert (H) to Macomber (H), "Congressional Briefings on SALT," quoted in *Administration Strategy toward Congress on Three Nuclear Arms Issues (Limited Test Ban Treaty, Nonproliferation Treaty, SALT I Agreements)*, Research project no. 1189, March 1978; also a confidential interview with author.

9. Joseph Coffey, "Strategic Arms Limitations and European Security," *International Affairs* 47 (October 1971): 692–707. See also John Newhouse, *Cold Dawn: The Story of SALT* (New York: Holt, Rinehart & Winston, 1973), 174–75, and Michael Stewart, "Britain, Europe and the Alliance," *Foreign Affairs* 48, no. 4 (July 1970): 653–54.

10. Smith, *Doubletalk*, 470.

11. Robert Schulzinger, *Henry Kissinger: Doctor of Diplomacy* (New York: Columbia University Press, 1989), 70.

12. John Sherman Cooper, interview with author, East Berlin, April 16, 1975. Platt, *The U.S. Senate and Strategic Arms Policy*, 19–21.

13. Confidential interview with author.

14. I. M. Destler to author, October 25, 1990.

15. Richard Perle, interview with author, Washington, D.C., July 28, 1976. For more details on Senator Jackson's role regarding SALT I, see Alton Frye, *A Responsible Congress* (New York: McGraw-Hill, 1975), 87–90; Peter Ognibene, *Scoop: The Life and Politics of Henry Jackson* (New York: Stein and Day, 1975), 202–3; and Platt, *The U.S. Senate and Strategic Arms Policy*, 23–30.

16. Nixon, *In the Arena*, 636.

17. "The White House—Remarks of the President at a Congressional Briefing on the Arms Limitation Treaty and Agreement," *White House Press Release*, June 15, 1972.

18. Newhouse, *Cold Dawn*, 159.

19. Ibid., 162–62. See also Smith, *Doubletalk*, 108–16.

20. Kissinger, *White House Years*, 43. Kissinger provided the rationale for controlling SALT policy-making in an article published shortly before he entered the Nixon administration.

> Because management of the bureaucracy takes so much energy and precisely because changing course is so difficult, many of the most important decisions are kept to a very small circle while the bureaucracy continues working away in ignorance of the fact that decisions are being made. . . . One reason for keeping the decisions to a small group is that when bureaucracies are so unwieldy . . . an unpopular decision may be fought by brutal means, such as leaks to the press or congressional committees. Thus, the only way secrecy can be kept is to exclude from the making of decisions all those who are theoretically charged with carrying it out.

"Bureaucracy and Policy Making: The Effect of Insiders and Outsiders on the Policy Process," in *Bureaucracy, Politics and Strategy*, ed. Henry Kissinger and Bernard Brodie, Security Studies Project no. 17 (Los Angeles: University of California Press, 1968. For a contemporary discussion of Kissinger's views on the bureaucracy, see Michael Charlton, "The President's Men at the NSC: Part I, The Kissinger Revolution," *National Interest* (Summer 1990): 101–8.

21. Newhouse, *Cold Dawn*, 216–17.

22. Ibid. and Smith, *Doubletalk*, 242–43.

23. Kissinger, *White House Years*, 810–23. The text of this Nixon ABM statement is reprinted in Smith, *Doubletalk*, app. 5, 485–86.

24. For a detailed discussion of this period, see Richard Haass and Nancy Kates, "SALT I: Getting from Nyet to Yes," Pew Case, no.339 (Cambridge: Kennedy School of Government, Harvard University, 1988). See also Fen Osler Hampson, "SALT I: Interim Agreement and ABM Treaty," in *Superpower Arms Control: Setting the Record Straight*, ed. Albert Carnesale and Richard Haass (Cambridge, Mass.: Ballinger, 1987), 65–103.

25. Smith, *Doubletalk*, 410.

26. *New York Times*, July 4, 1971.

27. Seymour Hersh, *The Price of Power: Kissinger in the Nixon White House* (New York: Summit Books, 1983), 481. See also, *New York Times*, November 18, 1971.

28. *Washington Post*, June 27, 1972.

29. Hersh, *The Price of Power*, 529.

30. Ibid., 550.

31. *New York Times*, June 2, 1972. See also Garthoff, *Détente and Confrontation*, 194–95.

32. U.S. Department of State, *Administration Strategy*.

33. Frye, *A Responsible Congress*, 15–46.

34. *Washington Post*, March 22, 1970.

35. Platt, *The U.S. Senate and Strategic Arms Policy*, 16. Confidential interview with author.

36. In the mid-1980s the Reagan administration reopened the issue of exactly what limitations were imposed by the ABM Treaty when it raised questions about the Senate's original interpretation of the treaty. For a detailed discussion of ABM Treaty interpretation issues, see U.S. Congress, Senate Committee on Foreign Relations, *The ABM Treaty Interpretation Resolution, Report*, 100th Cong., 1st sess., September 22, 1987. See also Sam Nunn, "ABM Reinterpretation 'Fundamentally Flawed,'" *Arms Control Today* (April 1987), 8–14.

37. U.S. Congress, Senate Committee on Armed Services, *Military Implications of the Treaty on the Limitation on Anti-Ballistic Missile Systems and the Interim Agreement on the Limitation of Strategic Offensive Arms, Hearings*, 92d Cong., 2d sess., June–July 1972, 415. See also Henry Jackson, "Weapons Agreements: A Senator Questions U.S. Concessions,"*Los Angeles Times*, June 25, 1972 and Duncan Clarke, *Politics of Arms Control* (New York: Free Press, 1979), 50–52.

38. Kurt Lauk, "Possibilities of Senatorial Influence: The Case of the Jackson Amendment to SALT I" (Stanford University, 1975), 13.

39. The full text of the Jackson Amendment is reprinted in *Strategic Arms Limitation Treaty (SALT): Legislative History of the Jackson Amendment, 1972*, i–ii. This document, compiled by Richard Perle of Senator Jackson's staff, includes the complete record of congressional consideration of the Jackson amendment.

40. Elmo R. Zumwalt, Jr., *On Watch* (New York: Quadrangle/New York Times Book Co., 1976), 405–7.

41. "Transcript of President Nixon's News Conference," *New York Times*, June 23, 1972. See also Garthoff, *Détente and Confrontation*, 300–1. Garthoff notes that the Soviets may have been "mouse-trapped" in this regard. He argues that there may have been a passing discussion in which both President Nixon and General Secretary Brezhnev declared that they would abide by the SALT I limitations and at the same time go forward with military programs consistent with the agreed limitations.

42. U.S. Congress, Senate Committee on Armed Services, "Testimony of Secretary of Defense Melvin Laird," in *Military Implications of the Treaty*, 151–52.

43. For further discussion of the linking of weapons modernization monies to SALT I ratification, see Jonathan Medalia, "The U.S. Senate and Strategic Arms Limitation Policymaking, 1963-1972" (Ph.D. diss., Stanford University, 1975), 155-59.

44. U.S. Department of State, *Administration Strategy*.

45. Kissinger, *White House Years*, 541.

46. For a discussion of increasing congressional assertiveness across a wide range of arms control issues, see Alan Platt and Lawrence Weiler, eds., *Congress and Arms Control* (Boulder, Colo.: Westview Press, 1978).

47. *Washington Post*, December 27, 1969.

48. Thomas Halsted, "Lobbying against the ABM, 1967–1970," *Bulletin of the Atomic Scientists* 27 (April 1971): 28.

49. "The White House—Remarks of the President at a Congressional Briefing on the Arms Limitation Treaty and Agreement," *White House Press Release*, June 15, 1972.

50. "The White House–Congressional Briefing by Dr. Henry Kissinger," *White House Press Release*, June 15, 1972.

51. Smith, *Doublespeak*, 443.

52. Quoted in *Congressional Quarterly*, June 15, 1974. See also Platt, *The U.S. Senate and Strategic Arms Policy*, 25-27; Smith, *Doulbletalk*, 442–44; and Clarke, *Politics of Arms Control*, 50-52.

53. Platt, *The U.S. Senate and Strategic Arms Policy*, 29-30.

54. "Soviet Grain Sale and Wheat Subsidy," *Congressional Quarterly Almanac, 1972* (Washington, D.C.: Congressional Quarterly Press, 1973), 822-24.

55. *Congressional Quarterly Almanac, 1972*, 589.

56. U.S. Congress, Senate Committee on Foreign Relations, "Statement of Hon. James L. Buckley," in *Strategic Arms Limitation Agreements, Hearings*, 92d Cong., 2d sess., 1972, 257.

57. Ibid., 269–70.

58. *Congressional Quarterly Almanac, 1972*, 589.

59. *New York Times*, November 18, 1971, and *Washington Post*, June 27, 1972.

60. Frye, *A Responsible Congress*, 22.

61. For a discussion of the role of the scientific community in the ABM debate, see Anne Cahn, *Eggheads and Warheads: Scientists and the ABM* (Cambridge: MIT Press, 1971).

62. For example, see Johan Holst and William Schneider, Jr., eds., *Why ABM?* (Elmsford, New York: Pergamon, 1969).

63. Abram Chayes and Jerome Wiesner, eds., *ABM: An Evaluation of the Decision to Deploy an Anti-Ballistic Missile System* (New York: Harper, 1969).

64. Frye, *A Responsible Congress*, 34.

65. U.S. Congress, Senate Committee on Foreign Relations, "Statement of Hon. Joseph Clark, Former U.S. Senator, Chairman of the Coalition on National Priorities and Military Policy," in *Strategic Arms Limitation Agreements, Hearings*, 272.

66. U.S. Congress, Senate Committee on Armed Services, "Testimony of Secretary of Defense Melvin Laird," in *Military Implications of the Treaty*, 152. It was estimated that the SALT agreements would result in a savings of $711 million in fiscal year 1973 as a result of canceled ABM construction and deployment. The $711 million in savings would be partially offset by $168 million used to accelerate a few strategic modernization programs. Total savings, accordingly, would then be roughly $543 million during the next fiscal year, as a result of approving the SALT I accords.

67. U.S. Congress, Senate, Committee on Foreign Relations, "Statement of George Rathjens, Council for a Livable World," in *Strategic Arms Limitation Agreements, Hearings*, 298–301.

68. "Statement of Phyllis Schlafly, Member, National Board of Directors, Association of Pro America,"328, and "Statement of James Dornan, Member, Board of Policy, Liberty Lobby,"306–18, in *Strategic Arms Limitation Agreements, Hearings*.

69. Lori Esposito Murray, *SALT I and Congress: Building a Consensus on Nuclear Arms Control* (Ph.D. diss., The Johns Hopkins University, 1989), 10–11, 450–54.

70. See Alan Platt, *The Politics of Arms Control and the Strategic Balance*, P-6825 (The RAND Corporation, 1982).

Selected Bibliography

Books and Articles

Cahn, Anne. *Eggheads and Warheads: Scientists and the ABM.* Cambridge: MIT Press, 1971.

Carnesale, Albert, and Richard N. Haass, eds. *Superpower Arms Control: Setting the Record Straight.* Cambridge, Mass.: Ballinger, 1987.

Chayes, Abram and Jerome Wiesner, eds. *abm: An Evaluation of the Decision to Deploy an Anti-Ballistic Missile System.* New York: Harper, 1969.

Clarke, Duncan. *Politics of Arms Control.* New York: Free Press, 1979.

Coffey, Joseph. "Strategic Arms Limitations and European Security" *International Affairs* 47 (October 1971): 692–707.

Congressional Quarterly Almanac, 1972. Washington, D.C.: Congressional Quarterly Press, 1973.

Frye, Alton. *A Responsible Congress.* New York: McGraw-Hill, 1975.

Garthoff, Raymond L. *Detente and Confrontation: American-Soviet Relations from Nixon to Reagan.* Washington, D.C.: The Brookings Institution, 1985.

George, Alexander L., ed. *Managing U.S.-Soviet Rivalry: Problems of Crisis Prevention.* Boulder, Colo.: Westview Press, 1983.

Halsted, Thomas. "Lobbying against the ABM, 1967–1970." *Bulletin of the Atomic Scientists* 27 (April 1971): 23–28.

Hersh, Seymour. *The Price of Power: Kissinger in the Nixon White House.* New York: Summit Books, 1983.

Holst, Johan and William Schneider, Jr., eds. *Why ABM?* Elmsford, New York: Pergamon, 1969.

Hyland, William G. *Mortal Rivals: Superpower Relations from Nixon to Reagan.* New York: Random House, 1987.

Kissinger, Henry. "Bureaucracy and Policy Making: The Effect of Insiders and Outsiders on the Policy Process." In *Bureaucracy, Politics and Strategy*, edited by Henry Kissinger and Bernard Brodie. Security Studies Project no. 17. Los Angeles: University of California Press, 1968.

———. *White House Years.* Boston, Mass.: Little, Brown & Co., 1979.

Labrie, Roger, ed. *salt Handbook: Key Documents and Issues, 1972–79.* Washington, D.C.: American Enterprise Institute, 1979.

Newhouse, John. *Cold Dawn: The Story of SALT.* New York: Holt, Rinehart & Winston, 1973.

Nixon, Richard M. *In the Arena.* New York: Simon and Schuster, 1990.

———. *RN: The Memoirs of Richard Nixon.* New York: Grosset and Dunlap, 1978.

Nunn, Sam. "ABM Reinterpretation 'Fundamentally Flawed,'" *Arms Control Today* (April 1987): 8-10.
Platt, Alan. *The Politics of Arms Control and the Strategic Balance*. P-6825. The RAND Corporation, 1982.
———. *The U.S. Senate and Strategic Arms Policy, 1969-1977*. Boulder, Colo.: Westview Press, 1978.
Platt, Alan, and Lawrence Weiler, eds. *Congress and Arms Control*. Boulder, Colo.: Westview Press, 1978.
Schulzinger, Robert. *Henry Kissinger: Doctor of Diplomacy*. New York: Columbia University Press, 1989.
Smith, Gerard C. *Doubletalk: The Story of the First Strategic Arms Limitations Talks*. Garden City, N.Y.: Doubleday & Co., 1980.
Willrich, Mason, and John Rhinelander, eds. *salt: The Moscow Agreements and Beyond*. New York: Free Press, 1974.
Wolfe, Thomas. *The SALT Experience: Its Impact on U.S. and Soviet Strategic Policy and Decision-Making*. R-1686-PR. The RAND Corporation, 1975.
Zumwalt, Elmo, Jr. *On Watch*. New York: Quadrangle/New York Times Book Co., 1976.

Government Publications

U.S. Congress. Senate. Committee on Armed Services. *Military Implications of the Treaty on the Limitation on Anti-Ballistic Missile Systems and the Interim Agreement on Limitation of Strategic Offensive Arms, Hearings*. 92d Cong., 2d sess., June-July 1972.
U.S. Congress. Senate. Committee on Foreign Relations. *Strategic Arms Limitation Agreements, Hearings*. 92d Cong., 1st sess., 1972.
U.S. Department of State. Office of the Historian. Bureau of Public Affairs. *Administration Strategy toward Congress on Three Nuclear Arms Issues (Limited Test Ban Treaty, Non-Proliferation Treaty, SALT I Agreements)*. Research project no. 1189. March 1978.

Unpublished Works

Haass, Richard, and Nancy Kates. "SALT I: Getting from Nyet to Yes." Pew Case, no. 339. Cambridge: Kennedy School of Government, Harvard University, 1988.
Lauk, Kurt. "Possibilities of Senatorial Influence: The Case of the Jackson Amendment to SALT I." Stanford University, 1975.
Murray, Lori Esposito. "SALT I and Congress: Building a Consensus on Nuclear Arms Control." Ph.D. diss., The Johns Hopkins University, 1989.

6 The SALT II Treaty

Dan Caldwell

On June 18, 1979, President Jimmy Carter and General Secretary Leonid Brezhnev signed the second Strategic Arms Limitation Treaty (SALT II) in Vienna. Carter considered the treaty to be very significant; a month before signing the treaty, he told a congressional delegation: "I will never have a chance so momentous to contribute to world peace as to negotiate and to see ratified this SALT treaty. And I don't believe that any member of the Senate will ever cast a more important vote than when a final judgment is made to confirm and ratify this negotiated treaty."[1] Members of Congress agreed. Senate minority leader Howard Baker (R-Tenn.) called SALT II "the most important treaty this country has undertaken since World War I."[2] Senator John Glenn (D-Ohio) concurred: "Not since Woodrow Wilson's time and the League of Nations debate has a treaty been so important, yet so contentious, as the SALT II Treaty."[3]

The formal debate on the treaty lasted for six and a half months, from the signing of the treaty on June 18, 1979, to January 3, 1980, when President Carter withdrew the treaty from the Senate's consideration. The informal debate on SALT II, however, had begun much earlier, soon after the SALT I agreements were signed in May 1972.

The first strategic arms limitation talks resulted in two agreements: the Anti-Ballistic Missile Treaty and the Interim Agreement to Limit Strategic Offensive Arms. (See chapter 5 of this volume.) Senator Henry M. ("Scoop") Jackson (D-Wa.) was concerned about the numerical advantage granted to the USSR by the latter agreement and pro-

The author would like to thank Lynn Davis, I. M. Destler, and Michael Krepon for their comments on a previous draft of this chapter.

posed an amendment that would prohibit future negotiators from granting the Soviet Union similar terms. The second round of SALT negotiations opened in November 1972 and continued under presidents Richard M. Nixon, Gerald Ford, and Jimmy Carter. As the negotiators met, U.S. and Soviet scientists and engineers continued their work to develop new nuclear weapons and launchers. Particularly problematic were modern, large ballistic missiles, cruise missiles, and the Soviet Backfire bomber.

Wanting to achieve dramatic progress on controlling nuclear weapons, President Carter authorized Secretary of State Cyrus Vance to present a "comprehensive proposal" for deep cuts in strategic nuclear arms to the Soviets in March 1977. This proposal had widespread support among liberals and conservatives, Republicans and Democrats; however, the Soviet leadership rejected it almost as soon as it was presented. After several months, the two sides resumed negotiations and developed a three-tiered approach to SALT II that included a treaty, a protocol to the treaty, and a statement of principles.

SALT II was not negotiated in a vacuum; the Carter administration was concerned about a number of other foreign policy issues. During the 1976 presidential campaign, Jimmy Carter had indicated his support for the Panama Canal treaties that were under negotiation at that time. When the Panamanian government indicated its willingness to conclude the treaties, President Carter readily accepted. The treaties were then presented to the Senate and barely ratified in 1978. Members of the Carter administration viewed the ratification of the treaties as a significant victory and as the template for future ratification efforts.

Since the early 1970s U.S.-Soviet relations had been affected and influenced by Sino-U.S. relations. During his visit to the People's Republic of China (PRC) in 1972, President Nixon signed the Shanghai Communiqué which laid the foundation for the normalization of relations between the two countries. Despite continued discussion of rapprochement throughout the Nixon and Ford administrations, the normalization of relations had not been achieved by the time that Carter entered office. Within two years of gaining power, however, the Carter administration formally recognized the People's Republic of China in December 1978. This action deeply concerned the Soviets and delayed the ongoing SALT II negotiations.

Signed in June 1979 and scheduled to remain in effect from the time it entered into force until December 31, 1985, the SALT II Treaty contained nineteen articles and was seventy-eight pages long.[4] It placed a limit of 2,400 (to be lowered to 2,250 by the end of 1981) on the number of "strategic nuclear launch vehicles"—intercontinental ballistic missiles (ICBMS), submarine-launched ballistic missiles (SLBMS), air-to-surface ballistic missiles (ASBMS), and long-range bombers—held by each side. Within this ceiling, no more than 1,320 ICBMS, SLBMS, ASBMS, and heavy bombers could be equipped with multiple independently targetable re-entry vehicles (MIRVS) or long-range cruise missiles. Within this sub-limit, no more than 1,200 ICBMS, SLBMS, or ASBMS could be MIRVed (e.g., equipped with MIRVS), and within this sub-limit, no more than 820 ICBMS could be MIRVed. In addition to these overall limits the treaty contained specific limitations on the throw-weight and launch weight of ICBMS; a limit on the testing and deployment of one "new type" of ICBM; a restriction on the number of warheads that could be deployed on each type of missile; and other detailed limitations. Whereas the SALT I agreements placed primarily quantitative limitations on strategic nuclear weapons systems, the SALT II Treaty placed both quantitative and qualitative restrictions on these systems.

The second part of the SALT II agreement consisted of a protocol, scheduled to remain in effect until the end of 1981, that banned the flight testing and deployment of ICBMS from mobile launch platforms; prohibited the deployment of land-based or sea-based cruise missiles with a range of more than 600 kilometers; and banned the testing and deployment of ASBMS. The third part of the SALT II agreement was a joint statement of principles concerning the next round of SALT negotiations.

Soon after the signing of the treaty, the domestic political debate within the United States over SALT II began in earnest. Congressional hearings were held during the summer of 1979, and by the end of August, at the conclusion of the major hearings, it appeared that the treaty would be ratified.

Three international events only indirectly related to SALT II then intervened to delay and ultimately to preclude the Senate's consideration of the treaty. At the end of August Senator Frank Church (D-Idaho) announced the discovery of a "Soviet combat brigade in Cuba." This created concern in Washington and delayed floor debate on the treaty. At the end of the first week of November a mob of Iranian "students" took over the U.S. embassy in Tehran and took fifty-two Americans hostage. Although this event was only tangentially related to SALT II, since the United States had two listening posts for gathering intelligence on Soviet missile tests in Iran, it raised questions in the minds of many Americans concerning the competence of the Carter administration in foreign policy. The final blow to SALT II was delivered by the Soviet Union in the form of an invasion of Afghanistan in late December 1979. Faced with what he characterized as one of the most significant events since the end of World War II, President Carter withdrew the SALT II Treaty from the Senate's consideration on January 3, 1980.[5]

International Political Context

The Carter administration entered office when the American public was disillusioned with international commitments and the Soviet Union was building up its military forces and pursuing an activist foreign policy in a number of areas. The Vietnam War had profound effects on Americans and their beliefs about foreign policy. The final fall of Vietnam occurred in April 1975, less than two years before Jimmy Carter's inauguration as president. The images of the final days of twenty-five years of U.S. involvement in Vietnam were simultaneously tragic and humiliating: U.S. Marines using their rifle butts to knock clinging Vietnamese from the landing rails of overloaded helicopters; South Vietnamese soldiers shooting at departing U.S. aircraft; and South Vietnamese who had worked for the Americans in tears. "No More Vietnams" had become the rallying cry of many Americans. The war had divided both the U.S. foreign policy establishment and the public, and these divisions had a deep-seated impact on the foreign policy of the Carter administration.

When they assumed office in January 1977, President Carter, Secretary of State Vance, and National Security Adviser Zbigniew Brzezinski agreed that the United States should move away from the Nixon-Ford-Kissinger balance of power–oriented approach to international relations and toward a "world order" approach. In contrast with the Nixon-Ford-Kissinger realpolitik, the Carter administration's approach placed greater emphasis on the role of economics and non-superpower states. According to this view, Japan and Western Europe had fully recovered from World War II, and as former colonial areas had become independent, the world had grown more complex, pluralistic, and interdependent.

During the 1976 campaign, Jimmy Carter had emphasized the need to conclude the Panama Canal negotiations, and after Carter's inauguration, the members of the National Security Council (NSC), at their first meeting, reached two important decisions that indicated U.S.-Soviet relations would not receive the highest priority of the new administration. First, the NSC decided to conclude the Panama Canal negotiations as quickly as possible, and, second, a decision was made to send Vance to the Middle East as early as the next month.[6] Carter was not completely free to choose which issues he would address, and as a result, SALT, Panama, the

Middle East, and other issues became competitors for attention and for the limited political capital with which Carter entered office.

During the Carter administration, "Presidential Review Memoranda" were used to task governmental agencies and departments with studies analyzing U.S. policies and options on various topics. Although the order in which these were assigned did not indicate the priority placed on each of these issues, listing the subjects of the first fifteen of these memoranda provides an overview of the administration's foreign policy concerns during its first months: (1) Panama Canal treaties, (2) SALT, (3) the Middle East, (4) South Africa, (5) Cyprus, (6) Mutual and Balanced Force Reduction arms control negotiations, (7) the economic summit, (8) North-South relations, (9) Europe, (10) U.S. military force posture, (11) U.S. intelligence, (12) conventional arms sales, (13) Korea, (14) the Philippines, and (15) nuclear proliferation.[7]

Despite the new administration's avowed interest in moving away from a preoccupation with U.S.-Soviet relations, it did have to develop an approach for dealing with the world's other most powerful state, and the conclusion of the SALT II Treaty was one of the key elements in the Carter administration's approach to the USSR. Conservatives pointed to the "relentless buildup of Soviet forces" throughout the 1970s and expressed deep concern over Soviet modern, large ("heavy") ballistic missiles such as the SS-9 and SS-18, and other Soviet ICBM modernization efforts. These critics argued that the United States needed to respond with a substantial buildup of its own. In addition to their military buildup effort, the Soviets and their allies' forces were active in a number of areas throughout the world, particularly in southern Africa and the Horn of Africa.

In responding to the Soviet Union's military buildup and foreign policy actions, President Carter emphasized five concepts during the early part of his administration. First, Carter stressed the need for arms control; in his inaugural address he expressed his hope of achieving the "ultimate goal—the elimination of all nuclear weapons from this earth." In enunciating this goal, Carter went beyond the arms control objectives of his predecessors, Nixon and Ford, who had negotiated with the Soviets at the SALT talks. The public and Congress overwhelmingly approved the SALT I agreements in 1972 soon after they were signed. However, as the decade of the seventies wore on, conservatives became more and more critical of arms control in general and SALT in particular. In their view arms control granted the USSR asymmetrical advantages and lulled the American public into complacency.

The conservatives' view stood in contrast with that of Jimmy Carter. In his first letter to Brezhnev after being elected president, Carter assured the Soviet leader that there were three areas where progress in U.S.-Soviet arms control could be made: SALT, the comprehensive test ban negotiations, and the Mutual and Balanced Force Reduction talks.[8] In March 1977, two months after writing this letter, the president sent Secretary Vance to Moscow to present a new arms control proposal calling for large cuts in Soviet and U.S. nuclear arsenals. Although a number of Democrats and Republicans supported his March 1977 comprehensive arms control proposal, Carter's emphasis on arms control and disarmament placed him at odds with those who were concerned about the Soviet military buildup and Soviet foreign policy activities around the world.

The second element of Carter's early approach to the Soviet Union was an emphasis on human rights. During the 1976 presidential campaign, Carter had made human rights the centerpiece of his foreign policy and thereby gained—during the first year of his administration—the support of both liberals and conservatives. In mid-February Carter received a letter from the eminent Soviet physicist and human rights activist Andrey Sakharov. Carter, having criticized Gerald Ford during the presidential campaign for failing to receive the great Russian writer and dissident Alexsandr Solzhenitsyn in the White House, and as a dramatic way of signaling his emphasis on human rights, replied to Sakharov's letter saying: "I am always glad to hear from you. . . . You may rest assured that the American people and our government will continue our firm commitment to promote respect for human rights not only in our country but also abroad."[9] In March the president received Soviet human rights activist Vladimir Bukovsky in the Oval Office, a dramatic gesture that underscored his emphasis on human rights. These actions disturbed Soviet leaders a great deal; they considered them to be "interference in the internal affairs of the USSR," which, the Soviets contended, was prohibited by the United Nations Charter.

The third element of President Carter's approach to the Soviet Union concerned linkage, a means of gaining diplomatic leverage that has existed since states began, but an approach that Nixon and Kissinger employed extensively. For example, Nixon and Kissinger would not agree to the opening of the SALT I negotiations until the Soviet Union agreed to work for the resolution of the conflicts in Vietnam and the Middle East. In contrast with Nixon and Kissinger, President Carter believed that arms control was so important that it should not be linked to other issues.[10]

Critics of SALT argued that the United States should not conclude an arms control agreement with the Soviet Union as long as it pursued interventionist policies around the world that were antithetical to the interests of the United States and its allies. Within the Carter administration, Zbigniew Brzezinski was the most prominent proponent of this view. Outside the administration, conservative critics of the SALT II Treaty widely held this view. Supporters of SALT II, such as Cyrus Vance, believed that the issue of nuclear arms control was so important that it should be de-linked from other issues of U.S.-Soviet relations.

A fourth element of Carter's approach to dealing with the Soviet Union was to de-emphasize anticommunism. In an address many consider to be the most important of his early speeches describing his approach to international relations—his commencement address at Notre Dame University in May 1977—Carter said: "We are now free of that inordinate fear of communism which once led us to embrace any dictator in that fear. . . . For too many years, we've been willing to adopt the flawed and erroneous principles and tactics of our adversaries, sometimes abandoning our values for theirs."[11]

A fifth element of Carter's approach to foreign policy concerned China. Within the administration, Zbigniew Brzezinski emphasized the need to develop better relations with PRC in order to place pressure on the Soviet Union. This emphasis culminated in the United States' formal recognition of the People's Republic of China in December 1978.

Jimmy Carter was the first U.S. president in twenty-five years who was not forced to confront the dilemmas that the United States faced in Vietnam. Carter chose to emphasize the importance of North-South relations and key regional powers, such as India, Iran, Brazil, and Nigeria, even before he was inaugurated president. The conclusion of the Panama Canal treaties became a symbol and the first tangible accomplishment of Carter's new "world order" approach to international relations.

Domestic Political Context

The defeat of the United States in Vietnam had domestic political effects within the United States as well as effects on broader international relations. The SALT II Treaty became the target of a number of conservatives, and the campaign against the treaty represented, according to former deputy national security adviser, David Aaron, "the revenge of the hawks."[12] Carter, therefore, had to try to deflect the ire of conservatives who were frustrated with the defeat in Vietnam and concerned by what they perceived to be growing Soviet adventurism abroad and ballooning Soviet strategic forces.

Vietnam was not the only demon that Jimmy Carter sought to exorcise from the American body politic; he also had to deal with widespread public disillusionment and disgust resulting from the Watergate scandal. In fact, Carter probably owed his election to Watergate; many Americans voted against Gerald Ford because he had pardoned Nixon. Once elected, Carter had to increase public confidence in the office of the presidency in order to implement domestic and foreign policies effectively.

The relationship of domestic and international political and economic issues became a burden to Carter. The downfall of the shah of Iran and the ensuing quadrupling of oil prices contributed to inflationary pressures in the United States. These economic problems, in turn, contributed to the fall in Carter's popularity.

When Carter took the oath of office, his only significant experience in international relations stemmed from his membership on the Trilateral Commission, a group formed in 1973 at the instigation of David Rockefeller by prominent business, political, and academic leaders from North America, Western Europe, and Japan to foster cooperation among these three regions on common economic, political, and social problems. Carter was the first governor and only one of six southerners among the sixty-five North American members invited to join the commission. Carter noted the value of his participation in the group to Hamilton Jordan. "Those Trilateral Commission meetings for me were like classes in foreign policy—reading papers produced on every conceivable subject, hearing experienced leaders debate international issues and problems, and meeting the big names like Cy Vance and Harold Brown and Zbig [Brzezinski]."[13] In addition to the "big names", Carter appointed a number of other Trilateral Commission members to his foreign policy team, including Vice President Walter Mondale, Treasury Secretary W. Michael Blumenthal, Director of the U.S. Arms Control and Disarmament Agency (ACDA) Paul C. Warnke,

Deputy Secretary of State Warren Christopher, Undersecretary of State Richard Cooper, Panama Canal treaties negotiator Sol Linowitz, and U.S. representative to the People's Republic of China Leonard Woodcock. By the time he assumed office, Carter had assembled a competent group of foreign policy makers. Cyrus Vance, Carter's selection to be secretary of state, was the quintessential "in-and-outer," having combined a successful Wall Street law practice with periodic service in government. He served as general counsel of the Department of Defense and secretary of the army in the Kennedy administration, negotiator and troubleshooter in Panama (1964), the Dominican Republic (1965), Vietnam (1966), Detroit (following the race riots of 1967), Korea (following the North Korean takeover of the USS *Pueblo* in 1968), and the Paris peace talks with the North Vietnamese (1968–69). Because of his training in law, his successful negotiation of a number of conflict-prone crises, and his involvement with Vietnam, Vance believed strongly in the efficacy of negotiations over the use of force in international relations. The dominant element in Vance's outlook, according to his biographer, was the threat of nuclear war.[14] Vance believed, as noted earlier, that the control of nuclear arms was so important that it should not be linked to other issues.

President Carter chose Zbigniew Brzezinski as his national security adviser, the son of a Polish diplomat, whose family immigrated to Canada following the communist takeover of Poland. Brzezinski graduated from McGill University in Montreal and went on to Harvard to earn his doctorate in government. Brzezinski focused his attention on the Soviet Union and Eastern Europe and wrote several books that reflected a hard-line view of Soviet foreign policy intentions. He served on the policy planning staff of the Department of State for two years during the Johnson administration and returned to Columbia University in 1970. He was named executive director of the Trilateral Commission, where he first met then-Governor Jimmy Carter.

During his tenure in office, President Nixon relied most heavily on Henry Kissinger in the making and implementing of foreign policy, and Secretary of State William Rogers was almost a figurehead. In a number of articles Brzezinski (as well as others) had criticized Kissinger's conduct of U.S. foreign policy as a "one-man show," and at the beginning of the Carter administration, he, Vance, and Carter agreed that they wanted to avoid a repetition of that pattern.[15] All three thought—as it turned out, very mistakenly—that conflict between Vance and Brzezinski would not be a problem; the two men had worked together on the Trilateral Commission and the Council on Foreign Relations and had both worked closely on Carter's election campaign. Ironically, given the conflict that developed between the two men, Vance recommended Brzezinski to Carter to serve as the president's assistant for national security affairs, and Brzezinski recommended that Vance be named secretary of state.[16]

According to Hamilton Jordan: "The President-elect was not worried about conflicts, and relished their different ideas and lively debate. The roles were clear to him: Zbig would be the thinker, Cy would be the doer, and Jimmy Carter would be the decider."[17] For his part, Vance supported a "collegial approach [to decision making] with one critical reservation. Only the president and his secretary of state were to have the responsibility for defining the administration's foreign policy publicly."[18] Initially, Brzezinski accepted his role as the administration's foreign policy "thinker," but over time, he increasingly became interested in becoming a "doer" and not just the provider of staff advice. There were also differences in personality between Vance and Brzezinski. A former NSC staff member observed, "If Vance was the steady, patient negotiator, Brzezinski was the theoretician and the manipulator."[19] Hamilton Jordan noted: "Vance didn't have an ounce of the self-promoter in him. He wasn't concerned with his image: he was there to serve his President and his country. And if Cy Vance didn't have an ounce of the self-promoter in him, then Zbig had several pounds."[20] The

differences between Vance and Brzezinski became
increasingly important. President Carter appointed Harold Brown to be his
administration's secretary of defense. Brown had served in the
Pentagon during the Kennedy and Johnson administrations.
Later, Brown served as a member of the U.S. delegation to
the SALT I negotiations and as president of the California
Institute of Technology. According to journalist Strobe
Talbott, Brown was Carter's "single most trusted adviser on
SALT."[21] As the conflict between Vance and Brzezinski
developed and sharpened, Brown at times became the "swing
vote."

President Carter named Paul C. Warnke the director of
ACDA and the chief negotiator at the SALT II talks. Warnke
proved to be a kind of lightning rod for conservatives, who
believed that he was weak on defense and would grant the
Soviet Union unilateral concessions. As a consequence, a
number of groups sponsored full-page advertisements in
major U.S. newspapers opposing Warnke's appointment.[22]
Warnke was eventually approved by the Senate, but the vote
was 58-40, a tally which was significantly shy of the
two-thirds majority that the administration would need to
obtain the ratification of any arms control treaty.

Carter realized that even if he was successful in negotiating
a treaty with the Soviets, he would then have to enter a new
set of "negotiations" with the Senate to obtain ratification of
the treaty. The president believed that if he could enlist the
support of one of the Senate's recognized experts in defense
policy, Henry M. Jackson, then others would follow Jackson's
lead. Jackson had played influential roles in the debates over
the most important previous arms control agreements, the
Limited Nuclear Test Ban Treaty and the SALT I agreements.

Carter's relationship with Jackson was mixed. At the 1972
Democratic convention Carter had made one of the speeches
nominating Jackson for president. Four years later, however,
Carter defeated Jackson in the Pennsylvania primary,
knocking him out of the race. After his nomination, President

Carter recalled: "I wound up the '76 campaign on fairly good terms with him [Jackson]. He was one of the six I seriously considered as vice president."[23] Several weeks after his inauguration, Carter invited Jackson to come to the White House to discuss SALT with him. After this meeting, Jackson and his foreign policy aide at that time, Richard Perle, prepared a twenty-three page, single-spaced memo concerning SALT.[24] They criticized the Nixon and Ford administrations for creating a "climate of urgency that made it difficult to think carefully about these complex issues" and noted that "it is essential to remember that not all negotiable agreements are in our interest; that some agreements may be worse than none; that the failure to obtain an agreement does not necessarily foreclose the possibility of doing so in the future; and that an unsound agreement now could make it difficult or impossible to obtain a sound one later."[25]

According to reports, Warnke dismissed the memo as a "first-class polemic."[26] President Carter, however, took the memo very seriously and sent it to Brown and Vance, who distributed it within their respective departments. President Carter noted: "Scoop came and met with me one time fairly early in my term . . . and brought me a long document that I kept in my private safe near the Oval Office outlining his draft of what a SALT II Treaty should be. I referred to that every now and then just to see if there were ways that I could accommodate Scoop's very ambitious demands, and sometimes I was able to."[27] In addition, Carter sent Jackson a number of handwritten, personal notes.[28]

In a further effort to win the support of Senator Jackson, President Carter retained Lieutenant General Edward Rowny as the Joint Chiefs of Staff (JCS) representative on the U.S. SALT II delegation. Senator Jackson and General Rowny had been friends for years; in fact, in 1960 Jackson had recommended then-Colonel Rowny to the Kennedy transition team for a position in either the White House or the Department of State's Bureau of Politico-Military Affairs.[29] General Rowny was originally appointed to the SALT II delegation following the replacement of virtually the entire top leadership of ACDA after the SALT I agreements were concluded. According to a member (and later chairman) of the SALT delegation, Ralph Earle II: "Rowny was an old friend of Dorothy Fosdick, Senator Jackson's principal foreign policy adviser, as well as a friend of Senator Jackson. One could only infer that Rowny had been in effect nominated by Jackson, and subsequent events were to make this very evident."[30] It was commonly understood that Rowny served as the eyes and ears of Senator Jackson and Richard Perle at SALT II.

When the new administration assumed office, it had the opportunity to remove Rowny, but it chose not to do so. In mid-January 1977, just before the administration assumed office, the Department of Defense transition team was considering the appointment of General Rowny as its sole representative on the SALT delegation. In the end the transition team did not choose to do so; however, General Rowny was reappointed as the JCS representative. Clearly, Carter's advisers had hoped to gain favor with Senator Jackson by reappointing Rowny, but, in retrospect, a number of administration officials and pro-treaty senators believed that President Carter and Secretary of Defense Brown made a serious error in failing to remove General Rowny from the SALT delegation at the beginning of the administration.

On the eve of Carter's departure for his meeting with Brezhnev in Vienna, Rowny announced that he was retiring from the army. At the time of his announcement many assumed that Rowny was resigning out of principle in order to campaign against the ratification of the SALT II Treaty, but this was a distortion of the facts. Rowny's reappointment to the SALT delegation and continued active service in the army had required a special waiver because by 1977 he had already served thirty-six years and was sixty years old. Army personnel regulations called for normal retirement after thirty-five years of service and age sixty. In fact, Rowny was scheduled to retire in the summer of 1979, and his retirement just before the Vienna summit was timed for the maximum political effect. According to a former senior Carter administration official, General Rowny's actions constituted "great selfishness for self-aggrandizement" rather than the altruistic picture that has previously been presented.[31]

There were several other individuals who played particularly important roles in the SALT II debate. Paul H. Nitze was one of the most respected national security experts in Washington and had served in a variety of positions dating back to the Truman administration, including a stint as a member of the SALT I delegation.[32] Nitze was offered a position in the Carter administration, but it was not a cabinet-level position, and he declined it. It is interesting to speculate what would have happened if Nitze had accepted a position in the Carter administration, as he had previously supported other arms control agreements in which he had some role. As it turned out, Nitze's detailed analyses of the various Carter administration SALT proposals became some of the most widely read and influential on Capitol Hill.

The Role of the President

Jimmy Carter and his closest advisers—Hamilton Jordan, Jody Powell and Gerald Rafshoon—engineered one of the most dramatic election campaigns in U.S. history. Carter went from being an obscure, one-term, southern governor (whom the press dubbed "Jimmy Who") in 1975 to being elected president in 1976. At the outset of his administration Carter had substantial public support, as figure 1 demonstrates. The high point in Carter's popularity occurred early in his administration, in March 1977. There was a gradual downward trend during the period of the SALT II negotiations.

One reason for Carter's declining popularity related to his decision to conclude the negotiations on the Panama Canal that had begun under President Lyndon B. Johnson and continued under presidents Nixon and Ford. During the 1976 presidential campaign, Carter emphasized the need for the Panama Canal treaties, and once in office, he pressed for the conclusion of the agreements, which transpired in September 1977. The treaties were quite controversial. Just prior to the signing of the agreements, NBC polled the general public and asked whether the United States should sign a treaty turning over control of the canal to Panama. Fifty-five percent replied that the United States should not do so, and only 27 percent supported such a treaty. When the Associated Press, a week after the treaty was signed, asked whether the Senate should ratify them, 50 percent replied negatively and 29 percent affirmatively.[33] Support for the treaties in the Senate was quite different; it appeared that there was substantial support. So the principal task facing the administration was to convince the public that the treaties were in the best interests of the United States.

Figure 1
President Carter's Popularity*

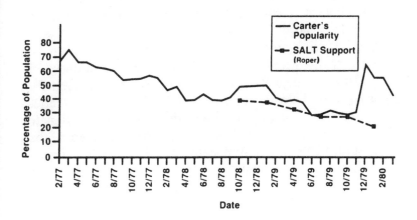

*Source: *The Gallup Opinion Index*, no. 182 (October/November 1980).

President Carter, like all presidents, had a limited amount of political capital to expend on the ratification of treaties that he concluded during his term of office, and both he and his advisers should have realized this political fact of life. Yet, in their memoirs and other writings, members of the Carter administration have not discussed whether the president and his advisers considered the feasibility and desirability of concluding the Panama Canal treaties before the SALT II Treaty. Landon Butler, Hamilton Jordan's deputy and one of those responsible for developing the administration's ratification strategy, explained:

> We were totally surprised that the Panama Canal treaties fell into our laps. . . . Sol Linowitz went down to negotiate; we took strong positions, and the Panamanians agreed with them. I don't think anyone expected the Panamanians to suddenly agree to the positions that we took as quickly as they did. . . . There was not much serious consideration given to dragging out the Panama Canal treaties for two or three years longer and do SALT first. There was just no way to know when or how we were going to get either one of them.[34]

The debate over the Panama Canal treaties was viewed by both proponents and opponents as extremely important; in fact, it was seen as a prelude to other significant foreign policy debates, including those over China and SALT II. Brzezinski believed, "If we had lost [the Panama Canal treaties], there is no doubt that our policy on SALT and most importantly the Middle East would have been dead ducks."[35] The Senate Foreign Relations Committee recommended the approval of the treaties by a vote of 14–1. Once the treaties were reported out of committee, they went to the Senate floor, where they were debated for twenty-two days, the longest foreign policy floor debate since the Versailles Treaty of 1919–20. The length of the debate indicated the contentiousness of the treaties. On April 18, 1978, the first Panama Canal Treaty was approved by a vote of 68–32, a single vote more than the necessary 67 to approve the treaties.

Brzezinski characterized the campaign for the ratification of the Panama Canal treaties as "difficult and personally draining, an uphill fight all the way to the end."[36] In the end, the support of moderate Republicans had been crucial. Former President Ford not only publicly supported the ratification of the treaties but also actively lobbied a number of Republican senators to vote for the treaties. Vance noted that Senate minority leader Howard Baker's "leadership was indispensable, and it [his vote in favor of the treaties] was an act of statesmanship."[37] Henry Kissinger had also supported the treaties, and after they were ratified, President Carter handwrote a letter to Kissinger thanking him for his support and noting, "Your help was crucial."[38]

In an excellent book about the ratification of the Panama Canal treaties, George Moffett III concludes: "In the end, of course, the administration did win in the Senate. Still, what the administration gained was in nearly every respect a Pyrrhic victory. In exhausting its political capital, it was forced to relinquish its leverage on other issues."[39] The administration had pressured moderate Republicans to vote in favor of the treaties, which went against the grain of many of their conservative constituents. Senator Baker and other moderates believed that they could not support any more of President Carter's foreign policy initiatives without losing the support of some of their important constituents.

In his memoirs President Carter recalled, "The lobbying campaign we mounted throughout the nation [for SALT II] . . made the Panama Canal treaties pale into relative insignificance."[40] For the most part, those members of the administration who worked on the ratification strategy for the Panama Canal treaties were the same ones who worked on the ratification campaign for SALT II. For example, Hamilton Jordan developed the ratification plan for the Panama Canal treaties and then developed the ratification plan for SALT II. He was also the chairman of the task forces established within the administration for the ratification of the treaties. Robert Beckel had worked as a liaison between the White House and the Senate during the Panama Canal debate and performed the same task during the SALT II debate, and George Moffett III, who directed the Committee of Americans for the Canal Treaties, joined the White House staff after the Panama Canal treaties were approved to work on the ratification of the SALT II Treaty.

Initially, the director of White House communications, Gerald Rafshoon, was given the responsibility to work out the administration's plan to ratify the SALT II Treaty. Rafshoon contacted the various groups within the administration working on SALT II and requested their recommendations. In the communications between Rafshoon and other officials some interesting differences are evident. For example, Matthew Nimetz, who was counselor of the Department of State and the chair of the department's SALT task force, wrote Rafshoon, "Members of Congress will, to a substantial degree, play a leading role in shaping public opinion towards the agreement."[41] This view differed in a fundamental way from the White House perspective (evident in Landon Butler's previously cited memo) that the key to ratification was to gain public support. Nimetz recommended that the White House "be involved in the ratification effort at an early date, and its direct participation would increase as the Congressional debate advances." Nimetz also noted that President Carter's personal contact with "key congressional leaders" and senior public figures would "be important to winning a broad consensus in support of SALT II."[42]

After receiving recommendations from a number of individuals and organizations, Rafshoon and his staff developed two plans: a communications plan for their office and an overall strategic plan for the administration. In the communications plan Rafshoon described an ambitious list of tasks to complete in support of SALT II, including establishing a speakers bureau, writing speeches and briefing papers, producing a film, arranging for presidential addresses and press conferences, coordinating media appearances by senior members of the administration, arranging interviews of high-level members of the administration by prominent columnists, and distributing positive editorials to members of the Senate.[43]

In early December Rafshoon wrote an "eyes only" memo to President Carter outlining a strategic plan to develop public support for the SALT II Treaty.[44] Rafshoon began the memo by emphasizing the importance of the agreement: "Continuation of the SALT process will be one of the most significant achievements of your Presidency." Reflecting the age-old adage that in politics timing is everything, Rafshoon hoped that the negotiations would be concluded before the State of the Union address in January and that the summit would then take place in late January or early February 1979. Rafshoon believed that the administration needed to develop *"simple and easily understood"* themes that would "strike a *responsive chord"* and appeal to the public's *"common sense."*[45] The goal of the ratification effort should not be "to educate the public either about the complexities of strategic planning or the details of the treaty." Rather, the administration's arguments "must make more sense— intuitively—than the opposition's. They must be supported by common sense." As in both his earlier memo and Landon Butler's, Rafshoon recommended the production of a pro-SALT film "as quickly as possible."

After considering Rafshoon's recommendations, President Carter gave Jordan the responsibility to develop the SALT II ratification strategy and to chair the SALT task force. By the end of January 1979 Jordan had prepared a "SALT II Ratification Work Plan" and sent it to Carter for his review.[46] The plan was broken down by time periods and functional tasks (congressional relations, public outreach, media, press, contacts with major public figures, and liaison with allied governments). This detailed document served as the blueprint for the administration's ratification efforts.

In the first months of 1979 members of the administration worked out detailed plans for the SALT ratification campaign. The White House chief of administration, Hugh Carter, developed a computerized master list of tasks to be completed and the person responsible for completing each of these tasks.[47] In early May Rafshoon accurately predicted that "the debate over SALT II will be long, rancorous and confused" and urged the president to "take the time to show that you are the country's foremost SALT expert."[48] As the summit approached, the administration stepped up activities related to the upcoming ratification debate. The White House Office of Congressional Relations sent each senator lengthy briefing books on SALT on May 10, May 29, and June 14.[49] Two weeks before the summit, Rafshoon launched the press component of the ratification campaign by sending a letter and materials on SALT II to forty-seven prominent journalists.[50]

In his January memo Jordan noted the importance of Carter's meeting with Brezhnev in Vienna: "The summit will provide our first opportunity to explain the full treaty to the American public. . . . Immediately after the summit, the administration's activities should leave no doubt that we plan an all out fight for ratification."[51] According to plan, as soon as Carter returned from Vienna, the administration's all-out campaign to ratify the treaty began.

Anne Wexler was the liaison between the White House and special interest groups, and during the SALT debate she was responsible for public outreach. Her office worked with business, labor, religious, local, and state leaders to broaden the pro-SALT coalition and support for the treaty. Because federal statute prohibits federal funds from being "used directly or indirectly to pay for any personal service, advertisement, telegram, telephone, letter, printed or written matter, or other devices intended or designed to influence in any manner a Member of Congress, to favor or oppose, by vote or otherwise, any legislation,"[52] Wexler's office worked through various nongovernmental pro-SALT groups such as Americans for SALT. Religious leaders were singled out for attention. Materials on SALT were sent to more than a thousand members of the clergy in the hope that they would preach sermons related to SALT. The administration actively sought popular evangelist Billy Graham's support, and Wexler recommended that the president and vice president invite Reverend Graham to the White House to discuss SALT. Wexler's office was part of a much broader effort within the federal government to win public support for SALT II. This effort quickly became known as "the selling of SALT" among both proponents and opponents of the treaty alike, and treaty opponent Kenneth L. Adelman referred to this campaign as "Rafshooning the Armageddon."[53] In May 1978 the Department of State created the SALT working group within the Bureau of European Affairs in order to respond to the anticipated increased public need for information about U.S.-Soviet relations following the conclusion of the SALT II negotiations. By the end of 1978 the group had furnished speakers for at least 138 engagements in forty-five states and 34 engagements in Washington, D.C.; distributed 400,000 copies of SALT-related documents available for public distribution; and organized nine major conferences throughout the United States.[54] The Department of State, ACDA, and Department of Defense estimated that their combined costs for SALT II public affairs expenditures during 1978 were approximately $600,000. During the first six months of 1979, the Department of State and ACDA officials had participated in another 650 speaking engagements in forty-eight states and the District of Columbia and had organized twenty-eight conferences at an estimated total cost of $624,000.[55] In addition to these expenditures several White House offices also distributed SALT materials and arranged conferences on SALT at a total estimated cost of $19,000.

Executive-Congressional Relations

Presidential candidate Carter had campaigned as a Washington outsider, trying to make a virtue out of his paucity of Washington experience. Once elected, Carter and his advisers did little to dispel the wariness that many members of Congress felt toward the new president. Neither Carter nor his senior staff and cabinet members enjoyed socializing with and cultivating the support of members of Congress. Carter and his principal cabinet members with foreign policy responsibilities, Cyrus Vance and Harold Brown, were cerebral and remote figures who did not enjoy interacting with members of Congress.

Carter's problems with Congress, however, were not simply due to personality conflicts. During the Ninety-sixth Congress (1977–79), Carter sought to deal with a number of complex and controversial issues, including windfall profits on oil production, comprehensive energy legislation, Taiwan, the Panama Canal treaties, defense spending, and Iran. It is interesting that despite his problems in dealing with Congress, Carter was able to accomplish a great deal. The Panama Canal treaties were ratified; sales of aircraft to Saudi Arabia and Egypt were approved; an arms embargo against Turkey was lifted; the sanctions against trading with Rhodesia were retained; the Taiwan Relations Act was passed; and the largest development assistance bill in history was passed. These victories were achieved at considerable cost, however.

Carter's problems with Congress were exacerbated owing to the ineffectiveness of the White House Office of Congressional Relations. Jimmy Carter had brought the director of the office, Frank Moore, with him from Georgia. Moore had no previous experience in Washington, and he received very poor reviews from many senators and staff members.

Early in the administration, senators Gary Hart (D-Colo.) and Alan Cranston (D-Calif.) went to the president and suggested that he appoint a senior official to act as a liaison between the White House and the Senate. They suggested that the president appoint Robert S. Strauss, who, as the special trade representative, had served as the administration's chief lobbyist for the legislation on the multilateral trade negotiations.[56] Senator William Proxmire (D-Wis.) believed that the president should have appointed the respected former Senate majority leader Mike Mansfield to such a position rather than naming him as ambassador to Japan.[57] Instead, the president relied on Frank Moore until it became obvious that he needed help. Robert Beckel, who had assisted with the ratification of the Panama Canal treaties, was brought in, and in early 1978 the White House decided that an overall coordinator for the SALT II ratification effort was needed. Matthew Nimetz, who was the number three person at the Department of State, was appointed. Finally, in August 1979 the president brought the respected Washington attorney Lloyd Cutler into the White House to act as the "SALT II ratification czar," but his appointment came late in the process. Cutler had little experience in national security matters and needed time to learn the issues, which were both multifaceted and complex.

The Basis for Support and Opposition

Those who supported the ratification of the SALT II Treaty argued that the terms of the treaty were advantageous to the national security of the United States for seven principal reasons. First, the treaty established equal numerical limits on the total number of strategic nuclear launch vehicles (ICBMs, SLBMs, ASBMs, and long-range bombers) for the United States and the Soviet Union. Second, the treaty placed qualitative limits on MIRVs deployed on ICBMs and SLBMs, weapons that many considered to be the most destabilizing in the Soviet and U.S. arsenals. Both sides were limited to deploying no more than fourteen warheads per SLBM and no more than ten warheads per ICBM. Many, including Secretary of State Vance, considered these limits on "missile fractionation" to be some of the most significant in the treaty.[58] Third, each side was limited to developing and deploying one "new type" ICBM. Thus, the United States would be free to develop and deploy a new, large ICBM to counter the Soviet large SS-18 ICBM.

Fourth, the treaty called for a reduction of the total number of Soviet strategic nuclear launch vehicles from 2,400 to 2,250 by the end of 1981. SALT II, therefore, was actually the first arms treaty that called for reductions in the number of nuclear weapons. Fifth, the treaty would save the United States money. Secretary of Defense Brown estimated that the SALT II Treaty would enable the United States to save approximately $30 billion over the life of the treaty. Sixth, treaty supporters argued that the SALT II Treaty would "pave the way" for other arms control agreements, possibly including a ban on antisatellite weapons and a comprehensive test ban treaty. Lastly, some observers noted that the greatest nuclear danger the world faced was that more and more states would develop, test, and deploy nuclear weapons. The Nuclear Nonproliferation Treaty, signed in 1968, had placed restrictions on the development of nuclear weapons by nonnuclear weapons states. However, the nuclear weapons states, including the United States and the USSR, had pledged in Article 6 of the treaty to work toward nuclear disarmament. The SALT II Treaty would be a step in that direction.

Treaty supporters noted a number of areas in which the Soviets had made concessions to the United States, including the Soviet decision to omit from the SALT II negotiations U.S. forward-based systems (U.S. nuclear weapons based in Europe that could reach the Soviet Union), the banning of the Soviet SS-16 mobile ICBM, the decision to publish a data base of Soviet and U.S. strategic forces, and the counting rule for cruise missiles deployed on bombers.[59]

The opponents of the treaty argued that the terms of the treaty were detrimental to the national security interests of the United States. First, opponents noted that the treaty allowed the Soviet Union to keep 308 modern, large (heavy) SS-18 ICBMs, which, they argued, meant that the treaty favored the USSR. Second, opponents argued that the SALT II Treaty granted the Soviet Union strategic superiority over the United States and that this was very important. Paul H.

Nitze claimed that it was principally U.S. strategic superiority that caused the Soviet Union to back down in the Berlin crisis of 1961 and the Cuban missile crisis of 1962. Third, opponents contended that SALT II weakened the U.S. commitment to defend its European allies. Fourth, a protocol to the treaty called for a three-year ban on the deployment of cruise missiles and mobile ICBMs. Opponents of the treaty argued that this protocol would create an impetus not to deploy these weapons. Fifth, opponents were quite concerned that the Soviet Backfire bomber was not included in the treaty, the Carter administration not having classified it as a long-range bomber. Sixth, opponents argued that the SALT II Treaty would not save the United States any money.

Treaty supporters believed that the verification procedures called for in SALT II represented one of the major advantages of the treaty, whereas opponents were specifically concerned about several verification issues related to the treaty. The latter noted that the treaty called for ceilings on the numbers of launchers and not on the actual numbers of missiles. Therefore, the Soviets could legally increase the number of missiles in their stockpile, and since several of the Soviet systems were "reloadable," the Soviets could, the opponents argued, achieve superiority over the United States. Given the closed, secretive nature of Soviet society and the vastness of the USSR, opponents were concerned that the Soviets would be in a much better position to cheat on the agreement than the United States would be. Treaty opponents did not have a high opinion of the performance of the Standing Consultative Commission, the U.S.-Soviet organization created to monitor the SALT I agreements.

Critics of the Carter administration contended that the president had ordered a number of actions that resulted in the weakening of U.S. national security. In particular, they pointed to the president's cancellation of the B-1 bomber, the slowdown of the construction of the Trident submarine and missile, the cancellation of the deployment of the enhanced radiation weapon (neutron bomb), and the closing of the country's only ICBM production line as evidence of their concern.

SALT II Treaty supporters pointed to strategic improvements that had taken place since the signing and approval of the SALT I agreements. The Minuteman III ICBM had been hardened and modernized with a new warhead, the Mark 12A, and a new guidance system. These improvements doubled warhead yield and accuracy. The United States had developed a new SLBM, the C-4 (also called the Trident I), and deployed it in Poseidon submarines. The United States had also improved the survivability and penetrability of B-52 bombers and equipped them with short-range, air-to-ground missiles. In addition, the Stealth bomber program was begun (although this program was not made public until 1980). The total number of strategic nuclear warheads deployed by the United States increased from 5,700 in 1972 to 9,200 in 1980, giving the United States an advantage in this important criterion of strategic power. Furthermore, the United States had moved ahead with the development of cruise missiles and the D-5 (or Trident II) SLBM.[60]

The major question mark in the Carter administration's defense program was a new ICBM labeled the "MX," which stood for "missile experimental." Treaty critics were particularly concerned about the 308 large SS-18 ICBMs that the treaty allowed the Soviet Union to retain and strongly advocated the development and deployment of a similar weapon by the United States. The critics contended and administration officials conceded that in the future the SS-18 could carry from twenty to thirty warheads.[61] In the months before the signing of the SALT II Treaty, "MX and SALT became as intertwined as the fibers of a rope," according to one Senate staffer.[62]

There were several questions concerning the MX. The first concerned whether the missile should be built at all. The answer to this question quickly became as much a domestic political issue within the United States as an issue of military policy. Vance pointed out, "I had long felt, since the 1977

cancellation of the B-1 bomber, that ratification of the SALT
II Treaty would be unlikely without a firm administration
commitment to the MX program."⁶³ The second debate took
place within the Carter administration and concerned the type
of missile that should be built. Zbigniew Brzezinski favored
building 100 large missiles that would carry 10 warheads each,
whereas William Perry, the deputy secretary of defense,
favored building 330 smaller missiles that would carry 3
warheads each.⁶⁴ Each plan called for the deployment of
approximately 1,000 warheads.

Although President Carter had stated publicly that efforts
to build support in the Senate for the treaty would not result
in new weapons programs, he came to the conclusion that he
would not be able to get the treaty ratified if he did not go
ahead with the MX. Consequently, on June 7, 1979, just eleven
days before he signed the SALT II Treaty, Carter announced
plans to develop and deploy 200 MX missiles that would be
shuttled among 8,000 to 9,000 hardened shelters so that they
would not be vulnerable to a first-strike attack. The president
had hoped that his choice of the Brzezinski option, the large
MX, would increase the chances that Nitze, Jackson, and other
conservatives would support the treaty, but that hope soon
proved unrealistic. Jackson and Nitze continued to criticize
the treaty even after Carter had announced his support for
the development and deployment of the MX.

The debate over SALT II was a symptom of the deeper
debate over the direction and objectives of post-Vietnam U.S.
foreign policy in general and U.S.-Soviet relations in
particular. Views concerning the proper U.S. policy toward
the Soviet Union ran a full spectrum: on the Left, some
believed that the United States was to blame for the onset of
the cold war and that the USSR simply responded to the U.S.
threat. Adherents of this view preferred a policy of
concessions toward the USSR. At the other end of the
spectrum, direct, pejorative parallels were drawn between the
Soviet Union and Nazi Germany and between the
Nixon-Ford-Kissinger policy of détente and Neville

Chamberlain's pre–World War II policy of appeasement.[65] These critics advocated a policy of competitive confrontation with the Soviet Union. Those in the middle of the political spectrum viewed U.S.-Soviet relations as characterized by both cooperation and competition and advocated a mixture of positive incentives and negative sanctions in dealing with the Soviet Union.

Support and Opposition within the Senate

Once the treaty was submitted to the Senate, four groups of senators emerged. One group was irreconcilably opposed to the ratification of SALT II in the form that it was submitted to the Senate. This group included, among others, Henry M. Jackson, John Tower (R-Tex.), Jake Garn (R-Utah), and Jesse Helms (R-N.C.). A second group consisted of senators who were strong supporters of the treaty and included Alan Cranston, John Culver (D-Iowa), Gary Hart, and Joseph R. Biden, Jr. (D-Del.). A third group that emerged during the treaty debate consisted of the liberal critics of SALT II who believed that the treaty did not do enough to control the arms race. This group was led by Mark Hatfield (R-Ore.), George McGovern (D-S.Dak.), and William Proxmire. The fourth and most important group consisted of the "undecideds." Their votes would determine whether the treaty was ratified or rejected. The most important members of this group were majority leader Robert Byrd (D-W.Va.), minority leader Howard Baker, Armed Services Committee Chairman John Stennis (D-Miss.), and Sam Nunn (D-Ga.).

Henry M. Jackson was the most prominent of the irreconcilable opponents of the treaty. During his forty-one years of service in Congress, Jackson had devoted his attention to two principal issues: energy and national security. He closely reviewed any matters concerning arms control and often influenced the way in which the Senate dealt with these matters. Paradoxically, during his service in the Senate,

Jackson voted in favor of every arms control agreement that was reported to the Senate for a final vote, including the Antarctic Treaty, the Limited Test Ban Treaty, the Outer Space Treaty, the Nuclear Nonproliferation Treaty, the Seabed Arms Control Treaty, the Anti-Ballistic Missile Treaty, the Interim Agreement to Limit Offensive Arms, the Biological Weapons Convention, and the Environmental Modification Convention.

Despite this apparent support for arms control, Jackson had demanded a price from the executive branch for his support for a number of these agreements. When the Limited Test Ban Treaty was considered by the Senate, Jackson demanded and received a promise from the Kennedy administration that the United States would continue nuclear tests underground at the same level or higher upon the entry into force of the treaty. Jackson authored the amendment to the 1972 Interim Agreement demanding that future agreements contain "equal aggregates" for the United States and the USSR. After the SALT I agreements were concluded, Jackson demanded that the Nixon administration replace almost all of the high-level officials at ACDA. It was during this "purge" of ACDA that Lieutenant General Edward Rowny replaced Lieutenant General Royal Allison as the JCS representative on the U.S. SALT delegation.

Columnist Rowland Evans has noted: "Of all the sources of power in Washington today, the most nearly invisible—yet in some ways the most influential—is the congressional staff. . . . a staff of professionals is no less essential to the care, feeding and orderly operation of Congress than Merlin was to King Arthur or Cardinal Richelieu to Louis XIII."[66] With allowances for journalistic license, Evans makes a valid point: the staff of members of Congress perform vital roles. Like other senators, Jackson had a group of staff members to assist him. Of all of Jackson's advisers, Richard Perle was the most influential and effective. Perle served Jackson in various professional and staff positions from 1969 to 1979, and he attracted the attention of officials at the highest level of the executive branch throughout that period. Henry Kissinger noted: "I actually considered Jackson a good friend, and I agreed with many of his analyses of Soviet intentions. The difference between Jackson and me was that he wanted all-out confrontation, under the influence of one of his associates, Richard Perle. *He* wanted all-out confrontation with the Soviets, and he liked a policy of constantly 'needling' of the Soviet Union."[67] Looking back on his presidency, Jimmy Carter noted, "I never did have much hope that I could convince Richard Perle that we needed the SALT II Treaty or [that we] ought to negotiate any treaty with the Soviet Union."[68]

Perle was hardly alone; there were a number of conservative staff aides working for other senators and some of these staff members began meeting regularly at the Madison Hotel for meals. This group hence became known as the "Madison group." The members of this group had very good ties to, and obtained sensitive information from, the Department of Defense. They sought to draft amendments that would result in the renegotiation of the treaty, so-called "killer amendments."

Senator Jackson and the other irreconcilable opponents worked against the SALT II Treaty even before it was concluded; five weeks before the treaty was signed Jackson issued a press release that stated: "From what I know of the SALT II treaty it is substantially unequal and unverifiable. It favors the Soviet Union. In its present form it is not in the security interest of the United States." Despite Jackson's opposition, President Carter tried to win his support for the treaty, but by the time the Senate was considering the treaty, Jackson's opposition was firm.

In order to defend against Jackson's and other critics' attacks on the treaty, senators Cranston, Culver, and Hart developed a substantive case for the treaty and a strategy for dealing with the critics' attacks. The case that they developed was based on the premise that the SALT II Treaty would increase the national security of the United States, rather than on the idea that arms control was inherently good or that it would contribute to détente. The "national security case for SALT" claimed that the treaty would cap the threat to the United States; that it would help the United States to assess the threat from the USSR; and that it would help the United States to evaluate Soviet capabilities better.

Supporters of the treaty invited twenty senators to form a group intended, according to the organizer of the group, Senator Cranston, "to consider the strengths and weaknesses of the treaty and to develop supporters within the Senate so that we would be ready to deal with counter-arguments."[69] The "Cranston group" met regularly with officials from the administration to discuss treaty issues. Just as the staff members who opposed the treaty formed the Madison group, the staff members who supported the treaty formed several groups of their own.

On March 2, 1979, senators Hatfield, McGovern, and Proxmire wrote to President Carter indicating, "After considerable thought we have concluded that the proposed SALT II treaty is very difficult, if not impossible, for us to support."[70] The "gang of three" was particularly concerned that "the price of SALT II" would be too high; that to gain the support of conservative senators, the administration would agree to develop and deploy new weapons systems such as the MX missile.

In an interview Senator Hatfield remarked: "We viewed our strategy as a way to slow down and perhaps stop the constant yielding and placating of the pro-military senators. . . . The more [the Carter administration] placated, then the more they demanded."[71] In fact, the Carter administration was not completely hostile to the criticism of the three senators. After they announced their position, several members of the White House Office of Congressional Relations met with the senators and their staff members on Capitol Hill. They indicated that the "White House would support strong language in the Treaty, if the Senate were to put it in, suggesting that the next round [of the SALT negotiations] have very deep reductions." According to one of Proxmire's staff members, who was present at this meeting, "We felt that this was a tactical victory of sorts, that we got their attention."

There were approximately thirty senators who had not decided whether they would vote for or against SALT II by the time that it was signed. The two most important among them were Robert Byrd and Howard Baker, the Senate's majority and minority leaders. Majority leader Byrd did not come out in favor of SALT II at the time that it was signed. Instead, he studied in great detail the hearings and considered the testimony before the Foreign Relations, Armed Services, and Intelligence committees. Byrd may have adopted his noncommittal approach in order to win over undecided senators. In early July Byrd led a delegation of senators to Moscow, where they were received by both Foreign Minister Andrey Gromyko and General Secretary Brezhnev. According to reports, Byrd was pleased with his trip to the USSR and with the answers to his questions that he received there. However, despite this, Byrd waited until late October to announce his formal support for the treaty.

The Senate minority leader, Howard Baker, had supported several arms control agreements, including the SALT I agreements and the Vladivostok Accord. In addition, he had supported President Carter on several important foreign policy issues, including the ratification of the Panama Canal treaties and the lifting of the embargo on arms shipments to Turkey. Perhaps because of this past support, Baker felt vulnerable to conservative attack within the Republican party. This was an important consideration at any time, but was even more significant in 1980, since Baker was seeking his party's nomination for president. He was also a member of the Senate Foreign Relations Committee.

At the beginning of 1979 Baker indicated that he was undecided on SALT II and that his vote would depend upon how the Soviets conducted themselves in the world.[72] Within several months Baker indicated that he was "leaning against" the treaty owing to his concerns about the restrictions placed on U.S. strategic programs, the Soviet Backfire bomber, and verification. As late as June 6 Baker was still publicly undecided; three weeks later, however, he announced his formal opposition to the treaty. On November 2 Baker formally announced his candidacy for the Republican nomination for president. One week later, in the Senate Foreign Relations Committee, he voted against reporting the treaty favorably to the full Senate.

Both critics and supporters of SALT II viewed Sam Nunn's role in the debate over the treaty as crucial. President Carter, just three weeks after his inauguration, sent Nunn a handwritten, "personal and confidential" note in which he assured the senator, "As you know, I will be the monitor and actual negotiator in arms limitation talks, & will stay close to you & others."[73] One White House official commented: "I can envision winning SALT without Jackson and possibly even without Baker. . . . But without Nunn, we're dead."[74] In January 1979 Frank Moore and Zbigniew Brzezinski wrote a memo to President Carter concerning the administration's ratification strategy in the Senate. They pointed out: "Nunn is, perhaps, the most crucial Senator in the SALT ratification battle. . . . He may be one of the only Senators who can effectively counter Jackson."[75]

During the Carter administration, Nunn criticized the president for unilaterally canceling the B-1 bomber program, and he was influential in persuading the Senate not to cancel the neutron bomb. Nunn was concerned about a number of aspects of the SALT II Treaty, including the vulnerability of U.S. land-based missiles, the Soviet Backfire bomber, the verification of the agreement, and the effect of the protocol to the agreement. To Nunn, the most important question was not the effect of the treaty on arms control but rather the effect of the treaty on U.S. defense programs. After the signing of the treaty, Nunn led the effort to pressure the Carter administration to increase the defense budget in exchange for supporting the SALT II Treaty. The administration was committed to a 3 percent increase, but

Nunn wanted an increase of 5 percent. President Carter recalled in an interview, "Sam used the SALT II Treaty in a legitimate fashion to extract from me promises for a higher level of defense expenditures, and I didn't particularly object to that."[76]

In addition to Byrd, Baker, and Nunn, John Glenn (D-Ohio) played an important role in the SALT II debate. Glenn was a Democrat, a member of the Senate Foreign Relations Committee, and a retired military officer and astronaut. Because of this background, a number of senators respected Glenn's opinion concerning the SALT II Treaty. Glenn was primarily concerned about one issue— verification—and was so focused on this issue that some within the administration derisively referred to him as "Johnny One-Note." Within the Senate, however, Glenn had a significant following.

The Committee Hearings

At the end of 1978 Senator John Sparkman (D-Ala.) retired, and Frank Church, with twenty-two years of experience on the Senate Foreign Relations Committee, became its chairman. Church and Carter had run against one another in several 1976 Democratic presidential primaries and harbored some resentment against one another as a result of these contests. Despite whatever ill will existed between Carter and Church, Carter indicated a desire to work closely with the Senate Foreign Relations Committee and its chairman by meeting with them before the inauguration, an unprecedented action for a president-elect.

After the 1978 congressional elections, there were two significant changes within the committee. First, three conservative Republicans—Jesse Helms, Richard Lugar (R-Ind.), and S. I. Hayakawa (R-Calif.)—joined the committee. The other three Republican members were Jacob Javits (the ranking Republican member from New York),

Charles Percy (R-Ill.), and Howard Baker. The nine Democratic members of the committee (in descending order of seniority) were Frank Church (chair), Claiborne Pell (D-R.I.), George McGovern, Joseph R. Biden, Jr., John Glenn, Richard Stone (D-Fla.), Paul Sarbanes (D-Md.), Edmund Muskie (D-Maine), and Edward Zorinsky (D-Nebr.). Senators Biden and Lugar were also members of the Senate Intelligence Committee, which reviewed the verification procedures of the treaty.

The second important change within the Senate Foreign Relations Committee occurred as the result of a decision to do away with the former bipartisan staff and to create a minority staff. As was the case with congressional staff overall, the staff of the Senate Foreign Relations Committee had grown significantly in the late 1960s and 1970s. In 1965 there were nine professional staff members for the committee; by 1979 the number of staff members had grown to thirty. Both the addition of the three conservative Republican members and the creation of a minority staff heightened partisan division within the committee.

On July 9, the Senate Foreign Relations Committee began hearings on the treaty. These hearings were held for a total of twenty-seven days from July through October. The public hearing record filled five volumes of 2,266 pages with the testimony of eighty-eight witnesses.[77] In addition, the committee held thirteen executive sessions, and the transcripts of these sessions totaled more than 1,200 pages. Six witnesses testified only in executive session, bringing the total number of witnesses who testified before the committee to ninety-four.[78]

Opponents of the SALT II Treaty were anxious to have a formal, public forum in which to review and criticize the treaty. Senator Jackson, a member of the Senate Armed Services Committee, persuaded Chairman Stennis to hold hearings on the treaty. Jackson's and Perle's files contain a number of memoranda concerning their preparations for these hearings. One memo, entitled "An Outline for the SASC

Hearings: What We Hope to Establish," noted the following:
"It should be our purpose in the hearings to demonstrate that
pivotal administration arguments are not supported by
evidence and/or logic, that the treaty is unequal and
unverifiable, that it is flawed with loopholes and ambiguities."
Another memo reviewed the strengths and weaknesses of
various Carter administration witnesses. Harold Brown was
viewed as "probably the administration's strongest witness."
The newly appointed director of ACDA, retired General
George Seignious, was portrayed as follows: "A weak witness—if
he claims that he is only recently involved we help make the
point that it is Warnke's treaty." Clearly, Jackson and Perle
wanted to characterize the treaty as Warnke's: "Even though
retired, Warnke should be called as the principal architect of
the treaty."

The Senate Intelligence Committee was created to oversee
executive branch intelligence operations and to consider
matters related to the intelligence capabilities of the United
States. Consequently, the Senate Foreign Relations
Committee requested that the Intelligence Committee review
the verification issues related to the SALT II Treaty. There
were three specific reasons for the request: (1) the issues
involved were of a highly sensitive nature, (2) verification was
clearly going to be a significant issue in the debate over SALT,
and it therefore deserved the most thorough and professional
treatment, and (3) the Intelligence Committee was set up to
deal with these issues.[79] Several members of the Intelligence
Committee were also members of either the Foreign
Relations Committee (Biden and Lugar) or the Armed
Services Committee (Jackson). According to William Miller,
the staff director of the Intelligence Committee in 1979:
"About one-third of the Senate reviewed the material
collected by the Intelligence Committee, and nine or ten of
these considered it very closely. . . . Senator Byrd was one of
those who was rigorous in reviewing the material."[80] The
issue of verification became an important one in the debate
over SALT II, and the Senate Intelligence Committee played

an important role in addressing this issue.

The Senate's Action

The Senate Foreign Relations Committee concluded its hearings and began its markup sessions on the treaty on October 15. The committee considered thirty-six conditions to the SALT II Treaty, dividing these conditions into three categories. "Category I" conditions were those that did not require formal notification to the Soviet Union. "Category II" provisions were those that "would be formally communicated to the Soviet Union as official statements of the position of the United States Government in ratifying the Treaty, but which do not require their agreement."[81] "Category III" provisions were those that would require the explicit agreement of the Soviet government in order for the treaty to enter into force.

Twenty-three of the thirty-six proposed conditions were adopted; of these, thirteen were "Category I" conditions, five were "Category II" conditions, and two were "Category III" conditions requiring the explicit approval of the Soviet Union (three of the adopted conditions were later withdrawn from consideration). The first of these "Category III" conditions was a reservation, adopted by the committee by a vote of 14–0, that stipulated that the agreed statements and common understandings contained in the SALT II Treaty and protocol would be of the same legal status as the treaty. The second "Category III" condition adopted by the committee was a reservation that the letter given by General Secretary Brezhnev to President Carter concerning the capabilities and production of the Backfire bomber would be legally binding on the Soviet Union.

On October 5, 1979, the Senate Intelligence Committee issued an unclassified, unanimous report that concluded, "Overall, the Committee finds that the SALT II Treaty enhances the ability of the United States to monitor those components of Soviet strategic weapons forces which are subject to the limitations of the Treaty."[82] Considering that the members of the intelligence committee included such hard-line members as senators Jackson, Garn, Lugar (who voted against the treaty in the Foreign Relations Committee), and Malcolm Wallop (R-Wy.), the unanimous approval of the Intelligence Committee's report significantly strengthened the claim of the Carter administration that the treaty was adequately verifiable.

On November 9, 1979, after four months of hearings, the Senate Foreign Relations Committee, by a vote of 9-6, voted to recommend the ratification of the treaty to the full Senate. Seven Democrats (Biden, Church, McGovern, Muskie, Pell, Sarbanes, and Zorinsky) and two Republicans (Javits and Percy) voted in favor of the treaty. Two Democrats (Glenn and Stone) and four Republicans (Baker, Helms, Hayakawa, and Lugar) voted against the treaty.

On December 17, 1979, nineteen undecided senators sent President Carter a letter in which they raised a number of concerns over "certain provisions" of the SALT II Treaty, including those concerning "heavy missiles," limitations on the basing modes of the MX, and the exclusion of restrictions concerning the Soviet Backfire bomber. In addition, the senators expressed their concern over the "precedential effect" of the three-year protocol to the treaty and its limitations on cruise missiles.

Three days later, over the objections of Senate Armed Services Committee Chairman Stennis, the committee adopted a report denouncing the treaty as "not in the national security interests of the United States." According to reports, Jackson and Perle were the principal authors of the report. The report specifically cited the following areas of concern: (1) certain inequalities, such as the Soviet advantage in throw-weight, the Soviet possession of modern, large ballistic missiles, the exclusion of the Soviet Backfire bomber, the inclusion of Western theater nuclear forces, and the potential precedents established by the protocol to the treaty, (2) loopholes concerning "new types" of ICBMS, (3) the verification of the treaty, and (4) ambiguities contained in the treaty. Ten senators voted in favor of releasing the report, and seven senators voted "present," in effect indicating their opposition to the release of the report. Although the report was released in December 1979, majority leader Byrd did not allow it to be filed officially with the clerk of the Senate until a year later. One Senate aide noted, "People in the White House were absolutely crushed by the vote in the Senate Armed Services Committee," and in an interview Anne Wexler confirmed that those in the White House viewed this vote as a major setback.[83]

It is interesting that Nunn voted with six other members of the Senate Armed Services Committee who were opposed to the committee's release of the report. By that time, although he never made a formal commitment on SALT II, Nunn was reportedly leaning toward supporting the ratification of the treaty.[84]

Estimates vary concerning the effect of the hearings on the fate of the SALT II Treaty. In retrospect Richard Perle remarked, "The treaty was dead after the hearings."[85] Senate staffer Larry Smith estimated that the vote after the hearings stood at fifty-seven in favor of the treaty, twenty-seven opposed, and sixteen undecided. Senator Cranston, known as one of the best vote counters in the Senate, estimated that shortly before the treaty was signed, the tally stood at twenty firmly against ratification, ten leaning against, forty leaning heavily toward, ten leaning slightly toward, and twenty undecided.[86]

Public Opinion and the Role of Interest Groups

A CBS/New York Times poll taken in June 1979 (the same month that the SALT II Treaty was signed) asked: "The Senate will debate the US treaty with the Soviet Union which limits strategic nuclear weapons—called SALT. From what you know about this SALT treaty, do you think that the Senate should vote for or against it, or don't you know enough about it to have an opinion?" Twenty-seven percent were in favor of the agreement, 9 percent were opposed, 10 percent did not have an opinion and 54 percent said that they did not know enough about the treaty.[87] In February 1978 the Opinion Research Corporation had asked respondents how much they had heard or read about the SALT negotiations. Sixty-one percent reported that they had heard or read very little or nothing at all, 29 percent a fair amount, and only 8 percent a great deal.[88] In a December 1978 survey only 34 percent of those questioned could correctly identify the two countries involved in the SALT negotiations.[89] Another poll taken in 1979 found that even fewer—23 percent—knew which two nations were involved in the talks.[90]

The public neither knew very much about SALT II, as the above polling information demonstrates, nor considered it particularly important. In May 1979, one month before the SALT II Treaty was signed, Louis Harris asked: "I'd like to ask you about some issues and problems that some people would like to see Congress do something about. If you had to choose, which one do you feel is most important for Congress to do something about?" Thirty-one percent responded "keeping inflation under control; 20 percent answered "passing an energy bill to make the U.S. more energy self-sufficient; and a minuscule 2 percent replied "backing a SALT agreement with Russia to control nuclear weapons." As is obvious from these results, the public did not consider a SALT agreement to be particularly important; indeed, the public ranked a SALT agreement at the bottom of the list of its concerns.[91]

Public opinion polls on SALT II are confusing. They indicate that the range of those supporting SALT ranged from a high of 81 percent (NBC poll of January 1979) to a low of 20 percent (Committee on the Present Danger poll of March 1979). Figure 2 indicates the wide variation of some of the polls conducted on SALT II. In its summary of SALT polls the editors of *Public Opinion* commented, "SALT polls are poles apart."[92] One can see the reason for this comment when figure 2 is examined.

There are several possible reasons why the results of these polls are so different. First, public opinion expert Daniel Yankelovich has pointed out: "Conventional survey techniques are most accurate when reflecting the public's state of mind on well-thought-through issues. They are not as sensitive in judging how the public might react after it has the opportunity to learn the facts, to listen to competing views, to think through the questions, and to see how well any

Figure 2
Public Opinion Polls on SALT II*

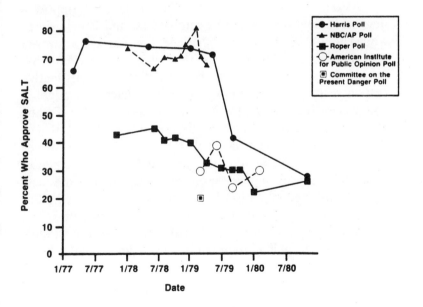

*Data taken from Thomas W. Graham, "The Politics of Failure: Strategic Nuclear in the United States, 1945-1985," Ph.D. dissertation, Massachusetts Institute of Technology, 1989. I would like to thank Dr. Graham for providing me with this data.

particular policy accords with their deeper values, attitudes, and beliefs."[93] Clearly, the public had not thought through the issues related to SALT II, and the wide divergence in the SALT polls reflects this. Second, research on public opinion indicates that there is a tendency for people to give positive responses when asked about unfamiliar issues, and this tendency is indicated in the SALT polls.

Third, many criticized the wording of a number of the polls on SALT. For example, the Committee on the Present Danger noted, "Highly generalized, hypothetical and simplistic questions with no effort to measure gradations of response provide data which furnish little insight into relevant public attitudes and are apt to be completely misleading."[94] Many of the questions supposedly concerning SALT really asked people what they thought about arms control in general rather than SALT II in particular. For example, an NBC/Associated Press poll asked, "Do you favor or oppose a new agreement between the United States and Russia which would limit nuclear weapons?" Eighty-one percent answered that they favored a new agreement, but it was not clear what people had in their minds when they indicated an affirmative response to this question. Did they have in mind a comprehensive test ban, the Nuclear Nonproliferation Treaty, SALT II, or some other agreement? Pollster Burns W. Roper was also critical of the NBC poll: "The NBC question comes very close to asking whether people would like to have peace. In fact by saying 'a new agreement' instead of 'the new agreement,' it could almost be interpreted as asking whether people would like to see the present draft renegotiated."[95]

Within the Department of State the Bureau of Public Affairs tracked public opinion on SALT II on a regular basis, and the assistant secretary of state for public affairs summarized polls and forwarded these summaries to the secretary of state, the director of ACDA and the counselor of the Department of State. President Carter, and the White House staff, relied primarily on the polls conducted by his own in-house pollster, Patrick H. Caddell. In his memoirs

Carter noted: "Caddell's polls, I knew from experience, were remarkably accurate."[96]

Department of State analysts believed that Roper "posed the most appropriately worded question," and they therefore gave "more credence to Roper's data than to the data produced by any of the other polls."[97] Roper himself thought that "most of the polls are conveying misleadingly high levels of approval," and his polls indicated support levels from a low of 20 percent to a high of 42 percent. (Figure 2 traces the result of the Roper polls on SALT II.)

While the Department of State relied primarily on Roper's polls, President Carter and the White House staff depended upon Caddell's polls. In a dramatic memo that Caddell sent to President Carter and Hamilton Jordan in May 1978, Caddell reported the results of his most recent poll as follows: "Since foreign policy/defense concerns have been secondary matters in recent years, nothing in our structured quantitative research prepared us for the below surface anxiety and concern over these issues that the open end interviews revealed." Caddell warned that *"for the first time since the Vietnam War, defense/foreign affairs is emerging"* and that the public was moving in a more conservative direction. Concerning SALT, Caddell predicted: *"SALT itself seems destined to be caught in the vertex [sic] of these larger concerns over our defense and foreign policy posture. I fear that a SALT agreement will not be judged on its own merits but rather become a vehicle for these concerns. Given the attitudes we see emerging, SALT could become a firestorm."* Caddell urged that the issue of "peace as well as defense" be considered.[98]

What is striking about this memo is that Caddell was surprised by his results. Public support for increasing the defense budget grew almost monthly from 1974 to 1981; whereas peace was the dominant concern of most Americans from 1964 to 1974, military strength became paramount from 1974 to 1981. Caddell urged the president to emphasize the issue of "peace," just as the public was moving in the opposite direction. The evidence of this movement was clear in public opinion polls of the time, except in Caddell's.

Caddell and the Department of State's public opinion analysts agreed that about 20 percent of the public opposed SALT II. However, Caddell's and the Department of State's conclusions differ in a very important respect. Whereas the Department of State argued that public support for "generic" arms control should not be confused with specific support for SALT II, Caddell concluded "that Americans support both arms limitation in general and SALT in particular." In retrospect, it appears that the information provided by the Department of State was more accurate than that provided by Caddell, but President Carter—to his detriment—believed Caddell's polls.

Interest Groups: Pro and Con

On November 11, 1976, just three days after Carter's electoral victory, the Committee on the Present Danger was formally founded. The 141 board members of the new organization read like a "Who's Who" of U.S. politics and included Douglas Dillon and Henry Fowler, both former secretaries of the treasury; General Andrew Goodpaster, former Supreme Allied Commander of NATO (the North Atlantic Treaty Organization); Lane Kirkland, then secretary-treasurer of the AFL-CIO (American Federation of Labor-Congress of Industrial Organizations); General Lyman Lemnitzer, former chairman of the Joint Chiefs of Staff; David Packard, former deputy secretary of defense; Norman Podhoretz, editor of *Commentary*; Dean Rusk, former secretary of state; and Admiral Elmo Zumwalt, Jr., former chief of naval operations. Sixty percent of its members were Democrats, and 40 percent were Republicans.[99] Fowler, Kirkland, and Packard were the cochairmen of the committee; Nitze was the chairman of policy studies; and Eugene V. Rostow was the chairman of the executive committee. Charles Walker was the treasurer, and Max Kampelman was counsel.

The budget of the committee was fairly small by Washington standards: $90,000 in 1977; $200,000 in 1978; and $300,000 in 1979.[100] Despite the committee's public pledge to limit annual contributions from any single source, conservative philanthropist Richard Mellon Scaife donated approximately $260,000 to the committee.[101]

After the founding of the committee, its leaders had to decide the tactics that the organization would adopt to get its message across. According to Rostow: "When we commenced operations in 1976, a considerable number of our founding members urged that we purchase media advertising including TV and radio time, employ direct mail, create regional and local chapters and the like to reach John Q. Citizen. Seeing our special function in quite another light, we firmly rejected that advice."[102] Instead, the committee focused its efforts on influencing the attentive public. According to former staff member Charles M. Kupperman, the committee was "not a grassroots organization. To the contrary, the Committee on the Present Danger deliberately focused on the upper echelon of American opinion leaders."[103] At its height the committee had a mailing list that consisted of about 13,000 names, hardly a large list by Washington interest group standards.

Shortly after the disastrous Vance trip to Moscow in March 1977, the committee published its first pamphlet, *What Is the Soviet Union Up To?* The committee distributed more than 1,400 copies of the report to influential citizens, newspaper reporters, and editorial writers. Drafted by Richard Pipes, the report ominously warned, "The ultimate Soviet objective–a Communist world order–requires the reduction of the power, influence, and prestige of the United States," and "Soviet nuclear offensive and defensive forces are designed to enable the USSR to fight, survive and win an all-out nuclear war should it occur."[104] The only reference to SALT in this first report was a brief note that SALT I had had "no visible effect on the Soviet [military] build-up." The report ended by warning that "if past trends continue, the USSR will within several years achieve strategic superiority over the United States." The committee fired its "first salvo in the SALT II debate" in July 1977 when it published a pamphlet entitled *Where We Stand on SALT.*

From the time of the founding of the Committee on the Present Danger through the end of December 1979, members of its executive committee and board participated in 479 television and radio programs, press conferences, debates, public forums, and speaking engagements. The committee distributed more than 200,000 copies of its pamphlets and reports. During the Senate's hearings on the SALT II Treaty, executive committee and board members testified on seventeen different occasions before the Armed Services and Foreign Relations committees.[105]

By all accounts the Committee on the Present Danger was the single most effective organization within the Washington beltway opposing the treaty; however, there were a large number of other groups allied with the committee, including, most prominently, the American Conservative Union, the American Security Council, and the Coalition for Peace through Strength. Whereas the Committee on the Present Danger focused on elite decision makers, these other groups focused on the mass public. According to Charles M. Kupperman, when the committee received a request for information from the general public, it passed this to the American Security Council for a response.[106] Thus, there was a clear division of labor among interest groups opposing the treaty.

Several of the opposition interest groups had substantial resources. For example, the American Conservative Union had 325,000 members and had spent an estimated $1 million opposing the ratification of the Panama Canal treaties.[107] During the SALT II debate, this group produced a thirty-minute anti-SALT film, which was shown on more than 200 television stations across the nation.

The most important single mass membership organization in the SALT II debate was the American Security Council, which had a membership of 200,000. Annual dues for members were $20 per person, and the budget of the organization in 1979 was $4 million. Unlike the Committee on the Present Danger, the American Security Council (founded in 1955) was a lobbying organization, not a tax-exempt, nonprofit organization. The council was led by John M. Fisher (president) and retired U.S. Army Lieutenant General Daniel O. Graham (executive director). In keeping with its focus on the mass public, the council produced a series of short, hard-hitting films designed to underscore dramatically the alleged military weaknesses of the United States. The first of these films, *Only the Strong*, was followed in 1978 by *The Price of Peace and Freedom* and in the summer of 1979, by *The SALT Syndrome*. Conservative organizations would purchase copies of these films and make them available to educational institutions, churches, civic groups, unions, and professional associations at nominal or no charge. *Only the Strong* was shown on television more than 800 times, and *The SALT Syndrome* was shown more than 600 times in 1979 alone. One scholar who studied the role of interest groups in the SALT II debate found that *The SALT Syndrome* had a greater impact on public opinion than any other single activity.[108] The Carter administration took *The SALT Syndrome* so seriously that it published and distributed a sentence-by-sentence rebuttal of the film.[109]

Conservatives had learned from two important previous skirmishes during the Carter administration: the confirmation battle over Paul C. Warnke's appointment and the Panama Canal treaties debate. They had learned that they could achieve greater influence by forming an ad hoc umbrella organization to oversee and coordinate the activities of like-minded conservative groups. Consequently, the Coalition for Peace through Strength was founded in August 1978 to coordinate the efforts of organizations and individuals who were concerned about the direction of U.S. defense in general and SALT II in particular. The coalition included 204 members of Congress, 106 national organizations, and 2,500 retired generals and admirals. In practice it was often hard to tell the difference between the American Security Council and the Coalition for Peace through Strength, for the two organizations worked hand in hand. The two organizations, for example, jointly produced and distributed *The SALT Syndrome*.

In opposing the treaty, the anti-SALT groups had several advantages. First, they were united in their opposition to SALT II; the same kind of unity did not characterize the pro-treaty groups. Second, the anti-treaty groups had superior resources and were more effective in organizing public opinion. Third, as Norman J. Ornstein and Shirley Elder have noted, "In a political system geared toward slow change with numerous decision points and checks and balances, a group's likelihood of success is enhanced if it focuses on blocking rather than initiating action."[110] The opponents of SALT II therefore had the advantageous position. Fourth, scholars have found that conservatives tend to write their legislators more than liberals and that those who are opposed to a policy tend to write more often than those who favor a policy.[111] SALT II was a case in which conservatives were opposed to ratification of the treaty, and, not surprisingly, mail to senators ran strongly against the ratification of the treaty.

Given the ways in which the Carter administration tried to influence the Senate, the administration itself resembled an interest group. Administration officials met extensively with senators to try to win their votes; they traveled throughout the United States giving speeches, press conferences, and radio and television interviews; and they met with leaders of pro-treaty interest groups. The activities of the European allies of the United States also closely resembled those of an interest group, and the Carter administration treated the allies accordingly. For example, the administration literally lobbied the Western European defense ministers and was able to obtain formal endorsements of the SALT II Treaty from Canada, France, Italy, NATO, Norway, the United Kingdom, and West Germany.

Within the United States there were a number of groups reflecting a diversity of interests that supported the ratification of the SALT II Treaty, including the AFL-CIO, the American Committee on East-West Accord, Americans for Democratic Action, the Arms Control Association, the Center for Defense Information, the Coalition for a New Foreign and Military Policy, Common Cause, the Communication Workers of America, the Council for a Livable World, the Federation of American Scientists, the Friends Committee on National Legislation, the International Association of Machinists, the National Council of Churches, Committee for a Sane Nuclear Policy (SANE), the Union of Concerned Scientists, the United Auto Workers, the United Steelworkers, and the U.S. Catholic Conference.

Despite the number and character of pro-treaty interest groups, there was no nongovernmental, pro-treaty analogue to the Committee on the Present Danger. There were, however, several umbrella organizations that were formed in order to support ratification of SALT II. The Religious Committee on SALT consisted of twenty-seven religious organizations, and the membership of the denominations represented by the committee included more than 50 million people. In September 1979 175 religious leaders representing many of the member groups of this committee met with President Carter and other cabinet members at the White House. After this meeting, they went to Capitol Hill to meet with senators to urge them to vote in favor of SALT II. Other prominent religious leaders also endorsed SALT II, including conservative evangelist Billy Graham. Perhaps influenced by Reverend Graham's support and President Carter's own evangelical religious beliefs, some groups that had not previously supported arms control efforts, such as the Southern Baptist Convention, came out in favor of ratification of the treaty. Like many interest groups, the Religious Committee on SALT was handicapped by limited financial resources; the budget for the committee for a two-year period was less than $20,000. Despite this limitation (and disproportionate to it), the committee had an impact on the SALT II debate, owing to the extensive network of the religious organizations that were associated with the committee.[112]

Just as anti-SALT groups learned certain lessons from the past, the pro-SALT interest groups had also learned that coalition building was an important key to success. During the summer of 1978, Americans for SALT was founded in order to generate "a national campaign for ratification of the SALT II Treaty." The sole goal of the organization was to lobby in favor of the treaty by organizing programs to increase the visibility of growing public support for SALT II, to coordinate local pro-SALT activities in communities and states with the efforts of national organizations, and to conduct extensive educational programs. Thus, the avowed focus of Americans for SALT was on the grass-roots level rather than on the attentive (or elite) public.

Americans for SALT was founded with the support of a number of organizations, including the American Committee on East-West Accord, the Arms Control Association, the Council for a Livable World, the National Council of Churches, several labor unions, and New Directions (a public interest group designed to be the "Common Cause of foreign policy). The cochairpersons of the committee were all distinguished in their respective fields and included former presidential adviser and Secretary of Defense Clark Clifford, University of Notre Dame President Father Theodore Hesburgh, former Pentagon official Townsend Hoopes, former Ambassador Henry Cabot Lodge, and former Ambassador Charles Yost. Americans for SALT organized a speakers bureau and offered speakers to organizations planning programs concerning SALT II. The committee published thirteen issues of an "action newsletter," *SALT Talk*, which carried news of the committee's activities, descriptions of the treaty, and suggestions for "what you can do." The committee also distributed special reports from time to time, including a rebuttal to a report published by the Coalition for Peace through Strength. Another special report consisted of a set of guidelines for organizing state and local organizations, planning a speaking event, writing letters to the editor, holding news conferences, and writing press releases. Three weeks after the SALT II Treaty was signed, Americans for SALT sponsored full-page advertisements in the *New York Times* and the *Washington Post* in which a number of prominent Americans announced their support for the treaty.[113] Ten days later, Americans for SALT convened a "field organizing conference" for more than 100 treaty supporters from twenty-four states in order to develop strategies to promote Senate ratification of the treaty. After the group was briefed by government experts, President Carter spoke to the group and stressed the need for ongoing citizen involvement in the ratification effort.

Americans for SALT, however, was hampered by several factors. First, the organization was created only one year before the SALT II Treaty was signed; many of the anti-treaty organizations had been founded much earlier. The Committee on the Present Danger, for example, was founded in November 1976 and began actively lobbying against the treaty in the summer of 1977. Second, Americans for SALT had major personnel problems during its first year of existence, when two executive directors and an assistant executive director were fired. A third problem was funding. Eventually, a total of approximately $300,000 was raised to support the activities and programs of Americans for SALT. A fourth problem concerned the nature of the pro-SALT coalition. As the former president of the nongovernmental interest group, the Arms Control Association, William Kincade, has pointed out: "The pro-treaty groups were not effective because they were not unified. Nobody on the left is satisfied with half a loaf, and consequently, they usually get nothing. That's what happened with SALT II."[114]

The disunity of the Left was evident when Jeremy Stone, the executive director of the Federation of American Scientists, a public interest lobby of scientists, published an article in the *New York Times* in March 1979 that criticized the emerging SALT agreement for failing to place meaningful limits on Soviet and U.S. strategic nuclear arsenals.[115] After the SALT II Treaty was signed, Stone refused to endorse the treaty, despite the fact that the Federation of American Scientists did so. Others followed Stone's lead. In May, Robert C. Johansen, the president of the Institute for World Order, published an article in *Harper's* magazine in which he argued, "The achievement of both SALT I and SALT II is to curtail relatively insignificant parts of a quantitative arms race so that more money and brainpower can be devoted to a significantly more dangerous qualitative arms race."[116] In March 1979 senators Hatfield, McGovern, and Proxmire published a critical assessment of the agreement, and in August *Progressive* magazine called for the outright rejection of the treaty on the grounds that it did not do enough to achieve "genuine" arms control.

President Carter and his advisers sought to gain public approval of the agreement in a number of ways. Central to the administration's ratification strategy was the White House effort to win the approval of influential citizens from states with undecided senators. The White House sponsored a number of briefings for such citizens in Washington, D.C. Typically, Cyrus Vance, Harold Brown, or Zbigniew Brzezinski, or some combination of these, would describe the elements of the treaty and then respond to questions from the audience. President Carter made an attempt to drop by these meetings in order to add to the aura. The administration hoped that these citizens would be so convinced of the need for the treaty that they would go home and urge their senators to vote in favor of the agreement.

In retrospect, the Carter administration would have been more effective in dealing with the Senate if it had concentrated its efforts on dealing with individual senators rather than attempting to bolster grass-roots support for SALT II through the White House briefings and SALT public information programs. Hamilton Jordan was immediately responsible for developing the SALT II ratification plan and is, therefore, responsible for this shortcoming. Ultimately, however, the "buck stops" on the president's desk, and President Carter was therefore responsible for the mistaken approach.

Conclusion

President Carter and his administration faced a number of significant challenges in concluding the negotiations and campaigning for the ratification of the SALT II Treaty. Broadly considered, these challenges can be placed in five principal categories: (1) the timing of the treaty negotiations and ratification effort, (2) shortcomings of President Carter and his administration, (3) indifferent public opinion and effective opposition from interest groups, (4) the Senate and executive-congressional relations, and (5) aggressive Soviet activities and other external events that affected the American public's assessment of the Carter administration.

The Administration's Timing

The administration's timing was critical in several areas of arms control. The decision to lay aside the SALT II agreement negotiated by the Nixon and Ford administrations and to present in March 1977 the "comprehensive proposal" calling for deep cuts, in retrospect, was a major error. The administration presented the comprehensive proposal as a take-it-or-leave-it deal. When the Soviets rejected this proposal, the administration tried to present a fallback position based on the Vladivostok Accord. The Soviets, however, were distrustful of Carter because he presented the comprehensive proposal without prior consultations and because of his emphasis on human rights. According to Senator Cranston: "Instead of seeking to conclude a treaty that was almost complete, Carter created almost a new treaty. This got things off to a bad start and destroyed the bipartisan opportunity that was there to have a Democratic president complete the work of two previous Republican presidents. This upset a good opportunity."[117] The March 1977 proposal became a benchmark for conservatives in the United States, and they evaluated all subsequent U.S. SALT proposals and draft agreements on the basis of this proposal. Thus, the comprehensive proposal alienated the Soviets and raised the expectations within the United States of what SALT II could accomplish.

Trying to meet conservative critics' negative assessment of the SALT II Treaty, the Carter administration pressed several points with the Soviets—for example, the classification of the Backfire bomber and verification procedures—that further delayed the signing of the treaty. In addition, the United States' recognition of the People's Republic of China caused a delay of three to six months. As Lloyd Cutler has noted: "The treaty was signed too late. In the first two years of [Carter's administration], he would have had a much better chance of getting sixty-seven votes.[118]

The administration's sequencing of the Panama Canal treaties and the SALT II Treaty also contributed to the outcome of the debates. Some moderate Republican and conservative Democratic senators believed that they could vote for one or the other of the agreements, and the conservative Democratic Senator Richard Stone told President Carter, "You don't ask a vulnerable politician to walk the plank twice."[119] When the Panama Canal treaties came first, the Carter administration put the pressure on, and some of these moderate and conservative senators voted in favor of them. The administration essentially spent its political capital on Panama, leaving little in reserve for the SALT II ratification effort.

Timing was also important during the SALT II debate itself. The treaty was signed in June and withdrawn from Senate consideration in January, a time frame of six and one-half months. Former Nixon and Ford NSC official William G. Hyland has commented, "The [Carter] Administration's handling of the ratification process was badly botched; no president should have allowed the Senate to dally over such a critical treaty."[120]

The President and His Administration

Jimmy Carter's personality had a significant effect on the SALT II Treaty ratification debate. During the 1976 election campaign, President Carter saw himself and presented himself to the American people as an outsider to Washington politics. Carter believed that his lack of experience with national and international affairs was an advantage rather than a disadvantage, and once elected, he did little to develop good working relations with the Washington community of present and past government officials, legislators, lobbyists, and journalists to support his programs.

According to former NSC staff member Gary Sick, President Carter "seemed to believe that if a decision was correct it would sell itself, and his disregard to the potentially dangerous political consequences of his programs at times appeared to border on recklessness."[121] As a consequence of this aspect of Carter's personality, the president was unwilling to spend much time meeting with members of Congress on an informal basis to cultivate relationships that could have perhaps helped him win congressional support of his programs.

Carter's shortcomings were magnified by several of his appointments. First, he appointed some policymakers with conflicting views that were in many respects mutually exclusive. Second, he appointed some people who were poorly qualified, especially in the key area of executive-congressional relations. Third, he did not appoint several prominent individuals to his administration who could have helped him win increased support among conservatives. Fourth, he appointed several advisers too late.

Because President Carter had little background in foreign affairs, he particularly needed a strong, well-coordinated team to assist him in this complex area. Yet the two men he selected for the most important foreign policy positions in his administration had very different views of the best ways of dealing with the Soviet Union. Zbigniew Brzezinski's instincts were toward competition and confrontation with the USSR. He acted in ways that suggested it was more important to seek to limit the expansion of Soviet influence in the world than to expeditiously negotiate and ratify the SALT II Treaty. For example, Brzezinski was principally responsible for linking SALT II to Cuban and Soviet activities in Africa in 1978; pushing for the United States to normalize relations with the People's Republic of China in late 1978; and pressing the U.S. intelligence community to investigate Soviet activities in Cuba and elsewhere in the spring and summer of 1979. In retrospect, some of the policies supported by Dr. Brzezinski appear to have slowed down or damaged the prospects for the ratification of the SALT II Treaty.

In contrast with Brzezinski, Cyrus Vance's instincts were toward negotiation and conciliation. He believed that the control of nuclear weapons was so important that SALT II should not be linked to other, secondary issues on the agenda of U.S.-Soviet relations. President Carter hurt his administration's effectiveness and the chances of ratifying SALT II by not choosing one approach or the other. Instead, he tried to follow two mutually exclusive policies during his four years in office.

The division of the Carter administration at the top was replicated at lower levels. In order to achieve his heartfelt goal of nuclear arms control, President Carter appointed a man known for his strong support of arms control, Paul C. Warnke, as director of ACDA and the chief U.S. negotiator at the SALT II talks. This appointment stimulated a great deal of controversy and opposition to the Carter administration in general and to SALT II in particular. A number of observers believe that this appointment was a mistake, because Warnke's appointment did little to win the support of undecided senators for SALT II and other arms control efforts. To try to placate conservatives, President Carter and his senior officials reappointed Lieutenant General Edward Rowny to his position as JCS representative to the SALT II negotiations. General Rowny then provided information on the negotiations to Senator Jackson, but his appointment did little to achieve Jackson's support for SALT II; in fact, it had precisely the opposite result.

Perhaps as damaging to the administration as appointments that were made were several appointments that were not made. The most important of those candidates who were not appointed was Paul H. Nitze. For four decades Nitze had been centrally involved in the planning and implementation of U.S. defense policy. He had advised every president since Harry S. Truman and had been an early supporter of Jimmy Carter in the 1976 election. However, Carter and Nitze had different views on arms control and national security. Nitze was offered a position in the Carter administration, but, as mentioned earlier, it was not at the cabinet level, and Nitze therefore did not accept the offer. Given Nitze's long ties to the Democratic party and his early support of Jimmy Carter, his opposition to SALT II was not inevitable and perhaps could have been prevented by appointing him to a senior, cabinet-level position. Ironically, this was the type of position to which both Rowny and Nitze were appointed during President Reagan's second term of office (after both had served as arms control negotiators during the first term).

President Carter appointed several advisers too late. It was clear to many that an overall "SALT II ratification czar" would be needed in order to obtain the ratification of the SALT II Treaty, but this appointment was not made until mid-August 1979 when the president appointed the respected Washington attorney Lloyd Cutler to this position. Cutler, however, was appointed at least a year too late; hearings on SALT II were already well under way, and opponents to the treaty had been working for more than a year. Several senior members of the Carter administration were critical of Cutler's appointment on the grounds that he was not familiar with the ways that Congress operated, with national security issues or the substance of SALT II. The President also appointed former *Time* magazine senior editor Hedley Donovan as a senior White House adviser. This appointment was designed to broaden the base of Carter's advisers, but like the Cutler appointment, it came too late.

Related to, but separate from, the personnel problems of the Carter administration were the substantive problems concerning the SALT II Treaty. Reflecting his deeply held personal values and convictions, President Carter made human rights the dominant theme of his administration's approach to foreign policy during his first several years in office. This emphasis attracted considerable public and congressional support within the United States; however, it alienated certain U.S. allies, such as the shah of Iran, and adversaries of the United States, such as Leonid Brezhnev.

Despite all of the problems related to Jimmy Carter's personality and his administration, the research conducted for this case study indicates that had the Senate voted on the treaty in mid-August, it would have been ratified. What factors contributed to the demise of the treaty?

Public Opinion and the Role of Interest Groups

During the mid-1970s, public opinion became more assertive and pro-military. This change in public opinion coincided with the rise of a number of conservative interest groups in the United States. Many of these had existed for years; others were founded in the 1970s to combat a perceived decline of support for strong U.S. defense and foreign policies. At least one—the Committee on the Present Danger—was founded as a direct response to the election of Jimmy Carter. Some of these conservative groups were well financed and well staffed; they were certainly better financed than their liberal, pro-arms control counterparts. Despite the resources of these groups, it would be an exaggeration to claim that they were able to turn public opinion around in a conservative direction. Rather, they encouraged trends already emerging at the time.

The conservative interest groups were able to take advantage of the rightward trend in public opinion for four major reasons. First, these groups began campaigning against SALT II long before it was signed, in contrast with the Carter administration, which did not begin its full-scale ratification campaign until after the treaty was initialed. Second, the conservative groups took full advantage of new technologies for contacting and influencing public and congressional opinion. In 1980, Richard Viguerie sent more than 70 million computer-based direct-mail appeals, which raised more than $20 million for conservative congressional candidates. Third, many of the conservative anti-SALT groups coordinated their efforts and thereby made more efficient use of their resources. These organizations also exchanged address lists for various mailings and solicitations for funds. Fourth, the conservative groups adopted an effective media campaign highlighted by the success of the popular anti-SALT film, *The SALT Syndrome.*

Clearly, the conservative interest groups won the battle against the pro-SALT moderate and liberal groups. Why was this the case? Because public opinion had shifted in a more conservative direction, the pro-SALT groups were fighting an uphill battle. In addition, as political scientist Miroslav Nincic has argued convincingly, the shift in public opinion may have resulted from "the politics of opposites; namely, that "other things being equal, the public will tend to prefer assertiveness in dovish presidents while seeking a more conciliatory stance in hawkish chief executives."[122] Throughout Carter's administration, public support for Carter's Soviet policy increased when he became more assertive and tended to decrease when he became more conciliatory.

The Senate and Executive-Congressional Relations

Given the constitutional requirement of a two-thirds majority vote in favor of treaties, the ultimate fate of the SALT II Treaty lay with the Senate. The Carter administration sought to influence public opinion in the hope that the influential citizens invited to the White House to hear a briefing on the treaty would then contact their senators to vote in favor of the SALT II Treaty. This was the strategy that the administration had used to gain the ratification of the Panama Canal treaties, and it had worked (although barely, since the Panama Canal treaties were ratified by a margin of one vote). As noted earlier, the members of the Carter administration used the ratification campaign for the Panama Canal treaties as the template for the ratification campaign for the SALT II treaty . This was an unfortunate error, for the situations were reversed in these two cases. In the Panama case, the Senate favored the treaties, and the public opposed them. It therefore made good sense for the Carter administration to target the public as the audience for its ratification campaign. In the SALT II case, the public favored the treaty, and the Senate did not. Rather than using the Panama strategy, it would have been far better for the members of the administration to devote most of their time, effort, and resources to convincing the Senate rather than the public of the need for the SALT II Treaty.

President Carter and his administration also erred in trying to win over certain members of the Senate, most notably, Henry M. Jackson. From the early days of his administration Jimmy Carter had sought Jackson's support, yet as Carter himself later recalled, it was very unlikely that Jackson would vote in favor of any SALT II Treaty. Jackson's support of SALT II would have been sufficient to ratify the treaty, but such support was extremely unlikely, and resources invested in Jackson were wasted. Perhaps part of the reason for Jackson's opposition was the influence of his staff members, particularly Richard Perle, who was extremely critical of arms control.

Quite rightly, Carter emphasized the need to gain the support of prominent, moderate senators, including majority leader Robert Byrd and Armed Services Committee member Sam Nunn. Both Byrd and Nunn carefully reviewed the advantages and disadvantages of the treaty. Senator Byrd announced his support of the treaty at the end of October, following the Soviet combat brigade episode. Senator Nunn appeared to be leaning in favor of voting for the treaty after Carter agreed to a significant increase in defense spending.

Senator Howard Baker would have been crucial had the Senate voted on SALT II. His support of the Panama Canal treaties had made ratification possible; it had also alienated many of his conservative supporters. Although some observers believe that Baker could not have voted for SALT II, given his support of the Panama Canal treaties, others believe that he could have been persuaded to vote in favor of SALT II if the administration had negotiated with him more seriously on the issues about which he was concerned, particularly Soviet heavy missiles.[123] The fact that Baker was running for the Republican presidential nomination in 1980 was also a key factor, and the near defeat of moderate Republican and incumbent President Gerald Ford by conservative Ronald Reagan at the 1976 Republican Convention was undoubtedly not lost on Baker. Given the international events of late August through December 1979, the question of Baker's support became moot; however, it does raise an important issue, namely, the crucial role that the majority and minority leaders of the Senate play in the ratification of treaties.

The Effects of International Events on the Ratification Debate

Because of the unpredictable nature of international events, foreign policy successes or failures are often the result of, to use the phrase of former Secretary of State Dean Acheson, "plain dumb luck." Acheson believed that this was the principal explanation for the Kennedy administration's success in the Cuban missile crisis. Many believe that the same factor accounts for the Carter administration's failure to ratify SALT II. The Senate would likely have ratified the treaty had a vote been taken before the end of August. However, following the "discovery" of the Soviet combat brigade in Cuba and the politicization of this issue by Senator Stone and Senator Church, the vote on SALT II was significantly delayed. The takeover of the U.S. embassy in Tehran during the first week in November raised more questions in the minds of the public about the Carter administration's competence in the foreign policy area, and the Soviet invasion of Afghanistan drove the final nail in the coffin of SALT II.

In assessing all of these reasons behind the failure to ratify SALT II, the administration's timing and the underlying shift in public opinion were the most important domestic factors. Even despite the errors that the Carter administration committed and the shift in public opinion, the administration was nevertheless able to gain significant support for the SALT II Treaty during the summer of 1979. Events in Cuba, Iran, and Afghanistan, however, precluded a positive vote on the treaty.

Notes

1. Jimmy Carter, *Keeping Faith: Memoirs of a President* (New York: Bantam, 1982), 240.

2. Howard Baker, "Press Conference on SALT II," unpublished transcript, June 27, 1979.

3. John Glenn, "SALT: A Congressional Perspective," unpublished press release, May 17, 1979, 1.

4. U.S. Department of State, *SALT II Agreement*, Selected Documents, no. 12A, June 1979.

5. For a comprehensive consideration of this case, see Dan Caldwell, *The Dynamics of Domestic Politics and Arms Control: The SALT II Treaty Ratification Debate* (Columbia: University of South Carolina Press, 1991).

6. Zbigniew Brzezinski, *Power and Principle: Memoirs of the National Security Adviser, 1977-1981* (New York: Farrar, Straus and Giroux, 1983), 73.

7. Ibid., 51–52.

8. Jimmy Carter to Leonid Brezhnev, January 26, 1977, quoted in ibid., 151–52.

9. Jimmy Carter to Andrey Sakharov, February 17, 1977, quoted by Sandy Vogelsang, *American Dream, Global Nightmare: The Dilemma of U.S. Human Rights Policy* (New York: W. W. Norton and Co., 1980), 103–4.

10. Edward Walsh, "Carter Stresses Arms and Rights in Policy Speech,"*Washington Post*, March 18, 1977, A1.

11. *New York Times*, May 23, 1977.

12. David Aaron, interview with the author, San Francisco, Calif., January 16, 1988.

13. Carter quoted by Hamilton Jordan, *Crisis: The Last Year of the Carter Presidency* (New York: G. P. Putnam, 1982), 45.

14. David S. McLellan, *Cyrus Vance* (Totowa, N.J.: Rowman and Allenheld, 1985), 41.

15. Zbigniew Brzezinski, "U.S. Foreign Policy,"*Foreign Affairs* 51, no. 4 (July 1973): 708–27, and Zbigniew Brzezinski, "The Balance of Power Delusion,"*Foreign Policy*, no. 7 (Summer 1972): 54–59.

16. Carter, *Keeping Faith*, 52.

17. Jordan, *Crisis*, 47.

18. Cyrus Vance, *Hard Choices: Critical Years in America's Foreign Policy* (New York: Simon and Schuster, 1983), 35.

19. William B. Quandt, *Camp David: Peacemaking and Politics* (Washington, D.C.: The Brookings Institution, 1986), 35.

20. Jordan, *Crisis*, 49.

21. Strobe Talbott, *Endgame: The Inside Story of SALT II* (New York: Harper & Row, 1979), 50.

22. Emergency Coalition Against Unilateral Disarmament, "Why Paul Warnke Should NOT be Confirmed as Director of the Arms Control and Disarmament Agency and Chief Negotiator for the Strategic Arms Limitation Treaties . . . an Open Letter to the United States Senate," *Washington Post*, February 22, 1977, A15 (emphasis in the original).

23. Jimmy Carter, telephone interview with author, April 12, 1988, unpublished transcript, 2.

24. Henry M. Jackson to Jimmy Carter, "Memorandum for the President on SALT,"February 15, 1977, accession no. 3560-5, box 315, folder 35, Henry M. Jackson Papers, University of Washington Libraries (hereafter cited as Jackson MSS).

25. Ibid., i.

26. Talbott, *Endgame*, 53.

27. See note 23 above.

28. See, for example, Jimmy Carter to Henry M. Jackson, April 5, 1977, accession no. 3506-6, box 36, folder 17, Jackson MSS, and Jimmy Carter to Henry M. Jackson, August 22, 1977, "Henry Jackson (Presidential),"WHCF–Name file, Jimmy Carter Library.

29. Resume of Edward L. Rowny and List of Recommended Appointees, Henry M. Jackson Papers, accession no. 3560-6, box 83, folder 19, Jackson MSS.

30. Ralph Earle II, "Chapter III,"unpublished manuscript on SALT II, February 28, 1983, 14. I am indebted to Ambassador Earle for allowing me to quote from this manuscript.

31. Confidential interview with author.

32. Paul H. Nitze with Ann M. Smith and Steven L. Rearden, *From Hiroshima to Glasnost: At the Center of Decision* (New York: Grove Weidenfeld, 1989), and Strobe Talbott, *The Master of the Game: Paul Nitze and the Nuclear Peace* (New York: Alfred A. Knopf, 1988).

33. Polling data cited George D. Moffett III, *The Limits of Victory: The Ratification of the Panama Canal Treaties* (Ithaca, N.Y.: Cornell University Press, 1985), 210, app. A.

34. Landon Butler, interview with author, Washington, D.C., October 21, 1987.

35. Brzezinski, *Power and Principle*, 138–39.

36. Ibid., 136.

37. Vance, *Hard Choices*, 151–52.

38. Jimmy Carter to Henry Kissinger, May 1, 1978, "Kissinger," name file, Jimmy Carter Library.

39. Moffett, *The Limits of Victory*, 207.

40. Carter, *Keeping Faith*, 88.

41. Matthew Nimetz to Gerald Rafshoon, memorandum, "SALT II through Solar Initiatives,"October 6, 1978, Gerald Rafshoon Files, box 60, Jimmy Carter Library.

42. Ibid.

43. Gerald Rafshoon, "SALT—Office Communications Plan," October 12, 1978, Gerald Rafshoon Files, "Rail Strike through Soviet Postcards,"box 6, Jimmy Carter Library.

44. Gerald Rafshoon to Jimmy Carter, memorandum, December 6, 1978, Carter Presidential Papers, Staff Offices, Assistant for Communications, subject files, SALT [5] folder, Jimmy Carter Library.

45. Ibid., 2 (emphasis in the original).

46. Hamilton Jordan to Jimmy Carter, memorandum, January 30, 1979, Carter Presidential Papers, Staff Offices, Chief of Staff (Jordan), subject file, "SALT Notebook [CF, O/A 648],"box 53, Jimmy Carter Library.

47. "SALT II Ratification Master Work Plan," April 11, 1979, WHCF, Hugh Carter files, box 77, Jimmy Carter Library.

48. Gerald Rafshoon to Jimmy Carter, memorandum, May 8, 1979, "FO 6-1, 5/9/79-5/15/79," WHCF–Subject Files, Foreign Affairs, Executive, box 70-41, Jimmy Carter Library.

49. "Reference Guide to SALT," accession no. 3560-6, box 50, folder 9, Jackson MSS.

50. Gerald Rafshoon to Shana Alexander and other journalists, June 4, 1979, "FO 6-1, 6/1/79-6/11/79," WHCF–Subject files, Foreign Affairs, Executive, box 70-41, Jimmy Carter Library.

51. See note 46 above.

52. 18 U.S.C. § 1913.

53. Kenneth L. Adelman, "Rafshooning the Armageddon: The Selling of SALT," *Policy Review*, no. 9 (Summer 1979): 85–102.

54. J. K. Fasick to Barry Goldwater, March 16, 1979, report no. ID-79-24 (Washington, D.C.: U.S. General Accounting Office, 1979).

55. J. K. Fasick to Barry Goldwater, August 27, 1979, report no. ID-79-50 (Washington, D.C.: U.S. General Accounting Office, 1979).

56. Larry Smith and Alan Platt, interviews with author, Washington, D.C., October 23, 1987.

57. William Proxmire, interview with author, Washington, D.C., June 4, 1987.

58. Cyrus Vance, interview with author, New York City, July 14, 1988.

59. U.S. Congress, Senate Committee on Foreign Relations, "Testimony of Ralph Earle II," *The SALT II Treaty, Hearings*, pt. 1, 96th Cong., 1st sess., 248–49.

60. U.S. Congress, Senate Committee on Foreign Relations, "Statement of Professor Robert Legvold," *The SALT II Treaty, Hearings*, pt. 3, 74–75.

61. U.S. Congress, Senate Committee on Foreign Relations, "Testimony of Cyrus Vance and Harold Brown," *The SALT II Treaty, Hearings*, pt. 1, 91, 104.

62. Larry Smith, interview with author, Washington, D.C., October 20, 1987.

63. Vance, *Hard Choices*, 365.

64. William Perry, interview with author, Menlo Park, California, January 15, 1988.

65. Richard Perle, "Echoes of the 1930s," *Strategic Review* 7 (Winter 1979): 11–15.

66. Rowland Evans, quoted by Harrison W. Fox, Jr., and Susan Webb Hammond, *Congressional Staffs: The Invisible Force in American Lawmaking* (New York: Free Press, 1977), vii.

67. Henry Kissinger, interview in Michael Charlton, *From Deterrence to Defense: The Inside Story of Strategic Policy* (Cambridge: Harvard University Press, 1987), 43 (emphasis in the original).

68. See note 23 above.

69. Alan Cranston, interview with author, Washington, D.C., June 5, 1987.

70. George McGovern, Mark Hatfield, and William Proxmire, to Jimmy Carter, March 2, 1979, reprinted in the *Congressional Record*, March 5, 1979, 2044.

71. Mark Hatfield, interview with author, Washington, D.C., June 4, 1987.

72. "Baker: Senate Undecided on SALT," *Washington Post*, January 15, 1979.

73. Jimmy Carter to Sam Nunn, February 14, 1977, "Executive, FG 264, 1/1/78-12/31/78." WHCF–Subject file, Federal Government–Organizations, box FG-209, Jimmy Carter Library.

74. Albert R. Hunt, "In the SALT Debate, Senator Sam Nunn's Role Could Prove Decisive," *Wall Street Journal*, March 22, 1979, 1.

75. Frank Moore and Zbigniew Brzezinski to Jimmy Carter, memorandum, January 23, 1979, "FO-6-1, 11/21/78-2/10/79," WHCF, Foreign Affairs, Executive, Jimmy Carter Library.

76. Jimmy Carter, telephone interview with author, April 12, 1988, unpublished manuscript, 3.

77. U.S. Congress, Senate Committee on Foreign Relations, *The SALT II Treaty, Hearings*.

78. U.S. Congress, Senate Committee on Foreign Relations, *The SALT II Treaty, Report*, 96th Cong., 1st sess., 1979, 52.

79. William Miller, interview with author, Washington, D.C., October 21, 1987.

80. Ibid.

81. U.S. Congress, Senate Committee on Foreign Relations, *The SALT II Treaty, Report*, 18.

82. U.S. Congress, Senate Select Committee on Intelligence, *Principal Findings by the Senate Select Committee on Intelligence on the Capabilities of the United States to Monitor the SALT II Treaty, Report*, 96th Cong., 1st sess., 1979.

83. Ronald Tammen, interview with author, Washington, D.C., June 4, 1987, and Anne Wexler, interview with author, Washington, D.C., October 28, 1988.

84. *Congressional Quarterly*, "Weekly Report," December 15, 1979.

85. Richard Perle, telephone interview with author, November 10, 1988.

86. Rudy Abramson, "GOP Liberals, Moderates Hold Fate of Arms Pact," *Los Angeles Times*, May 11, 1979.

87. CBS/New York Times poll, June 1979, cited by Thomas W. Graham, "The Politics of Failure: Strategic Nuclear Arms Control, Public Opinion, and Domestic Politics in the United States, 1945–1985" (Ph.D. diss., MIT, 1989).

88. Cited by David W. Moore, "The Public Is Uncertain," *Foreign Policy*, no. 35 (Summer 1979): 70.

89. Ibid.

90. Robert Erikson, Norman Luttbeg, and Kent L. Tedin, *American Public Opinion*, 2d ed. (New York: John Wiley and Sons, 1980), 19.

91. Louis Harris poll of May 1979, cited by Graham, "The Politics of Failure."

92. *Public Opinion* (March–April 1979), 27.

93. Daniel Yankelovich, "Cautious Internationalism: A Changing Mood Toward U.S. Foreign Policy,"*Public Opinion* 1, no. 1 (March–April 1978): 16.

94. Committee on the Present Danger, *Public Attitudes on SALT II: The Results of a Nationwide Scientific Poll of American Opinion*, (Washington, D.C., March 1979), 4.

95. Burns W. Roper to Frank Church, March 2, 1979, attached to a memorandum from William J. Dyess to George Seignious and Matthew Nimetz, "SALT II through Solar Initiative," April 4, 1979, Gerald Rafshoon files, box 60, Jimmy Carter Library.

96. Jimmy Carter, *Keeping Faith*, 114.

97. William J. Dyess to George Seignious and Matthew Nimetz, memorandum, "SALT II through Solar Initiative,"April 4, 1979, Gerald Rafshoon files, box 60, Jimmy Carter Library.

98. Patrick H. Caddell to Jimmy Carter and Hamilton Jordan, memorandum, May 10, 1978, Gerald Rafshoon files, box 60, "SALT [5], Rail Strike through Soviet Postcards" folder, 1, Jimmy Carter Library (emphasis in the original).

99. Nitze, Smith, and Rearden, *From Hiroshima to Glasnost*, 354.

100. Charles Tyroler II, interview in Kupperman, "The SALT II Debate" (Ph.D. diss., University of Southern California, 1980).

101. Karen Rothmyer, "Citizen Scaife," *Columbia Journalism Review* (July–August 1981): 41.

102. Eugene V. Rostow to the members of the Committee on the Present Danger, memorandum, October 13, 1987, 2.

103. Kupperman, "The SALT II Debate," 192.

104. Committee on the Present Danger, *What Is the Soviet Union Up To?* (Washington, D.C., April 1977), 6, 8–9.

105. "Memorandum from Eugene V. Rostow, Chairman, Executive Committee, to Friends and Supporters of the Committee," December 5, 1979.

106. Charles M. Kupperman, interview with author, Washington, D.C., June 5, 1987.

107. *Time*, January 8, 1979, 21.

108. David Carl Kurkowski, "The Role of Interest Groups in the Domestic Debate on SALT II" (Ph.D. diss., Temple University, 1982).

109. "The SALT Syndrome: Charges and Facts: Analysis of an Anti-SALT 'Documentary,' " *Congressional Record*, July 30, 1980, 10366–71.

110. Norman J. Ornstein and Shirley Elder, *Interest Groups, Lobbying and Policy-Making* (Washington, D.C.: Congressional Quarterly Press, 1978), 66.

111. Lewis A. Dexter, "What Do Congressmen Hear: The Mail," *Public Opinion Quarterly* 20 (Spring 1956): 17–27.

112. Kurkowski, "The Role of Interest Groups," 121.

113. "7 out of 10 Americans Approve of the SALT II Treaty," *Washington Post*, July 9, 1979, A15.

114. William Kincade, interview with author, Washington, D.C., July 13, 1988.

115. Jeremy Stone, "SALT, in Perspective," *New York Times*, March 11, 1979.

116. Robert C. Johansen, "Arms Bazaar,"*Harper's*, May 1979, 21.

117. Alan Cranston, interview with author, Washington, D.C., June 5, 1987.

118. Lloyd Cutler, interview with author, Washington, D.C., October 27, 1988.

119. William Bader, interview with author, Arlington, Va., October 20, 1987.

120. William G. Hyland, *Mortal Rivals: Superpower Relations from Nixon to Reagan* (New York: Random House, 1987), 225.

121. Gary Sick, *All Fall Down: America's Tragic Encounter with Iran* (New York: Penguin, 1986), 262.

122. Miroslav Nincic, "The United States, the Soviet Union, and the Politics of Opposites," *World Politics* 40, no. 4 (July 1988): 469.

123. Alton Frye, interview with author, Washington, D.C., July 12, 1988.

Selected Bibliography

Books and Articles

Brzezinski, Zbigniew. *Power and Principle: Memoirs of the National Security Adviser 1977-1981*. New York: Farrar, Straus and Giroux, 1983.

Burt, Richard. "The Scope and Limits of SALT." *Foreign Affairs* 56, no. 4 (July 1978): 751-70.

———, ed. "A Strategic Symposium: SALT and U.S. Defense Policy." *Washington Quarterly* 2, no. 1 (Winter 1979).

Caldwell, Dan. *The Dynamics of Domestic Politics and Arms Control: The SALT II Treaty Ratification Debate*. Columbia: University of South Carolina Press, 1991.

Carter, Jimmy. *Keeping Faith: Memoirs of a President*. New York: Bantam, 1982.

Church, F. Forrester. *Father and Son: A Personal Biography of Senator Frank Church of Idaho by His Son*. New York: Harper & Row, 1985.

Colby, William E. "Verifying SALT." *Worldview* 22 (April 1979): 4-7.

Cutler, Lloyd, and Roger Molander. "Is There Life After Death for SALT?" *International Security* 6, no. 2 (Fall 1981): 3–20.

Destler, I. M. "Treaty Troubles: Versailles in Reverse." *Foreign Policy*, no. 33 (Winter 1978–79): 45–65.

Duffy, Gloria. "Crisis Mangling and the Cuban Brigade." *International Security* 8, no. 1 (Summer 1983): 67–87.

Flanagan, Stephen J. "The Domestic Politics of SALT II: Implications for the Foreign Policy Process." In *Congress, the Presidency and Foreign Policy*, edited by John Spanier and Joseph Nogee, 44–76. Elmsford, N.Y.: Pergamon, 1981.

Ford, Gerald R. *A Time to Heal: The Autobiography of Gerald R. Ford*. New York: Harper and Rowe, 1979.

Fosdick, Dorothy, ed. *Staying the Course: Henry M. Jackson and National Security*. Seattle: University of Washington Press, 1987.

Garn, Jake. "The SALT II Verification Myth." *Strategic Review* 7 (Summer 1987): 16–24.

Garthoff, Raymond L. *Detente and Confrontation: American-Soviet Relations from Nixon to Reagan*. Washington, D.C.: The Brookings Institution, 1985.

Gray, Colin S. "SALT II: The Real Debate." *Policy Review*, no. 10 (Fall 1979): 7–22.

Haig, Alexander M., Jr. "Judging SALT II." *Strategic Review* 8 (Winter 1980): 11–17.

Heginbotham, Stanley J. "The President's Double Bind: The Politics and Alliance Diplomacy of Arms Control." In *Defending Peace and Freedom: Toward Strategic Stability in the Year 2000*, edited by Brent Scowcroft, 69–96. Lanham, Md.: University Press of America, 1988.

Hyland, William G. *Mortal Rivals: Superpower Relations from Nixon to Reagan*. New York: Random House, 1987.

Johnson, U. Alexis, with Jef Olivarius McAllister. *The Right Hand of Power*. Englewood Cliffs, N.J.: Prentice-Hall, 1984.

Kissinger, Henry A. *For the Record: Selected Statements, 1977-1980*. Boston, Mass.: Little, Brown & Co., 1981.

Kistiakowsky, George B. "False Alarm: The Story Behind SALT II." *New York Review of Books* 26, March 22, 1979, 33–38.

Krepon, Michael. *Strategic Stalemate: Nuclear Weapons and Arms Control in American Politics*. New York: St. Martin's Press, 1984.

Kruzel, Joseph. "SALT II: The Search for a Follow-on Agreement." *Orbis* 17, no. 2 (Summer 1973): 334–63.

Laird, Melvin R. "SALT II: The Senate's Momentous Decision." *Reader's Digest* (October 1979): 101–5.

Lodal, Jan. "SALT II and American Security." *Foreign Affairs* 57, no. 2 (Winter 1978/79): 245–68.

——. "Verifying SALT." *Foreign Policy*, no. 24 (Fall 1976): 40–64.

Luttwak, Edward. "Ten Questions About SALT II." *Commentary* (August 1979): 21–32.

Mandelbaum, Michael. "In Defense of SALT." *Bulletin of the Atomic Scientists* 35 (January 1979): 15–21.

McLellan, David S. *Cyrus Vance*. Totowa, N.J.: Rowman and Allanheld, 1985.

Moore, David W. "The Public Is Uncertain." *Foreign Policy*, no. 35 (Summer 1979): 69–73.

——. "SALT: A Question of Trust." *Public Opinion* (January– February 1979): 49–51.

Newhouse, John. "Reflections: The SALT Debate." *The New Yorker*, December 17, 1979.

——. *War and Peace in the Nuclear Age*. New York: Alfred A. Knopf, 1989.

Newsom, David D. *The Soviet Brigade in Cuba: A Study in Political Diplomacy*. Bloomington: Indiana University Press, 1987.

Nitze, Paul H. "Assuring Strategic Stability in an Age of Equivalence." *Foreign Affairs* 54, no. 2 (January 1976): 207–32.

——. "Deterring Our Deterrent." *Foreign Policy*, no. 25 (Winter 1976–77): 195–210.

Nitze, Paul H., with Ann M. Smith and Steven L. Rearden. *From Hiroshima to Glasnost: At the Center of Decision*. New York: Grove Weidenfeld, 1989.

Nixon, Richard M. *RN: The Memoirs of Richard Nixon*. New York: Grosset and Dunlap, 1978.

Perle, Richard. "Echoes of the 1930s." *Strategic Review* 7 (Winter 1979): 11–15.

Pipes, Richard. "Why the Soviet Union Thinks It Could Fight and Win a Nuclear War." *Commentary* (July 1977): 21–34.

Platt, Alan. *The U.S. Senate and Strategic Arms Policy, 1969–1977*. Boulder, Colo.: Westview Press, 1978.

Podhoretz, Norman. "The Present Danger." *Commentary* 69, no. 3 (April 1980): 27–40.

Potter, William C., ed. *Verification and SALT: The Challenge of Strategic Deception*. Boulder, Colo.: Westview Press, 1980.

Ranger, Robin. "SALT II's Political Failure: The U.S. Senate Debate." *RUSI: Journal of the Royal United Services Institute for Defence Studies*, no. 617 (June 1980): 49–56.

Robinson, Clarence A., Jr., ed. *Aviation Week and Space Technology on SALT*. New York: McGraw-Hill, 1979.

Rostow, Eugene. "The Case Against SALT II." *Commentary* 67, no. 2 (February 1979): 23–32.

Rowny, Edward L. "Negotiating with the Soviets." *Washington Quarterly* 3

(Winter 1980): 58–66.

Sanders, Jerry W. *Peddlers of Crisis: The Committee on the Present Danger and the Politics of Containment.* Boston, Mass.: South End Press, 1983.

Slocombe, Walter. "A SALT Debate: Hard but Fair Bargaining." *Strategic Review* (Fall 1979).

Smith, Gaddis. *Morality, Reason, and Power: American Diplomacy in the Carter Years.* New York: Hill and Wang, 1986.

Smith, Gerard C. *Doubletalk: The Story of the First Strategic Arms Limitation Talks.* Garden City, NY: Doubleday, 1980.

Sullivan, David S. "The Legacy of SALT I: Soviet Deception and U.S. Retreat." *Strategic Review* 7 (Winter 1979): 26–41.

Talbott, Strobe. *Deadly Gambits: The Reagan Administration and the Stalemate in Nuclear Arms Control.* New York: Alfred A. Knopf, 1984.

———. *Endgame: The Inside Story of SALT II.* New York: Harper & Row, 1979.

———. *The Master of the Game: Paul Nitze and the Nuclear Peace.* New York: Alfred A. Knopf, 1988.

Vance, Cyrus. *Hard Choices: Critical Years in America's Foreign Policy.* New York: Simon and Schuster, 1983.

Warnke, Paul. "Apes on a Treadmill." *Foreign Policy*, no. 18 (Spring 1975): 12–29.

Wolfe, Thomas. *The SALT Experience.* Cambridge, Mass.: Ballinger, 1979.

Government Publications

(Please note that all of these documents were published by the U.S. Government Printing Office in Washington, D.C., unless otherwise noted.)

U.S. Congress. House. Committee on Armed Services. *SALT II: An Interim Assessment, Report.* 95th Cong., 2d sess., 1978.

U.S. Congress. House. Committee on International Relations. *Strategic Arms Limitation Talks: Hearings and Briefings,* 95th Cong., 2d sess., 1979.

U.S. Congress. Senate. Committee on Armed Services. *Military Implications of the Treaty on the Limitation of Strategic Offensive Arms and Protocol Thereto (SALT II Treaty), Hearings.* 96th Cong., 1st sess., 1979, 4 pts.

———. *Military Implications of the Proposed SALT II Treaty Relating to the National Defense, Report.* 96th Cong., 2d sess., 1980.

U.S. Congress. Senate. Committee on Foreign Relations. *The SALT II Treaty, Hearings.* 96th Cong., 1st sess., 1979, 5 pts.

———. *The SALT II Treaty, Report.* 96th Cong., 1st sess., 1979.

U.S. Congress. Senate. Select Committee on Intelligence. *Principal Findings by the Senate Select Committee on Intelligence on the Capabilities of the United States to Monitor the SALT II Treaty, Report.* 96th Cong., 1st sess.,

1979.

U.S. Department of Defense. *Annual Report of the Secretary of Defense.*
1972–80.

U.S. Department of State. *Compliance with SALT I Agreements.* Special
Report, no. 55. July 1979.

———. *Salt One: Compliance. Salt Two: Verification.* Selected Documents,
no. 7, February 1978.

———. *SALT II Agreement.* Selected Documents, no. 12A. June 1979.

———. *Verification of SALT II Agreement.* Special Report, no. 56. August
1979.

———. *Vienna Summit.* Selected Documents, no. 13. June 1979.

Unpublished Works

Coalition for Peace through Strength. "The SALT Syndrome." Boston, Va.:
American Security Council Educational Foundation, n.d.

Graham, Thomas W. "The Politics of Failure: Strategic Nuclear Arms
Control, Public Opinion, and Domestic Politics in the United States,
1945–1985." Ph.D. diss., MIT, 1989.

Koontz, Theodore James. "The SALT II Debate: An Analysis of Senatorial
Decision Making." Ph.D. diss., Harvard University, 1985.

Kupperman, Charles Martin. "The SALT II Debate." Ph.D. diss., University
of Southern California, 1980.

Kurkowski, David Carl. "The Role of Interest Groups in the Domestic
Debate on SALT II." Ph.D. diss., Temple University, 1982.

7 The INF Treaty

Janne E. Nolan

The U.S.-Soviet agreement to eliminate intermediate-range (500–5,000 kilometers) nuclear weapons, known as the INF Treaty, was signed on December 8, 1987, and ratified by the Senate on May 27, 1988. The agreement was the culmination of a protracted domestic and international debate about the role of U.S. nuclear weapons in Europe and, more generally, about the basic legitimacy of U.S.-Soviet arms control agreements.

Although the actual negotiation of the agreement has a long and fractious history, its ratification was swift and won the support of all but five members of the U.S. Senate.[1] As the first agreement between the two sides to eliminate—rather than simply reduce or constrain—an entire class of weapons, the INF Treaty is popularly believed to be a major arms control success story. It was the first U.S.-Soviet arms control treaty to be ratified by the Senate since 1972, when the Anti-Ballistic Missile (ABM) Treaty was approved.

The INF Treaty owes its genesis to a decision taken by the NATO (North Atlantic Treaty Organization) alliance in the last months of the Carter administration to deploy new nuclear weapons in Europe.[2] In the effort to counter the growing superiority of Soviet nuclear forces targeted against Western Europe, especially the three-warhead SS-20 missile, the NATO alliance agreed in 1979 that 108 Pershing II and 464 cruise missiles would be deployed in five European countries.[3]

To temper opposition from European publics and from the Soviet Union, NATO members also agreed that these deployments should be accompanied by arms control negotiations. The so-called "dual-track" decision was to form "two parallel and complementary approaches" to the quest for nuclear stability and a credible U.S. nuclear umbrella in

The author gratefully acknowledges the assistance of Brian Cux in compiling research material for this study.

Europe. These limitations were to be pursued after the conclusion of the second treaty arising from the Strategic Arms Limitation Talks (SALT II), an agreement that was never submitted for ratification and was replaced under the Reagan administration by the Strategic Arms Reduction Talks (START) and separate negotiations on INF.[4]

When Ronald Reagan assumed office in January 1981, the impending INF deployments were facing strong opposition from the Soviet Union and waning support from some of the European allies, many of whom were facing growing pressures from domestic peace movements. Determined to proceed with nuclear force modernization, the administration at first delayed the resumption of INF negotiations. Bound formally to abide by the commitment to seeking arms limitations, however, and facing growing pressures to do so from European leaders, the administration submitted its first INF proposals in February 1982. Embracing the concept of "zero-zero," the United States offered to cancel the impending missile deployments in return for Soviet elimination of all intermediate- and medium-range missiles deployed in Europe and Asia.[5]

Heralded by Reagan officials as the first step toward "real" arms control, the proposal was quickly rejected by the Soviet Union. Trading prospective deployments for forces in place, the Soviets argued, was unprecedentedly one-sided and inequitable. This opinion was shared by many analysts in the United States and Europe, who believed that the zero-zero formula was intended to sabotage any prospects for arms control.

Soviet proposals pressed instead for staged reductions in European-based forces, including French and British forces and U.S. air- and sea-based nuclear-capable forces dedicated to NATO's defense.[6] Although the West had always insisted that only U.S. and Soviet land-based systems be included in the negotiations, the Soviet Union maintained that any system capable of targeting Soviet territory should be counted.

The United States modified its position several times

between February 1982 and November 1983 to allow some Soviet INF systems to remain and to permit a smaller deployment of U.S. forces to go forward. The much publicized July 1982 "walk in the woods" proposal discussed by U.S. negotiator Paul H. Nitze and his Soviet counterpart, Yuri Kvitsinsky, for instance, would have traded a reduced number of SS-20s for fewer U.S. cruise missiles and zero Pershing IIs.[7]

Although the Soviets would not concede the legitimacy of any new U.S. deployments, they also tempered their proposals during this period, eventually proposing a limit on the number of SS-20s to equal the number of French and British missiles (calculated at 140) and a freeze on SS-20s in Asia, in return for a halting of U.S. deployments. Faced with a fundamental stalemate over U.S. resolve to proceed with the scheduled deployments, however, the Soviets walked out of the negotiations as the first missiles were introduced in Europe in November 1983.

Despite the sporadic demarches of the two sides between 1983 and mid-1985, no breakthroughs in the INF talks were believed possible until after Mikhail Gorbachev assumed control of the Soviet government in 1985. Following a steady campaign of ambitious disarmament proposals, which the United States dismissed as propaganda ploys, Gorbachev began in 1986 a progressive softening of the formal Soviet INF position. Over time, European forces were excluded from Soviet proposals, and implicitly the Soviets moved to accept the concept of zero missiles in Europe.[8] By the time of the Reykjavík summit in October 1986 the two sides had agreed on a framework for INF restrictions that approximated zero-zero, although an agreement was forestalled by Soviet insistence that progress in INF be linked to agreements in START. By February 1987, however, the Soviets dropped this precondition, and serious negotiations on INF resumed.

The vital importance of ratification politics for the final outcome of the INF Treaty was particularly evident in decisions taken between February 1987 and May 1988. Faced with sudden and unexpected Soviet acceptance of its proposals, the United States had to face for the first time the domestic and international controversies that could ensue from an agreement to eliminate U.S. missiles in Europe and from the far-reaching verification schemes it had put forward in 1986, which included unprecedented Soviet access to Western military installations.

Although the agreement elicited widespread support from the public, debate over the ratification of the INF Treaty revealed fundamental disagreements about its merits among administration officials, members of Congress, and conservative commentators. Despite the relatively modest scope of the agreement—affecting less than five percent of U.S. nuclear forces—and the disproportionate cuts it imposed on the Soviet Union, the agreement became a lightning rod for critics of U.S.-Soviet détente. In essence, the INF Treaty served as a referendum on arms control in an administration that had resisted reaching any accommodation with the Soviet Union for seven years. For conservative critics, the treaty's ratification spelled the end of the Reagan era.

International Political Context

Formally a bilateral accord, the INF Treaty was from the beginning a multinational event. Because the weapons in question were deployed or slated for deployment in Europe and Asia, the discussion of limitations impinged directly on vital military and political interests of the NATO allies and Japan. Consequently, allied political opinion was always a central factor in the formulation of U.S. policy, whether or not U.S. decisions proved to be consonant with or sensitive to the allies' views.[9] Allied opinion, in turn, was directly elicited by the Reagan administration to help sell the treaty domestically during the ratification debate.

The INF Treaty was also inseparably linked to internal

upheavals occurring in the Soviet Union during the 1980s. This was a time of turbulence for the Soviet government, with three changes in leadership between 1982 and 1985. Whereas Yuri Andropov and Konstantin Chernenko did little more than replicate the hard-line policies of Leonid Brezhnev, the ascendance of General Secretary Mikhail Gorbachev transformed U.S.-Soviet relations, ushering in a new era of conciliation and making highly publicized, radical arms limitations proposals the new currency of arms control. The revolutionary steps toward democratization in the Soviet Union and Eastern Europe initiated by Gorbachev served as the backdrop for the INF ratification debate, accounting in large measure for the relative ease with which the treaty was approved.

The international context in the early 1980s, by contrast, did not augur well for the successful conclusion or ratification of an INF treaty for several reasons. The declaration of U.S.-Soviet strategic parity in the late 1970s, codified in SALT II, had prompted heightened attention to the military balance in Europe. With the development of more capable Soviet nuclear weapons targeted against Western Europe, including the SS-20 missile and the Backfire bomber, European governments began to express their concerns publicly about force disparities in the European theater and, as they charged, U.S. indifference to new European security threats.

This long dormant source of controversy within the NATO alliance, the perceived failure to consider adequately the implications for Europe of U.S. defense and arms control policies, had emerged as a full-blown cause célèbre by the time President Reagan assumed office in 1981. Despite the NATO decision to adopt the dual-track approach in 1979, consensus among the allies about the new nuclear deployments was extremely fragile, belying major differences among various European governments and between them and the United States.[10] The dual-track decision captured what one analyst has termed a European "cycle of anxiety."

The INF Treaty

> Lack of confidence in a particular administration often surfaces as demands for tighter defense and security guarantees. When the response comes in the shape of a new generation of nuclear weapons, however, the pendulum of concern soon swings back to expose the underlying fears of entrapment, generating spirited European opposition to NATO's over-reliance on nuclear weapons and renewed calls for East-West détente.[11]

Whereas Carter had had to contend with the earlier phase of this cycle, the pendulum had swung well in the other direction by the time Reagan became president. Growing European peace movements had unified against the scheduled deployments, and the Soviet Union sought to capitalize on this sentiment and sow dissent within the NATO alliance with an aggressive propaganda campaign.

The allies began pressuring the Reagan administration about INF as early as January 1981, when West German Chancellor Helmut Schmidt, facing a domestic peace movement and a fractious parliament, stated publicly that the United States had to give Europe a binding assurance that negotiations on INF would resume without delay.[12] The administration at first questioned whether it was bound by the Carter 1979 agreement, or whether, as some Reagan officials hoped, the United States could embark on a full-scale rearmament program before engaging in any discussion of arms control in Europe or elsewhere. In May 1981 White House counsellor Edwin Meese announced that the administration did not believe it was legally bound by any prior accord on strategic forces, including SALT I or SALT II.[13] For an administration bent on repudiating its predecessor's agenda, especially in the area of arms control, the 1979 dual-track decision was a political albatross.

Hard-line administration advisers believed that European nuclear deployments were an urgent U.S. military priority which should not be hindered by European opinion, especially pacifist sentiments. Letting the Europeans participate in what should have been a U.S. force modernization decision had been a mistake, they argued, allowing the United States to be "pushed around" by allies who showed dangerous signs of appeasement towards the Soviet Union. As one Reagan official described the burgeoning peace movement in West Germany in 1981, "[It is] largely in the Socialist party, the party of the left."[14]

When the administration resolved to pursue INF negotiations in 1981, it was clear that this was a reluctant political concession needed to ensure the scheduled deployments, not an enthusiastic embrace of the dual-track decision. The U.S. formulation of the zero option, moreover, was aimed at appeasing European opinion while buying time to ensure that the deployments proceeded on schedule.[15] As crafted by the assistant secretary of defense for international security policy, Richard Perle, the U.S. version of the zero option was sold as a way to end-run the Soviet Union and to defuse the European anti-nuclear movement, providing maximum appeal to public opinion. Secretary of State Alexander Haig later stated, "[Secretary of Defense Caspar] Weinberger argued for adoption of the zero option on the basis of its potential for attracting public support." Haig, however, believed the initiative "would . . . generate suspicion that the U.S. was only interested in a frivolous propaganda exercise or, worse, that it was disingenuously engaging in arms negotiations simply as a cover to build up its nuclear arsenal."[16]

Despite the absence of agreement among administration advisers about the zero option's substantive or political merits, the formula's simplicity and the appearance of a radical departure in arms control was appealing to Ronald Reagan. For some, it also provided diplomatic cover for what they believed should be the administration's real agenda. As one commentator put it, "By paying lip service to the ideal solution of zero, the U.S. could hold the high ground in the propaganda war with the Soviets even as it set about negotiating toward a realistic goal—perhaps in the neighborhood of 600 warheads against the same number of Soviet ones."[17]

From 1981 to 1985 the negotiations were carried out

against a backdrop of deteriorating U.S.-Soviet relations. Convinced that the Soviet Union was intent only on generating opposition in Europe to the scheduled deployments in any case, the administration was not disposed to take Soviet INF negotiating proposals too seriously. In September 1983 the Soviets shot down a Korean civilian airliner that had strayed into Soviet airspace, incurring bitter denunciation from the United States and forestalling congressional amendments on behalf of arms control.[18] Progress in other arms control negotiations, including the Mutual Balanced Force Reduction talks on conventional forces in Europe, were practically at a standstill.

By November 1983 there was nothing in Geneva to provide a pretext for stopping the deployments. The Soviets walked out of the talks on November 23, the day after the first Pershing arrived in West Germany. The Soviet walkout led to the suspension of START talks as well, followed by a two-year hiatus in negotiations. As relations between the United States and the Soviet Union grew increasingly strained, the propects for any kind of agreement seemed remote.

In 1986, however, the international context changed dramatically as the United States and Soviet Union began the process of improving relations, paving the way to the Soviet Union's unconditional acceptance of the zero option. By the time the treaty was submitted for ratification, the two sides had agreed to a comprehensive global ban on INF, eliminating both intermediate- and short-range nuclear missiles from Europe and Asia. The agreement was heralded by the administration as an unprecedented victory for its arms control strategy.

The perception of U.S. success in gaining Soviet agreement to its proposal, however, had to compete with a sudden awareness of the potential liabilities of the zero option—allegations that the administration had difficulty countering, given its own contradictory views on the subject. The substantive problems of this formula, which had not previously been accorded sufficient importance to prevent it from becoming U.S. policy, began to surface more prominently in anticipation of the ratification debate: zero missiles meant that the United States and Europe were still "de-coupled" ; the elimination of U.S. missiles heightened the significance of East-West disparities in short-range nuclear forces and in conventional forces; and SS-20s in Asia absent compensating U.S. systems would exacerbate the nuclear threat to Asian allies. When Gorbachev said he also would eliminate short-range nuclear forces, he precipitated even more controversies.[19]

Despite mixed reactions, the allies were quick to support the treaty's provisions in deference to U.S. pressure and European public opinion. West German Chancellor Helmut Kohl, for example, a conservative opponent of the zero option, endorsed it as sound policy. In the haste to conclude a deal, the United States forestalled allied actions that could have imposed delays or complicated ratification, such as linking NATO acceptance of the missile ban to a declaration that no further nuclear reductions could occur without Soviet reductions in conventional forces.[20] Disingenuously or not, the administration also claimed that quick resolution of INF issues would pave the way toward an agreement on strategic forces, which Reagan purportedly hoped to sign at the May 1988 summit.[21] West German Foreign Minister Dietrich Genscher expressed optimism than a START agreement could be concluded in this time frame, a prognosis that proved to be wrong.

International opinion played an important role in the administration's strategy for INF ratification throughout the debate. Having fostered the appearance of unanimous NATO support, the administration moved quickly to defuse domestic critics by pointing to the adverse effects that a failure to ratify the treaty would have on West European politics. Kohl, among other prominent Europeans, was called on to meet with congressional leaders to press for prompt ratification.[22] General Secretary Gorbachev also contributed to the administration's public diplomacy campaign for INF. At the

December 1987 Washington summit Gorbachev and Reagan stood side by side proclaiming their joint triumph in INF, cementing a public perception of a new era of U.S.-Soviet friendship in which the INF Treaty was a critical foundation.

Domestic Political Context

The Reagan administration assumed office with a determination to repudiate the U.S.-Soviet arms control policies of its predecessors, which it viewed as dismal failures. Hard-line critics of the Soviet Union and arms control made up most of the new president's cabinet; many of them were veterans of the highly successful anti-SALT lobby, the Committee on the Present Danger. In addition to INF negotiator Paul H. Nitze, the committee's chairman, other committee members included National Security Adviser Richard Allen; CIA Director William Casey; U.S. Ambassador to the United Nations Jeane Kirkpatrick; Undersecretary of Defense for Policy Fred Iklé; Secretary of the Navy John Lehman; U.S. Arms Control and Disarmament Agency (ACDA) Director Eugene V. Rostow and his successor, Kenneth L. Adelman; and Assistant Secretary of Defense for International Security Policy Richard Perle.[23]

In keeping with its campaign promises the administration pledged to restore the military strength of the United States, a pledge underscored by an unprecedentedly ambitious military modernization program.[24] Officials engaged in harsh rhetoric about the Soviet Union's hegemonic ambitions, its record of alleged consistent cheating in arms control agreements, its disregard for human rights, and its determined efforts to defeat the United States militarily. A central theme for the administration, in words that were to come back to haunt it in the INF ratification debate, was any agreement with such an "evil empire" was automatically suspect.

In the early 1980s domestic opinion about arms control

was contradictory. Pollsters noted that Americans did not quarrel with Ronald Reagan's assessment that the Soviet Union had gained "a definite margin of superiority," but a clear majority also supported a mutual freeze on Soviet and U.S. nuclear weapons. Following a number of ill-advised remarks by administration officials in 1981–83, including a statement by Haig that the United States might use nuclear weapons as a "demonstration shot" in a crisis, public anxieties about the administration's bellicose policies seemed to tilt opinion toward arms limitations.[25] A CBS/New York Times poll in April 1983 concluded that 64 percent of Americans favored efforts to moderate the U.S.-Soviet competition, including a nuclear freeze.[26]

Based on the administration's own polls, administration advisers initially interpreted the public mood differently. Advisers such as Meese and National Security Adviser William P. Clark believed "that Mr. Reagan's hard-line is the right one, and that he can carry the public with him if he persists."[27] This view was to prevail among Reagan's advisors throughout the president's first term.

Underlying the general agreement about the administration's agenda were deep divisions among administration advisers. Many of the clashes became acrimonious and personal and were aired publicly. In part, this was because Reagan did not establish a formal structure for foreign policy decision making. For the first year Reagan preferred to leave it to his "triumvirate" of trusted political aides, Edwin Meese, James Baker, and Michael Deaver, to coordinate the competing lines of bureaucratic jurisdiction.[28] Efforts by Secretary of State Haig to create a more coherent structure, which included putting himself at the helm, were thwarted by Meese and never materialized.

Although the Reagan foreign policy apparatus improved in later years, it remained a battleground of powerful personalities vying for the president's attention. Selling an idea to the president required an ability to translate complex issues into simple proposals that promised public appeal.

Although this decision-making process was hardly optimal for formulating sensitive foreign policy, the president's popularity with the public protected the administration from charges that its policies were ill-advised or unrealistic. This factor helps explain the administration's adoption, and the Senate's subsequent approval, of an INF Treaty based on the zero option, any substantive or political liabilities notwithstanding.

The content of the INF Treaty is a microcosm of the way in which fundamental disagreements over arms control philosophies were worked out among the individuals surrounding Reagan, only to resurface during the ratification debate. In the first phase of INF policy formulation the two main camps that found themselves in opposition included Weinberger, Iklé, and Perle, on the one hand, and Haig, Assistant Secretary of State for European Affairs Lawrence Eagleburger, and the director of the Department of State's Bureau of Politico-Military Affairs, Richard Burt, on the other. Their differences revealed the disparate preoccupations of Reagan hard-liners and career foreign policy professionals, a division that was to persist during the ratification debate.

To the former group, excessive accommodation of pacifist trends in Europe was a form of capitulation and could undercut domestic credibility. Although Iklé and Perle had substantive objections to the dual-track decision, they mostly objected to the idea that they were being pressured to honor an agreement forged by a prior and discredited administration.[29] This view was shared by most of Reagan's "California team," the officials who had been instrumental in the election campaign and who occupied senior positions in the White House and cabinet. National Security Adviser Richard Allen used words like "blackmail" and "pressure tactics" in reference to the European insistence on arms limitations, while Perle cautioned against giving the Europeans "veto over our negotiating position," as he put it in 1981.[30]

By contrast, Haig, Eagleburger, and Burt believed that European views had to be taken fully into consideration for the alliance's INF consensus to survive. U.S. indifference to European views, they argued, not only might lead the Europeans not to proceed with the deployments but could destroy NATO cohesion for years to come. According to one analysis, "The State Department saw as its task ensuring that the Reagan administration did not repudiate the dual-track decision."[31]

Initially, the Weinberger-Perle camp was ascendant. Perle, far more adept at bureaucratic infighting than the others, and possessing extensive expertise in security issues, used his skills to advantage to create support for the zero option. By November 1981 President Reagan was persuaded that Perle's position was the correct one.

The president revealed the U.S. zero option in a speech on November 18, to almost universal acclamation from the Congress. As one commentator put it the day after: "From House Speaker Thomas P. ["Tip"] O'Neill to the most conservative Republicans in the Senate, plaudits for Reagan's address echoed around the Capitol. . . . [The speech] enabled him to please congressional hawks while disarming others who have been critical of the administration's previous bellicosity."[32] Critics were almost nonexistent. Senator Gary Hart (D-Colo.) alone cautioned both that the proposal might suggest to the allies that the United States was not serious about reducing INF and that "it might take another NATO summit meeting to get Western unity on the subject."[33]

Still, the decision to adopt the zero option ensured that the INF negotiations would be controversial. U.S. negotiators not only had to contend with Soviet intransigence and European political turmoil but also were hampered by bureaucratic infighting at home and a lack of high-level attention. Nitze's "walk in the woods" initiative in mid-1982, for example, was the culmination of his frustrations with what he perceived to be the administration's halfhearted interest in achieving progress in INF.[34] Whatever the merits of Nitze's informal demarche, the administration's abrupt rejection of it had domestic political repercussions, and these played a role in the ratification debate.[35] As the administration had reason to fear, the incident was portrayed as a struggle between a pro–arms control visionary and an intransigent administration, and it left the impression that an early breakthrough in INF might have been possible, and on terms that were perhaps more militarily advantageous to the United States than the zero option.[36]

Beginning in 1985 the domestic political context of INF began to change markedly. Although the Democratic party was soundly defeated in the 1984 presidential election, the campaign debate had launched spirited attacks on the administration's arms control failures. The return of the Senate to Democratic control in 1986 lent new impetus to congressional activism on behalf of arms limitation. Partisan conflicts over key administration priorities, including nuclear testing, the deployment of the controversial MX missile, and the Strategic Defense Initiative (SDI), were garnering wider support. The departure in mid-1987 of several administration arms control opponents, including Weinberger, Perle, and ACDA Director Kenneth Adelman, suggested that moderate, pro–arms control officials would have greater freedom to press for an agreement.

The political liabilities inherent in the administration's INF position, however, were soon to surface in the ratification debate. First was the very nature of the zero option, which had never been fully accepted by key advisers as a realistic bargaining ploy and certainly never for its substantive merits. Domestic critics began to raise doubts about its effect on NATO security, charging that the allies were being "blackmailed" into an agreement that would leave them vulnerable to superior Soviet conventional and short-range nuclear forces.[37] In March 1987 Brent Scowcroft, James Woolsey, and John Deutch, considered moderates on the arms control political spectrum, warned of "The Danger of the Zero Option," in an article in the *Washington Post*.[38]

Opposition to the INF Treaty gained momentum as the 1988 presidential election campaign began in earnest in early

1987.[39] Not coincidentally, one key critic was Senate minority leader Robert Dole (R-Kans.), who was seeking his party's presidential nomination. Of the five other Republican presidential candidates, including Representative Jack Kemp (R-N.Y.), former Secretary of State Alexander Haig, former Delaware Governor Pete du Pont, religious leader Pat Robertson, and Vice President George Bush, only Bush did not express severe reservations about, or outright opposition to, the treaty.

Other critiques of the agreement were offered by former Reagan advisers. Perle, in particular, launched sustained attacks against the zero option, decrying the wisdom of the proposals that he had had the most influence in devising.[40] Rostow, the new chairman of the Committee on the Present Danger, urged the Senate to defer action on INF ratification pending Soviet concessions in START.[41]

Another contentious ratification issue was verification. In 1986, the Reagan administration had put forward unprecedentedly stringent verification standards for INF. Verification, especially on-site inspection, was a cause célèbre for administration hard-liners. It was an issue on which they permitted little compromise. If the Soviets were sincere, it was implied, they would open their borders to U.S. inspections, something they had always refused to do; their refusal to agree to such inspections simply demonstrated their intention to cheat. As it was, all previous administrations had been so mesmerized by the alleged benefits of arms control, the hard-liners maintained, that they had failed consistently to enforce agreements or to challenge the Soviets when they violated accords.

Throughout the 1980s, verification standards and allegations of Soviet noncompliance became a litmus test of partisan loyalty and toughness toward the Soviet Union. In 1983 Congress passed an amendment requiring the administration to issue annual reports on Soviet treaty violations. Backed by conservatives, this initiative was designed to force the administration to take explicit positions on sensitive compliance issues, thereby ensuring a firm foundation for opposing future agreements until these matters had been settled. The unclassified versions of these reports, hammered out in bitter interagency disputes, helped to publicize charges and to politicize verification and compliance issues to an unprecedented degree.

This high profile accorded compliance issues led to the unusual appearance of senior CIA officials at open hearings of the Senate Armed Services and Appropriations committees and to congressional requests for the CIA to conduct unclassified studies documenting Soviet cheating. One such study in 1987 alleged that arms violations were part of "Moscow's carefully planned strategic military and intelligence operations," as one journalist reported. "Considering the current U.S. practice, which, de facto, is to provide the Soviets with all the benefits that accompany the spirit of arms control without any penalties," the report charged, "the Soviets have little to risk by continuing just to negotiate for the indefinite future."[42]

Critics consistently argued that compliance issues, which had previously been worked out in diplomatic channels, were usually too complex and ambiguous to provide conclusive evidence of Soviet violations. Their voices, however, were muted until the INF Treaty was concluded. The administration eventually acknowledged that no verification agreement could ever be technically foolproof, but it had difficulty undoing the bitter partisanship over this issue that its own rhetoric had helped to create.

Having sold verification as an end in itself, the administration obscured for years the difficulties posed by ambitious on-site inspection schemes. Assuming that the Soviets would never agree to its proposals, the administration badly misjudged the domestic complexities associated with intrusive verification measures. The prospect that Soviet inspectors would have free access to Western military installations "anywhere, anytime" was anathema to U.S. and allied militaries, not to mention defense industries and even the communities that the Soviets could be expected to visit. Even before Soviet agreement, the Joint Chiefs of Staff (JCS) had raised objections to the first package of verification proposals put forward for INF in 1986. The whole idea of Soviets appearing unannounced to roam around the United States on "espionage shopping expeditions," as one official put it, was an intelligence and security nightmare.

These concerns forced a change in the U.S. position in mid-1987, in the form of restricting inspections to a few designated sites under strict procedures. The "walk-back" created the appearance of U.S. retreat, however, which INF critics duly exploited. Perle charged that the restriction of short-notice inspections to designated areas was worse than useless: "The last place the Soviets would choose to hide missiles is in the relatively few areas that we would be permitted to inspect. . . . Something like 99.999 percent of Soviet territory would be off limits to U.S. inspectors."[43] These arrangements, Perle stressed, would lull the United States into a false sense of complacency while giving the Soviets license to cheat. The debate seemed to have come full circle. Whereas on-site inspection was once considered the only way to ensure that the Soviets would not dupe the West, the belief now was that it could serve as the very method by which to do so.

Verification controversies loomed large in the impending ratification debate. In August 1987 a Department of State report detailing Soviet failures to account for or redress alleged violations of arms control treaties was deliberately leaked in an apparent effort to undercut Senate support for INF.[44] The Department of State was facing steady attacks from conservatives about its retrenchment from the original verification package. Its officials countered that Soviet acceptance of the zero option justified loosening verification requirements: a ban on missiles was less difficult to verify, and the Soviets now "had less incentive to cheat." In truth, the decision to alter the verification package was the result of objections from U.S. intelligence agencies and from allies.[45]

Despite initial reservations, the JCS formally endorsed the INF Treaty.[46] Testifying before the Senate Armed Services Committee in December 1987, JCS Chairman Admiral William J. Crowe stated that "The JCS have unanimously concluded that, on balance, this treaty is militarily sufficient and effectively verifiable. In turn . . . they strongly recommend its ratification by the U.S. Senate."[47] Crowe went on to spell out the military risks of failing to ratify the agreement, including the proliferation of more advanced SS-20s, SS-23s, and the SS-X-24 ground-launched cruise missiles (GLCMs) in Europe.[48] Although General Bernard Rogers, former supreme allied commander for Europe, argued against the treaty after he resigned in 1987, his argument that it weakened NATO security did not prove decisive in the ratification debate.[49]

Role of the President

The INF Treaty, perhaps more than any other single international agreement, owes its domestic success to a powerful and extraordinarily popular president who staked his personal prestige on the treaty's conclusion and ratification.[50] As the most conservative and anti-Soviet president since Richard M. Nixon, Ronald Reagan had consderable credibility with which to champion this agreement, and this credibility had an inestimable impact on the success of the treaty ratification debate.

President Reagan's personal commitment to the accord reflected his growing concern that his legacy as president would be marred if it did not include progress toward peaceful accommodation with the Soviet Union. Beginning in 1987, rumors circulated that his wife, Nancy, had persuaded him to pursue arms control initiatives before the end of his presidency.[51]

The zero option also was the product of Ronald Reagan's

unique approach to arms control. Like his vision of the SDI, it seemed simple, innovative, and bold. It demonstrated U.S. determination to "replace the language of arms control" with real reductions, not just arcane technical regulations that managed the arms race.[52] For these reasons, Reagan believed, it met the ultimate litmus test: the public would support it. Ronald Reagan may have been the only official in the White House who believed that the zero option was a sincere and negotiable proposal. As it happened, he was proved correct.

Fortuitously or otherwise, the Soviet acceptance of U.S. proposals suggested a vindication of an arms control strategy that the president had long espoused, embracing "toughness" at the negotiating table on behalf of comprehensive reductions. As Perle put it: "However one regards the INF Treaty, it is the treaty that Ronald Reagan set out to get in 1981. His will and resolve and that of our allies has vindicated the judgment that the Soviets could be pressed to abandon their intermediate missiles in exchange for ours."[53] Although many have since argued that it was Gorbachev's willingness to accept U.S. proposals, not U.S. strategy, that delivered these results, the view expressed by Perle persists as dogma in conservative circles.[54]

The administration's ratification strategy from the outset tried to capitalize on the president's popularity by depicting the treaty as Ronald Reagan's personal achievement. As White House Chief of Staff Howard Baker put it: "It's Ronald Reagan's treaty. So I'm sure that the president will be anxious for the Senate to ratify this treaty in this form because he negotiated it."[55] Although Reagan's actual stewardship of the negotiations had been remote, at best, the message to critics was clear: attacks on the INF agreement were attacks on Ronald Reagan. Even before the treaty was signed, the president announced publicly that he intended to insist on Senate ratification of the treaty "without reservations or amendments, including those to be offered by conservative Republicans seeking to block the pact."[56] By scheduling a summit in May 1988, moreover, he helped create a sense of urgency for prompt ratification. Regardless of the nature of disputes, few in Congress wanted to be seen as undercutting the president while he was engaging in sensitive diplomacy with the Soviet Union. President Reagan, ever conscious of the power of public opinion, took his case for INF directly to the American people. In a televised network interview in November 1987 Reagan excoriated right-wing critics of the pact. Accusing them of believing that "war is inevitable," Reagan said they were "ignorant of the advances that have been made in verification." Although he continued to caution at other times that the Soviets were still "our adversaries," he had clearly parted company with many of his old supporters. A White House official noted, "Reagan isn't going to convert right wingers but he can go over their heads and speak directly to their constituency."[57]

Aside from making a few well-timed speeches, however, President Reagan left it to others to turn the Reagan mystique into political victory. It was Reagan's popularity and standing as a staunch defender of U.S. national security that was critical to the treaty's success, not his direct intervention in or stewardship of the administration's ratification strategy.

Executive-Congressional Relations

Ronald Reagan's landslide electoral victory in 1980, which gave the Republicans control of the Senate for the first time in twenty-six years and added more than a dozen Republican seats in the House of Representatives, helped ensure the success of most administration defense priorities for more than five years. Yet while the majority in Congress seemed to favor a defense buildup and renewed assertiveness toward the Soviet Union, countless efforts were launched by pro-arms control liberals and moderates to try to temper perceived excesses of the administration's anti-Soviet posture.

After a fifteen-month hiatus in arms control, a grass-roots campaign calling for a freeze on U.S. and Soviet strategic arms won some support in Congress in 1982, although never enough to win a binding vote or majority support from the Senate.[58] A nonbinding freeze resolution was passed in the Democratically controlled House in 1981. In 1982 Congress voted to eliminate funds for production of the MX missile.

The controversy over the MX led Reagan to appoint a bipartisan commission of experts, directed by former national security adviser Brent Scowcroft, to try to forge a consensus on the future of land-based missiles. By the end of 1983 a renewed congressional attack on the MX prompted Reagan to alter the U.S. negotiating position in START, saving the missile by a close margin.[59]

Still, until the mid-1980s, moderates and liberals could not interfere too severely with the momentum of the administration's defense programs. Their efforts were mostly geared toward damage limitation, especially toward preventing actions that could lead to the abrogation of existing arms control treaties. They tried to ensure continued adherence to the SALT II accord, and to prevent a breakout from the ABM Treaty, and they pressed for ratification of existing treaties to limit nuclear testing.

Conflict between Congress and the administration over INF was modest, and debate about European missiles infrequent. Between 1981–83 two efforts by House liberals to block Pershing deployments garnered few votes and elicited almost no public attention.[60] As Edith B. Wilkie, executive director of the Congressional Arms Control and Foreign Policy Caucus, characterized INF in 1987: "INF is an issue that Congress has never understood or cared about. It is essentially a European issue or an arms control experts' issue and not a political issue."[61]

The active involvement of the Senate arms control observer group in the INF deliberations beginning in 1981 also helped temper mainstream opposition to INF policies. The twelve-member group was an important conduit of information between the administration and Senate moderates. As Senator Sam Nunn (D-Ga.) told reporters in March 1985, the group's active contact with negotiators helped to build confidence about the process and ensure that any treaty was "not a surprise to anyone."[62]

As the INF Treaty neared conclusion in mid-1987, however, congressional politics had changed. In the debate over the fiscal year 1988 defense authorization bill Congress was gearing up for a major assault on Reagan's strategic priorities. For the first time since Reagan had assumed office, both houses adopted binding amendments affecting two major arms control issues: a ban on weapons tests that would violate the ABM Treaty, and a provision which would prevent the United States from deploying new weapons which exceeded limits of the SALT II Treaty.[63] These amendments provoked bitter partisan divisions and reflected new strains in executive-congressional relations.

Even more pointedly, the Reagan administration was facing unprecedented challenges to its foreign policy credibility, including the release in mid-1987 of the Tower Commission's report detailing the administration's actions in the Iran-Contra affair. The successful conclusion of the INF Treaty presented Reagan with the opportunity both to demonstrate international leadership and to deflect attention from this controversy. It was against this backdrop that the INF Treaty moved to political center stage.

After years of battling the administration on arms control, the Democrats were initially faced with a dilemma concerning the INF pact. "With a treaty within reach," one commentator noted, "the Democrats, in control of both houses of Congress for the first time in the Reagan Presidency, are scrambling to find a way to retain the offensive on arms control without ceding the high ground to President Reagan."[64] Senate majority leader Robert Byrd (D-W.Va.) sounded a note of caution to the administration's optimism about the INF pact in mid-1987, suggesting that Reagan might be pursuing the treaty to deflect attention from the Iran-Contra affair.[65]

It was not, however, the ascendance of the Democratic party that posed the main challenges to concluding or ratifying an INF treaty. Not surprisingly, the most vocal criticism came from the conservative wing of the Republican party, the traditional stronghold of Reagan supporters who had embraced Reagan for his hard-line views. The perception that Reagan had "sold out" by reaching an agreement with the Soviets—even one made up of unprecedentedly generous Soviet concessions—was pervasive in these circles. In what proved to be only the opening salvo in a protracted Republican assault on the treaty in 1987, former President Richard M. Nixon and his former secretary of state, Henry Kissinger, attacked the emerging treaty in an article in the *Los Angeles Times*.[66] To the consternation of the administration, former Reagan loyalists waged a sustained assault while liberals and moderates lined up in praise.

Although the administration's outward posture was that it expected minimal problems in ratifying the accord, it set in motion an elaborate political campaign as soon as the treaty was signed. Reagan met in December with a group of Senate Republicans to urge their support and tried to capitalize on the positive impression made by Gorbachev when he had visited Washington for the December summit.[67] Clearly, the president and his advisers understood the political delicacy of a conservative administration having to defend itself against its own party and were anxious to contain the potential damage to Republicans in an election year.

The administration tried to co-opt Senate opposition by offering maximum cooperation. As Secretary of State Shultz wrote in a letter to senators, "The administration is eager to work with the Senate to scrutinize this treaty from every angle." According to press reports, a group of twenty officials from the Department of State began on January 1 to meet daily to discuss ratification strategy, including ways to defuse efforts by the Senate to link the treaty to past Soviet arms violations, the Soviet presence in Afghanistan, human rights, or the East-West conventional balance. They in turn reported to two more senior groups, one chaired by White House Chief of Staff Howard Baker and the other by then–National Security Adviser Colin Powell.[68]

The administration also appointed former Senator John Tower (R-Tex.), who had served his last term as chairman of the Senate Armed Services Committee, to help guide the treaty through the ratification process. A seasoned veteran of congressional wars and a hard-liner, Tower was to allay the fears of conservatives about the verifiability of the INF Treaty and "to prevent any crippling amendments or reservations" that could force renegotiation of the treaty's terms.[69]

The three executive branch groups, as part of their work, "canvassed and briefed dozens of Senate staffers, prepared testimony for administration witnesses, and compiled a record of treaty negotiations for the Senate."[70] Included with the treaty package submitted to the Senate was a 120-page, line-by-line analysis of the treaty's provisions, eight other supporting documents, and nearly 200 diagrams and pictures of U.S. and Soviet nuclear installations, which had been exchanged in the last stages of the talks.

To some officials, this strategy was far too accommodating to Congress. They objected to sharing the negotiating record, in particular, fearing that this would give critics extra ammunition. Former INF negotiator Maynard Glitman, who replaced Nitze in 1986, said "if you go through a negotiating record you're going to get a lot of ins and outs and you're going to see a lot of posturing that both sides did in order to make certain points, and I think it'd be easy to misread the actual flow of what was happening."[71] As it was, the administration had little choice in the matter. Nunn and Byrd had threatened to hold up INF ratification hearings if the record was not forthcoming.[72] On the Republican side, Dole demanded in December 1987 that Shultz hand over the treaty for Senate inspection, threatening that "the Senate will have to go over the treaty with a fine tooth comb."[73]

The administration may have complicated its own task by

initially appearing to treat the INF Treaty as a fait accompli. In November 1987 Howard Baker alluded to his apparent conviction that the treaty inevitably would be ratified. "Stopping a treaty is not as easy as you think," he argued, referring to a range of parliamentary maneuvers that could thwart an anti-INF filibuster.[74] Other administration efforts to pressure Senate critics, including a January 1988 letter from former INF negotiator Nitze urging prompt ratification, helped to create an impression that Senate views were seen by the administration as simply a hindrance to the momentum of this historic victory.

In response, Perle charged in 1988 that "if the administration has its way, ritual Senate ratification will mark an era of rubber stamp diplomacy that will make the Supreme Soviet . . . seem like a great deliberative body by comparison."[75] Rankling at White House pressures to ratify the treaty before the upcoming summit, Senator Malcolm Wallop (R-Wyo.) said "Let the public relations deadline in Moscow be damned."[76]

Before the full Senate considered the INF Treaty, extensive hearings were held in the Senate Armed Services, Foreign Relations, and Intelligence committees. All three approved the treaty by a majority vote, but each issued detailed reports raising questions about certain elements of the agreement.

Both the Armed Services and Intelligence committees raised concerns about the INF verification package. Administration witnesses were pressed to explain how it would ensure compliance, given the lower standards adopted in the last days of negotiations. Senators also urged that the benefits of intrusive verification should not be oversold in future agreements, and they pressed the administration to redefine "how much verification is enough."[77] The Intelligence Committee used the occasion to press the administration for additional funding for satellite surveillance and other intelligence functions, stressing that there was a gap between the administration's verification objectives and intelligence capabilities.[78]

Another issue that generated controversy was the treaty's
ban on conventionally armed ground-launched cruise missiles.
The ban was deemed necessary because of the difficulty of
verifying whether GLCMs were carrying conventional or
nuclear warheads. Conservatives argued that this system was
vital to NATO defenses and that the ban would magnify East-
West disparities in conventional forces. All the committees,
however, concurred that INF should not allow deployment of
these systems and an effort by Senator Ernest Hollings (D-
S.C.) in floor debate to reverse this decision was soundly
defeated.[79]

The Joint Chiefs of Staff did not impose the usual
requirements for "safeguards" that have come to be expected
as the price of their support for an arms control treaty. Some
defense programs were "recommended" as necessary
compensations for the INF reductions, including the Lance
land-based nuclear missile and air- and sea-launched cruise
missiles, but no demands were placed as conditions for
approval.[80]

Although Democratic opinion was firmly in favor of the
treaty, a major outstanding issue concerned the Senate's
authority for treaty ratification. A decision by the
administration in 1985 to reinterpret the meaning of the 1972
ABM Treaty unilaterally, based purportedly on a
reexamination of the "negotiating record," had provoked a
bitter feud between the administration and key Democrats,
notably the new chairman of the Senate Armed Services
Committee, Sam Nunn. Claiming that the review revealed
fundamental errors of interpretation, the administration
attempted to free itself of the legal obligation to abide by key
ABM Treaty restraints. This move was revealed to the Senate
without prior consultation. For several months the
administration rebuffed entreaties from a bipartisan group of
senators to look at the documents on which these conclusions
had been based. Eventually, the Senate gained access to the
ABM negotiating record, and Nunn offered a point-by-point
refutation of the administration's claims.[81]

The administration's bungling of the ABM treaty reinterpretation issue practically ensured that the Senate would use its leverage over INF Treaty ratification to restate its authority. The demand that the INF Treaty negotiating record be made available for Senate review owed its genesis to the ABM flap. Complete treaty negotiating records had been considered the exclusive domain of the executive branch, too sensitive to be shared with Congress. The administration's contention that the discrepancies in ABM Treaty provisions were based on statements made by negotiators in the 1970s, however, opened the way for Nunn to argue that he could not approve the INF Treaty without full access to the INF record, in order to avoid such discrepancies in the future.

After complicated parliamentary maneuvering, the Senate adopted an amendment to the INF ratification resolution in which it reaffirmed that no president could repudiate or alter a treaty unless the Senate approved.[82] Crafted by several members of the Senate Foreign Relations Committee, which was led by Senator Joseph R. Biden, Jr. (D-Del.), the "Biden Condition" stipulated that the Constitution required that the interpretation of a treaty should derive from the "shared understanding" between the executive branch and the Senate of the treaty's text at the time of ratification.[83] Although it passed by an overwhelming majority, this initiative met with fierce opposition from the administration.

The most severe campaign against the treaty was led by several conservative senators, including Jesse Helms (R-N.C.), Ernest Hollings (the only Democrat to vote against the pact), Dan Quayle (R-Ind.), Alan Simpson (R-Wyo.), Steven Symms (R-Idaho), and Malcolm Wallop. They fashioned numerous "killer amendments" in early 1988, measures that would have required a return to the negotiating table. Trying to delay the ratification until after the summit, Helms and other hard-line Republicans tried countless maneuvers to link INF approval to the record of Soviet misdeeds.[84] Hard-liners were worried that the conclusion of INF would encourage Reagan to push for a START agreement as well, in a reenactment of the

Reykjavík "October surprise," when Reagan and Gorbachev had to be restrained from concluding a comprehensive arms agreement abolishing ballistic missiles, if not all strategic weapons.

The appearance of last-minute compromises on verification was a major focus of Senate attacks. Wallop charged, "the administration is willing to accept a lower level of confidence than it set out to have."[85] Helms noted during committee hearings that "in the closing weeks of deliberations, almost 100 unresolved items were concluded. The United States gave up what had been considered fundamentally important issues during this period . . . including the right to inspect suspect sites."[86] Verification, however, was only a conduit to press the view that any agreement with the Soviet Union was a bad idea. As Helms put it, "We must not get lost in the details of verification, compliance, and missile technology" but should instead "examine all aspects of the U.S.-Soviet relationship."[87]

Helms led the charge with a series of amendments geared toward a filibuster. Among them was a requirement that the president certify that the data base estimating the number of SS-20s was accurate (an amendment arising from the allegation that the number contained in the treaty appendix was too low); a proposal to invalidate the treaty on the grounds that Gorbachev was not legally the head of the Soviet government; and a provision that would allow either side to withdraw from the treaty in fifteen days after discovering a "material breach" of the treaty's terms. These and other "killer amendments" were overwhelmingly defeated, but the protracted debate threatened to leave Reagan in Moscow without a ratified treaty. When the summit delegation left on May 25, Baker was left behind in the hope that he could rush to Moscow with a concluded treaty before the summit was over.

On May 26, with the summit in session, Byrd stopped Helms's delaying campaign by threatening to invoke cloture, a parliamentary maneuver, which would prohibit "killer" amendments and restrict debate on the text of the treaty to thirty hours. Cloture had not been invoked for a treaty since the 1919 Treaty of Versailles.[88] Byrd agreed to allow Helms to offer amendments to the "resolution of ratification," the document on which the Senate would actually give its consent. Helms, having also extracted a promise from Reagan earlier in the week that he would slow down START discussions, backed down. "I would admit I am licked," he said bitterly.[89]

Public Opinion and the Role of Interest Groups

Despite an initial hostility to arms control, the Reagan administration became progressively more receptive to public pressures for arms agreements over the course of incumbency. After a number of early skirmishes with Congress, especially over the MX missile, the administration seems to have decided that a more mainstream approach to arms control would make it easier to secure support for its defense programs. The hiatus in arms talks for fifteen months after the election clearly was unpopular. The resumption of START talks in late 1983, by contrast, helped forestall congressional actions that could have scrapped the MX missile altogether. From then on, the administration tried to walk a fine line between accommodating public pressures for arms control and avoiding actions that would antagonize its supporters on the Right.

In the first part of the administration it was the steady drumbeat of European public opinion that influenced the administration's INF policies, not domestic opinion. In 1982 Paul H. Nitze marshaled statistics about European anti-nuclear sentiment to press his case for greater flexibility in the INF talks. A United States Information Agency poll indicated that only 6 percent of Europeans were in favor of the impending deployments, 30–35 percent were in favor of these as a means of getting an agreement, and 25 percent were completely opposed. The deployments, Nitze suggested, would be at the expense of NATO's political survival.[90]

Not all of Reagan's advisers were convinced. Rostow had tried to minimize the seriousness of the mass demonstrations in West Germany against the deployments, suggesting that the demonstrators knew nothing about the meaning of "dual-track." When the case for arms control was made by European governments, however, especially by such conservative leaders as Prime Minister Margaret Thatcher and Chancellor Helmut Kohl, the seriousness of the peace movement and its effects on the stability of NATO were difficult to refute.

Grass-roots arms control lobbies in the United States paid little attention to the INF negotiations until 1987. At a strategy conference in St. Louis, Missouri, in February 1983, the national freeze campaign had adopted a resolution calling for a one-year delay in Pershing II and GLCM deployments to allow more time for arms control negotiations. Representative Edward J. Markey (D-Mass.), a leading voice in Congress for the freeze movement, organized meetings in early 1983 with European critics of the deployments, including former West German Chancellor Willy Brandt and former British Defence Minister Denis Healey, to help build domestic support for a pause in deployments.[91] Yet, as even freeze leaders admitted, this issue was a political sideshow. One observer noted, "Liberal arms control advocates . . . have concentrated their political energy on other fights—for nuclear weapons freeze and against the MX intercontinental missile—rather than intermediate range nuclear forces based and aimed at targets in Europe."[92]

The sudden thaw in U.S.-Soviet relations in late 1987, epitomized by Gorbachev's shaking hands with Reagan on American television in November, changed public opinion toward the Soviet Union and galvanized attention to and support for the INF Treaty. A CBS/New York Times poll just before the conclusion of the INF agreement reported that Americans favored Gorbachev 2-1 and that two thirds supported the emerging treaty.[93]

Pro-arms control lobbies lined up to support the president from the outset. A coalition of peace groups headed by the president of Common Cause, Fred Wertheimer, met in mid-November 1987 to marshal liberal backing for the treaty's ratification. Their objective was "to translate positive poll numbers [indicating support for the treaty] into a sense that there is some intensity to it."[94] It is doubtful that the administration welcomed their efforts, however, given the White House's already difficult task of consolidating support from the Right.

Conservatives dissatisfied with Reagan's new peace offensive hastily assembled their own lobbies. In December 1987 Republican strategist Richard Viguerie announced the formation of the Anti-Appeasement Alliance on behalf of conservatives who felt "alienated, abandoned, and rejected by the president."[95] Viguerie tried to activate "top key conservative activists throughout the nation," sending out more than 100,000 letters.[96] The American Security Council, an existing pro-defense group, collected more than 1,000 signatures from retired military personnel for a petition opposing INF, while the Conservative Caucus, which had accused Reagan of being "a dupe of dovish advisers," ran full-page newspaper ads with pictures of Reagan and Gorbachev next to pictures of Neville Chamberlain and Adolf Hitler. The headline over the pictures read, "Appeasement is as unwise in 1988 as it was in 1938."[97]

Summarizing conservative's sense of betrayal over the INF Treaty, right-wing activist Paul Weyrich, head of the Committee for a Free Congress, noted the demise of the "great conservative dream," in which Ronald Reagan, unencumbered by a reelection campaign, "would set the stage for a conservative revolution." Reagan had instead done the opposite, Weyrich charged, "endangering what he has already accomplished and behaving in a way that will have a harmful effect on the future."

Conservatives found a voice in the 1988 presidential

campaign, in which all the candidates except Bush were
initially vitriolic in their attacks on the treaty. Having to tread
a fine line between loyalty to the president and his own
political ambitions, Bush staked his future with Republican
moderates who favored the agreement. Kemp, by contrast,
referred to INF as "nuclear Munich," warning that
compromises on European missiles would give SDI critics the
leeway to press for agreements to kill strategic defenses.[98]

The administration, however, was unconvinced that
majority opinion, even among conservatives, was against the
treaty. White House polls in late 1987 suggested that most
conservative voters sided with the president. "If you say no
treaty with the Soviets, that's not where the public is," said a
White House official. "It's a different party now."[99]

A poll conducted by the private firm Martilla and Kiley,
for instance, seemed to confirm this view. The poll found not
only that 74 percent of Republicans were in favor of the
accord, but that 69 percent also believed that a military
buildup had made this possible.[100] For the White House, the
polls on the INF agreement vindicated the success of Reagan's
strategy of achieving "peace through strength."

In early 1987 public criticism of the Reagan administration
for its handling of the Iran-Contra affair may also have
influenced INF policy. With polls indicating that his popularity
had dropped to an all-time low, Reagan may have seen the
INF accord as a way to help deflect negative press
attention.[101] His political problems were seen to be
jeopardizing support for Republicans in a presidential election
year. Others have argued that Gorbachev may also have been
influenced by Reagan's political problems, seizing the
opportunity to advance a bold proposal that a weakened
Reagan would have difficulty in refusing.[102]

By the time of the Senate ratification debate the public
seemed to be overwhelmingly lined up behind INF. According
to a poll conducted by the Daniel Yankelovich Group in
March 1988, 77 percent of Americans approved of the treaty.
Underlying this apparent consensus, however, were some

qualifications. Fifty-four percent of those polled said they would favor an amendment to the treaty to require Reagan to certify that the Soviets were adhering to all prior arms control pacts, even if this meant killing the treaty. Forty percent would have supported an amendment requiring the USSR to lift restrictions on the emigration of Jews before the treaty could take effect.[103]

Conclusion

In the end, the ratification of the INF Treaty could be seen as the story of an administration that succeeded in spite of itself. According to Strobe Talbott, "INF was doomed to success," despite the best efforts of so many administration insiders. Public acclamation for U.S.-Soviet conciliation, underscored by the INF Treaty, seems to have been an important factor in dissuading negative votes or harmful amendments in the Senate. The public was clearly in favor of a new era of U.S.-Soviet relations and trusted Reagan's credibility on defense too much to believe charges that he had made a bad deal.

The administration's strategy for INF ratification was carefully tuned to political considerations. The existence of the treaty, in fact, owes much to the spread of anti-nuclear sentiment in the West, without which the administration might have been free to avoid arms control for several more years. Any lessons to be drawn from this experience for other treaties, however, must consider the remarkable influence of the sweeping changes that were occurring in the Soviet Union. Absent the ascendance of Mikhail Gorbachev and the willingness to accede to even the most stringent U.S. demands, the INF Treaty might well still be languishing in the shadows of SALT and START.

The peculiar convergence of events that account for the success of the INF Treaty would be difficult to replicate. The INF accord succeeded politically in part because it allowed everyone to declare some kind of victory. As Pat Towell noted at the time: "It gives Reagan a major arms accord in the final year of his presidency, when his sights are trained on his place in history. It gives Republicans a popular election-year defense vote and helps them argue that events have vindicated their past support for Reagan's peace-through-strength defense budgets. And for Democratic arms control advocates, having the INF Treaty negotiated by a hard-liner such as Reagan lends the force of bipartisanship to their cause."[104]

It is not hard to imagine that under different circumstances, the inherent liabilities of the zero option might have resulted in the Senate's refusal to ratify the treaty, at least without significant amendment or reservation. None of the issues that the original dual-track decision in 1979 had set out to solve were in fact resolved, and the role of nuclear weapons in Europe, though now vastly diminished, remained open to controversy. The extent to which U.S. strategy at the negotiating table was decisive in securing the dramatic Soviet concessions that led to success, as such, is open to question. The administration radically altered its negotiating posture several times over the course of the negotiations and was ready to abandon or indefinitely delay consideration of the zero option until the Soviets forced its hand. With a less popular president the mistakes and reversals of the United States at the negotiating table would likely have invited far harsher criticism and, perhaps, failure.

The negotiation and ratification of the INF Treaty reveal how much the character of the arms control process changed in the 1980s. What had once been largely the domain of secret diplomacy between two superpowers was transformed into an overt struggle for international public opinion. It was a new game, in which appeals for public support for proposals often preceded their introduction at the negotiating table. Neither U.S. nuclear objectives nor NATO's security concerns were decisive in setting the terms of the INF accord. Instead, the force of public opinion, bolstered by a new Soviet leader determined to cement his influence in the West and by a U.S.

president preoccupied with his personal legacy, prevailed. As General Bernard W. Rogers argued bitterly in 1988, "The political credibility of [NATO's European leaders] took a higher priority than that of deterrence of NATO."[105]

Notes

1. Senators voting against the INF Treaty were Jesse Helms (R-N.C.), Ernest Hollings (D-S.C.), Gordon Humphrey (R-N.H.), Steven Symms (R-Idaho), and Malcolm Wallop (R-Wyo.).

2. For additional discussion of the evolution of nuclear forces in Europe, see, for instance, Jane M. O. Sharp, "Understanding the INF Debacle: Arms Control and Alliance Cohesion," *Arms Control* (September 1987): 96–127.

3. U.S. and Soviet parity in the strategic balance and increasing force disparities in the European theater, it was argued, meant that the U.S. nuclear guarantee to Europe was no longer credible. It was further argued that without European-based weapons of sufficient range and accuracy to reach targets in the Soviet Union, the only U.S. response to Soviet aggression against NATO would be the use of strategic forces, a situation that might inhibit U.S. leaders in crisis and "de-couple" U.S. and European security. For additional discussion, see, for instance, U.S. Congress, House Committee on Foreign Affairs, *The Modernization of NATO's Long-Range Theater Nuclear Forces*, Report prepared for the Subcommittee on Europe and the Middle East, 1980.

4. See Dan Caldwell's chapter on the SALT II Treaty, chapter 6 of this volume.

5. On the Soviet side this included 500 land-based SS-4, SS-5, and SS-20 missiles, with almost 1,100 warheads targeted against Western Europe and Asia. For further details of the nuclear balance in Europe, see International Institute for Strategic Studies (IISS), *The Military Balance 1981-1982* (London: IISS, 1982), 89–90.

6. The Soviet Union did not agree that there was an imbalance in forces in Europe, as U.S. forward-based systems and the nuclear weapons deployed by France and the United Kingdom could reach targets in the Soviet Union.

7. For additional discussion of this and subsequent INF proposals, see Strobe Talbott, *Deadly Gambits: The Reagan Administration and the Stalemate in Nuclear Arms Control* (New York: Alfred A. Knopf, 1984).

8. In January 1986 Gorbachev proposed elimination of INF missiles in Europe by the year 2000, as part of a nuclear disarmament scheme. See William B. Vogele, "Tough Bargaining and Arms Control: Lessons from the INF Treaty," *Journal of Strategic Studies* 12, no. 3 (September 1989): 262.

9. Discussions of European-based nuclear forces traditionally had been subsumed under the larger rubric of U.S.-Soviet negotiations on strategic forces and were either excluded from consideration or left as "residual" issues for later negotiation. The SALT II Treaty was a prime example of this practice, papering over disagreements about European-based systems in protocols that pledged their resolution at a later time. The clear implication was that thorny issues of European security should not be allowed to interfere with the higher priority of achieving limitations on strategic armaments.

10. Among the countries that reserved judgment about deployments, pending possible progress in negotiations, were Belgium, Denmark, the Netherlands, and Norway. See Frederick Donovan and James Goodby, "Choosing Zero: Origins of the INF Treaty," Pew Case, no. 319 (Washington, DC.: Georgetown University Institute for the Study of Diplomacy, 1988), 15.

11. Sharp, "Understanding the INF Debacle," 100.

12. Addressing the Bundestag, Schmidt said: "I have to point out that the double-track decision of 1979 is to date the only existing American commitment in the Alliance to arms control negotiations which . . . deals with weapons in an area directly relevant to Europe and also to West Germany. The United States of America must continue to uphold this obligation." Cited in Donovan and Goodby, "Choosing Zero," 27.

13. The administration also said that it would not move to undercut either accord unless the Soviets did so first. Adherence to the two agreements remained a chronic source of controversy in executive-congressional relations and among different elements of the bureaucracy for the remainder of the administration and played a role in the INF ratification debate. See Bernard Gwertzman, "US Says It Is Not Bound by 2 Arms Pacts With Soviets," *New York Times*, May 20, 1981, A11.

14. U.S. Congress, House Committee on Foreign Affairs, *Review of Administration Initiatives on Strategic, Theater, and Conventional Arms Control*, November 20, 1981, 12.

15. When it had first emerged as a West German initiative in 1981 and was pushed through the West German government by Foreign Minister Hans-Dietrich Genscher, the zero option was received positively in Europe but instantly denounced by U.S. officials, including Secretary of State Alexander Haig and National Security Adviser Richard Allen. Allen described it as

"illusory" and likely to be acceptable only to "pacifist" elements. See Talbott, *Deadly Gambits*, 57.

16. Alexander Haig, *Caveat: Realism, Reagan, and Foreign Policy* (New York: Macmillan Co., 1984), 229.

17. Talbott, *Deadly Gambits*, 58.

18. See, for instance, Pat Towell, "House Panel Keeps 'Big-Ticket' Defense Items," *Congressional Quarterly*, October 22, 1983, 2169.

19. The "second zero," as it was called, precipitated West German fears of being left as the only European state with battlefield nuclear weapons, and thus the potential nuclear battleground in Europe. France and the United Kingdom were concerned that this would lead to a West German decision to eliminate tactical nuclear forces—a third zero. U.S. military commanders argued that this decision spelled the end of the U.S. ability to provide an extended nuclear deterrent in Europe. For further discussion, see, for instance, James M. Markham, "Bonn's Tactical Stand Worries Some NATO Allies," *New York Times*, October 9, 1987, and Michael Gordon, "Commander of NATO Is Opposed to Ridding Europe of All Missiles," *New York Times*, June 24, 1987.

20. Pat Towell, "Shultz, Soviets Draw Nearer to Agreement on Euromissiles," *Congressional Quarterly*, April 18, 1987, 718.

21. Bill McAllister, "Reagan Enlists Tower's Help to Win INF Treaty Approval," *Washington Post*, January 22, 1988, A8.

22. Martin Sieff, "Kohl to Urge Delay in Nuclear Upgrade," *Washington Times*, February 18, 1988, A1.

23. Donovan and Goodby, "Choosing Zero," 21.

24. The Reagan defense buildup was slated to cost $1.6 trillion over five years.

25. See, for instance, Hedrick Smith, "Growing Nuclear Debate," *New York Times*, April 9, 1982.

26. Leslie H. Gelb, "Poll Finds Doubt Over Responses to Soviet Threat," *New York Times*, April 15, 1983, A1.

27. Ibid., A13.

28. Haig, *Caveat*, 57–59.

29. Richard Perle, in particular, believed that the political and economic cost to be paid for the deployments, which he referred to as a "marginal military fix," were out of proportion to any tangible benefits. See Talbott, *Deadly Gambits*, 44.

30. Ibid., 51.

31. Donovan and Goodby, "Choosing Zero," 29.

32. Robert G. Kaiser, "Reagan Proposal Draws Praise From Broad Cross-Section on Hill," *Washington Post*, November 19, 1981, A7.

33. Cited in ibid.

34. In a private discussion with his Soviet counterpart, Kvitsinsky, during a walk in the Swiss mountains, Nitze proposed a package that would limit both sides to 75 missile launchers, eliminate Pershing II deployments, and restrict SS-20s in Asia in return for a ceiling of 150 on nuclear capable aircraft. For further discussion, see Talbott, *Deadly Gambits*, 124–41.

35. Perle was bitterly opposed to Nitze's plan and worked tirelessly to discredit it. The ban on Pershing IIs also was opposed by the president, who had the impression that "slow-flying" cruise missiles were not an adequate counter to the SS-20. Although the joint chiefs of staff did not overtly repudiate Nitze's ideas, they had expressed misgivings about giving up the Pershing II, especially if it presaged the United States giving up the right to deploy ballistic missiles in Europe.

36. After the "walk in the woods" formula was killed as an initiative, even Perle acknowledged its merits. See Strobe Talbott, *The Master of the Game: Paul Nitze and the Nuclear Peace* (New York: Alfred A. Knopf, 1988), 180.

37. See, for instance, Mary Belcher and Warren Strobel, "Shultz Hopes for Autumn Summit," *Washington Times*, April 24, 1987, A1.

38. *Washington Post*, March 31, 1987.

39. See, for instance, *Congressional Quarterly*, "Background Weekly Report," November 10, 1987, 2123.

40. Vogele, "Tough Bargaining and Arms Control."

41. *Congressional Quarterly Editorial Research Reports*, January 29, 1988 (Washington, D.C.: Congressional Quarterly Press, 1988), 46.

42. Bill Gertz, "Arms Violations Fit Soviet Strategy," *Washington Times*, February 11, 1987.

43. Quoted in *Congressional Quarterly*, December 5, 1987, 2971.

44. Michael Gordon, "Behind Issue of Soviet Compliance," *New York Times*, August 7, 1987, A16.

45. See, for instance, Warren Strobel, "New Missile Plan Is Not a Retreat, State Insists," *Washington Times*, August 26, 1987, 1.

46. In 1981 the chiefs had opposed the zero option, arguing that discussions of shorter-range Soviet systems would prompt the Soviets to raise the issue of U.S. shorter-range systems and of aircraft. In a characteristic act of a master tactician, Perle threatened that if the JCS rejected his proposal, he would see to it that limits on aircraft were added to the U.S. proposals. The JCS backed down. See Donovan and Goodby, "Choosing Zero," 33.

47. Admiral William J. Crowe, "Why the Joint Chiefs Support the INF Treaty," *Arms Control Today* 18, no. 4 (April 1988): 6.

48. Ibid.

49. See, for instance, Peter Almond, "Rogers Says Europe Will Suffer Over Treaty," *Washington Times*, December 7, 1987, B5, and George C. Wilson, "US Should Build New Missiles for Europe to Offset Treaty, General Says," *Washington Post*, January 23, 1988, A21.

50. In the 1980 presidential election Reagan won forty-four states and 489 electoral votes. In 1984, he won by an even more impressive margin, taking forty-nine states and 525 electoral votes.

51. Bernard Weinraub, "Nancy Reagan's Power Is Considered at Peak," *New York Times*, March 3, 1987, A1.

52. *Department of State Bulletin* 88, February 1988, 3, cited in Donovan and Goodby, "Choosing Zero," 1.

53. U.S. Congress, Senate Committee on Foreign Relations, "Testimony before the Senate Committee on Foreign Relations," *The INF Treaty*, pt. 3, 5.

54. For additional discussion on conservative views about INF bargaining strategy, see Vogele, "Tough Bargaining and Arms Control."

55. David Hoffman, "NATO Is Halting Deployment," *Washington Post*, November 26, 1987, A1.

56. David Hoffman, "Reagan to Insist on Ratification Without Changes by Senate," *Washington Post*, November 26, 1987, A1.

57. Lou Cannon, "Soviets Hint at Major Shift in Military Policy," *Washington Post*, November 30, 1987, A1.

58. See, for instance, "Foreign Affairs Committee Turns Down Nuclear Freeze and Weapons Build-Down," *Congressional Quarterly*, September 24, 1983, 1967.

59. "Reagan Faces Squeeze on Nuclear Arms Policy," *Congressional Quarterly*, January 21, 1984, 101.

60. Pat Towell, "Europe's INF: The 'Other' Nuclear Debate," *Congressional Quarterly*, October 1, 1983, 2031.

61. Pat Towell, "Soviet Offer Breaks Logjam on Euromissiles," *Congressional Quarterly*, March 7, 1987, 427.

62. "US Negotiators Head for Geneva," *Congressional Quarterly*, March 9, 1985, 438.

63. Pat Towell, "White House, Conferees Near Deal on Arms Control Disputes," *Congressional Quarterly*, November 7, 1987, 2722.

64. Linda Greenhouse, "Democrats in Short- and Long-Range Dilemma," *New York Times*, April 23, 1987, Washington Talk page.

65. Steven V. Roberts, "Many Lawmakers Back Missile Plan," *New York Times*, April 22, 1987, A12.

66. See Jack Nelson, "Nixon, Kissinger Warn Reagan on Arms Control," *Los Angeles Times*, April 26, 1987, 1.

67. *Congressional Quarterly Editorial Research Reports*, January 29, 1988, 43.

68. R. Jeffrey Smith, "Girding for Battle on INF Treaty," *Washington Post*, January 24, 1988, A18.

69. McAllister, "Reagan Enlists Tower's Help."

70. Smith, "Girding for Battle."

71. Quoted in ibid.

72. See Peter Adams, "Nunn May Request INF Negotiating Record," *Defense News*, May 11, 1987, 10. See also "Nunn, Byrd Abandon Plan to Delay INF Treaty," *Congressional Quarterly*, February 13, 1988, 308.

73. Ralph Z. Hallow, "Dole, Shultz Lock Horns Over Treaty," *Washington Times*, November 4, 1987, A1.

74. Hoffman, "Reagan to Insist on Ratification Without Changes by Senate," A1.

75. Richard Perle, "What's Wrong With the INF Treaty," *U.S. News & World Report*, March 21, 1988, 28.

76. Paul Bedard, "GOP Hard-Liners Opposing Swift Approval of INF Treaty," *Washington Times*, May 20, 1988.

77. The Intelligence Committee report noted a "tension between monitoring requirements and overall strategic needs" in such decisions as the exclusion of "anywhere-anytime" inspection measures because of the concerns these raised about Soviet counterintelligence. See U.S. Congress, Senate Select Committee on Intelligence, *The INF Treaty: Monitoring and Verification Capabilities*, 100th Cong., 2d sess., May 1988, unclassified report.

78. Susan F. Rasky, "Senate Begins Debate on Missile Treaty," *New York Times*, May 18, 1988, A3.

79. Bedard, "GOP Hard-Liners."

80. See Barry S. Pavel, "JCS Involvement in Nuclear Arms Control," paper P-2037 (Alexandria, Va.: Institute for Defense Analyses), 28.

81. See, for instance, "Nunn Blasts Administration on ABM Treaty," *Congressional Quarterly*, March 14, 1987, 457.

82. Pat Towell, "Senate Votes 93–5 to Approve Ratification of the INF Treaty," *Congressional Quarterly*, May 28, 1988, 1431.

83. For further discussion, see Joseph R. Biden, Jr., and John B. Ritch, "The Treaty Power: Upholding a Constitutional Partnership," *University of Pennsylvania Law Journal* 137, no. 5 (May 1989).

84. Paul Bedard, "Foes May Deal INF to Forestall Summit Surprise," *Washington Times*, May 24, 1988, A1.

85. Strobel, "New Missile Plan Is Not a Retreat," A1.

86. Quoted in *Congressional Quarterly*, January 30, 1988, 197.

87. Smith, "Girding for Battle," A18.

88. Paul Bedard, "Helms Gives Up on Blocking INF," *Washington Times*, May 26, 1988, A1.

89. Susan F. Rasky, "Helms Ends Fight Against Arms Pact," *New York Times*, May 26, 1988, A1.

90. Cited in Donovan and Goodby, "Choosing Zero," 41.

91. Towell, "Europe's INF," 2031.

92. Ibid.

93. Cited in Pat Towell, "Conciliation Colors the Pre-Summit Picture," *Congressional Quarterly*, December 5, 1987.

94. Pat Towell, "Arms Controllers Line Up With Reagan on INF," *Congressional Quarterly*, November 14, 1987.

95. Towell, "Conciliation Colors the Pre-Summit Picture."

96. Peter LaBarbera, "Conservatives Assemble Forces to Defeat or Amend INF Treaty," *Washington Times*, January 22, 1987.

97. Ibid.

98. Peter Adams, "Administration Deflects Blows to INF Proposals," *Defense News*, May 25, 1987, 9.

99. Cannon, "Soviets Hint at Major Shift in Military Policy," A32.

100. Ibid.

101. E. J. Dionne, "Poll Shows Reagan Approval Rating a 4-Year Low," *New York Times*, March 3, 1987, A1.

102. See, for instance, Robert Hunter, "Soviet's Euromissile Proposal," *Defense News*, March 9, 1987, 19.

103. *Americans Talk Security*, March 1988, 30–31.

104. Towell, "Senate Votes 93–5 to Approve Ratification of the INF Treaty," 1432.

105. Cited in Vogele, "Tough Bargaining and Arms Control," 267.

Selected Bibliography

Books and Articles

Allison, Graham, and Albert Carnesale. "Can the West Accept Da for an Answer?" *Daedalus* (1987): 69–93.

Arms Control Association. "Summary and Text of the INF Treaty and Protocols." *Arms Control Today* 18, no. 1, INF Supplement (January/February 1988): 1–12.

Biden, Joseph R., Jr., and John B. Ritch. "The Treaty Power: Upholding a Constitutional Partnership." *University of Pennsylvania Law Journal* 137, no. 5 (May 1989).

Blackwell, James R. "Contributions and Limitations of On-Site Inspections in INF and START." In *Arms Control Verification and the New Role of On-Site Inspection*, edited by Lewis A. Dunn with Amy E. Gordon. Lexington, Mass.: Lexington Books, 1990.

Davis, Lynn. "Lessons of the INF Treaty." *Foreign Affairs* 66, no. 4 (Spring 1988): 720–34.

Dean, Jonathan. "Gorbachev's Arms Control Moves." *Bulletin of the Atomic Scientists* 43, no.5 (June 1987): 34–40.

———. *Watershed in Europe: Dismantling the East-West Military Confrontation*. Lexington, Mass.: Lexington Books, 1987.

Donovan, Frederick, and James Goodby. "Choosing Zero: Origins of the INF Treaty," Pew Case no. 319. Washington, DC: Georgetown University Institute for the Study of Diplomacy, 1988.

Gordon, Michael R. "Dateline Washington, INF: A Hollow Victory?" *Foreign Policy*, no. 68 (Fall 1987): 159–79.

Kaufman, Joyce P. "US-Soviet Arms Control and Politics." *Arms Control* 8 (1987): 278–94.

Perle, Richard. "What's Wrong With the INF Treaty." *U.S. News & World Report*, March 21, 1988, 46.

Rasky, Susan F. "Senate Rebuffs Foes of the Missile Treaty." *New York Times*, May 21, 1988, A3.

Sharp, Jane M. O. "Understanding the INF Debacle: Arms Control and Alliance Cohesion." *Arms Control* (September 1987): 96–127.

Talbott, Strobe. *Deadly Gambits: The Reagan Administration and the Stalemate in Nuclear Arms Control.* New York: Alfred A. Knopf, 1984.

———. "The Road to Zero." *Time*, December 14, 1987, 18–30.

Thompson, James A. "The LRTNF Decision: Evolution of US Theatre Nuclear Policy, 1975–1979." *International Affairs* (1984): 601–14.

Towell, Pat. "Conciliation Colors the Pre-Summit Picture." *Congressional Quarterly*, December 5, 1987, 2967–71.

———. "Senate Votes 93-5 to Approve Ratification of INF Treaty." *Congressional Quarterly*, May 28, 1988, 1431.

———. "Soviet Offer Breaks Logjam on Euromissiles." *Congressional Quarterly*, March 7, 1987, 427–30.

Vogele, William B. "Tough Bargaining and Arms Control: Lessons from the INF Treaty." *Journal of Strategic Studies* 12, no. 3 (September 1989): 257–72.

Government Publications

U.S. Arms Control and Disarmament Agency. Office of Public Affairs. *Understanding the INF Treaty.* Washington, D.C.: GPO, 1988.

U.S. Congress. Senate. Committee on Armed Services. *NATO Defense and the INF Treaty, Report and Hearings,* l00th Cong., 2d sess., 1988, vols. 1–4.

U.S. Congress. Senate. Committee on Foreign Relations. *The INF Treaty, Report and Hearings,* 100th Cong., 2d sess., 1988, 6 pts.

U.S. Congress. Senate. Select Committee on Intelligence. *The INF Treaty: Monitoring and Verification Capabilities,* 100th Cong., 2d sess., 1988, unclassified report.

Conclusions
Michael Krepon

The task of drawing conclusions from the seven case studies presented in this volume is a daunting one. Although an effort has been made to supplement these cases with additional examples of executive-congressional relations and the arms control treaty ratification process, the total number of cases remains small, reflecting the comparatively few instances in which such treaties have been presented to the U.S. Senate for that body's advice and consent.

Moreover, each case is clearly unique. Presidents Warren G. Harding and Ronald Reagan may have shared some traits, but the Senate changed markedly during the sixty-five-year interval between its deliberations over the Washington Naval Treaties and the Intermediate-range Nuclear Forces (INF) treaty. In the mere seven years between Senate consideration of the Anti-Ballistic Missile (ABM) Treaty and the second treaty arising from the Strategic Arms Limitation Talks (SALT II), the domestic and international contexts for the Senate's deliberations were strikingly different, as were the outcomes of the treaties in question.

Finally, the outcome of a ratification debate can turn on many different variables. For example, perceptions of the president's stewardship of national security, the substantive value of the treaty under consideration, and the trustworthiness of prospective treaty partners are all key to the success or failure of a ratification effort. How can analysts rank order these factors, or even determine which among

The author wishes to acknowledge the helpful comments and suggestions of Barry Blechman, Thomas H. Buckley, Dan Caldwell, Stephen Flanagan, Alton Frye, Benjamin S. Loeb, Alan Platt, Howard Stoertz, and William C. Widenor. The author is also grateful for the research and editorial support provided by Page Fortna, Fred von Lohmann, John Parachini, and Amy Smithson.

them are the most important?

The focused comparison method of analysis borrowed from Alexander L. George and others has helped considerably in the comparing and contrasting of these cases. Yet it has by no means removed the subjective elements to such an inquiry, nor has it provided clarity as to the rank ordering for the most important components of success or failure in the cases. What follows is an evaluation of these disparate cases, based on seven excellent studies and the comments received from the case study authors and outside reviewers. The author hopes that it will provide the reader with greater clarity or new insights. If it stimulates other readers to refine or alter the list of lessons learned, or encourages further scrutiny of this and related subjects, so much the better.

On the basis of the cases of arms control treaty ratification that have been investigated, five keys to success appear particularly prominent. First, the more a treaty appears to provide tangible benefits to the nation's security, such as mandated reductions of threatening weapons systems or a halt to activities that are widely perceived to be dangerous, the more likely the Senate will be to provide its consent to ratification. Second, presidential popularity appears to be a critical component of success, covering a multitude of sins, including chief executive's lack of familiarity with the substance of the agreement negotiated under his auspices. Third, presidents who are widely perceived as staunch defenders of U.S. national interests are ideally suited to succeed in the tangled web of executive-congressional relations during the treaty ratification process. Presidents who lack this credential can expect very difficult sledding on Capitol Hill. Fourth, a perception in the legislative branch and the public at large of the president as an experienced hand in international politics and successful practitioner of the art of diplomacy is important. Fifth, a president's ability to work with Congress is obviously a critical key to success. Presidential micro-management in support of treaty ratification appears to be no vice—as long as the chief executive has sure political instincts in his dealings with Capitol Hill.

The more presidents lack these keys to success, the more they will be hurt by dissension within the ranks, which can become corrosive during treaty ratification debates. The more presidents lack these keys to success, the greater their dependence on highly competent advisers, a nonthreatening international environment, and a degree of luck regarding domestic and international events. Other important elements of successful arms control treaty ratification strategies are the president's handling of, and support from, the Senate leadership; the absence of, or support from, a "pivotal" senator who can either lend considerable credence to a treaty or badly undercut criticism of it; the support, no matter how lukewarm, of the Joint Chiefs of Staff (JCS); and the judicious use of "safeguards" to minimize the presumed risks of a treaty without undercutting its basic objectives and purposes. These conclusions will be elaborated in the pages to follow.

International Political Context

As Dan Caldwell's case study of the SALT II Treaty indicates, the Soviet Union's troubling international behavior badly compounded the domestic misgivings that had been fostered about the agreement by the Kremlin's mistreatment of religious and ethnic minorities. President Jimmy Carter was not widely perceived as being "tough" enough in protecting U.S. interests abroad; presidents benefiting from greater standing as staunch defenders of U.S. security have had considerable latitude in dealing with the misbehavior of negotiating partners.

The SALT II case is instructive in this regard: the treaty's provisions were no more than "modest but useful" in the estimation of the joint chiefs,[1] the president and his negotiating team were under strenuous attack as being insufficiently attentive to national security requirements, the Kremlin was embarked on an activist foreign policy, and Soviet military expenditures were disturbingly high and continuing to increase. Even so, the Carter administration had plausible hopes of securing a bare two-thirds majority vote of support from the Senate, until the Soviet Union made ratification impossible with its invasion of Afghanistan.

Soviet behavior before the conclusion of the Limited Test Ban Treaty was far worse than in the mid- to late-1970s. In the twenty-three months before Governor W. Averell Harriman's successful mission to Moscow, the Kremlin had been responsible for two of the most nerve-racking and dangerous acts of the Cold War—the construction of the Berlin Wall and the secret emplacement of ballistic missiles in Cuba. Yet, as the lopsided vote to consent to ratification of the LTBT indicated, senatorial and public concerns over the Kremlin's erratic behavior were overridden by widespread relief over recently improved superpower relations and a desire to halt nuclear fallout from atmospheric tests.

Although a correlation between troubling behavior by a negotiating partner and the demise of ratification chances is difficult to prove, the reverse is not: good behavior clearly begets improved prospects for arms control treaties in the Senate. When Prime Minister Margaret Thatcher declared that the West could do business with Mikhail Gorbachev in December 1984, more than one third of the U.S. Senate appeared to remain skeptical of this assertion. Yet when President Ronald Reagan was similarly convinced by Soviet deeds and developed a personal relationship with the new Soviet leader, opposition to the INF Treaty in the Senate shrank. Ultimately, just five senators voted against the accord. Concerns over verification and the Kremlin's compliance practices, so prominent during Reagan's first term in office, lost their newsworthiness against the backdrop of the Soviet withdrawal from Afghanistan, acknowledgment that the Krasnoyarsk radar constituted an outright violation of the ABM Treaty, and a willingness to accept unprecedented verification procedures in the new accord.

Good behavior by a negotiating partner may not only assist the politics of ratification but also simplify future negotiations by lessening pressures for "safeguards." These assurances often accompany arms control accords and take the form of commitments for increased defense spending, improved intelligence collection efforts, and readiness to resume practices barred by the treaty in question. As discussed below, some safeguards have been helpful, while others have undercut the objectives and purposes of an accord, making subsequent agreements more difficult and less meaningful to negotiate.

When a traditionally hostile negotiating partner is acting responsibly abroad and reducing its military might, the stimulus for safeguards is reduced considerably, especially when domestic economic considerations militate against larger defense expenditures. Thus, in stark contrast with previous nuclear arms control agreements, no safeguards accompanied the INF Treaty. The absence of safeguards does not mean that follow-on accords are assured of the Senate's consent. Nevertheless, the absence of ill-chosen safeguards may mean that subsequent presidents will face smaller hurdles in securing the consent of two thirds of the Senate for future accords.

Aversion to War and Military Spending

Arms control treaties can receive a powerful boost from the public's strong aversion to war, but war weariness is not necessarily enough to secure the consent of two thirds of the senators present and voting. It certainly was not sufficient in the case of the League of Nations, when Woodrow Wilson squandered a consensus of most Americans and their elected representatives in support of a peace treaty through an ill-advised negotiating strategy with both the leaders of Europe and the U.S. Senate. Wilson left for Paris in the role of peacemaker, but he became less and less of one the longer the Senate debated his handiwork. (One disaffected Department of State aide, William C. Bullitt, noted, "I can see at least eleven wars in it.")[2]

War breeds fear of new wars. Even when these fears pass, as was the case during the 1920s, an aversion to new military spending can linger. This political fact of life shaped the negotiating strategy President Warren G. Harding endorsed and Secretary of State Charles Evans Hughes executed during the Washington Conference on the Limitation of Armaments. Critics of the resulting treaties bemoaned provisions that required the United States to forgo new capital ship construction and fortification of U.S. outposts in the Pacific, but they had been overwhelmed by senatorial and public opposition to such expenditures. By insisting that the obligation to observe a ten-year holiday on capital ship construction be multilateral, Hughes had made a virtue out of necessity.

Later, when war clouds began to form ominously on the horizon, new negotiating efforts were made to extend naval constraints. In the politics of treaty ratification, however, the fear of war is a poor substitute for a favorable and stable international environment. As Thomas H. Buckley has indicated in his case study, Charles Evans Hughes was able to negotiate so successfully, despite the electorate's unwillingness to build a big navy, because of the international environment: he could play on British fears of losing a naval arms race to the United States and on Japanese interests in maintaining the status quo in the Pacific.

Aversion to new naval expenditures deepened after the Washington Conference. Only nine senators voted against the London Naval Treaty of 1930, which extended and slightly modified the terms negotiated at the Washington Conference. Critics of arms control later blamed these accords for constraining U.S. naval posture, but during Senate debate over the London Naval Treaty, a reservation calling for the country to build up to treaty strength by the end of 1936 garnered just eleven votes.[3]

The London Treaty, negotiated by Secretary of State Henry L. Stimson for President Herbert Hoover, turned out to be the last strategic arms control agreement for more than forty years. By 1935 fascist and militarist governments in Germany and Japan had publicly renounced all of their treaty obligations, and last-ditch efforts to salvage naval arms limitations inevitably faltered.[4]

The fear of war is sufficient to convene diplomatic conferences, but it cannot produce useful accords when states have hostile intent and are unalterably opposed to the status quo. After wars have been fought, they generate support for formal compacts to prevent their recurrence and breed revulsion against some of the instruments of warfare used. Just as the Geneva Protocol banning the use of chemical weapons traces its lineage to World War I, efforts to curtail nuclear weapons derive from the gruesome and foreboding events that ended World War II. The Senate's consent to ratification of the LTBT rested in part on public's health-related fears about fallout and its desire to place U.S.-Soviet relations on a more hopeful path.

The relationship between fears of nuclear war and subsequent ratification efforts is more difficult to track. Polling data do not suggest that concerns about nuclear war were a major factor in the Senate's deliberations over the ABM Treaty or SALT II.[5] Nevertheless, the record on this point is somewhat clouded.

When the electorate has perceived strategic modernization programs to be making the prospect of nuclear war less remote, it has become more insistent upon improved superpower relations and arms control accords. In this way, as Alan Platt recounts in his case study, the Johnson and Nixon administrations' plans to deploy ballistic missile defenses created public support for the ABM Treaty. Thereafter, efforts to pursue "nuclear war-fighting" strategies of deterrence—the development of new weapons systems with greater accuracy and more discriminate nuclear weapons effects—energized pro-arms control senators throughout the 1970s. Similarly, the Reagan administration's loose talk about "winning" a nuclear war, pursuing backyard civil defense programs, and firing nuclear warning shots fueled the movement to "freeze" all nuclear programs.

In other words, nuclear nightmares appear to be a subliminal and constant factor in U.S. politics, occasionally bubbling to the surface during presidential campaigns. The public's uneasiness with nuclear threats remains part of the background noise of U.S. politics; the electorate's fears can provide an impetus to nuclear negotiations and constrain strategic modernization programs. Future administrations would be well advised, however, not to use nuclear nightmares as a basis for seeking ratification of new agreements. Each of the thousands of nuclear weapons deployed in the field potentially has a nightmare attached to it, and if one's negotiating partner is that trigger-happy or dangerous, how can a treaty help? As a result, administrations have not promoted arms control treaties as a means to avoid nuclear holocaust.[6] Future attempts to do so can easily backfire rather than succeed.

The Leadership Factor

U.S. leadership in shaping the negotiating agenda has been a decided plus during ratification debates. Secretary of State Hughes, by surprising other delegations (and most members of the Harding administration) with his dramatic call for scrapping naval combatants at the outset of the Washington Conference, controlled the agenda of the talks. His high-risk strategy also stood in sharp contrast with the bargaining tactics employed by President Woodrow Wilson in Paris. Unlike Wilson, whose agenda was widely perceived to have been swallowed up by European intrigues, Hughes could demonstrate to the Senate that his negotiating objectives were largely reflected in the final accords.[7]

Likewise, Reagan administration officials could take pride in demonstrating to the Senate that their negotiating objectives, articulated at the outset of the INF Treaty negotiations, were clearly met in the agreement signed by the Soviet Union. President Jimmy Carter had no such basis to seek the Senate's consent to the SALT II Treaty. Torn between moving rapidly to conclude an accord inherited from the Nixon and Ford administrations, or opting for deeper reductions, he chose the latter but was forced to fall back quickly to the former. In the process, he undermined his leadership position by deferring to the Soviet negotiating agenda and so provided a massive opening for his domestic critics.

Other openings followed when Carter decided not to produce the B-1 bomber or deploy enhanced radiation weapons in Europe. A strong analytical case could be made for these decisions, but in both international and domestic political contexts these decisions were costly. Presidential leadership in bilateral arms control negotiations has usually been equated with "toughness," whether by the choice of negotiating strategy or by White House decisions relating to the weapons that are the subject of the negotiations.

One way presidents can demonstrate toughness is to proceed with nuclear weapons systems that are believed to provide leverage in the negotiations, provide insurance against their demise, or safeguard comparable capabilities to those presumably already deployed or sought by the Kremlin. Jimmy Carter, by rejecting this standard and deciding on the B-1 solely on the technical merits and problems of the bomber as he saw them, wounded himself in the ratification debate that followed, a wound deepened by his vacillation on the "neutron bomb" issue. Carter's decision in the final months of negotiations to proceed with the MX missile and to boost defense spending came too late to salvage a leadership position lost in earlier decisions.

Two tough presidential decisions during the SALT I negotiations, on the other hand, certified Richard M. Nixon's leadership position, making criticism of the ABM Treaty and the Interim Agreement difficult to sustain in the Senate. By mining Haiphong harbor and resuming the U.S. bombing campaign over North Vietnam on the eve of a summit meeting in Moscow, at which the SALT I accords were to be signed, Nixon projected a willingness to sacrifice the presumed centerpiece of his reelection campaign in order to prosecute an unpopular war. No one could then effectively argue that Nixon had negotiated poorly on behalf of the United States for his own political reasons, despite the artificial deadline the president imposed to complete the negotiations in time for the fall campaign.

Earlier, Nixon had rejected the advice of many in the Senate and elsewhere that he wrap up an agreement solely on strategic defenses. He insisted on an accord that also restrained offenses. The Kremlin eventually agreed, sustaining the president's judgment and strengthening his hand against complaints that the Interim Agreement did not go far enough in curtailing Soviet rocketry. In defense of the latter agreement Nixon administration officials argued that the accord made the best of an unfortunate situation defined by high Soviet and low U.S. production rates. Disaffected senators like Henry M. ("Scoop") Jackson (D-Wa.) seethed at this argument, but they approved the accords with the proviso that sufficient safeguards would have to be endorsed by the executive branch.

When the Carter administration pursued a similar line of argumentation in the SALT II debate, maintaining that the United States would be better off with the agreement than without, a key block of disaffected senators could no longer be appeased by safeguards. Only a president with strong credentials as a guardian of U.S. interests abroad can effectively argue that he has made the best out of a poor situation. Jimmy Carter could not plausibly make this case; many in the Senate blamed him, unfairly or not, for the negotiating hand that he held.

Linkage

There are numerous examples of formal or tacit linkage in U.S. arms control negotiations either pursued or accepted by the executive branch.[8] For example, the Washington Naval treaties codified linkage between fleet levels and naval fortifications in the Pacific: Japan was willing to accept inferiority in the ratios of naval combatants negotiated in Washington only if the United States and the United Kingdom pledged not to improve defenses of their Pacific holdings. The implications of these terms were clearly understood and accepted by all parties; they became the source of great contention when, in the 1930s, Japan ceased to accept the status quo in the Pacific.[9]

Arms control treaty supporters and skeptics periodically argue over the value of linkage, but most recognize that tacit linkage is a political fact of life, at least during the months preceding ratification and especially during the Senate debate: if the negotiating partner behaves badly, senators are more likely to provide an administration with advice rather than consent. The classic example of this remains the Carter administration's difficulties in securing ratification of SALT II at a time when the Kremlin was busily seeking to expand its sphere of influence in Africa, Asia, and Latin America.

The Kremlin ultimately wounded itself more than the United States by these adventures. In the short term, however, treaty skeptics and opponents were bolstered by Soviet adventurism, the impact of which was especially apparent in Henry Kissinger's testimony. This previously staunch opponent of legislative encroachments on presidential authority now suddenly argued for a set of congressionally mandated principles of linkage and for periodic votes on Soviet compliance.[10] A majority of the Republicans on the Senate Foreign Relations Committee agreed, concluding that the administration's "failure to establish linkage was a mistake, and the Senate should not ratify that mistake."[11]

Attempts by senators to move beyond de facto linkage to the imposition of constraints on Soviet international behavior have periodically been made, without success. During the LTBT debate, Senator Barry Goldwater (R-Ariz.) offered a reservation to postpone the effective date of U.S. ratification until the USSR removed its military and technical personnel from Cuba, and Senator John Tower (R-Tex.) proposed waiting until the Soviets paid up their UN dues.[12] Before the ratification debate over SALT II was shelved owing to the Soviet invasion of Afghanistan, treaty opponents were preparing efforts to insert limitations on the Backfire bomber into the treaty and to reduce the number of the Kremlin's "heavy" missiles—objectives that U.S. negotiators failed to achieve across three administrations.

Treaty supporters now call such efforts "killer amendments," thinly disguised efforts to defeat a treaty other than by a direct up or down vote on the treaty itself. Killer amendments are still very difficult to adopt, however. As Henry Cabot Lodge (R-Mass.) confided to the irreconcilable William Borah (R-Idaho) during plans to oppose President Wilson's League of Nations, "A straight vote in the Senate, if taken immediately, would be hopeless, even if it were desirable."[13] Ever since, the strategy of senators wishing to make their mark on a treaty has been to craft understandings, reservations, and conditions that minimize the damage they perceive will result from the accord or that establish more congenial negotiating objectives for subsequent agreements.

Examples of these tactics abound. They include the safeguards packages accompanying the LTBT and the SALT I accords and the 1972 Jackson amendment calling for equal force levels in subsequent agreements. These approaches have not foreclosed ratification efforts; indeed, they have ultimately gained the support of the executive branch and helped to provide overwhelming votes for ratification.

Other senatorial attempts to impose linkage have a quite different purpose, to block ratification of the treaty in question. Ostensibly, these efforts reflect heartfelt positions by

senators to alter the international behavior or reduce the
military capabilities of a miscreant negotiating partner, usually
the Soviet Union. Language is crafted that reflects widely held
aspirations and that sounds reasonable enough to most
Americans while being deeply objectionable to the Kremlin.
For irreconcilable opponents of a treaty this indirect approach
has much value: If linkage is accepted by a majority of the
Senate, the treaty is likely not to go into effect. If, on the
other hand, the attempt fails, it still calls attention to Soviet
misbehavior, demands adherence to positions most Americans
intuitively support, and forces treaty supporters to explain why
bad behavior is being condoned.

Even with this framework for debate, linkage amendments
viewed as hostile by the executive branch have fared poorly.
All concerned have known that, no matter how attractively
packaged, such linkage amendments are a surrogate for
negating a treaty. Support for these efforts usually does not
extend beyond irreconcilable treaty opponents, and sometimes
not even that far. For example, the Goldwater reservation to
the LTBT requiring the Soviets to leave Cuba gained just
seventeen votes, and Senator Tower's effort to make the
Kremlin pay up its UN dues garnered only eleven votes.

Perhaps in the future a weakened administration with poor
credentials for protecting U.S. interests abroad will face a
Senate coalition of moderates and irreconcilables, aligned in
support of a linkage amendment. It was such a coalition that
President Wilson helped to create and refused to bargain
with. Senator Lodge's battle against Article 10 of the League
Covenant proposed the reverse of linkage: Lodge's coalition
assumed further misbehavior abroad and insisted that the
United States not be drawn into the resulting fray without
congressional authorization.

In summary, the chances of the Senate's imposing arms
control linkage over the opposition of the executive branch
during a ratification debate are remote. Strenuous opposition
can be expected at home as well as abroad. If the imposition
of linkage suggests a repudiation of the executive branch's

negotiating strategy, strenuous opposition will be required to avoid a potential loss of control during the remainder of the ratification debate; if a majority of the senators present and voting elect to support linkage despite the White House's opposition, treaty opponents will be encouraged to assert their position in other areas as well. President Nixon chose to avoid this battle in SALT I, linking up with Senator Jackson instead.

Even when the White House chooses to accept a linkage amendment, the target of these efforts may not be so accommodating, unless that country strongly desires the agreement's implementation. Arms control accords, however, are not gifts given with new strings attached at the eleventh hour; they are compacts that reflect a balancing of interests achieved only after difficult and usually extended bargaining. For this simple reason, attempts by the Senate to alter the terms of a treaty unilaterally invite counter-conditions and stalemate. After a successful negotiation, a powerful and proud foreign country cannot accept linkage imposed by the legislative branch without inviting further humiliating gestures.

Senators who are masters of the art of bargaining and compromise know this, but they are not the prime movers behind linkage amendments designed to block treaty implementation. Proponents of such amendments are usually not concerned with securing the adherence of a negotiating partner with new terms imposed by the Senate. They are concerned primarily with securing a majority of the Senate behind their amendment; if this can be achieved, the rejection of the treaty by an injured party can be considered a success.

Domestic Political Context

Article 2, Section 2 of the Constitution, which enables just thirty-four senators to kill a treaty, seems, on its face, to be an onerous requirement. Gerard C. Smith, the head of the U.S. team that negotiated SALT I, has said, "If a majority vote of both Houses of Congress is sufficient to make war, it should be sufficient to make agreements having peaceful purposes."[14] The requirement to secure the support of two thirds of the Senate rather than a simple majority appears to place an unreasonable burden on the executive branch. After all, the two-thirds requirement was born of unique historical circumstances that became irrelevant long ago—the desire of western states at the Constitutional Convention to block agreements inimical to their trading interests, like the Jay-Gardoqui Treaty.[15]

The two-thirds requirement has clearly been a difficult one for the executive branch to meet for treaties governing the foreign relations of the United States. The Jay Treaty with Great Britain over post–Revolutionary War grievances barely survived Senate scrutiny, as did the peace treaty with Spain ending the War of 1812. More recently, Senate irreconcilables and President Wilson combined to sink the Versailles Treaty, and the Panama Canal treaties narrowly survived the ratification process. Given the infrequent occurrence of ratified arms control treaties, it is natural to blame these periods of drought on the two-thirds requirement.[16]

In the final roll-call votes, however, arms control treaties have usually sailed through the Senate with many votes to spare. In the end, only one senator voted against the Washington Naval Treaty establishing fleet ratios and limits, nine voted against the London Naval Treaty of 1930, nineteen opposed the LTBT, two voted against the ABM Treaty, and five opposed the INF Treaty. When viewed in historical perspective, the SALT II Treaty experience was atypical. The Coolidge administration's botched effort to secure senatorial consent for the Geneva Protocol in 1926 was even more so—the only instance of failure when the same political party controlled the White House and the Senate.

Although the two-thirds requirement has usually not been onerous during the final roll-call vote, it has been an important factor during negotiations leading up to an agreement and during negotiation with the Senate. For example, President John F. Kennedy reluctantly relinquished his goal of a comprehensive test ban when faced with the concerns of the joint chiefs and a preliminary head count suggesting such a ban would fall ten votes short of a two-thirds majority.[17] President Carter in the latter stages of the SALT II negotiations, made several less consequential decisions that many associated with his uphill search for sixty-seven votes, including the decision to proceed with the largest of all candidate designs for the MX missile.

The White House's readiness to agree to safeguards minimizing perceived risks associated with arms control accords has been another mechanism to ensure more than the necessary two-thirds vote. Until the INF Treaty, every nuclear arms control agreement receiving the Senate's advice and consent was linked to a package of safeguards negotiated with deference to defense-minded senators and the JCS. In President Kennedy's case, as noted in Benjamin S. Loeb's study on the LTBT, one object of the safeguards was to generate an overwhelming vote to provide impetus for a comprehensive treaty. Ironically, one of the safeguards—carrying out an "aggressive" underground test program—undermined that objective. Similarly, the Nixon administration mortgaged the future of strategic arms control when it eased passage of the SALT I accords with commitments to proceed with multiple independently targeted reentry vehicles (MIRVs) and nuclear-armed cruise missiles, both of which made subsequent limitations harder to achieve and more difficult to verify.

In response to these and other safeguards, including the Trident submarine and B-1 bomber, Senate Foreign Relations Committee Chairman J. William Fulbright (D-Ark.) opened the hearings on SALT I by voicing the concern that the Nixon administration's actions posed the "danger of having our actions belie our words."[18] Fulbright's qualms, however, mattered considerably less than Henry M. Jackson's. Similarly, in the final months of the SALT II debate, senators William Proxmire (D-Wis.), George McGovern (D-S.Dak.), and Mark

Hatfield (R-Ore.) laid down a marker that the Carter administration's concessions to defense-minded senators could cost the treaty their support.

In the end, however, pro–arms control senators can usually be counted upon to vote for a treaty, whereas defense-minded senators require assiduous courting. Until the INF Treaty debate, when budget deficits, the warming of the cold war, and an increasing lack of interest in new nuclear modernization programs made safeguards difficult to propose, safeguards were the means of choice to sway fence-sitting senators. Even in the case of the INF Treaty, safeguards in the form of improved intelligence collection capabilities were demanded and provided. For supporters of arms control the central question is usually not whether two thirds of the United States Senate will consent to ratification, but whether the agreement will be worth the price incurred during bargaining for its ratification.

Bipartisanship

In a classic study of the Senate's role in the treaty ratification process, written almost sixty years ago, W. Stull Holt concluded that partisanship and jealousy over senatorial prerogatives were the two biggest factors in the demise of treaties.[19] Holt's conclusions remain valid today. The requirement to secure the assent of two thirds of the senators present and voting means that a treaty must have bipartisan support. Otherwise, it will fail miserably.

Partisan appeals by the executive branch, therefore, are a clear sign of desperation and a poor omen for critical vote counts in the Senate. The classic case of faulty executive judgment in this regard is Woodrow Wilson's performance during and after the negotiation of the Treaty of Versailles. As William C. Widenor notes in his case study of the Versailles Treaty, Wilson badly compounded the errors of excluding Republican senators from his negotiating team and not harkening to their advice in Washington. In an extraordinarily maladroit move, the president cabled members of the Foreign Relations Committee from Paris, inviting them to dine with him upon his return and imploring them to withhold judgment about the treaty until he was able to brief them. Then he chose Boston as his debarkation point—the home base of his principal antagonist, Senator Henry Cabot Lodge—to deliver a rousing speech for the treaty, before proceeding to the White House to entertain the questions of the chairman, Senator Lodge, and his fellow committee members.[20] This partisan move contributed to solidifying Republican opposition.

President Nixon had a better idea: returning from the Moscow summit, where the SALT I Interim Agreement and ABM Treaty were signed, he went immediately to Capitol Hill to deliver a speech to a joint session of Congress. President Carter employed the same tactic upon his return from the Vienna signing of SALT II. President Kennedy de-emphasized partisanship when he decided not to go to the signing ceremony for the LTBT in Moscow, inviting a bipartisan group of senators to attend instead.

The blessing of both the Senate majority and minority leaders is a requirement for sufficient bipartisan support. Wilson's dealings with Lodge were doubly myopic, given the latter's twin roles as majority leader and chairman of the committee handling Senate consideration of the peace treaty. By Lodge's count, Wilson approached at least fifteen Republican senators to try to enlist their support, but not once did he deign to bargain with their majority leader.[21]

It is especially critical for Democratic presidents to gain the support of the Republican leader in the Senate. Otherwise, they risk facing a coalition of moderates and irreconcilables such as defeated Wilson. John F. Kennedy succeeded where Jimmy Carter failed: by enlisting the support of the Senate minority leader, Everett Dirksen (R-Ill.), he ensured that the treaty would not become a partisan issue.

Jimmy Carter tried and succeeded in gaining the support of

Dirksen's son-in-law, minority leader Howard Baker (R-Tenn.), during the Senate's consideration of the Panama Canal treaties, but Baker chose not to lend his support during the bitter campaign over SALT II. Carter was unwilling to accord Baker—who was certain to be a presidential candidate in 1980—the role of broker during the ratification debate, and Baker cast his lot with those pursuing crippling amendments to the treaty.

The old adage that Democratic presidents should negotiate treaties and Republican presidents should oversee ratification campaigns is at least half correct: in the seventy-year period covered in these case studies, Republican presidents have found it easier to demonstrate their credentials as tough defenders of U.S. national security than have their Democratic counterparts. Just as important, they have had far more success in peeling off moderates from oppositionist ranks within the Republican party and limiting opposition to hard-core irreconcilables.

Without the bipartisan support of the Senate leadership a treaty can be delayed for long periods through parliamentary maneuvers, a favored tactic of opponents facing a popular agreement. With enough time, critics can hope to build an effective case against specific provisions, chipping away at popular support. Henry Cabot Lodge controlled the clock during consideration of the League of Nations, using two full months to review treaty provisions, including two complete weeks to have the treaty text read aloud. This was considered undue delay by supporters of the league, but it was hardly dilatory compared with the formal debate over the SALT II Treaty, which lasted six and one-half months. The longer treaty critics debated SALT II, the more they found international events working in their favor.

Timing has not been a problem with a conservative Republican in the White House and a Democratic majority in the Senate—a successful electoral combination for ratification purposes. Republican presidents have never faced Woodrow Wilson's and Jimmy Carter's predicament—the disaffection of the opposition party leadership. With the thinning out of the ranks of pro-defense Democrats like Henry M. Jackson, most Democrats in the Senate have invariably voted for ratification and against crippling amendments. When this block of votes has combined forces with a vocal, anticommunist, pro-defense president, ratification has been assured. The overwhelming votes in support of the ABM and INF treaties attest to the power of this bipartisan combination.

The most lopsided vote for ratification of an arms control treaty occurred when there was a Republican in the White House and a Republican majority in the Senate. Despite lingering ill will toward the United Kingdom and nascent concerns over Japan, the Harding administration was able to secure, with just one dissenting vote, an agreement establishing ratios for these countries' naval combatants. Secretary of State Hughes's adeptness at securing the Senate's overwhelming consent to the Washington Naval treaties was nowhere more apparent than in his choice of a negotiating team, which included Henry Cabot Lodge as well as the Senate's minority leader, Oscar W. Underwood (D-Ala.).

A Republican in the White House working with a Republican majority in the Senate is still no guarantee for ratification, as the case of the Geneva Protocol attests. In 1926 the Coolidge administration failed to convince the Senate to consent to essentially the same agreement banning chemical warfare that it had approved four years earlier as part of the Washington Naval treaties. As Rodney J. McElroy notes in his case study, the laissez-faire attitudes of President Coolidge and Secretary of State Frank B. Kellogg, together with Senator William Borah's iconoclastic leadership of the Foreign Relations Committee, proved no match for the determined lobbying efforts of the Chemical Warfare Service and veterans groups. Borah's chairmanship was anything but a coalition-building enterprise; a standard joke in Washington was to express amazement that he consented to face the same direction as his horse during frequent rides in Rock Creek Park.[22]

Key Constituencies and Pivotal Senators

Two constituencies have usually mattered most in arms control ratification debates: pro-defense but undecided senators and the most senior officers of the U.S. military establishment, the joint chiefs of staff. In the LTBT debate the key block of uncommitted but somewhat skeptical senators followed the lead of Henry Jackson and Everett Dirksen. When they signed on, Senate consent to ratification was ensured. During the elongated debate over SALT II, the Carter administration's hopes rested on the noncommittal shoulders of Sam Nunn (D-Ga.), having previously lost the critical support of Howard Baker and Henry M. Jackson.

The fate of treaties that succeeded or failed in the Senate by close margins has often turned on the concerted efforts of one key senator. For example, the outcome of the debate over the League of Nations was sealed not just by Woodrow Wilson's obtuseness but also by Henry Cabot Lodge's narrow nationalism. In 1898 William Jennings Bryan (D-Nebr.) played this pivotal role; without Bryan's support for the peace treaty with Spain, President William McKinley would not have achieved his razor-thin margin for ratification.

For arms control treaties the most pivotal senator has usually been either the Republican leader in the Senate or someone with standing, seniority (either in the Armed Services Committee or the Foreign Relations Committee), and an image as a staunch supporter of U.S. national security interests abroad. Only a few individuals have fit this profile in the case studies under review: Lodge, Dirksen, Jackson, Baker, and Nunn. If a senator fitting this profile chooses to oppose a treaty with all of the skills and devices at his disposal, the president faces a severe challenge.[23]

Pivotal senators generally can command the votes of their

colleagues who have not yet declared a position in the late stages of debate. In addition, criticism of an accord by outside experts can become far more damaging when a pivotal senator concurs. In the SALT II debate, for example, several private citizens, most notably Paul H. Nitze, effectively disparaged the accord, but their campaign against SALT was less decisive than that waged on Capitol Hill by Henry M. Jackson and his staff.

Without the leadership of a pivotal figure in the Senate, treaty opponents face a steep uphill battle—even if public figures with considerable stature weigh in against a treaty. This was clearly evident in the LTBT debate, in which Edward Teller testified against the agreement as "possibly a step towards war."[24] His opinion usually carried considerable weight on Capitol Hill, but on this issue it was negated by the decisions of senators Jackson and Dirksen to support President Kennedy.

The positioning of pivotal senators and the bloc of undecided senators they sway has often been linked to the position of the JCS. When the joint chiefs have supported an arms control treaty, no matter how warily, it has become more difficult for a pivotal senator and most of his undeclared colleagues to oppose the accord effectively. The preferred alternative for the White House, the chiefs, and the pivotal senator has been a private, three-way accommodation to manage ratification with minimal risk. Thus, safeguards packages have often been negotiated in private and then presented to the full Senate in the final stages of the ratification process. Such tripartite negotiations were not possible in the case of SALT II, when Senator Jackson's strident opposition could not be mollified by safeguards or muted by the joint chiefs' mild endorsement. Private negotiations aimed at salvaging a two-thirds vote centered on Senator Nunn but were stillborn with the Soviet invasion of Afghanistan.

Since the creation of the JCS in 1947, no active-duty member of the chiefs has testified in outright opposition to a signed arms control treaty. Undoubtedly, the chiefs have concluded that their qualms are more usefully expressed privately during the negotiations or in consultations with the White House and pivotal senators over appropriate safeguards. Concerns expressed privately by the chiefs have resulted in important modifications in U.S. negotiating positions, such as in the acceptance of a partial rather than a comprehensive nuclear test ban, and in numerous other changes of lesser consequence. Concerns expressed by the chiefs have also led to generous safeguards attached to the LTBT and SALT I accords.

The extent of past efforts to satisfy the concerns of the joint chiefs of staff speaks volumes about how crucial the White House has considered their support to be. President Gerald Ford was quite explicit in this regard, noting how he declined to conclude a SALT II Treaty because of the misgivings of Secretary of Defense Donald Rumsfeld and the chiefs: "I recognized that they held the trump card. The Senate would have to ratify the new accord. If Rumsfeld or the Joint Chiefs testified against it, there was no way that the Senate would ever go along with it."[25]

Instances of outright opposition or the expression of serious reservations to an arms control treaty by senior military officers on active duty have been rare, such as the testimony of General Thomas S. Power, commander-in-chief of the Strategic Air Command, and General Bernard A. Schriever of the U.S. Air Force Systems Command during Senate consideration of the LTBT. In contrast, retired senior officers have often testified against arms control treaties, including such former JCS chairmen as General Nathan Twining (LTBT) and Admiral Thomas Moorer (SALT II). Their critiques have often been based on operational concerns heightened by tours of duty before retirement. For example, General Bernard W. Rogers's testimony expressing deep misgivings about the INF Treaty dwelt on its implications for the strategy of flexible response espoused by NATO (the North Atlantic Treaty Alliance), a concern heightened by eight years of duty as supreme allied commander for Europe.

Rogers's testimony gave new expression to a long and honorable tradition whereby senior officers, recently retired, declare adverse professional and personal judgments about treaties that would limit U.S. military options in the event of war. Rear Admiral H. A. Wiley, formerly commander-in-chief of the United States Fleet, strengthened the foundation for this tradition in 1930 when he strongly opposed a provision in the London Naval Treaty extending the ban on U.S. fortifications in the Pacific.

In all, the Senate Committee on Naval Affairs took 450 pages of (at best) lukewarm testimony from naval officers on the London Naval Treaty, but this testimony did not affect the outcome; just as the concerns of noted civilians require a pivotal figure in the Senate to have particular force, the misgivings of retired military leaders require the measured support of senior active-duty officers. Thus, when the acting commander-in-chief of the United States Fleet and a naval adviser to the U.S. delegation, William V. Pratt, pronounced the London Naval Treaty "most satisfactory," the qualms expressed by retired naval officers did not damage prospects for ratification.[26]

Senior military officials whose misgivings cannot be assuaged by modifications in U.S. negotiating positions or agreed safeguards are in a quandary: they can swallow their reservations and provide qualified support in public testimony, as General Curtis LeMay did during the LTBT hearings, publicly oppose their commander-in-chief, or retire from active service. One military adviser to the London Naval Treaty negotiations, Rear Admiral Hilary P. Jones, chose the second route. His testimony raised questions of propriety when he provided the Senate Committee on Naval Affairs with his internal memoranda to the U.S. delegation. Lieutenant General Edward Rowny played a similar role when he retired at the end of the SALT II negotiations and testified how his advice went unheeded and how the positions of the joint chiefs had eroded over time.

These breaches of confidentiality were minor compared with William C. Bullitt's performance during the Senate's debate over the League of Nations. This disgruntled former attaché to the American Commission provided Senator Lodge with sensitive memoranda of conversations between members of the U.S. delegation, as well as with early drafts of President Wilson's proposals for the league. The defections of negotiating team members, whether military or civilian, always wound the executive branch. They need not, however, be fatal, as long as pivotal senators and senior members of the U.S. military remain firm in their support of the treaty.

Electoral Politics

The adage that it is unwise for a president to submit an arms control treaty to the Senate during the last year of his term is only half true: to date, late timing has bedeviled Democratic presidents far more than Republicans. Even if Woodrow Wilson could somehow have seen the wisdom to compromise after failing to capture sufficient votes for the league, he ran out of time to do so. Stymied by Henry Cabot Lodge and his own rigidity, Wilson tried to make the 1920 elections a referendum on the league and failed miserably. The electorate overwhelmingly preferred Warren G. Harding's bloviations about a nebulous "association of nations" and the Republican party's vague platform supporting "agreement among nations to preserve the peace of the world."[27]

In 1980 President Jimmy Carter similarly found that the electorate was willing to see him leave office, despite the argument that the fate of the SALT process rested on his reelection. Indeed, two of Carter's crucial supporters on the Senate Foreign Relations Committee, Chairman Frank Church (D-Idaho) and ranking minority member Jacob Javits (R-N.Y.), also went down to defeat in the 1980 elections when candidates were swept into office on a wave of conservative sentiment. By 1979 Carter was a seriously wounded president. As Dan Caldwell notes in his case study of the SALT II Treaty, the delays incurred during the negotiations proved exceedingly costly, both to the treaty and to the president.

With the exception of Gerald Ford, Republican presidents have been able to send arms control treaties successfully to the Senate floor in election years. Indeed, when presidents with reputations as staunch defenders of U.S. national security interests have turned swords into plowshares, the conservative wing of the Republican party has been effectively silenced, and electoral dividends have invariably followed. The political timing of Richard M. Nixon's SALT I signing ceremony in late May 1972 was impeccable politically, even though it meant negotiating against a self-imposed deadline, ill-staffed back-channel deals, and other imprudent steps. All was forgiven during an election year: the SALT I hearings were recessed for the political conventions, after which the senators returned to Washington to approve the accords overwhelmingly.

As Janne E. Nolan notes in her case study, Ronald Reagan was similarly free to propose that the Senate consent to ratification of the INF Treaty in an election year. All of the Republican presidential candidates who opposed the treaty or equivocated their support for it during the primary campaign fell by the wayside; the lone supporter, George Bush, became the party's standard-bearer and cruised to victory in the November election. Only one Republican president apparently felt stymied from having concluded an arms control treaty at the time of an approaching election. In this case the unelected president, Gerald Ford, was subject to attack from the political Right for allegedly having fallen under the spell of Henry Kissinger and for signing the Helsinki Accords "ratifying" Soviet domination of Eastern Europe. This exception seems now to underscore the general rule that Republican presidents are free to conclude arms control treaties during an election year.

Role of the President

Presidential standing on arms control issues derives from at least three critical elements. First, the president may enjoy standing owing to a perception that he is a staunch defender of U.S. national security interests (which has been especially true in the periodic confrontations with the Soviet Union and the People's Republic of China that characterized the Cold War). Second, standing can also derive from a perception that the president is knowledgeable about the issues being negotiated and from a reputation that he is a keen observer of international politics. Finally, standing can derive from a president's overall popularity, which can translate into greater clout on substantive issues. Each of these sources of presidential standing have helped immeasurably in facilitating the White House's ability to work effectively with the Senate during the treaty ratification process.

Occupants of the White House who have combined staunch national interest or anticommunist credentials with substantive knowledge of the arcane issues of nuclear diplomacy, such as Richard M. Nixon and John F. Kennedy, have been ideally positioned to secure the high ground in ratification debates with treaty opponents. Future presidents who lack both of these qualities will find themselves and their treaties inviting targets on Capitol Hill. On the other hand, presidents perceived as firm defenders of U.S. interests abroad and were popular at home have not needed to be well versed in negotiating history or international diplomacy to fare well in treaty ratification debates. In such circumstances presidents have maintained their standing as long as they were able to rely on trusted, experienced advisers.

For example, the consensus view of historians is that Warren G. Harding had little to do with U.S. negotiating strategy for the Washington Conference; as Thomas H. Buckley recounts, Harding's rare comments on the treaties during the Senate's deliberations suggested a lack of appreciation of international and domestic political sensitivities. Yet the treaties were steered through the shoals of Senate debate by none other than Henry Cabot Lodge, whom Secretary of State Charles Evans Hughes had shrewdly chosen as a member of the negotiating team.

Likewise, Ronald Reagan's grasp of INF negotiating issues was often questioned, especially by experienced observers who worried publicly about the treaty's negative implications for NATO's strategy of flexible response and the future deployment of other nuclear weapons on the continent.[28] Reagan's off hand remarks about complicated diplomatic and negotiating matters were periodically a source of embarrassment for administration officials but rarely for the president or his legions of admirers. During the Senate's debate, the INF Treaty's ratification was a foregone conclusion, owing to the president's popularity and reputation as a staunch foe of communism.

Conversely, a deep knowledge of negotiating issues does not guarantee sufficient presidential standing in the Senate, particularly if the occupant in the White House is not personally popular or is perceived as weak in defending U.S. national interests abroad. No president was better versed in the details of negotiations than Jimmy Carter, but hampered by Soviet adventurism, he fared poorly in his dealings with the Senate. As Dan Caldwell notes, Carter's lack of personal popularity, his reputation as a vacillating figure in dealing with the Kremlin, and a weak congressional relations team handicapped the president's recruitment of undecided senators.

Jimmy Carter's experience suggests that a president lacking in popularity and national security credentials could well find his standing further weakened as a result of arms control treaties completed under his auspices. The contentious ratification of the Panama Canal treaties constituted a Pyrrhic victory, since they weakened the president's stature as a defender of U.S. interests abroad.[29] Conservative groups that mobilized during this debate successfully honed their tactics for the SALT II controversy to follow, during which Carter's standing was eroded still further by political ferment in Iran. Woodrow Wilson's popularity and stature also suffered as a result of his role in the negotiation of the Treaty of Versailles. Wilson left for Europe as a peacemaker; he returned as a dealmaker who got caught up in Old World intrigues, alienating a number of domestic ethnic groups in the bargain. In contrast, Richard M. Nixon's standing was enhanced by the SALT I accords: his popularity and electoral prospects improved, despite the fact that he was prosecuting an increasingly unpopular war while the Watergate storm front was appearing on the horizon. Similarly, John F. Kennedy's popularity was boosted as a result of the signing and ratification of the LTBT. Where presidential standing is concerned, conservatism on national security issues has, as it does in so many other aspects of politics of treaty ratification, multiple rewards.

Consensus-Building

Consensus-building begins in the executive branch, since divisions within the president's official family can open up avenues of attack from Capitol Hill and make coalition-building in the Senate more difficult. This was clearly the case in the Carter administration, where divisions within the executive branch, especially the corrosive differences between Secretary of State Cyrus Vance and National Security Adviser Zbigniew Brzezinski, contributed to the SALT II Treaty's demise.

Yet the Reagan administration was beset by more open and deeper divisions, beginning with the most basic question of whether to negotiate with the Soviet Union. Department of State and Pentagon officials conducted intense bureaucratic warfare over negotiating strategies, tactics, and the value of existing accords; secretaries of state Alexander Haig and George Shultz sparred openly with Secretary of Defense

Caspar Weinberger. Yet none of these awkward divisions harmed the ratification prospects of the INF Treaty.

Clearly, divisions within the executive branch are not always disabling. When the president has been personally popular and widely perceived to be protective of U.S. interests, and when the treaty that has been negotiated under his auspices has been generally viewed as worthwhile, embarrassing internal disputes have been no bar to successful results in the Senate. Presidents who have not been widely popular or who have been perceived as uncertain defenders of U.S. interests abroad have had far less leeway on Capitol Hill. For them, divisions within the ranks have had real costs: if a chief executive has been suspected of being "weak" in negotiating with adversaries of the United States, the appearance of poor discipline among cabinet officers and their subordinates has only strengthened this perception, further eroding presidential standing in the Senate.

Presidents have used a variety of strategies in seeking to mold consensus despite potential or actual divisions within the executive branch. Wilson and Nixon stifled debate within their official families and made key decisions in consultation with only one trusted adviser. In contrast, Carter and Reagan let discordant voices ring. During negotiation of the Washington and London naval treaties, presidents Harding and Hoover avoided discord within the executive branch by delegating extraordinary authority to their negotiating teams.

During negotiations over the Nuclear Non-Proliferation Treaty, President Lyndon B. Johnson built consensus by making sure that the concerns of the joint chiefs of staff were taken into account: the chiefs conducted no less than nineteen formal reviews of the evolving treaty text.[30] President John F. Kennedy adopted the opposite approach in negotiating a test ban treaty, consciously not asking the chiefs for their collective opinion on the wisdom of an atmospheric test ban before W. Averell Harriman's was dispatched to Moscow.[31]

Exclusionary tactics did not harm negotiation and ratification prospects for the agreements that emerged from the Washington Conference. In this instance, Secretary of State Hughes stunned nearly everyone with his opening statement, which called for a ten-year naval holiday for capital ship construction and the scrapping of approximately seventy naval combatants. According to one chronicler of the Washington Conference, no foreign delegates were given advance notice of the speech, and fewer than a dozen men—including the president—knew of its content in any detail. No printed copies of Hughes's proposal were made until the day of the speech.[32] By using the element of surprise, Hughes astutely established the conference agenda and accomplished his objectives.

In stark contrast, Wilson's use of secrecy did not help his cause in the Senate, as Secretary of State Robert Lansing's lukewarm testimony (and his polite but damning published account of the peace negotiations) attests.[33] In the short run, Nixon's exclusion of his cabinet and frequent bypassing of his negotiating team succeeded: the ABM Treaty and the SALT I Interim Agreement were approved by overwhelming majorities. These tactics, however, activated powerful opposition currents to the SALT process while strengthening perceptions that Nixon's willing helper and agent, Henry Kissinger, was not suitable for subsequent cabinet-rank appointments.

In any event, secrecy of the kind employed by Wilson and Nixon is no longer an option. Interagency reviews have become ritualized, the media follow negotiating gambits closely, and even if secrecy can be maintained in Washington, leaks have now become commonplace in Moscow and other capitals. Attempts to bypass the secretary of state, as demonstrated by the awkward exclusion of Robert Lansing and William Rogers from arms control negotiations, seem a thing of the past: since the Ford administration presidents have relied primarily on secretaries of state to push arms control treaties to closure.

Other tactics once employed in pursuit of executive branch cohesion are also implausible today. It is inconceivable that future heads of U.S. delegations will pride themselves on their near complete lack of oversight from Washington, as Charles Evans Hughes and Henry L. Stimson did while negotiating naval treaties on behalf of the United States. Furthermore, future presidents who choose to hold the joint chiefs at arm's length during arms control negotiations, as Kennedy did, will do so at great risk.

With exclusionary tactics no longer a reliable option, presidents appear stuck for the foreseeable future with an inherently untidy and potentially fractious interagency process. If the president chooses his closest advisers and key cabinet officials carefully, he will not be damaged by bureaucratic infighting when he tries to convince two thirds of the Senate to consent to ratification. Presidents whose national security credentials are suspect will do well to impose order among the ranks; popular presidents representing right-of-center constituencies can afford more chaos within the official family.

A consensus within the executive branch on an arms control agreement will not be very helpful if the country at large and the Senate, in particular, are deeply divided about the value of the accord. The president's responsibility for coalition-building begins in the executive branch but must quickly orient outward to include key senators. The decentralization of power on Capitol Hill has clearly made the president's job more difficult.

In the past the critical lines of communication and consensus-building between the president and the Senate were fairly simple: starting at 1600 Pennsylvania Avenue, they ran through the secretary of state to the offices of the majority and minority leaders on Capitol Hill and then to the chairman of the Senate Foreign Relations Committee. If a lack of consensus existed within this core group, as was the case between Woodrow Wilson and Henry Cabot Lodge on the league issue, ratification was in jeopardy. When this core group supported a treaty, even the opposition of important committee chairmen proved not to be disabling. For example, the Senate consented to the ratification of the 1930 London

Naval Treaty, despite the staunch opposition of the chairman of the Committee on Naval Affairs, Frederick Hale (R-Maine). Similarly, the LTBT was ratified over the objections of the formidable Richard Russell (D-Ga.), chairman of the Armed Services Committee. As Benjamin S. Loeb notes in his case study, Russell's opposition was muted—easing the Kennedy administration's problems considerably.

In recent decades the critical lines of communication and consensus-building have become considerably more complex within the executive branch. Now consensus must be shaped with the president's national security adviser as well as with the secretary of state. Presidents also must now deal with the secretary of defense, his top aides, and the joint chiefs of staff instead of, as formerly, with the secretary of war and his top army and navy officers. In addition, the consensus should include various ambassadors serving as U.S. negotiators and the director of the U.S. Arms Control and Disarmament Agency.

Critical lines of communication and consensus-building have become even more convoluted in the legislative branch, particularly with the diffusion of power in the Senate and the decline in the stature of the Senate Foreign Relations Committee. Now, presidents in search of consensus must assiduously seek the support of the committee chairmen and ranking minority members of three key committees—Armed Services, Intelligence, and Foreign Relations—as well as the Senate leadership. Few presidents will enjoy the support of every one of these key senators. For example, in the voting on the INF Treaty, even Ronald Reagan lost the support of the ranking minority member of the Senate Foreign Relations Committee, Jesse Helms (R-N.C.), an irreconcilable opponent of arms limitation accords with the Soviet Union. Presidents, however, cannot afford many defections from the ranks of this expanded core group of senators, and none from the inner circle of Senate leaders and pivotal senators, whose opposition can cause widespread disruption in a president's consensus-building efforts.

Presidential Roles

Presidents have vastly increased their chances of securing the Senate's consent to ratification depending on the way they have gone about breaking negotiating deadlocks at home and abroad, by working with the Senate before and during the ratification debate, and by setting the terms of public debate during the Senate's deliberations. The execution of all these roles has been difficult when presidents have become too directly involved in the negotiations, as the case of Woodrow Wilson attests. Wilson decided to lead the U.S. delegation, he alone briefed members of the Senate Foreign Relations Committee upon his return from Paris, and he personally undertook a whistle-stop campaign to sway public attitudes toward the league. Indeed, Wilson was so personally invested in the league debate that when he was most in need of judicious staff support and fallback positions, he had none. At the other extreme, Calvin Coolidge's aloofness contributed heavily to the Senate's failure to consent to ratification of the Geneva Protocol in 1926. As Rodney J. McElroy shows in his case study, Coolidge allowed an agreement very similar to the one approved overwhelmingly in the Senate during the Harding administration to be bottled up in the Foreign Relations Committee for one year, and then made little discernible effort to rescue it from a surprisingly persuasive campaign waged by the U.S. chemical industry, veterans groups, and the army's Chemical Warfare Service.[34] Modern-day presidents seeking to secure the Senate's consent to ratification must operate between these two extreme cases.

A central responsibility of the president is to break deadlocks over critical issues when his official family cannot reach consensus or when negotiations are at an impasse. These decisions have invariably been made in the face of considerable political pressure from both ends of the political spectrum. When presidents have chosen to assuage domestic concerns raised by conservative circles, they have often facilitated agreements in the short run but generated problems in the longer term. A classic example is the decision made by President Kennedy late in the nuclear test ban negotiations to shift the objective from a comprehensive to a partial ban. This choice to forgo a comprehensive test ban was later regretted by Kennedy and rued by arms control supporters. Nevertheless, it was based on hard political realities at the time of decision. As Benjamin S. Loeb shows in his case study, concerns that a comprehensive test ban could not be verified and the strong misgivings of the joint chiefs reaffirmed head counts that there were not enough votes in the Senate for a complete ban on testing. In the short run Kennedy secured an important agreement, but one of the safeguards he approved in order to ease concerns of conservative critics, an aggressive program of underground tests, worked against his goal of an early comprehensive test ban.

A comparable presidential decision was President Nixon's choice during the SALT I negotiations to allow MIRVs to proceed without constraints. In this case Nixon and Kissinger harkened to the warnings of the joint chiefs as well as to powerful and conservative senators on Capitol Hill who were "passionately in favor" of MIRVs.[35] As Kissinger noted in his memoirs, at the time the Soviet Union's strategic arsenal was growing at a rate of 200–300 missiles per year while U.S. deployments were relatively static, awaiting completion of the MIRV testing program. Deployment of MIRVs was to be the means of multiplying the size of U.S. forces and countering the Kremlin's massive building program. Nixon and Kissinger decided not to pursue meaningful limits on MIRVs strenuously, a fateful judgment that, in William G. Hyland's estimation, was the "key decision in the entire history of SALT, given the difficulties that ensued trying to brake the buildups of U.S. and Soviet strategic forces."[36] Kissinger offered a more dramatic appraisal: "There can be no doubt that the age of MIRVs has doomed the SALT approach."[37]

When presidents have chosen to assuage domestic concerns expressed by liberal circles, the resulting agreements, at a

Conclusions

minimum, have faced tougher scrutiny on Capitol Hill. In extreme cases such agreements may fail to receive the support of two thirds of the Senate, as was the fate of the Geneva Protocol for almost fifty years. When this accord was first debated in the Senate in 1926, liberal sentiment strongly favored a flat prohibition against the use of chemical weapons, but the argument for military preparedness offered by the Chemical Warfare Service, the American Legion, and the Veterans of Foreign Wars carried the day. The decision by President Carter to cancel the B-1 bomber in the midst of the SALT II negotiations raised a similar outcry from the Right. As Cyrus Vance later recalled, this decision may have been right on the merits, but it constituted "a millstone around the administration's neck" during the ratification debate.[38]

There are no free rides when breaking deadlocks during critical points in the negotiating process: when presidents have chosen sides on critical issues, they have alienated important constituencies. True wisdom in the art of breaking deadlocks involves not only planning for the support of two thirds of the Senate but also making decisions that facilitate short-term agreements without badly mortgaging the future. Presidents who are masters of their craft combine these tactical and strategic skills.

Arms control agreements, like other public policy decisions, have always come with at least small mortgages. Such payments may be reflected in commitments to build new weapons or to refrain from doing so, either of which could be costly to the security of the nation. The Washington and London naval treaties avoided large public outlays for capital ship construction but required pledges not to fortify U.S. possessions in the Pacific; the ABM Treaty mandated comparable restraint in building defenses against ballistic missile attack; the INF Treaty effectively foreclosed the deployment of nuclear-armed missiles in Europe; the LTBT legitimated hundreds of underground nuclear tests; and so on. To best serve U.S. national security interests and advance the process of arms reductions, presidents must not only have the political skills to break deadlocks in ways that secure a strong domestic consensus but also have the foresight to reject mortgage payments that defeat the objectives and purposes of the agreements they sign.

A second critical role of the president in the arms control treaty ratification process is establishing the themes and the overall strategy that will ensure popular support and a favorable vote in the Senate when an agreement is reached. Presidents who neglect this responsibility invite opposing senators to fill the vacuum.

The Wilson and Harding administrations, for example, relayed messages about international negotiations directly to the public via speeches or through the newspapers. The Hoover administration had the opportunity to employ a new tool of mass communications—the radio—with the U.S. delegation to the London Naval Treaty conference broadcasting negotiating updates back to the United States, courtesy of the Columbia Broadcasting Company. By the time of the test ban negotiations, television was the ubiquitous medium for transmitting presidential messages, as well as opposing views, about arms control. Presidents would be wise not to wait until the ratification debate is at hand to make public addresses that build consensus and stress central themes. Given the executive branch's other preoccupations, however, the prospect of a treaty-signing ceremony has usually been needed to focus its members on the desirability of framing the terms of debate.

As Janne E. Nolan recounts in her case study, the INF negotiations began as an exercise in cynicism; they ended as an object lesson in the effective use of the media to set the terms of debate for treaty negotiation and ratification. The Reagan White House publicized clear and compelling objectives at the outset of the negotiations and then was able to make their achievement the centerpiece of its ratification campaign. It was far easier to rally congressional and public support behind the goal of deep reductions than the vague notions of greater stability and predictability that were central to the Carter administration's case for SALT II.

President Carter and his advisers generally chose to refrain from making exaggerated claims for the SALT II Treaty in their public speeches and congressional testimony.[39] In light of the treaty's "modest but useful" accomplishments, administration officials would have had difficulty adopting a hard sell. President Kennedy chose to build the case for the LTBT as a hopeful first step. The administration's lead witness, Secretary of State Dean Rusk, rejected a defense of the treaty in grandiose themes and stressed the more modest accomplishments of slowing the spiral of the nuclear arms race, containing the spread of these weapons, and reducing fallout.[40] Secretary of State Henry L. Stimson adopted a similarly low-key approach in his defense of the 1930 London Naval Treaty.[41]

In contrast, President Nixon chose to make strong claims for the SALT I accords, which he characterized as central symbols of how the U.S.-Soviet relationship had changed from confrontation to negotiation. The president and Henry Kissinger equated the accords with the promotion of nothing less than world peace.[42] In Senate testimony Secretary of State William Rogers hailed the agreements as breaking the "action-reaction" phenomenon that fueled the nuclear arms race.[43] The Harding administration adopted similar rhetorical tactics in rallying Senate support for the Five-Power Naval treaty, with Secretary of State Hughes declaring that the accord "ends, absolutely ends, the race in competition in naval armament.[44]

The Harding administration did not have to make grandiose claims for the Washington treaties, which provided tangible benefits at a time of relative peace and tranquility in international affairs. In contrast, administrations that have offered modest characterizations of treaties when international conditions appeared threatening have run the risk of being defeated by opponents who have had little to lose by overstating their case. Treaty advocates who take their cues from the president can exaggerate an agreement's accomplishments, the negative consequences of failing to ratify it, or both. In the case of the Carter administration, low-key approaches were adopted on both fronts. Meanwhile, Jimmy Carter steadily lost ground to vocal opponents of SALT II throughout the ratification debate.

Presidents who have chosen to make strong claims for arms control agreements have positioned themselves so as to place their opponents on the defensive and to capture the high ground in congressional and public debates. This approach has lacked credibility, however, when the agreement's benefits have been undeniably modest and when executive branch warnings about the terrible consequences of a failure to ratify have lacked plausibility. Serious downside risks have been associated with overstating an agreement's worth—in particular, public disenchantment with the arms control process—when, inevitably, the promised benefits (such as peace dividends) have not been achieved. Still, future presidents will be drawn to overselling, in part because of the perceived needs of the moment, in part because the backlash from unfulfilled expectations invariably falls on succeeding administrations.

Presidents who have been able to negotiate arms control treaties of compelling worth have clearly been in the best position to convince the Senate and the public of their value. As Alan Platt notes in his case study of the ABM Treaty, given the considerable cost of, technical difficulties with, and public opposition to ballistic missile defenses, a treaty that permitted the United States to catch up to the Soviet Union and deploy equal but low numbers of defensive deployments appeared to be a treaty well worth having. Similarly, when President Reagan was able to offer the complete abolition of entire classes of nuclear-tipped missiles in the INF Treaty, most senators found counterarguments about damage to nuclear weapons employment policies and doctrine to be unpersuasive.

Just as substantive achievement has been a strong argument

for ratification, minimal achievement has occasionally led to great difficulties in the Senate. The Threshold Test Ban Treaty and the Peaceful Nuclear Explosions Treaty, negotiated by presidents Nixon and Ford, respectively, remained on the Senate's calendar for more than a decade before garnering the Senate's consent to ratification. While there were a number of reasons for this delay, including concerns over verification, a primary cause for the treaties' lengthy deferral was the lack of compelling reasons for entry into force.

Arms control treaties with compelling rationales have allowed presidents to reinforce their standing or to gain new standing during the treaty ratification process. They have provided presidents with the option of not having to make exaggerated claims that would have fostered subsequent public disaffection. As the Coolidge administration's mishandling of Senate consideration of the Geneva Protocol suggests, however, substance has not been a substitute for process. Presidential skills in working effectively with the Senate to secure ratification have been essential. The negotiation of substantive treaties has made the president's task simpler while increasing the margin for error in dealing with the legislative branch.

The third critical role of the president in the arms control treaty ratification process, smoothing relations with the legislative branch, is considered below.

Executive-Congressional Relations

President Richard M. Nixon and his principal adviser, Henry Kissinger, kept senators at arm's length during the entire SALT I negotiations. Repeated efforts by members of the Senate Foreign Relations Committee and its Arms Control Subcommittee to receive briefings from the administration were rebuffed.[45] It was not until after the SALT I accords were signed that members of Congress were invited to the Old Executive Office Building to be briefed about agreements negotiated without their input. Nevertheless, this strategy met with a remarkable degree of success: senators, administration officials, and even U.S. negotiating team members groused about their exclusion, but in the end they acquiesced in supporting the accords.

Similar tactics backfired when Woodrow Wilson employed them fifty years earlier in negotiating the Treaty of Versailles. As William C. Widenor notes in his case study, while in Paris Wilson largely ignored the Senate, his cabinet, and all but one of his negotiating team, Colonel Edward House. He made one attempt to elicit from Senator Lodge suggestions for changes in the draft League Covenant, an approach that Lodge rebuffed. While making concession after concession to other delegations in Paris, Wilson yielded only once to the entreaties from Americans back home, responding affirmatively to the cablegram advice of former President William Howard Taft that several changes be made in the League Covenant, including the insertion of language formally recognizing the Monroe Doctrine. When Wilson finally left France, he was determined not to compromise further.[46]

President Nixon dealt with the pressure building in the Senate as a result of his negotiating decisions and exclusionary tactics by bargaining with Henry M. Jackson during the ratification process and supporting an amendment requiring that future treaties not limit the United States to levels of intercontinental strategic forces inferior to those of the Soviet Union. President Wilson dealt with the pressure building in the Senate by standing fast and by taking his case to the voters. In so doing, Wilson helped defeat that which he worked so hard to achieve while breaking himself in the process.

Wilson's tactics provide an object lesson in how not to deal with the Senate's penchant for adding reservations and understandings to treaty texts. In the dispute over the league Wilson argued that reservations were unnecessary because their meaning was inherent in the treaty text and that other states might add their own reservations in response to the Senate's action. The weakness of Wilson's argument suggests that there were deeper reasons behind his obstinacy: after all, if the Senate's reservations merely reaffirmed existing obligations, there was no need to oppose the initiatives and no reason for other states to react negatively to them.

Successful presidents have had the political sensitivity and strategic sense to know when to stand fast and when to compromise in order to convince sixty-seven senators to consent to treaty ratification. Successful senators wishing to add reservations or amendments to treaty texts have known the value of indirect approaches that appeal to high-minded ideals, national traditions, and Senate prerogatives. The task of treaty opponents has been aided by a change in the Senate's standing rules in 1868 allowing all "motions and questions" regarding treaties to pass with a simple majority instead of a two-thirds majority vote.

Most reservations, understandings, and conditions passed by the Senate have not directly undercut the executive branch's position or required a major course correction in future negotiations. Reservations of this kind have usually been the product of quiet negotiations between key senators and White House officials and have served as the mortar by which overwhelming votes for ratification have been built. For example, during debate over the Washington Naval treaties, the Harding administration calmed public fears by accepting a reservation offered by Senator Frank Brandegee (R-Conn.), which stated that the United States was accepting no commitments to use armed force abroad or to join alliances—critically contentious issues during the League of Nations debate three years earlier. Likewise, the Hoover administration dealt with criticism over its failure to provide the Senate with a complete negotiating record of the London Naval Treaty by consenting to a reservation that no documents or side agreements existed that modified treaty provisions.

The differences between Woodrow Wilson and Henry Cabot Lodge over the League of Nations were too deep to be bridged in this way. Lodge's tactics provide a textbook case of how to add reservations against the will of the chief executive. He advised the irreconcilable wing of his party that he did "not think it would be wise for us at this stage to make it a party issue, not to confront it with a blank negative."[47] Instead, he crafted reservations that were designed to appeal to the broadest coalition possible.

With regard to the momentous controversy over Article 10 of the League Covenant, Lodge's reservation required congressional assent before U.S. military forces could be used in support of the league's obligation to "preserve as against external aggression the territorial integrity and existing political independence" of member states. For good measure, Lodge added reservations providing for the unconditional right of withdrawal from the league, the right to declare certain questions within the sole jurisdiction of the United States, and the right to decline arbitration over any question relating to the Monroe Doctrine. By defining the issue in terms of U.S. constitutional law and national tradition, Lodge denied Wilson exclusive possession of the moral high ground in the league debate.

The passage of the Jackson amendment in the debate over SALT I constituted another masterful senatorial performance. Jackson was deeply troubled by Nixon and Kissinger's methods of diplomacy and by the accords they reached but he was faced with the clear prospect of the Senate's consent. He quickly succeeded in capturing the high ground of political debate by asking his colleagues the seemingly irrefutable question "What is wrong with parity?"[48] Despite the implicit criticism in the Jackson amendment, Nixon and Kissinger wisely chose not to oppose this pivotal senator's efforts, choosing instead to haggle in private over the language of the amendment to be introduced. From Jackson's perspective, passage of a simple amendment demanding equality made the best out of a bad bargain while positioning its author to become the arbiter of subsequent agreements.

As Janne E. Nolan notes in her case study, Senator Robert Byrd (D-W.Va.) and his allies were similarly astute in demanding, as the price of the Senate's consent to the INF Treaty, the implicit repudiation of the Reagan admininstration's previous unilateral reinterpretation of the ABM Treaty. Seeking to loosen the ABM Treaty's strict constraints against testing, some administration officials had concocted—and the president had approved—a "broad" interpretation of the treaty's terms, which was at considerable variance with the testimony of Nixon administration officials during the Senate's treaty ratification hearings.

With a date already set for a summit signing ceremony in Moscow, Byrd engineered a vote stipulating that the Senate's advice and consent was based on the executive branch's prior testimony and that any reinterpretation of the INF Treaty would require the Senate's consent. Even senators supportive of the Strategic Defense Initiative (the program geared toward deployment of space-based defenses, which ultimately would necessitate violations of the ABM Treaty) found it difficult to oppose an appeal based on common sense, constitutional law, and the Senate's prerogatives. Despite the implicit rejection of its position on the ABM Treaty, the Reagan administration opted for a treaty-signing ceremony in Moscow and accepted Senator Byrd's proposal.

Senate Consultation

By properly informing and consulting the Senate about the status of negotiations, the executive branch can reduce the prospect of embarrassing reservations or crippling amendments passing during a treaty ratification debate. Not all senators can be involved in the takeoff, and some will choose not to be in on the landing. Yet presidents who wish to make the latter as smooth as possible have little choice but to involve key senators early in the negotiating process. In any event, wholesale exclusion of the Senate of the kind practiced by presidents Nixon and Wilson is no longer a viable option.

As William C. Widenor notes in his case study, Wilson's exclusionary tactics were evident in his choice of a negotiating team. Wilson elected to bring a team of only four commissioners to Paris, only one of whom, Henry White, was a Republican. Moreover, White's background was in diplomacy, not politics. Wilson did not invite any senators to serve on the U.S. delegation, and before the negotiations began, an effort led by Albert Cummins (R-Iowa) to have eight senators go to Paris to acquaint themselves with the negotiations was shelved on procedural grounds.[49] Republican stalwarts like former President William Howard Taft were also left on the sidelines.

The Harding administration chose a far different approach for the Washington Conference, with Secretary of State Hughes enlisting the direct participation of Henry Cabot Lodge and the minority leader of the Senate, Oscar W. Underwood, who was also a member of the Foreign Relations Committee. As Thomas H. Buckley notes, by choosing senators of this stature to serve with him, Hughes ensured bipartisan support and completely undercut the Senate's irreconcilables. Moreover, including both the majority and minority leaders excused Harding and Hughes from inviting the prime instigator of the talks, Senator William Borah, who was seen as being "too independent, impulsive, and unpredictable."[50]

Similarly, the Hoover administration promoted consensus by enlisting the participation of two senators on the Foreign Relations Committee, Joseph Robinson (D-Ark.) and David Reed (R-Pa.), to serve on the U.S. delegation to the London Naval Treaty negotiations. Robinson was the senate minority leader; Reed was the chairman of the Senate Committee on Military Affairs. Hoover and Secretary of State Stimson were constrained in their choices, since Borah had by then become chairman of the Foreign Relations Committee and since the committee's ranking majority and minority members, in addition to the chairman of the Naval Affairs Committee, were opposed to the prospective treaty. Robinson and Reed proved to be instrumental in building a consensus in the Senate supportive of the agreement reached in London.

Sitting members of Congress have not served as delegates to international security negotiations since the San Francisco Conference at which the United Nations Charter was negotiated. The prolonged and increasingly complex nature of arms control talks and the greater demands of congressional incumbency preclude senators from becoming directly involved in this way. Instead, consensus-building and executive branch consultations with senators have been grounded in formal briefings, private chats, and occasional visits by congressional delegations to the negotiations.

Presidents who have worked assiduously and deftly at encouraging the support of senators during the negotiations have been better positioned to reap rewards during ratification debates. President Carter was often criticized for his habit of detailed management, but this trait was also shared by President Kennedy in his pursuit of sixty-seven votes for the LTBT. As Benjamin S. Loeb notes in his case study, Kennedy's attention to detail was extraordinary, including daily reviews of detailed negotiating accounts and numerous White House meetings and telephone calls to enlist the support of senators.[51] Judging from Kennedy's performance, micro-management in the pursuit of a consensus in the Senate need not be counterproductive. Indeed, it can be quite helpful as long as the president has sure political instincts and astute knowledge of the senators to be courted.

In 1985 a formal mechanism to promote Senate involvement was arranged between Senator Byrd and the Reagan White House, building on prior arrangements established in 1977 but which later fell into disuse. Arms control observer groups were formed in both houses of Congress to receive briefings and visit delegations on a regular basis. The observer group in the Senate, which included leading figures from the Foreign Relations, Armed Services, and Intelligence committees, began to assume a collective identity as a result of its many briefings and trips. These observers can serve as a sounding board for negotiating initiatives and as an early warning system to sensitize the executive branch about the degree of importance senators are likely to attach to particular issues. Senate observers may also serve to reaffirm and thereby strengthen executive branch positions during their frequent meetings with Soviet delegations.

When senators have not considered themselves meaningfully consulted by the executive branch, or when consultations have not led to negotiating initiatives preferred by senators, the legislative branch has had a wide variety of responses. One important instrument of suasion has been the congressional resolution. During the SALT I negotiations, sense of the Senate resolutions were passed expressing that body's interest in constraining MIRVs and suspending offensive and defensive strategic deployments. A resolution offered by Senator Borah for 50 percent cuts in naval building programs was instrumental in convincing the incoming Harding administration to embrace the cause of disarmament, and the nuclear freeze resolutions introduced in both houses of Congress helped persuade the Reagan administration to restart negotiations on nuclear weapons.

When such resolutions have failed to produce their desired effects, Congress has employed the power of the purse to influence the executive branch's negotiating objectives. The Senate has been reluctant to stop weapons systems that the executive branch has claimed are necessary for negotiating leverage, if not U.S. security. Yet the more the White House has rejected congressional sentiment on preferred negotiating outcomes, the more it has invited an assertive response on defense authorization and appropriation bills.

The Nixon administration experienced this action-reaction phenomenon when its funding requests for a twelve-site continental missile defense system barely survived in the Senate. As a result, Nixon and Kissinger had little choice but to negotiate tight constraints on ballistic missile defenses in the ABM Treaty. Similarly, when Reagan administration officials attempted to replace the ABM Treaty with space-based defenses, congressional majorities refused to permit funding for the necessary testing. During the better part of the Reagan administration, the fervor of some top officials to dispense with existing arms control agreements was matched by congressional initiatives to cut the Pentagon's strategic modernization programs.

There are many ways for senators to convey messages to an inattentive White House. When Woodrow Wilson returned from a break in the Paris negotiations to defend his handiwork and proclaim his "fighting blood" in Henry Cabot Lodge's hometown, the Senate majority leader countered with a round-robin letter, signed by thirty-nine Senate Republicans, highlighting concerns about the draft League Covenant. Henry M. Jackson adopted a more indirect approach in his struggle against SALT II, using the hearings on Paul C. Warnke's nomination to be President Carter's chief SALT II negotiator as a platform to air concerns over the new administration's lack of toughness in dealing with the Kremlin. Although Warnke was confirmed, Jackson's allies persuaded more than one third of the Senate to vote against him, a clear signal of trouble to come on any treaty votes. Warnke resigned before the conclusion of the SALT II negotiations, in part to remove himself as a divisive issue in the Senate's debate, but by this time Jackson's bill of particulars against the treaty had grown considerably.[52]

Given all of the devices disgruntled senators and distinguished experts can use against a treaty, presidents have been well advised to consult early and often with the majority and minority leaders and with pivotal senators and key public figures. Ratification debates are replete with examples of how such individuals have effectively opposed agreements in which they had no personal stake but convincingly supported treaties to which they had contributed in some way. The Reagan administration alone provides several examples of this phenomenon. Senator John Tower and Ambassador Richard

Burt had been deep skeptics of arms control during the Carter administration but became effective negotiators of the START (Strategic Arms Reduction Talks) agreement; Paul H. Nitze and Lieutenant General Edward Rowny, ardent critics of SALT II, were given negotiating portfolios in the Reagan administration and became supporters of the INF Treaty, despite the clear damage that would ensue, some critics argued, to U.S. nuclear strategy and doctrine. Of course, the reverse is also true, as typified by Henry Kissinger, who has expressed great unease about every nuclear arms control treaty negotiated since he left office.

A classic case of this variation on the time-honored maxim "Where you stand depends on where you sit" is that of Henry Cabot Lodge. This ardent nationalist and ally of then-Vice President Theodore Roosevelt was a staunch supporter of the 1898 peace treaty with Spain that ceded the Philippine Islands to the United States. In a letter to Roosevelt about the bruising treaty debate Lodge wrote: "I cannot think calmly of the rejection of that Treaty by a little more than one-third of the Senate. It would be a repudiation of the President and humiliation of the whole country in the eyes of the world, and would show we are unfit as a nation to enter into great questions of foreign policy."[53]

Little more than twenty years later, driven by a personal hatred of Wilson and the same nationalist tendencies that led him to support the annexation of the Philippines, Lodge conspired to shelve the League Covenant, counting on Wilson's inflexibility to secure this result. In so doing, he helped engineer the very type of damage he had feared during the debate over the peace treaty with Spain. Then, having been chosen as a U.S. delegate to the Washington Conference, Lodge again became a powerful force for ratification in the Senate, arguing against efforts by irreconcilables to resurrect some of the same reservations employed so successfully against the League Covenant. In one heated exchange on the Senate floor irreconcilable James Reed (D-Mo.) argued that it was foolish for Lodge to oppose language he once championed. Lodge replied: "It may strike the Senator as foolish. He did not make [the treaty]."[54]

Coalition-Building and Safeguards

Historically, irreconcilable opposition in the Senate to arms control agreements has been insufficient to block entry into force: men such as Jesse Helms and William E. Borah are oppositionists by nature, not politicians capable of building a coalition of thirty-four senators. At the same time, ardent treaty supporters have usually been too few to secure the Senate's consent. The battle between presidents and irreconcilables has usually been waged over an uncommitted block of pro-defense or nationalist-minded senators, leery of both limitations on U.S. forces and foreign entanglements. A treaty's fate has been determined by whether the president or the principled opposition has been able to build a coalition with this crucial block of uncommitted senators.

In the contest over the League of Nations it was Henry Cabot Lodge rather than Woodrow Wilson who forged this crucial alliance; and in the bitter debate over SALT II Jimmy Carter was close to failure before the Soviet invasion of Afghanistan made the possibility of coalition-building moot. In both instances irreconcilable treaty opponents were led by a senator of sufficient standing, seniority, and substance to be able to compete successfully with the White House for uncommitted votes. Without the leadership of such a pivotal senator irreconcilables have little hope of blocking a president's wishes.

Very few senators have been in a position to make or break arms control treaties. Listing the handful that were in a position to play this role in the case studies reviewed in this volume—Lodge, Dirksen, Russell, Jackson, Howard Baker, and Sam Nunn—suggests the importance for the White House of building bridges early in the negotiating process with the Senate leader of the opposing party and with a pivotal senator (if one exists) on the Armed Services Committee or the Foreign Relations Committee.

Coalition-building between presidents and pivotal senators has rarely been consummated during the course of negotiations; typically, this has been a period in which presidents have tried to address at least some of the concerns expressed by key senators while the latter maintained lines of communication with both the executive branch and irreconcilable treaty opponents. It was the advent of ratification hearings that first presented opportunities for presidents and pivotal senators to expound central themes and to explore private deals to bridge their public differences.

Indeed, the way in which hearings have been organized has reflected the struggle between the White House and key senators over the public airing of competing themes. The first time that the Senate committee hearings and floor debates were made open for public consumption was during the debate over the League of Nations, courtesy of Senator Lodge. For the 1930 London Naval Treaty the Senate Foreign Relations and Naval Affairs committees held concurrent hearings, with divergent appraisals of the accord. During the LTBT ratification debate, the Foreign Relations Committee invited members of the Armed Services Committee and the Joint Committee on Atomic Energy to attend its hearings, but the Armed Services Committee also conducted separate reviews of the treaty's military implications, a practice that has since become standard. Since the SALT II Treaty another set of hearings has been conducted by the Senate's Select Committee on Intelligence.

Successful efforts at coalition-building between the White House and key senators have usually been unveiled formally on the Senate floor, after committee hearings have provided testimony concerning the military risks associated with the agreement in question. Here, for example, at the eleventh hour, Everett Dirksen and Henry M. Jackson pledged their support for the LTBT, and after passage of his amendment, Jackson decided to support the SALT I Interim Agreement.

The crucial mechanism for coalition-building in these and other instances has been safeguards, which have been designed to minimize the risks presumed to be associated with treaty commitments, especially with agreed constraints on U.S. military programs, and the potential of noncompliance by other signatories. In the debate over the League, Wilson refused to negotiate a package of assurances with Lodge, so the latter introduced them in the form of reservations. During the final stages of the LTBT debate, Kennedy agreed to four safeguards brokered by Senator Jackson on behalf of the Joint Chiefs: funds for an aggressive underground test program, maintenance of modern nuclear weapons laboratories and programs, preparations for resumed atmospheric tests in the event of Soviet noncompliance, and improved intelligence collection efforts.[55]

The SALT I accords were accompanied by an extremely large safeguards package, starting with the Nixon administration's decision to refrain from limiting MIRVs in the Interim Agreement in order to counter Soviet strategic modernization programs and mollify conservative critics concerned about trends in the strategic balance. In addition, the joint chiefs, Pentagon civilians, and pro-defense senators secured three broad assurances from the executive and legislative branches: improved intelligence collection efforts to provide high confidence in monitoring Soviet compliance, "aggressive improvements and modernization programs," including planning for rapid force augmentation, if needed, and vigorous research and development programs.[56] In specific terms, Secretary of Defense Melvin Laird tallied the price for the SALT I accords as funding for the Trident submarine program, the B-1 bomber, strategic defenses permitted by the ABM Treaty, and sea-launched cruise missiles.[57]

Planned safeguards for the SALT II Treaty were far more modest. The prospect of a difficult Senate debate undoubtedly contributed to the Carter administration's decisions to press ahead with a large variant of the MX missile and a mobile basing scheme for it, programs that elicited statements of concern from Soviet negotiators. Nor could President Carter's commitments toward a futuristic bomber, several new cruise missile variants, and long-range theater nuclear forces be considered in isolation from the need to shore up Senate support for the beleaguered treaty. Jimmy Carter, however, had previously decided to kill the B-1, cut defense spending, and forgo deployments of enhanced radiation weapons—decisions that provided essential ammunition to opponents of SALT II. A formal safeguards agreement accompanying the treaty was never consummated, since Soviet misbehavior obviated the effort.

In stark contrast with the safeguards packages negotiated among White House staff, Pentagon officials, and pivotal senators from the LTBT to the SALT II treaties, Senate consent to the INF Treaty was accompanied by no such assurances. The absence of formal commitments was clearly related to the unwillingness of America's European allies to accept deployments of new nuclear weapons systems—the traditional means of offsetting negotiated reductions or limitations. This episode constitutes a reminder that safeguards have not always been required for treaty ratification, particularly during periods of fiscal austerity and improved international relations. The executive branch did not ask for, and the Senate did not demand, safeguards for the Washington and London naval treaties.

Clearly, one of the most important tests of leadership and political skill facing a president is the negotiation of safeguards with pivotal senators and key Pentagon officials. Failure to negotiate a safeguards package can result in solidifying Senate opposition to a treaty; an overly generous safeguards package can cement a two-thirds majority vote but make future agreements more difficult to negotiate and less meaningful. Wilson erred on one side during the league debate: by electing not to set aside personal enmities and build bridges with Lodge, Wilson allowed his nemesis to form a coalition between mild reservationists and irreconcilables. Nixon and Kissinger committed the opposite error in the

SALT I Interim Agreement, undermining the strategic arms reduction process by safeguarding deployments of MIRVs and nuclear-armed cruise missiles.

Wilson and Nixon invited these negative consequences during ratification debates because they kept the Senate at arm's length during the preceding negotiations. Yet presidents who avoid repeating this error may still face difficult choices regarding safeguards, since consultations alone cannot guarantee the support of the joint chiefs and two thirds of the senators present and voting. At the eleventh hour the essence of clarity is knowing what proposed safeguards are necessary to carry the chiefs and a sufficient number of undecided senators and what proposed safeguards badly undermine the objectives and purposes of the treaty in question. Presidents must then make proper, balanced judgments about which safeguards to bless and which to oppose during the treaty ratification process.

These may be the most difficult choices a president makes. After all, an arms control treaty constitutes a way station on the course toward a preferred end state; it should not only stand on its own merits but also facilitate subsequent steps required to fulfill its promise. The negotiating trade-offs inevitably reflected in hard bargaining with senators may be justified if the basis has thereby been laid for better agreements in the future and if they accord with an administration's overall military strategy. No step can be taken, however, if one third plus one of the senators present and voting disagree. Thus, another set of trade-offs may be required, as when John F. Kennedy accepted the safeguard of aggressive underground testing, thereby making the possibility of near-term negotiation of a comprehensive test ban treaty remote.

In this perverse way arms control agreements can themselves contribute to the arms race. The failure, however, may be one of faulty strategic judgment as well as hard political reality. Distinctions between the two will be easier to make if future debates over safeguards are framed in terms of whether the proposed steps would undermine basic objectives and purposes. For example, in the case of the LTBT, improved intelligence collection efforts, the maintenance of modern laboratories, and a readiness to resume atmospheric testing did not undercut Kennedy's cherished objective of a comprehensive test ban; the commitment to undertake an extensive program of underground tests did. Yet even this would not necessarily have barred such a ban if subsequent presidents had been willing to make it a high enough priority. The Nixon administration's acceptance of safeguards did not jeopardize the ABM Treaty, but it did jeopardize the long-term process of strategic arms reductions ostensibly launched by the Interim Agreement. Given safeguards such as those accepted, the SALT II Treaty was marked at birth for a bitterly contentious Senate debate.

Framing presidential alternatives as choices between short-term political necessities and long-term negotiating objectives does not resolve the White House's dilemma over safeguards: difficult choices still have to be made, ideally by presidents who combine tactical vote-counting prowess with sound strategic sense. If presidents will consider the questions facing them in this way, however, some unhelpful safeguards may be avoided and the resulting damage lessened. That being said, if it becomes apparent that safeguards deeply injurious to the basic objectives and purposes of an agreement are the price of ratification, presidents will be hard-pressed to resist opting for short-term accomplishments.

Public Opinion and the Role of Interest Groups

Woodrow Wilson, America's most renowned educator-turned-president, provided the clearest lessons for posterity about the role of public opinion in the treaty ratification process. Unfortunately for backers of the League of Nations, Wilson invariably demonstrated how not to proceed. Presidents who wish to solicit the Senate's consent to treaty ratification need to avoid two things above all else: appearing to be partisan and affronting the Senate's prerogatives.[58] Wilson's actions offended the Senate on both counts; as William C. Widenor's case study demonstrates, Wilson refused to acknowledge the Senate's legitimate role in attaching reservations and understandings to a treaty text, and he turned a policy debate that was inherently above politics into a partisan issue.

Had Wilson sought the advice of former President William Howard Taft, he might have avoided what Arthur S. Link has called the "supreme" error of making the League issue "a hostage of party loyalty and politics."[59] Taft had earlier concluded arbitration treaties with Great Britain and France, which were heavily amended by the Senate to exclude issues relating to aliens, the territorial integrity of the United States, indebtedness questions, anything having to do with the Monroe Doctrine, and a vague category of "governmental policy" issues. Taft refused to accept these changes, shelving the treaties rather than renegotiating them. He took his case to the people, and lost handily. Taft learned to his chagrin that eleventh-hour appeals to the public over the heads of their elected representatives face extremely long odds on treaty ratification issues. Wilson, having declined to solicit Taft's advice during the ratification debate, after declining to add him to the U.S. negotiating team, proceeded to repeat the former president's mistakes, but for much higher stakes and on a far grander scale.

Treaties are ratified or blocked in the Senate, not at the ballot box. Yet Wilson repeatedly scorned deal-making with the Republican majority leader and chairman of the Senate Foreign Relations Committee; he visited personally with a pitifully small number of Republican senators, and he rejected all proposals for reservations. Having helped to create polarities rather than working coalitions in the Senate, Wilson then embarked on a cross-country speaking tour to sway public opinion—a futile and, for him, life-threatening gesture.

Senators have considerably more freedom to cast their votes

on arms control treaties than on issues of lesser magnitude. Senatorial latitude derives in large part from the intrinsic importance of these issues: the electorate is likely to be more forgiving of an unpopular vote on an arms control treaty based on principle than of a vote on a local dam or water project. Conversely, because of the perceived importance of treaty ratification votes, any hint of vote-trading for concessions on unrelated issues, such as the nomination of judges or the support of public works projects of statewide interest, can discredit a senator at the polls.

Senators also have considerable leeway in casting their votes on arms control treaty ratification issues because of the intrinsic complexity of these issues and the public's general inclination to leave such important matters to the "experts." Only when the stakes associated with the fate of an agreement are perceived to be particularly high or the outcome in considerable doubt, as in the cases of the League of Nations and the SALT II Treaty, has public interest overridden a natural deference to expertise. In such cases divisions within the ranks of experts has also encouraged public deliberation. Thus, although senators cannot be unaffected by voter sentiment on arms control treaties, they need not respond slavishly to it either.

Senators engaged in difficult reelection campaigns in states in which alleged Soviet misconduct has constituted a potent electoral issue have obviously been more inclined to respond to voter sentiment than those who have been reelected by comfortable margins and who have accumulated large war chests for future campaigns. In the SALT II debate, for example, Senator Richard Stone (D-Fla.) broke ranks with the Democratic majority on the Foreign Relations Committee, opposing the treaty on the grounds that it provided too many advantages to the Soviet Union while not providing for "genuine" arms reductions.[60] In committee hearings Stone focused on tangential issues relating to Soviet military operations in the Western Hemisphere, especially in Cuba. More important, the committee's chairman, Frank Church, helped to elevate the importance of the Soviet "combat" brigade in Cuba by announcing its presence while on the campaign trail in Idaho.

Both Stone and Church lost their reelection battles, a fact suggesting that tactical shifts in ratification debates may not be helpful at the polls; long-standing supporters can easily feel offended by such changes, and voters inclined to vote for another candidate may be unlikely to be swayed by votes cast on the perceived basis of political expediency.[61] Nor have senators with presidential ambitions been able to parlay participation in arms control treaty ratification debates toward achievement of their objective, as Barry Goldwater, Henry M. Jackson, Howard Baker, Robert Dole (R-Kans.), John Glenn (D-Ohio), and others can attest. The voting public may be uneasy about negotiating with the Soviet Union, but they are also uncomfortable with national candidates who oppose arms control.

Despite this record, presidential hopefuls in the Senate have found treaty ratification debates to be a useful springboard to gain national attention and to highlight issues for anticipated political campaigns. Moreover, treaty ratification debates can become important fund-raising vehicles for political candidates and for interest groups committed to support or oppose the agreements in question. Thus, as Dan Caldwell shows in his case study, the conservative movement gained new vitality with the Panama Canal and SALT II treaty debates.

These activities have had considerable repercussions, even if they have not resulted in changes during roll-call votes. The politics of arms control treaty ratification matters most for interest groups and for selected senators running for reelection or for higher office. If senators are skillful enough in opposing or supporting a treaty, they can perhaps gain the media spotlight, acquire additional leverage with the executive branch, secure commitments to specific weapons systems and future negotiating tactics, and build large war chests and mailing lists for subsequent political campaigns.

In the most narrow sense, however, the politics of treaty ratification are virtually a closed loop: the only votes that count are in the Senate, not on the hustings, where Taft, Wilson, and Carter searched for them in vain. Public opinion usually provides the background and theme music for the Senate's deliberations; rarely does it alter specific votes. During arms control negotiations, public opinion can build for a successful result, as was the case for the Washington Naval treaties, the Limited Test Ban Treaty, and the ABM Treaty. Yet as the SALT II Treaty case indicates, when Americans became increasingly troubled about Soviet behavior during the course of negotiations, public pressures grew against the treaty being negotiated. The ratification process then became a Senate and public referendum on the state of U.S.-Soviet relations. In such instances the executive branch has tried to mold public opinion concerning the treaty in question, but in successful efforts the primary focus has remained on influencing the votes of individual senators. Efforts to shape public opinion by the executive branch have remained extremely important, however, if for no other reason than to counter anti-treaty campaigns: without strenuous efforts by the executive branch, critics can establish the terms of debate, particularly through sophisticated media campaigns that drive up negative perceptions of the treaty in question.

Efforts to sway public opinion help reinforce the executive branch's efforts on Capitol Hill, but they cannot substitute for them. Some senators may be influenced by a select group of influential citizens whose judgment they respect, but few will cast critical votes on which hang the life or death of treaties primarily on the basis of public sentiment. The inclination of most senators not to be tied to polling data was particularly evident in the case of the Panama Canal treaties, which garnered the support of two thirds of the Senate and less than 30 percent of the general public.[62]

Senators cannot be asked to vote against popular sentiment too often, however, and it was Jimmy Carter's misfortune as well as accomplishment to have negotiated seriatim the

Panama Canal treaties and the SALT II Treaty. During the harsh Senate debate over the prospective "giveaway" of the canal, the Carter administration was able to solicit the backing of former President Gerald Ford and such luminaries in the national security firmament as Nelson Rockefeller, Matthew Ridgway, Paul H. Nitze and William C. Westmoreland. In addition, popular figures such as John Wayne were enlisted to support ratification. In the divisive debate over SALT II President Carter was unable to secure such help.

The role of public figures and Republican stalwarts in support of the unpopular Panama Canal treaties attests to the virtues of enlisting commanding or popular figures in ratification debates. Even if the formation of distinguished citizens' committees does not influence Senate voting, it still can provide important bipartisan support and protective cover to the executive branch and a counterweight to negative public opinion. In the case of the canal treaties, the citizens' panel included former secretaries of defense Clark Clifford and Melvin Laird as well as such pillars of the establishment as John J. McCloy and Douglas Dillon.

Distinguished citizens' committees—the League to Enforce Peace and the Committee to Defend America by Aiding the Allies—fulfilled similar roles at critical junctures in World Wars I and II. Presidents wishing to convey bipartisan and broad support for arms control agreements have occasionally adopted this time-honored practice. Warren G. Harding's advisory commission for the Washington Conference was headed by former Senator George Sutherland (R-Utah) and included Herbert Hoover, John L. Lewis, General John J. Pershing, and Theodore Roosevelt, Jr. President Kennedy worked behind the scenes to create the high-powered Citizens' Committee for a Nuclear Test Ban. During the Carter administration, another group of distinguished citizens was formed, Americans for SALT.

Despite its considerable efforts, Americans for SALT was outspent and otherwise overmatched by an array of public education and lobbying groups that made the defeat of the

SALT II Treaty a high priority. The most prominent public education group, the Committee on the Present Danger, consisted of prominent critics of détente and arms control from both political parties. Several of their most effective representatives, like Paul H. Nitze and Admiral Elmo Zumwalt, Jr., had been associated with the SALT I negotiations during the Nixon administration.

The Committee on the Present Danger competed effectively with the Carter administration in setting the terms of debate on ratification. Many of its prominent associates had close ties with senators; others were widely recognized experts whose views carried considerable weight in policy circles. As a result, the arguments set forth in committee pamphlets were echoed on Capitol Hill, and the committee's representatives were given many opportunities to present the case against SALT II in congressional hearings and in the media.

Outside of the Washington Beltway the most effective lobbying group against SALT II was the American Security Council, which at the peak of its campaign had a full-time staff of 106 working against ratification. Its television documentaries, *Peace Through Strength*, *The Price of Peace and Freedom*, and *The SALT Syndrome*, became highly effective fund-raising devices, the latter alone earning $2 million from more than 2,000 showings in various television markets. Altogether, the American Security Council spent approximately $6 million in its anti-SALT crusade.[63] The extent of this effort suggests that in campaigning against SALT, conservative groups were able to build on tactics that had been developed in earlier crusades against Warnke's nomination and the Panama Canal treaties.

The Carter administration attempted to counter the American Security Council's effective, anti-SALT documentaries with public speakers and with detailed, factual rebuttals, but these efforts had little impact; "talking heads" from the executive branch were no match for stirring electronic images with appropriate commentary and musical scoring. The American Security Council's campaign, along with other anti-SALT efforts, established the tone and cadence for this national debate. Carter administration officials, try as they might to sound upbeat about SALT II, were increasingly drowned out by the ominous staccato from the drum and horn section, orchestrated by conservative groups through the electronic media.

Highly contentious treaty ratification debates in the future will no doubt generate new direct mail and electronic media campaigns by freshly created opposing groups or by existing organizations activated for this purpose. Traditionally, the executive branch has been slow in organizing itself to explain its position and seek congressional and public support for arms control treaties; last-minute negotiating difficulties and crises of the moment have understandably received a higher priority. Energized treaty opponents, therefore, can have significant opportunities to shape the terms of public debate and establish negative themes that place the executive branch on the defensive. In the case of the Geneva Protocol and the Coolidge administration, for example, opponents appear to have had the entire field to themselves; the Carter administration's experience in SALT II was more typical. In both cases the end result is instructive.

With the marriage of electronic media and treaty ratification campaigns, the penalties for slow, ineffective rebuttals by treaty supporters have become more severe. Treaty opponents can fill the airwaves with powerful documentaries and thirty-second spots, duplicating tactics that have debased some U.S. political campaigns. The executive branch can respond to these campaigns through senior officials and public statements, but its ability to respond in kind to costly and sophisticated media campaigns is constrained by public law. Title 18 of the United States Code, Section 1913, the "Anti-Lobbying Act," prohibits the use of appropriated funds, directly or indirectly, for publicity or propaganda purposes. Previous interpretations of this legislation by the Department of Justice allow the executive branch only to provide information to, and solicit the support of, members of Congress, and to provide background material to the public in support of policy. The provision for thirty-second spots, if not documentaries, in support of treaty ratification would appear to stretch the clear meaning of this act. The responsibility to create media spots and documentaries on behalf of a treaty therefore falls heavily on private groups. Like treaty opponents, they have to organize themselves during the negotiations to carry out fund-raising appeals and to prepare media presentations. The executive branch needs to help outside groups organize themselves and to provide them with information, just as the Carter administration did with Americans for SALT.

As already noted, the executive branch would also be well advised not to wait until a treaty-signing ceremony to begin its ratification campaign. Despite all of the other distractions they face, the president and key administration figures clearly benefit by establishing central themes and framing the terms of debate during the negotiations. The longer they wait to engage in the varied tasks associated with treaty ratification, the harder their job can become.

Summary

It may seem unfair that ratification hinges on the consent of two thirds of the senators present and voting, but most arms control treaties ultimately have passed this severe test with votes to spare. The most difficult presidential decisions invariably occur well before the final roll-call vote, when, in support of consensus, critical trade-offs must be confronted in negotiations at home and abroad. As a result, supporters of arms control have periodically found themselves asking whether the price of new treaties has been too great. Their answer, in most cases, has been in the affirmative. Thus, the focus of ratification efforts has naturally turned to pro-defense but uncommitted senators who have a record of skepticism about the value of arms control treaties with long-standing foes.

The Republican party leadership in the Senate and pivotal senators—those with particular standing on national security issues and seniority on the relevant committees—have therefore represented the most critical votes in the determination of the outcome of ratification debates. Presidents have often turned to the adoption of safeguards to assuage senatorial and public concerns over arms control agreements. This tactic, however, has occasionally undermined the objectives and purposes of negotiated accords, making subsequent agreements less meaningful and more difficult to achieve.

Highly popular presidents who have enjoyed the widespread perception of being experienced and staunch defenders of U.S. national security interests, and who have demonstrated a sure hand in dealings with Congress, have been ideally suited to mollify senatorial and public concerns about arms control treaties. The more presidents have filled this profile, the more latitude they have been granted by the Senate and by the general public during ratification debates. Under such favorable circumstances, presidential lapses demonstrating unfamiliarity with the issues under negotiation or a poor understanding of an agreement's terms have not harmed ratification prospects; nor has dissension within an administration's ranks badly undermined a treaty's chances in the Senate.

Conversely, the more presidents have lacked these key traits, the more difficulties they have encountered during the arms control treaty ratification process. Presidents who have experienced waning popularity, who have not enjoyed reputations as being experienced and staunch defenders of U.S. national security interests, and who have not demonstrated a sure hand in dealings with Congress have found the search for sixty-seven votes to be a daunting task. Presidents most vulnerable to second-guessing have had the least margin for error in difficult negotiations at home and abroad; their precarious standing has been whittled away further in the inevitable process of making negotiating trade-offs. These presidents have also been most damaged by dissension within the ranks.

Presidents who have lacked standing have faced the most difficult choices of all: they, in particular, have needed tangible benefits in the treaties negotiated under their auspices, yet they have been most susceptible to pressures from pivotal senators and military leaders whose support for a treaty was critical for securing the Senate's consent. Presidents with suspect standing have been able to calm senatorial qualms somewhat by enlisting skilled cabinet officers and advisers in the negotiations, but they have also been most susceptible to backlash generated by negative developments at home and abroad. Luck has therefore played a role in the treaty ratification process, particularly with respect to the timing of favorable or unfortunate international developments.

The Table 1 provides a summary of how key factors affected the outcome of the seven case studies presented in this volume. The letter *Y* indicates a condition supporting treaty ratification; the letter *N* indicates a condition working against ratification. Although this table cannot begin to capture the nuances developed in the case studies, it does suggest lessons for future arms control treaty ratification efforts. The overwhelming Senate votes to consent to ratification of the Five-Power Naval Treaty and INF Treaty were accomplished without resorting to safeguards and occurred despite widespread acknowledgment of a poor presidential grasp of international politics and negotiating issues. These cases attest to the value of presidential popularity, a nonthreatening international environment, skilled advisers, and treaties that can easily be defended on substantive grounds.

The extraordinary level of Senate support for the ABM Treaty is evident from the factors depicted in the table. The Threshold Test Ban Treaty negotiated at the end of the Nixon administration fared quite differently. This treaty appeared quite modest in its benefits, left a major loophole (peaceful nuclear explosions) unclosed, and was negotiated under the auspices of a badly weakened president with thoroughly depleted skills in executive-congressional relations. When the Peaceful Nuclear Explosions Treaty was subsequently negotiated by President Ford, it added insufficient luster to a package that included the Threshold Test Ban Treaty to warrant prompt ratification.

President Wilson's handling of the Versailles Treaty negotiations at home and abroad remains a source of enduring fascination. In this case a popular president succeeded in negotiating an accord of widely acknowledged value during a period of U.S. ascendancy abroad. Yet Wilson failed to secure the Senate's consent, clarifying for posterity the critical importance of presidential skills in handling executive-congressional relations. President Coolidge re-affirmed this lesson in his quite different, but equally ineffective, handling of Senate consideration of the Geneva Protocol. Both accords were presented to the Senate without safeguards by presidents who did not seek the help of those who could help with votes on Capitol Hill or in national debates over ratification.

In stark contrast, President Kennedy shepherded the Limited Test Ban Treaty through the Senate with a keen appreciation for the strengths and weaknesses of his position. The latter led him to support what may be considered an overly generous package of safeguards to secure ratification. Presidents Harding and Hoover eschewed safeguards against noncompliance with the Washington and London naval treaties, yet they succeeded with the help of powerful senators recruited to serve on U.S. negotiating teams.

President Carter's experience during the SALT II negotiations points to the inability of safeguards to sway the Senate when so many other factors weigh heavily against ratification. In this instance what was sufficient to garner the support of the joint chiefs of staff was insufficient to convince two thirds of the Senate. During the ratification debate over the SALT II Treaty, Carter was unable to recoup presidential standing lost during the preceding period of negotiations.

Table 1
Key Factors in Selected Ratification Debates

	Versailles Treaty	Washington Naval Treaties	Geneva Protocol (1926)	LTBT	ABM	SALT II	INF
Perception of substantive treaty benefits	Y	Y	Y	Y	Y	N	Y
Presidential popularity	Y	Y	N	Y	Y	N	Y
Perception of president as defender of U.S. national security interests	N	Y/N	N	Y	Y	N	Y
Perception of president as experienced in foreign affairs	N	N	N	N	Y	N	N
Presidential skill in handling executive-congressional relations	N	Y	N	Y	Y	N	Y
Quality of presidential advice	Y	Y	N	Y	Y	Y	Y
Favorable international environment	Y	Y	Y	Y	Y	N	Y
Support of Senate leadership and pivotal senators	N	Y	N	Y	Y	N	Y
Support of military leadership	Y	Y	N	Y	Y	Y	Y

If politics is the art of the possible, the politics of arms control treaty ratification is a rare, but essential, art form.

During debate over the 1930 London Naval Treaty, an editorial writer for the *Norfolk Virginian Pilot* wryly noted, "It seems that every time our diplomats bring home a peace treaty, war breaks out in the Senate."[64] Behind the hyperbole lies a fundamental truth: full-scale wars during arms control treaty ratification debates are rare, but skirmishes between the executive and legislative branches happen frequently, before and after a treaty is placed on the Senate's calendar. If presidents and those who work for them are wise, they will manage these skirmishes in ways that permit two thirds of the senators present and voting to consent to ratification without sacrificing a treaty's basic objectives and purposes. The stakes involved in these endeavors are sufficiently high that both the policy and academic communities can find rewards in reviewing previous arms control treaty ratification efforts.

Notes

1. U.S. Congress, Senate Committee on Foreign Relations, *The SALT II Treaty, Hearings*, 96th Cong., 1st sess., 1979, pt. 1, 374.

2. Will Brownell and Richard N. Billings, *So Close to Greatness: A Biography of William C. Bullitt* (New York: Macmillan Co., 1987), 94.

3. The reservation was offered by Senator David I. Walsh. See *Congressional Record*, 71st Cong., special sess., July 14, 1930, 319–20, and July 21, 1930, 370–1; cited in Gerald E. Wheeler, *Prelude to Pearl Harbor: The United States Navy and the Far East, 1921-31* (Columbia: University of Missouri Press, 1963), 185.

4. In 1933 the Japanese government announced its intention to withdraw from the League of Nations. One year later it announced that it would cease to abide by its obligations under the Five-Power Naval Treaty. In 1935, Adolf Hitler renounced the Versailles Treaty.

5. See, for example, the 1984 Public Agenda Foundation/Brown Center for Foreign Policy Development poll, "Voter Options on Nuclear Arms Policy: Briefing Book for the 1984 Elections" (New York: Public Agenda Foundation, 1984).

6. In contrast, elementary confidence-building measures, such as the "hotline" agreement, are clearly linked to concerns of avoiding accidental wars and nuclear escalation.

7. Hughes proposed the scrapping of almost 2,000,000 tons of naval combatants in existence or under construction. The Five-Power Naval Treaty scrapped 1,716,000 tons. Richard Dean Burns and Donald Urquidi, *Disarmament in Perspective: An Analysis of Selected Arms Control and Disarmament Agreements Between the World Wars, 1919-1939*, vol. 3 (Washington, D.C.: U.S. Arms Control and Disarmament Agency, 1968), 30.

8. For a more complete discussion of linkage, see Kiron D. Skinner, "Linkage," in *Superpower Arms Control: Setting the Record Straight*, ed. Albert Carnesale and Richard N. Haass (Cambridge, Mass.: Ballinger, 1987), 275-302.

9. Naval authorities criticized the commitment not to fortify U.S. possessions in the Pacific, including Pearl Harbor, during debate over the Washington and London treaties. The poor level of preparedness by the U.S. Navy as well as its Pacific bases before World War II has often been blamed on the lulling influence of these accords. Such critiques overlook the political fact of life in the 1920s and 1930s that congressional majorities had no interest in funding fortifications in the Pacific or building the fleet up to treaty limits. Nor did the United States act to defend its interests in the Pacific after 1934, when it was free to act after Japan renounced its treaty commitments.

10. U.S. Congress, Senate Committee on Foreign Relations, *The SALT II Treaty, Hearings*, pt. 3, 222-23.

11. U.S. Congress, Senate Committee on Foreign Relations, *The SALT II Treaty, Report*, 96th Cong., 1st sess., 1979, 491.

12. *Congressional Record*, September 23, 1963, 17723, 17732.

13. Henry Cabot Lodge, *The Senate and the League of Nations* (New York: Charles Scribner's Sons, 1925), 147.

14. Gerard C. Smith, "There Is No Other Way," *Arms Control Today* 11, no. 1 (January 1981): 5.

15. See Benjamin S. Loeb, "Amend the Constitution's Treaty Clause," *Bulletin of the Atomic Scientists* (October 1987): 38-41.

16. In the view of Herbert F. York, "Arms control policy is developed not with an eye to a national consensus or even to a majority of the Congress, but rather with the objective of somehow capturing the support of those five or six senators who are two-thirds of the way over toward the 'no' end

of the political spectrum." "Bilateral Negotiations and the Arms Race," *Scientific American*, (October 1983): 159.

17. See Glenn T. Seaborg with the assistance of Benjamin S. Loeb, *Kennedy, Khrushchev and the Test Ban* (Berkeley: University of California Press, 1981), 227.

18. U.S. Congress, Senate Committee on Foreign Relations, *Strategic Arms Limitation Agreements, Hearings*, 92d Cong., 2d sess., 1972, 1.

19. W. Stull Holt, *Treaties Defeated by the Senate* (Baltimore, Md.: The John's Hopkins University Press, 1933), 154.

20. William C. Widenor, *Henry Cabot Lodge and the Search for an American Foreign Policy* (Berkeley: University of California Press, 1980), 305.

21. Lodge, *The Senate and the League of Nations*, 157.

22. Ralph Stone, *The Irreconcilables: The Fight Against the League of Nations* (1970; reprint, New York: W. W. Norton and Co., 1973), 183.

23. President Kennedy was fortunate in that a senator of similar stature, Richard Russell (D-Ga.), chairman of the Armed Services Committee, chose not to oppose the LTBT strenuously.

24. U.S. Congress, Senate Committee on Foreign Relations, *Nuclear Test Ban Treaty, Hearings*, 88th Cong., 1st sess., August 12-27, 1963, 418.

25. Gerald R. Ford, *A Time to Heal: The Autobiography of Gerald R. Ford* (New York: Harper & Row, 1979), 357.

26. U.S. Congress, Senate Committee on Naval Affairs, *London Naval Treaty of 1930, Hearings*, 71st Cong., 2d sess., May 1930, 54.

27. John Chalmers Vinson, *The Parchment Peace, The United States Senate and the Washington Conference, 1921-1922* (Athens: University of Georgia Press, 1955), 40.

28. See, for example, Richard M. Nixon and Henry A. Kissinger, "An Arms Agreement—on Two Conditions," *Washington Post*, April 26, 1987, D7.

29. For an elaboration of this theme, see George D. Moffett III, *The Limits of Victory: The Ratification of the Panama Canal Treaties* (Ithaca, N.Y.: Cornell University Press, 1985).

30. U.S. Congress, Senate Committee on Armed Services, *Military Implications of the Treaty on the Non-Proliferation of Nuclear Weapons*, 91st Cong., 1st sess., 1969, 14.

31. Seaborg and Loeb, *Kennedy, Khrushchev and the Test Ban*, 228-29.

32. Vinson, *The Parchment Peace*, 138.

33. Robert Lansing, *The Peace Negotiations: A Personal Narrative* (Boston, Mass.: Houghton Mifflin Co., 1921).

34. French opposition to the prohibition against the use of chemical weapons blocked entry into force of the 1922 agreement.

35. Henry Kissinger, *White House Years* (Boston, Mass.: Little, Brown & Co., 1979), 540.

36. William G. Hyland, *Mortal Rivals: Superpower Relations from Nixon to Reagan* (New York: Random House, 1987), 43.

37. Henry A. Kissinger, "A New Approach to Arms Control," *Time*, March 21, 1983, 25.

38. Vance, *Hard Choices: Critical Years in America's Foreign Policy* (New York: Simon and Schuster, 1983), 58.

39. The exception was Secretary of State Vance's testimony that he was not sure if NATO could survive absent the SALT II Treaty. U.S. Congress, Senate Committee on Foreign Relations, *The SALT II Treaty, Hearings*, pt. 1, 221.

40. U.S. Congress, Senate Committee on Foreign Relations, *Nuclear Test Ban Treaty, Hearings*, 19.

41. Stimson's testimony defined the Hoover administration's objectives as cooperating with other delegations to limit all classes of warships, assuring equality of combatant naval strength with Great Britain, and arranging a satisfactory relationship between the U.S. and Japanese navies. U.S. Congress, Senate Committee on Naval Affairs, *London Naval Treaty of 1930, Hearings*, 3.

42. U.S. Congress, Senate Committee on Armed Services, *Military Implications of the Treaty on the Limitation on Anti-Ballistic Missile Systems and the Interim Agreement on Limitation of Strategic Offensive Arms, Hearings*, 92d Cong., 2d sess., June–July 1972, 113–15.

43. U.S. Congress, Senate Committee on Foreign Relations, *Strategic Arms Limitation Agreements, Hearings*, 5. In later testimony Rogers offered more moderate objectives for the SALT I Interim Agreement: the achievement of a "sound strategic posture" and a "more stable strategic relationship" with the USSR. U.S. Congress, House Committee on Foreign Affairs, *Agreement on Limitation of Strategic Offensive Weapons, Hearings*, 92d Cong., 2d sess., 1972, 3.

44. Thomas H. Buckley, *The United States and the Washington Conference, 1921-1922* (Knoxville: University of Tennessee Press, 1970), 172.

45. Kissinger continued this practice after the SALT I accords as well. From 1973 to 1976 he evaded requests to discuss in detail the SALT II negotiations. See Alan Platt, *The U.S. Senate and Strategic Arms Policy, 1967-1977* (Boulder, Colo.: Westview Press, 1978), 56.

46. Arthur S. Link connects Wilson's refusal to compromise with the Senate to "a great burden of guilt" he felt, owing to his acceptance of so many other compromises in Paris. *Woodrow Wilson, Revolution, War, and Peace* (Arlington Heights, Ill.: Harlan Davidson, Inc., 1979), 106.

47. Lodge to former Senator Albert J. Beveridge (R-Ind.), February 18, 1919, cited in Widenor, *Henry Cabot Lodge and the Search for an American Foreign Policy*, 308.

48. *Congressional Record*, August 3, 1972, 12615.

49. *Congressional Record*, December 2, 1918, 3-5.

50. A characterization by Charles D. Hilles, one of Harding's advisers. Vinson, *The Parchment Peace*, 118.

51. Fred Kaplan, "Tapes Reveal JFK Efforts on Test Ban," *Washington Post*, October 9, 1988, A10.

52. Jackson's warning shot was reminiscent of the effort by Senator Strom Thurmond (R-S.C.), who called on the U.S. government to maintain and protect its sovereign rights over the Panama Canal Zone. Thurmond's resolution, which was backed by thirty-seven sponsors, slowed diplomatic efforts in the Ford administration but failed to dissuade the Carter administration from concluding treaties that narrowly received the Senate's consent.

53. Lodge to Theodore Roosevelt, December 7, 1898. Henry Cabot Lodge, ed., *Selections from the Correspondence of Theodore Roosevelt and Henry Cabot Lodge: 1884-1918*, vol. 1 (New York: Charles Scribner's Sons, 1925), 368, cited in Holt, *Treaties Defeated by the Senate*, 165.

54. *Congressional Record*, March 8, 1922, 3554.

55. U.S. Congress, Senate Committee on Armed Services, "Testimony of the Chairman of the Joint Chiefs, General Maxwell Taylor," *Military Aspects and Implications of Nuclear Test Ban Proposals and Related Matters, Hearings*, 88th Cong., 1st sess. 1963, pt. 2, 6-7.

56. See U.S. Congress, Senate Committee on Armed Services, *Military Implications of the Treaty on the Limitation of Anti-Ballistic Missile Systems and the Interim Agreement on Limitation of Strategic Offensive Arms*, 447.

57. U.S. Congress, Senate Committee on Armed Services, *Fiscal Year 1973 Authorization for Military Procurement, Research and Development, Construction Authorization for the Safeguard ABM, and Active Duty and Selected Reserve Strengths, Addendum No. 1, Amended Military Authorization Request Related to Strategic Arms Limitation Agreement, Hearings*, 92d Cong., 2d Sess., 1972, 4194.

58. Holt, *Treaties Defeated by the Senate*, 154.

59. Link, *Woodrow Wilson, Revolution, War, and Peace*, 125–26.

60. U.S. Congress, Senate Committee on Foreign Relations, *The SALT II Treaty, Report*, 489.

61. See I. M. Destler, "Treaty Troubles: Versailles in Reverse," *Foreign Policy*, no. 33 (Winter, 1978–79): 65.

62. Moffett, *The Limits of Victory*, 118–19.

63. Greg Hilton (American Security Council), telephone interview by Amy Smithson, November 26, 1990.

64. Cited in *Literary Digest*, July 19, 1930, 13.

Index